Getting The Most From Your Laptop

Other Computer Titles

by

Robert Penfold

BP470 Linux for Windows users
BP484 Easy PC Troubleshooting
BP495 Easy Windows Troubleshooting
BP503 Using Dreamweaver 4
BP504 Using Flash 5
BP507 Easy Internet Troubleshooting
BP518 Easy PC Peripherals Troubleshooting
BP521 Easy Windows XP Troubleshooting
BP523 Easy PC Interfacing
BP527 Using Flash MX
BP530 Using Dreamweaver MX
BP531 Easy PC Upgrading
BP534 Build Your Own PC
BP536 Using Photoshop 7
BP537 Digital Photography with your Computer
BP539 Easy PC Web Site Construction
BP540 Easy PC Security and Safety
BP541 Boost Your PC's Performance
BP542 Easy PC Case Modding
BP549 Easy PC Wi-Fi Networking
BP556 How to Transfer Computer Data and Settings
BP559 How to Set Up Your New Computer
BP561 Using iPod, MP3, and WMA with your PC
BP564 Getting the Most from Your iPod and MP3 Player
BP605 How to Find Anything on the Internet for the Older Generation
BP608 Looking After Your Computer for the Older Generation
BP611 Digital Video for the Older Generation

Getting The Most From Your Laptop

Robert Penfold

Bernard Babani (publishing) Ltd
The Grampians
Shepherds Bush Road
London W6 7NF
England
www.babanibooks.com

Please note

Although every care has been taken with the production of this book to ensure that any projects, designs, modifications, and/or programs, etc., contained herewith, operate in a correct and safe manner and also that any components specified are normally available in Great Britain, the Publisher and Author do not accept responsibility in any way for the failure (including fault in design) of any projects, design, modification, or program to work correctly or to cause damage to any equipment that it may be connected to or used in conjunction with, or in respect of any other damage or injury that may be caused, nor do the Publishers accept responsibility in any way for the failure to obtain specified components.

Notice is also given that if any equipment that is still under warranty is modified in any way or used or connected with home-built equipment then that warranty may be void.

First Published - November 2006
Reprinted - January 2007

British Library Cataloguing in Publication Data

A catalogue record for this book is available from the British Library

ISBN 978 0 85934 572 9

Cover Design by Gregor Arthur

Printed and bound in Great Britain by Cox and Wyman

Preface

Laptop PCs have been in existence for many years, but until quite recently they were not very popular. It is easy to see why this should be, with a typical laptop having a mediocre specification and a high asking price. There were actually some laptop PCs that had quite impressive specifications by the standards of the day, but they were so expensive as to be well beyond the reach of the average PC user. Things have moved on, and sales of laptop PCs surpassed those of desktop PCs in 2005, and have strengthened further since then. The obvious conclusion from the sales data is that large numbers of people need to use a computer while away from home or the office.

To an extent this is true, and large numbers of laptop PCs are used by people who need to work with a computer while on the move. On the other hand, an increasing number of laptop PCs are sold to people who will mainly or exclusively use them as normal home or small office PCs. This reflects the fact that the specifications of laptop PCs have improved to the point where they are now capable of running most types of software very well. Also, they have reduced in cost even faster than desktop PCs, making them much more competitive in this respect.

One of the main advantages for most users of laptops is that they require comparatively little space. Having finished work with a laptop PC you can close the lid and put it away in a drawer or small cupboard. This is clearly not an option with a desktop PC! With houses being filled with more and more gadgets, a lack of space to accommodate everything is becoming a common problem. Having a computer that you can use and then tuck away out of sight in a drawer or cupboard is a big selling point for many people.

Another advantage of buying a laptop PC is that it leaves your options open. A laptop that is normally used as a home or office PC can be used in the garden, on holiday, or just about anywhere you feel like using it. Using a desktop PC wherever the fancy takes you is not an option. Of course, there are a few drawbacks to using a laptop, such as a slightly higher price than a comparable desktop computer, but for many users the advantages far outweigh the drawbacks.

While buying and using a laptop PC is to a large extent the same as using a desktop type, there are plenty of differences as well. Whether you will use a laptop as a home/small office PC, on the move, or some combination of these, this book will help you to buy a suitable model. It will also help you to get your new laptop PC set up properly and working efficiently.

This book applies to laptop PCs running under Windows XP or Windows Vista. The Vista software used was the latest pre-release version available at the time of writing, but as the software evolves, small changes could be introduced by Microsoft. With reference to the topics covered in this book, in many cases the difference between the two versions is minor, and I have then referred to a machine running Windows XP. In places where the differences may be considered greater I have covered both versions of Windows.

Robert Penfold

Trademarks

Microsoft, Windows, Windows Media Player, WMA, WMV, Windows XP, Windows Vista, Windows Me, Windows 98 and Windows 95 are either registered trademarks or trademarks of Microsoft Corporation.

Real Player and Real Audio are registered trademarks of Real Networks Inc.

All other brand and product names used in this book are recognised trademarks, or registered trademarks of their respective companies.

Contents

1

2

Setting up your laptop 37

3

8

Security 237

9

Networking 279

1

Laptop basics and selection

Times past

At one time you would only buy a portable PC such as a laptop or notebook if you really needed the ability to compute while on the move. The drawbacks of mobile PCs were many, while the advantages were few. In fact there was probably only one significant advantage, which was the ability to work away from a mains power point. Even this advantage was not all it could be. The battery life of portable PCs tended to be very limited, and even if a spare battery was carried you soon needed a mains supply.

Apart from their portability, laptop and notebook PCs tended to compare very unfavourably with desktop PCs. Many of the drawbacks centred on the usability of portable PCs, or perhaps it would be more accurate to say their lack of usability. One of the main points of contention was the poor screens fitted to most of the devices. Most had monochrome screens that were all right for basic business applications such as spread sheets and word processing, but were of little use for things such as photo editing and most graphics applications. The lack of colour could still be something of a drawback in the more simple applications, and it was certainly a very undesirable feature.

Colour screens were actually available quite early in the development of portable PCs, but at a price. That price was often so high that only the "well heeled" amongst us could seriously consider buying one. Whether a colour or monochrome screen was chosen, its performance was likely to be quite poor in most respects.

One advantage of the LCD (liquid crystal display) screens used in most portable PCs is that they do not have the distortions associated with normal CRT (cathode ray tube) screens. A straight line is displayed as such even if it is close to one edge of the screen. Even the most expensive

CRT screens tend to produce noticeable curvature when displaying this type of thing. Of course, these days many desktop PCs are equipped with LCD screens, but this was not the case a few years ago. LCD screens were little used outside the field of portable computing.

In other respects the screens of early portable PCs left a lot to be desired. The LCD screen technology meant that everything was very precise, but a lack of contrast often gave the perception of a rather fuzzy picture that lacked detail. The screens were small and often operated at relatively low resolutions, which added to the impression of fuzziness and lack of detail.

The main complaint of most users seemed to be the very narrow viewing angles of these early LCD screens. In order to get the best results from these screens they had to be viewed from directly in front. The brightness dropped dramatically if you moved slightly out of position. With some screens it looked as if the computer had been switched off if you moved your head slightly to one side!

Another problem was that the screens were relatively dim. In direct sunlight the screen often looked completely blank. In fairness to the LCD technology of the day, a CRT screen would probably look equally blank if operated in direct sunlight. With a portable PC you expect it to operate wherever you happen to be at the time, but this is probably not being realistic. With any computer screen it is necessary to find somewhere that provides reasonable operating conditions. The real problem with the early LCD screens was that they were difficult to view in any fairly bright conditions. This could make it difficult to find somewhere that the display could be viewed reasonably well.

At a price

Probably the biggest drawback of portable computers has been their price. The best portable PCs cost thousands of pounds and were not something that the average PC user could afford. Unfortunately, at the budget end of the market the prices were still relatively high. A portable PC having a specification that roughly matched a "run of the mill" desktop PC would usually cost at least twice as much, and carefully comparing the two sets of specifications would probably reveal that using the portable PC involved a few compromises.

There were various reasons for the high cost of portable PCs. Probably the main contributor to the problem was the high cost of the LCD screen. At the time, practically every desktop PC had a monitor that used an ordinary CRT, and was relatively cheap. The LCD screen of a portable PC could easily cost more than a typical desktop PC complete with its CRT based monitor. This meant that there was no way that portable PCs could compete with desktop computers on price.

Of course, many of the components in a portable PC had to be much smaller and lighter than the standard items used in desktop PCs, and this inevitably made them more expensive to produce. The fact that portable PCs sold in relatively small numbers also meant that the savings due to high volume production were not as great as with desktop PCs.

Other drawbacks

Some drawbacks of portable PCs are built-in to this type of computing, and are not easily solved by improvements in the technology. One of the big selling points of the original PCs was that they were easily expanded. In addition to adding external units via the computer's ports, there were several integral expansion slots that could take various types of expansion card. A lack of physical space means that it is difficult for a portable PC to offer much scope for internal expansion.

The keyboards of portable PCs have been a contentious issue with many users. While the keyboards supplied with many desktop PCs are of dubious quality, there is usually no difficulty in unplugging the supplied keyboard and connecting one of your own choosing in its place. This is not really an option with a portable PC, where the keyboard is normally built-into the main unit. You can add an external keyboard to most portable PCs, but using a separate keyboard is only a practical option if it will never be necessary to use the computer on the move.

With a desktop PC it is not usually too difficult to change any part of the system if you find it difficult to work with, or it becomes out of date. Even internal parts of the unit such as drives and the display card can usually be changed quite easily. The same is not true of portable PCs. This is not to say that changes can not be made at all, but in general things are less flexible with portable PCs. It is usually impossible to change some parts of the system, and changing others can be quite difficult and expensive.

Due to this lack of flexibility it is important to make sure that you are reasonably happy with the system in its original form. Changing anything that is not to your liking might not be a practical proposition. In fact it is highly unlikely that it will be possible to change anything major that you do not like. Your only choices will be to put up with the problem or buy a new laptop PC.

Up to speed

Portable PCs have tended to lag behind desktop PCs in terms of raw computing power. The speed of desktop PCs has increased dramatically over the years, but so has the complexity of the microprocessors and other components such as the video processor. Despite improvements in the technology, this complexity has generally meant an attendant increase in the power consumption of the computer. While this increase in power consumption is unhelpful, with desktop PCs it is not a major problem. It is just a matter of equipping the computer with a bigger power supply and improving the cooling system to deal with the extra heat that is generated.

The situation is very different with portable PCs. There is no space for larger power supplies and cooling systems. This is academic anyway, since a portable PC that had a power consumption of a few hundred watts would run the battery flat in a few minutes! The need to keep the power consumption within reason has resulted in portable PCs tending to have lower levels of performance than desktop computers.

Times change

Things move on in the world in general and in the sphere of computing, and this has resulted in portable PCs becoming more competitive with desktop PCs. Many people now buy portable PCs even though they will not need to do any computing on the move, but are laptops really a practical alternative to desktop PCs? This is to some extent a "how long is a piece of string?" style question. It depends on the way in which you intend to use your PC.

Taking the speed issue first, it is probably still the case that a typical desktop PC is significantly faster than a typical laptop. However, in the past the computing power of a typical desktop PC was barely sufficient to run many of the application programs that would be installed on it. This is not really the case any more, and even a budget desktop PC has ample computing power to handle standard office applications such as word processor and spreadsheet programs.

In fact a modern low-cost PC is quite capable of handling more demanding applications such as drawing, media player, and photo editing programs. Most can even do a good job with a high-power application such as video editing. The only common application where budget and mid-price PCs do not function well is computer gaming, which really requires both a powerful processor and a top quality 3D video card.

Since the average desktop PC has a degree of overkill when used in most everyday applications, raw computing power is no longer a major issue for most users. Although a budget or mid-price laptop PC might not provide anything approaching the ultimate in computing power, it should be perfectly adequate for most applications. For gamers there are laptop PCs that have powerful processors and "state of the art" graphics systems, but the average laptop is not really well suited to playing computer games. Even these up-market specials are not really the ideal choice for computer gaming unless portability is essential.

Running costs

The cost of running a PC is something that was not a major consideration in the past. Although the amount of power consumed by a typical desktop PC was not insignificant, it was not that high either. Early PCs probably consumed about the same amount of power as a 100 watt light bulb. The monitors of the day were based on CRTs and typically consumed a bit more than the PC base unit. The total consumption was therefore quite low, as was the relative cost of each unit of electricity.

Running costs have steadily increased over the years, with electricity tending to become much more expensive, and computers becoming bigger and better. The power consumption of a modern desktop PC can easily be 300 watts or more, and a large CRT monitor probably has a power consumption that is comparable to this. In other words, using a modern desktop PC with a large CRT monitor results in a unit of electricity being used every hour or so. This makes running costs quite high even for those using a PC an hour or two per day. It makes the running costs very high for those that use a PC all day and practically every day.

The rise in the popularity of flat panel monitors is partially due to the fact that they have much more modest power requirements than the CRT variety. The LCD technology used in flat panel monitors actually requires very little power at all, and I presume that most of the power going into this type of monitor is actually consumed by the lighting unit. Even for a large flat panel monitor, the typical power consumption only seems to be about 30 to 40 watts. In other words, about a tenth of the power needed to run an equivalent CRT unit.

In fact, for those using a PC for many hours a day it makes economic sense to dispose of a CRT monitor and replace it with a flat panel unit. This gives the advantages of the more accurate geometry and generally better picture quality associated with this type of monitor, plus much lower running costs. Over a period of time the reduction in the electricity bills should more than pay for the new monitor.

Using a laptop PC instead of a desktop PC takes the cost savings a stage further. In order to obtain a reasonable battery life it is necessary for a portable PC to have reasonably low power consumption. The lower the rate at which power is drained from the computer's battery, the less likely you are to find that the battery has gone flat before you have completed the current task. In these days of expensive electricity, very low power consumption is clearly a big advantage even for users who will never use their laptop on the move.

The actual power consumption seems to vary greatly from one laptop to another, but something like 60 to 65 watts seems to be typical. Bear in mind that this is the consumption of the entire computer, including the monitor. It is therefore about one tenth of the power consumption of a typical desktop PC and CRT monitor. In comparison to a typical desktop PC plus flat panel monitor the power consumption is only about a fifth as much. You could run a laptop PC all day and all night on little more than a single unit of electricity. Running one continuously during normal working hours would only use about one unit of electricity every two days.

With such a large difference in the power consumptions of typical laptop and desktop PCs, any added cost when initially buying a laptop will be recouped fairly rapidly. In fact the total cost of ownership of a laptop PC is likely to be very much less than that of a desktop PC. Obviously the comparative costs depend largely on how much the computer is used, but assuming it is not used a few times and then put away in a cupboard for a few years, the laptop should always be cheaper in the long term.

Open options

An advantage of portable PCs that should not be overlooked is that they can be used on the move, as a home PC, or a combination of the two. Clearly a desktop PC does not provide the same degree of versatility. If you buy a laptop PC for use at home but decide to take it on holiday for playing games or DVDs on wet afternoons, you can do so. Taking a desktop PC on holiday is unlikely to be a practical proposition!

Fig.1.1 A modern laptop combines the base unit with the monitor, keyboard, and pointing device

Space-saving

I suspect that the main reason for the massive rise in the popularity of laptop PCs for home use is that they require less space. The manufacturers of electrical and electronic goods seem to come up with an endless stream of new gadgets. Modern life is incomplete unless you obtain practically all of these must-have devices. Unfortunately, the rooms in our houses do not expand slightly each time a new gadget comes along.

Fig.1.2 A laptop occupies little space when the case is closed

Most desktop PCs are substantial pieces of equipment. Matters are made worse by the fact that a conventional desktop PC actually consists of three main units (base unit, monitor, and keyboard). In a real-world system there are likely to be other items in the system such as a mouse and a printer. This all takes up a substantial amount of space. The situation can be eased slightly by using a flat panel monitor, but the system as a whole still requires a fair amount of space.

There are PCs that have small base units, and these are worth considering if space is strictly limited. However, bear in mind that the potential for internal expansion with these diminutive PCs is often limited or non-existent. Also, even a PC based on a small base unit might take up a fair amount of room. In other words, it is easy to end up with the worst of both worlds when using one of these PCs. You lose much of the potential for internal expansion, but there is no great saving in the amount of space needed to accommodate the system.

A laptop PC is genuinely space-saving, since it effectively combines the keyboard, base unit, and monitor in a single unit of modest dimensions

Fig.1.3 A laptop keyboard is not a standard PC type

(Figure 1.1). You can use it on the kitchen table or practically any flat surface that you can find. Having finished a computing session the laptop can be folded up (Figure 1.2) and put away in a drawer or cupboard. Although the folded width and depth of a laptop PC are not particularly small, the tiny height makes it easy to find a suitable storage space. Using a laptop removes the need to have an area of a room that is dedicated to computing.

Of course, in practice it might not be as simple as that. If the laptop is used with printers and other gadgets, it is unlikely that it will be possible to store these away in a drawer or cupboard along with the laptop. This depends on the nature of the add-on devices, and in the case of printers it is certainly possible to obtain portable units that are small and light enough to be stored out of sight with the laptop. Even if one or two full-size peripherals are used with a laptop, the small size of the computer itself helps to ease problems with fitting everything into your home.

Downside

Laptop PCs certainly have plenty of advantages for many users, but it is inevitable that there will be a few drawbacks as well. Some of these can be avoided by making sure that you buy the most suitable type of laptop. For example, a laptop that has quite a small screen is not a good choice if you will need it for graphics applications or your eyesight is not very good. Something like a 15.4 or 17 inch screen is more appropriate in either case.

For most users, actually getting information into a laptop is probably the main bone of contention. A conventional PC keyboard is something in the region of 450 millimetres wide, which most users would probably

Fig.1.4 The standard PC keyboard layout is too wide for a laptop PC

consider to be far too much for a portable PC. It is therefore inevitable that the built-in keyboards of laptop PCs are non-standard to a certain extent. In fact real-world laptop keyboards are well removed from the conventional PC variety. This is demonstrated by Figures 1.3 and 1.4 which respectively show typical laptop and conventional PC keyboards.

Of course, the standard QWERTY part of a PC keyboard is to be found on a laptop, and it is usually something close to the size of the equivalent part of a conventional PC or typewriter keyboard. The function keys will also be present, but possibly with a small amount of relocation. Beyond that, it is likely that the keyboard will only have a passing resemblance to a normal PC, or that it will be almost completely different.

The non-standard nature of a laptop keyboard is just something you have to accept. The physical constraints mean that the only way of having a full-size PC keyboard would be to have a rather elaborate system of folding it up into something of standard laptop proportions. Such keyboards have been produced, but never achieved popularity. I suppose that there has to be some doubt about the reliability of any system of this type, although such worries are perhaps unfounded. Probably the main reason for their lack of success is that the unfolded laptop is relatively large, which is not very convenient for those using the unit on the move.

Any laptop PC you buy these days will almost certainly have a non-folding keyboard. Most laptop PCs have provision for using an external keyboard, or have a USB port that can be used with an ordinary PC keyboard that has this type of interface. If you are familiar with a conventional PC keyboard and will be using your laptop at home, using an external PC keyboard is an attractive proposition. There is a huge range of keyboards to choose from, so it should not be difficult to find one that suits your needs.

This is not necessarily the best approach though. Although initially you might find that the built-in keyboard is difficult to use, it is likely that you will become accustomed to it over a period of time. The same is true if you are not entirely happy with other characteristics such as the springiness of the keys. It is possible that you will never feel completely happy using the keyboard, but it is more likely within a fairly short period you will be able to use it without any problems.

Mouse

The aspect of laptop computing that is most likely to give problems to new users is the mouse. To be more accurate, it is the lack of a mouse that tends to be a problem. A laptop PC normally has some form of built-in pointing device and no mouse is supplied. In fact a mouse will probably be offered as an optional extra, or you can connect a standard PC mouse to one of the computer's USB ports. Like an external keyboard, adding a mouse is an attractive proposition if you will be using your laptop at home. You can control the onscreen pointer in the normal way, and there is no need to adjust to the laptop's built-in pointing device.

If you have problems using the built-in pointing device I would certainly recommend using a mouse instead. When using the laptop at home there should be no difficulty in finding adequate space to use the mouse on the desktop. Using a mouse on the move is less convenient, but could be worthwhile if you will normally work with the laptop where it will not be too difficult to accommodate the mouse.

Price

The cost of computers in general has been steadily reducing in recent years, which is perhaps surprising considering that the specifications have getting ever more ambitious. What were once expensive optional extras such as CD and DVD writers are now included as standard. While it is still the case that laptop PCs are more expensive than the desktop variety, the difference has narrowed in both relative and absolute terms.

You can now buy good laptop PCs at prices that are very reasonable, and well within the budgets of most PC users. Consequently, price is no longer a major drawback unless you are operating on a very tight budget.

Portable alternatives

A laptop PC has its advantages and a few drawbacks as an alternative to a desktop PC. In a similar vein, there are alternatives to laptop PCs for mobile computing, and these have their advantages as well as some drawbacks. This book is primarily about laptop computers, and alternative forms of mobile computer will not be considered in detail. However, you certainly need to consider the alternatives, which offer cheaper and neater solutions for some users. Accordingly, these other types of mobile computer will be briefly assessed here.

Notebook

The terms "laptop" and "notebook" seem to cause a certain amount of confusion these days, and the differences between the two have decreased over the years. In fact the differences have been eroded to the point that these two terms are largely interchangeable. In the past, a laptop PC was larger than a notebook type, and physically was much the same as a modern laptop. The technology has moved on over the years, and a modern laptop is better specified while perhaps being a bit smaller, but the generally appearance and concept remain the same.

Notebook computers were significantly smaller than the laptop variety, but still had screens of reasonable dimensions and a proper QWERTY keyboard. This made them more portable, but made them relatively fiddly and difficult to use. Modern notebook PCs have tended to grow in size, meaning that they are now little different to laptops. In fact some manufacturers do not seem to differentiate between the two, and seem to use whichever term takes their fancy. This means that for most practical purposes there is no difference between the two any more.

A few manufacturers do produce laptop and notebook PCs, with a slight difference between the two ranges. When folded, a notebook is a bit thinner than a laptop. The difference is not usually very great, but it apparently enables notebooks to fit into special compartments in some briefcases, camera bags, etc. A chunkier laptop will not always fit into one of these cases. There is little practical difference between the two types, although the smaller size of a notebook PC means that it is likely

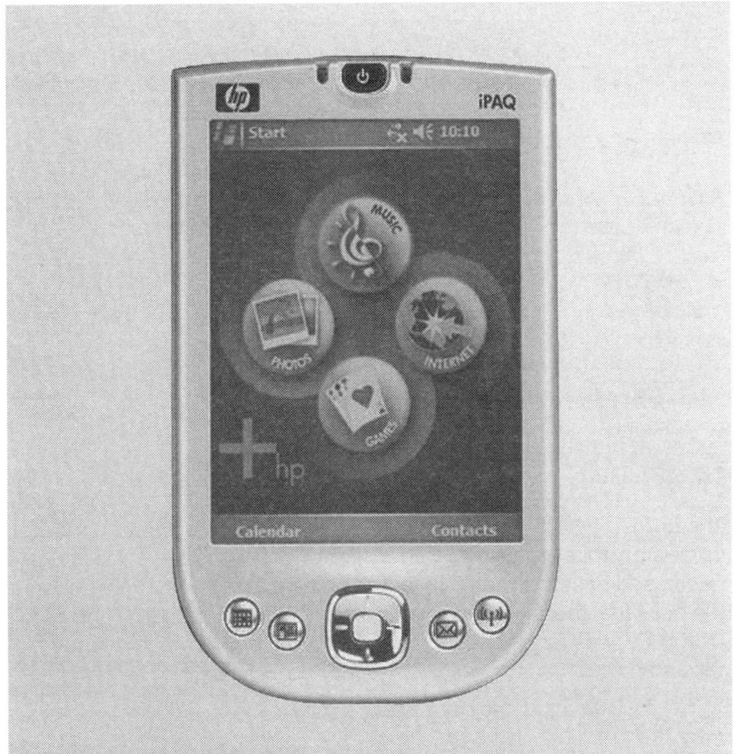

Fig.1.5 An HP iPAQ handheld computer

to have a shorter battery life. In this book the term "laptop" is used to cover laptop and notebook PCs.

Ultra-light

You might encounter references to "ultra-light" laptops, which are laptops that have the highest possible specification packed into a casing that is a bit smaller than that of a conventional laptop PC. The screen size is about 10 to 12 inches. This is a strange development, which seems to be reinventing the old notebook concept under another name. A computer of this type could be a good choice where maximum portability is required and the relatively small screen size is tolerable.

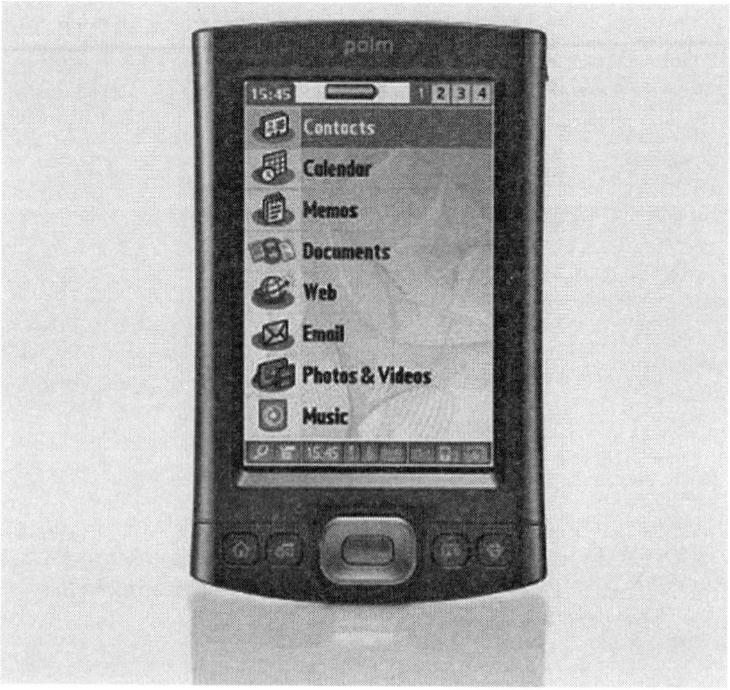

Fig.1.6 A Palm handheld computer

Handheld

A modern laptop is a powerful computer that can handle most of the tasks undertaken using a desktop PC, but this is reflected in its size and weight. These are both remarkably small considering the typical specification of a laptop. On the other hand, you are not going to slip a laptop PC into your pocket. If you require a computer that is really small and light it is necessary to opt for some form of handheld device, such as a PDA (personal digital assistant) or palmtop (Figures 1.5 and 1,6).

With many of these you are moving well away from normal PC computing, and the operating system used might not be some form of Windows. Also, with a really small computer there are inevitable compromises in the size and resolution of the screen, and with the keyboard. Actually, the compromises touch virtually every aspect of the computer, including

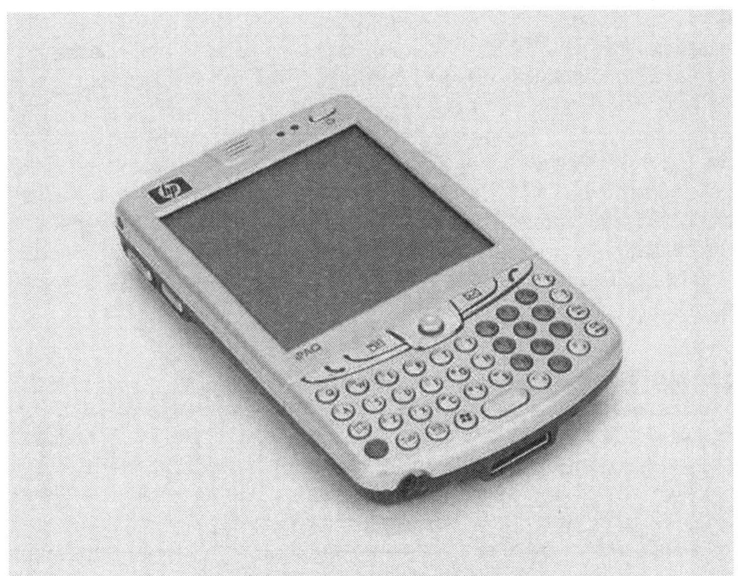

Fig.1.7 Some handheld devices have a QWERTY keyboard, like this HP multifunction device

such things as the speed of the processor, and the amount of memory fitted. Do not expect to get something that is small enough to fit in your pocket but can handle everything that a desktop PC can do.

Handheld computing is an area where Microsoft and Windows do not reign supreme. Many of these devices use an operating system called Palm OS. Palm OS is a relatively simple operating system, but this is not necessarily a bad thing when applied to a handheld computer. It only requires a relatively small monochrome display, and it runs quite quickly on computers that have only a modest amount of computing power and memory.

The main alternative to the Palm OS is one of the cut-down versions of Windows, as used in Pocket PCs. These use Windows CE or Windows Mobile as the operating system and have colour screens. The Pocket PC versions of Windows are probably less easy to learn than Palm OS if you are a complete beginner. On the other hand, they should be quick and easy to learn if you are familiar with the Windows operating systems used on desktop PCs.

Some handheld computers have a miniature keyboard of sorts, as in the example of Figure 1.7, but most rely on touch screens and handwriting recognition software. Where appropriate, the recognition software is usually included with the device, and it will probably be built into the operating system. Recognition software called Graffiti comes as part of the Palm OS, while Pocket PCs are supplied complete with a program called Transcribe. Note that with most software of this type it is necessary to do things in the manner dictated by the software, rather than expecting the software to understand your normal handwriting. In other words, you have to learn to form the characters using predefined sets of pen strokes.

Bundled software

Handheld computers are normally supplied with plenty of bundled software, so you should not need to buy standard applications such as a word processor or spreadsheet. Of course, if you need something that is not bundled with the device, or you are not happy with the supplied application software, there are plenty of third-party programs available. These include normal commercial, shareware, and freeware programs. There are versions of many popular PC programs that will run on handheld computers that run a version of the Windows operating system. These include scaled down versions of Microsoft Word and Excel.

As you would probably expect, there is plenty of software that will help to pass the time while travelling. A media player should be supplied with the device, enabling it to play MP3 and other audio files. Playing movie files might also be possible, but this is clearly dependent on the unit having a suitable screen and adequate computing power. A wide range of software for use on the move is available, including games, crosswords and other puzzles, maps, etc.

Multifunction

Manufacturers seem to be determined to combine as many functions as possible into a single device, and computing now has numerous multifunction gadgets that print, scan, send faxes, make the tea, or whatever. In a mobile computing context I suppose that there are genuine advantages in having two or three functions combined in a single unit. If you really need the extra functions, then something like a combined handheld computer, mobile phone, and camera is well worth considering.

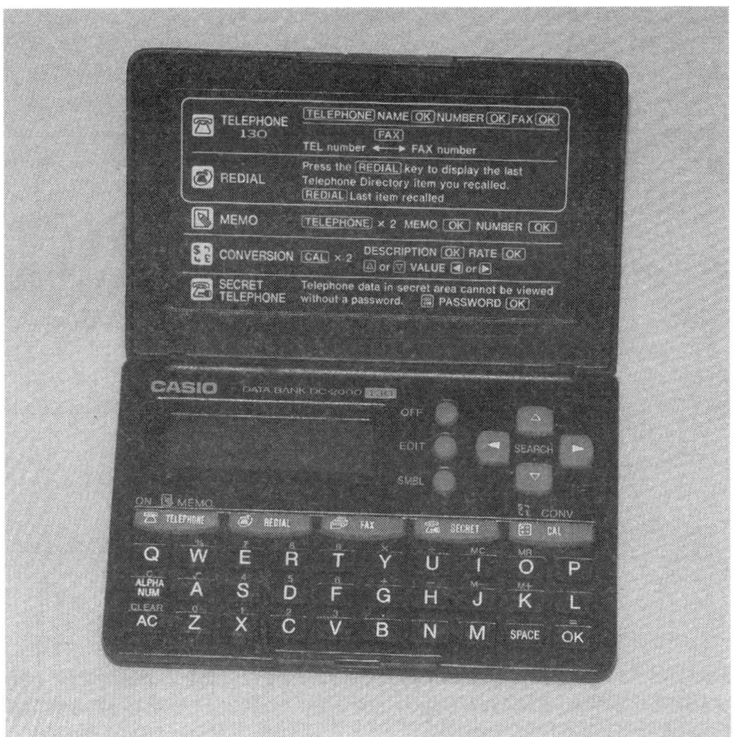

Fig.1.8 This organiser is really just a simple electronic database

However, make sure that the capabilities of each section fully meet your requirements.

Organisers

This is a rather vague term that is used to describe a variety of electronic gadgets. In the days of the now defunct Psion Organiser, it often referred to a quite potent computer that could handle word processing and many other computing applications. These days it is more likely to refer to a very simple device that is really just an electronic database (Figure 1.8). This can be used to store addresses, telephone numbers, store memos and notes, etc. There will often be other features such as currency conversion and calculator facilities.

No doubt many users find electronic organisers very helpful. They are mostly very small indeed and unlike most other portable computing devices the batteries have very long operating lives. However, a simple electronic organiser is not really a viable alternative to laptop PCs and handheld computers if some serious computing must be done, such as word processing, or using a spreadsheet. They lack the wherewithal to handle this type of thing.

Laptop or handheld

Modern handheld computers are mostly very impressive units that provide remarkable results considering their diminutive size and weight. On the other hand, they are not suitable for all. Where a handheld device will do an adequate job it is probably a better choice than a laptop. A handheld computer is much smaller and lighter than a laptop, and will probably be very much cheaper as well. However, you need to be sure that a handheld device really will do the job properly, or it could just be a waste of money.

To some extent you can gauge the suitability of a handheld computer by looking carefully at its specification, the software supplied with it, and the other useful information provided in the manufacturer's advertising literature. You can certainly use this information to eliminate devices that do not have everything you need, and which are therefore unsuitable. The fact that a handheld computer has a likely looking specification and software bundle does not mean that it will necessarily suit your needs though.

Usability is an important factor with any computer, but it tends to be of even greater importance with miniature types. The device will be of little practical value if the keyboard is so small that you can not use it effectively, you find the handwriting recognition system difficult to use, the screen is too small for you to see it properly, or something of this nature. You might be able to put up with this type of thing if it will only be necessary to enter or read small amounts of data, but good ergonomics are essential where large amounts of data will be involved. Ideally you should go to a shop that will demonstrate some likely looking handhelds and allow you to try them for yourself. In this way you can avoid buying one that you will never be able to use effectively.

Choosing a laptop

A laptop computer will almost certainly be a necessity if you will need to do large amounts of heavyweight computing on the move, or a small

Fig.1.9 Even the built-in Windows wordprocessor (Wordpad) can handle simple graphics

alternative to a desktop PC is required. Choosing a laptop is probably easier than selecting a handheld computer. Handhelds come in a wide variety of shapes and sizes, but laptops all adhere to the same basic scheme of things. This is not to say that all laptops are the same or that choosing one is easy.

When choosing any computer you need to consider the way in which it will be used, and the applications programs that will be run on it. There is no point in buying a top-of-the-range laptop and then using it for nothing more than word processing or playing Solitaire. A relatively simple and inexpensive laptop can handle basic applications such as these. There is also no point in buying a very basic laptop and then trying to run high-end applications on it. Even if your application programs will run on it, they are unlikely to work in a really usable fashion.

Word processing

Modern word processors are more sophisticated than the early programs for the PC that were strictly text-only and had no graphics capability. Apart from some very basic programs that are really text editors, word processors that run under Windows provide WYSIWYG (what you see is what you get) displays. In other words, the text is displayed in the correct font, style, colour, and so on. Also, these programs can handle graphics elements of various types, such as diagrams, photographs, and charts.

The demands on the hardware vary enormously depending on the type of word processing that is undertaken. Little loading is placed on the processor when undertaking straightforward word processing that does not include any graphics content. A WYSIWYG text display requires much more processing power than a basic text-only screen, but it is something that any reasonably modern laptop should be able to handle with ease.

For this type of thing it is not even essential to buy any word processor software. The WordPad program built into Windows (Start – All Programs – Accessories – WordPad) is suitable for basic word processing. In fact you can even add graphics to the text (Figure 1.9). However, for anything other than fairly basic word processing tasks it is advisable to obtain some good quality software.

If a laptop is needed for taking notes, and even if large amounts of text will be accumulated, a very basic laptop should be more than sufficient. A basic laptop is also adequate for more serious word processing that has no more than a small amount of graphical content. For word processing that includes a fair amount of graphics it is probably best to opt for at least a mid-range laptop that has a fairly large screen (15 inches or more).

DTP

DTP (desktop publishing) software has similar requirements to the word processing variety. A significant amount of word processing work actually entails using the program as a sort of pseudo DTP type. The difference between these two types of program has become blurred in recent years. In general though, DTP programs require a bit more processing power and memory in order to run really well.

Using a DTP program to do page layouts that only contain text is not very demanding on the hardware, and any reasonably up-to-date laptop should be able to handle it. More complex DTP work that involves a significant graphical content requires a more upmarket laptop. This means at least a mid-range unit with a 15-inch or larger screen, a minimum of 512 megabytes of memory, and preferably 1024 megabytes of memory.

Business applications

Other standard business applications such as databases and spreadsheets do not require a particularly powerful PC. Bear in mind that the use of graphics will place higher demands on the processor. Some types of graphics require a reasonably large screen, but in other respects any laptop should be able to handle standard business programs.

CAD

CAD stands for computer aided design or computer aided drawing, and it is software for producing technical drawings. Producing two-dimensional drawings is not demanding on the processor, but a large screen is needed when producing complex drawings. A 15 to 17-inch screen is adequate for many types of drawing, so a laptop with a large screen is just about suitable for some two-dimensional CAD work.

Three-dimensional CAD is far more processor intensive than the two-dimensional variety, and it almost invariably requires a very large screen. Consequently, it is an application where even an upmarket laptop would probably prove to be inadequate. In fact a laptop is less than ideal for most CAD work. Unless portability is essential, this is one application where a desktop PC will normally be a much better choice.

Internet

There seems to be a popular misconception that a fairly powerful PC is needed in order to surf the Internet. This is possibly due to the slightly dubious advertising used by some PC manufacturers when the Internet really started to become popular. It was sometimes suggested that a powerful PC would give quicker and more reliable surfing, which is not really the case. In this context the speed and reliability is largely dependent on the speed and quality of the Internet connection. A fairly modest laptop PC should be perfectly adequate for surfing the Internet, even when using a fast broadband connection.

It is not even essential to have a large screen in this application. Many Internet sites seem to be optimised for quite low screen resolutions such as 640 by 480 pixels or 800 by 600 pixels. Few require anything beyond 1024 by 860 pixels. Most laptop PCs can handle screen resolutions of this order. Any laptop having a screen size of 14 inches or more should certainly be able to do so.

Photo editing

The increase in the popularity of digital cameras has resulted in a similar rise in the popularity of photo editing programs such as Photoshop Elements and Paint Shop. Programs of this type mostly require a fairly high screen resolution, so a laptop having a resolution of at least 1024 by 860 pixels will probably be required. A screen size of 15 inches or more and a somewhat higher resolution is preferable.

The amount of memory and the processor power required for photo editing depends on the nature of the images that will be processed. Low-resolution images for use on the Internet are not very demanding in either respect. The same is not true of high-resolution images of the type produced by most modern digital cameras. A mid-range or upmarket laptop having a suitably large screen should do very well in a photo editing application where high resolution images are involved. At least 512 megabytes of memory will probably be required for good results, and 1024 megabytes is preferable.

Multimedia

With desktop PCs there are specials that are primarily designed for use in multimedia applications. There are also fancy media PCs that are designed to blend into the average living room rather better than a typical desktop PC. Last, and by no means least, there are laptop PCs that are primarily designed for multimedia applications. These are usually supplied with the Windows Media Edition operating system instead of the more usual Windows XP. Laptops that have a suitable specification sometimes have Windows Media Edition as an optional extra. Note that these laptops often provide something less than a full implementation of the features available from Windows Media Edition. You have to carefully read the "fine print" in order to ascertain whether all the facilities you require are actually included.

A multimedia laptop is the obvious choice if you require a portable PC that will mainly be used for multimedia applications. On the other hand, one of the non-portable media PCs might be a better choice where portability is not important. One of these units should have a full implementation of the facilities supported by Windows Media Edition.

Bear in mind that practically any modern laptop PC s should be capable of playing MP3 and other audio files, as well as audio CDs, DVDs, and movies in AVI, WMV, and the other popular formats. Obviously the specification must include a DVD drive of some kind if you will need to play DVDs, but these are now included as standard with many laptops. Some have a CD writer, and it is worth paying for an upgrade to a DVD writer even if you are not much interested in multimedia applications. The higher capacities of DVDs when compared to CDs means that they are much better suited to backing up you hard disc drive and data.

In most cases you will not have to buy any software for playing media files. The built-in player of Windows XP and Windows Media Edition can handle many requirements, and free players such as Apple's iTunes can handle most of the rest. There might be other multimedia software bundled with the computer, so it is worth checking to see if there are any useful extras of this type.

Games

As pointed out previously, most laptop PCs are not well suited to playing computer games. I suppose that their suitability is to some extent dependent on the types of game that you will be playing. Things like Solitaire, old "classic" action games, and puzzles do not usually require a great deal of computing power and high-speed graphics cards. The latest games with high resolution animations of almost photographic quality do require a top-notch graphics card and processor.

Of course, most of the latest action games can be run at lower resolution and with fewer colours, and the demands on the hardware are then much reduced. Consequently, a mid-range or top-end laptop should be able to handle most games, but not necessarily in a form that will be to your satisfaction. This type of laptop should be adequate if you are happy with something less than optimum graphics quality, as many people are.

There are a few laptops that have potent processors and fast three-dimensional graphics cards, and these are specifically aimed at those requiring a good games performance from a mobile PC. No doubt these work very well, but they should as they are very expensive. Large amounts of computing power tend to consume similarly large amounts of power, so a powerful laptop can reasonably be expected to have a very large battery and (or) a short battery life.

Bear in mind that laptop PCs lack the internal upgrade and expansion potential that can be taken for granted with desktop PCs. Upgrading a laptop games computer by (say) fitting a new graphics card is unlikely to be possible. A complete new laptop will be required if you decide that your laptop is a year or two old and can no longer handle the latest games releases to your satisfaction.

Second-hand?

There is a thriving market for second-hand PCs, and the current popularity of laptop PCs means that there is a particularly buoyant second-hand market for this type of PC. Unfortunately, this is not good news from the buyer's point of view. Strong demand means high prices, and bargains are hard to find. While I would not go as far as to say that you should never buy a pre-used laptop computer, I would generally recommend buying a new one if at all possible.

Modern laptops are mostly quite powerful PCs that are very capable, and even the lower cost types will run most PC software. As already pointed out, they are not well suited to all types of software, but they will run most programs in a usable fashion. The same is not true of many laptop PCs from a few years ago. One of the more upmarket laptops from that period will no doubt still give good results today provided it is in reasonable order, but the lower and mid-range units might be found wanting.

Before buying a second-hand laptop it is definitely a good idea to make comparisons with new budget units. When making the comparison, bear in mind that the new unit should last several years longer than the second-hand laptops.

Check to see what software, if any, is supplied with the pre-used PC. It could end up costing more than a new laptop if the latter is supplied with lots of good bundled software while the former is supplied with little or no software. Also check that a second-hand laptop is supplied with any essential accessories such as a battery and mains adapter/charger. Another point to note is that replacement batteries for laptops can be very expensive, and usually are. Make sure that a second-hand unit is supplied with a battery that is in good condition, and ideally it should come complete with a new battery.

Specifications

In many respects the specifications of laptops are no different to those of desktop PCs, and if you understand one then you understand the other. There are some important differences though, and these are discussed in the following sections. For the benefit of those who are new to computing, some general information about PC specifications will also be provided.

Clock speed

On the face of it, the clock speed of the processor used in a PC should give a good guide to the speed of the PC itself. In practice matters are not as simple as that, and for a number of reasons it is not safe to assume that a PC having a clock speed of (say) 2.6 gigahertz is twice as fast as one that is clocked at 1.3 gigahertz. The main reason for this is that there are several processors currently being used in laptop computers, and these have totally different designs. Some require more clock cycles than others for a given task.

Even when comparing two computers that have the same make and type of processor, clock speed is not a totally reliable guide to the speed of the computer as a whole. There are other factors that govern the operating speed of a computer. They generally exercise far less control over the operating speed than the processor, but their influence can still be very significant. The speed of the graphics card is crucial when any complex graphics is involved, especially when the graphics is of the three-dimensional variety. In fact this is one instance where the speed of the processor could be of secondary importance.

The amount of memory fitted to the computer is also an important factor. In general, the greater the amount of memory fitted, the faster it will run most software. However, these days most PCs are equipped with a substantial amount of memory as standard. This is something where the laws of diminishing returns apply, and using a larger amount of memory will not necessarily make a great amount of difference to the operating speed.

Another factor that can be of significance is the chip set that is used to support the processor. The chip set provides things like the input/output ports, and generally helps the processor to communicate efficiently with the memory and other parts of the PC. Some chipset and processor combinations work better than others.

Where high performance is essential you really need to read reviews of any laptops that are of interest. These are fairly easy to find on the Internet, and they are also to be found in computer magazines. Any review should include a speed test that shows how well the laptop as a whole compares to some other computers when running various types of software. This enables the relative speeds of the computers to be assessed in a realistic fashion.

Screen

The size of a monitor or television screen is its diagonal measurement. In the case of a monitor or television that is based on a CRT it is not the true diagonal measurement. CRTs tend to have rounded corners, and the size measurement is based on the tube having notional square corners. In other words, the quoted screen size is greater than the actual diagonal measurement of the display area. In specifications for CRT monitors you will sometimes find the visible or usable screen size quoted, and this is the true diagonal measurement of the screen.

LCD screens have perfect geometry, so the notional size and the actual diagonal measurement are the same. A 14-inch LCD screen is equivalent to a CRT screen size of a little over 15 inches, and a 15-inch LCD screen is roughly equivalent to a CRT screen size of about 16 inches or so. A 14 or 15 inch display does not give a particularly large viewing area by current desktop PC standards, but it is good enough for most purposes. As most modern software works best at quite high screen resolutions, I would suggest opting for a screen size of 15 inches or more.

Viewing angle

One advantage of CRTs is that they are bright when viewed at virtually any angle. The same is not true of LCD displays, which give optimum brightness when viewed from precisely in front. As pointed out previously, a huge drawback of the early units was that they rapidly dropped in brightness when viewed even slightly away from the optimum position. Also, the colours then tended to become oversaturated unless the picture was viewed from something close to the optimum position. This made it almost impossible for two people to simultaneously view the screen properly.

Modern LCD screens are much better, but there is still a significant reduction in brightness if the screen is viewed off centre. Some screens perform much better in this respect than others. The monitor I am using while writing this piece gives very little change in brightness even if I move well off centre. My other LCD monitor is far less accommodating.

The viewing angle gives an indication of how far you can go off centre before the brightness and general display quality significantly degrades. The vertical and horizontal viewing angles are generally different, and so they will usually be specified separately. A high viewing angle is better than a small one, but there is more to display quality than the viewing angle. Screen quality is a very subjective matter, so ideally you should see a laptop in action and try it for yourself before actually buying it.

Native resolution

An LCD screen is designed to operate at a specific screen resolution, which for many 14-inch screens is 1024 by 768 pixels. This is known as the native resolution, and it is the highest that can be used. It is the setting that will provide the best results in most applications, but it can sometimes be advantageous to switch to a lower screen resolution. For example, some games give smoother action if set for a lower screen resolution. It is usually possible to use at least one or two lower resolutions, but these inevitably involve some compromises and might not give quite the picture quality that you would expect. It is not possible to use a resolution that is higher than the native resolution.

Battery life

There are two versions of the battery life parameter. The batteries used to power laptop PCs are of the rechargeable variety, and using primary cells is not a practical proposition as the running costs would be too high. One version of the battery life figure is the number of times that the battery can be recharged before it degrades and will no longer hold a charge properly. This figure is usually the minimum number of charge/discharge cycles that will be provided. The battery will typically last much longer than this figure would suggest provided it used in accordance with the manufacturer's recommendations.

The other version of the battery life figure, and the one that is of more practical significance, is the time that a fully charged battery can run the computer before it has to be recharged again. The power consumption of a laptop PC varies considerably depending on the task being undertaken, so this version of the battery life figure tends to be something of a guesstimate. It should therefore be taken as nothing more than a general guide.

The power consumption of laptop PCs is very high by the standards of battery powered equipment. Despite the fact that the batteries are quite large, the typical battery life is only two or three hours. An extra battery is costly, but it has to be regarded as essential when computing on the move.

PCMCIA/PC Card

PCMCIA stands for Personal Computer Memory Card International Association, and it is the type of expansion slot/card used with many laptop PCs. As its name suggests, it was designed as a means of using memory cards with computers. In practice it has only been used to a significant degree with laptop computers and other portable electronic gadgets, and has never been used very much with desktop computers. Also, its use has spread to accommodate a wider range of applications than additional memory. These days PCMCIA cards are used in applications such as wi-fi adapters, advanced sound systems, and to provide additional ports.

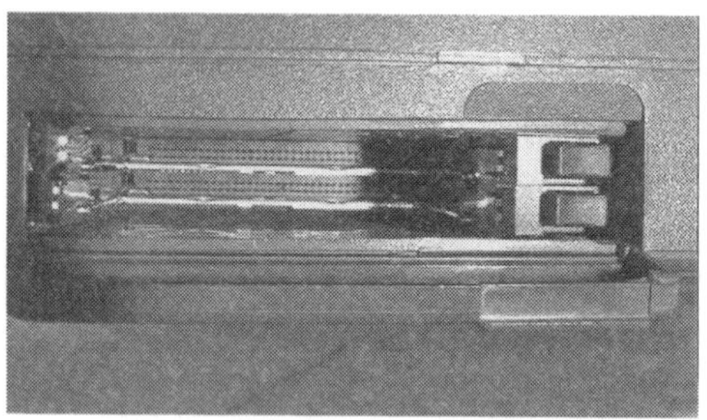

Fig.1.10 A double PCMCIA slot

The original PCMCIA name has been largely dropped now. Various alternative names have been used, but PC Card seems to be the one that has gained the most widespread acceptance. Since there are now some alternative types of expansion card, you need to take due care to obtain one of the right type for your laptop.

These days there is often the choice of using a USB port for expansion purposes rather than fitting a PC card. The advantage of the PC card method is that the card fits right into the PC, and effectively becomes part of it. A USB add-on is an external unit that either connects to the

Fig.1.11 An ExpressCard expansion slot

computer via a lead, or plugs straight into the port and protrudes on one side of the laptop. Therefore, a PC card is generally the better choice for a laptop that will be used on the move. It avoids the need to plug anything into the computer and remove it again each time you set up the computer and pack it away again. Using a PC card has little or no advantage where a laptop is used as a home or small office computer.

Most laptops that use this type of expansion have one PC card slot, but a few have two (Figure 1.10). Probably only a fairly small percentage of laptop users ever need even one expansion slot. It is possible to obtain laptops that are equipped with things such as integrated wi-fi adaptors and Firewire ports. It is only necessary to add them via an expansion slot if you buy a laptop that lacks these features initially.

Ideally you should assess your requirements before buying a laptop, and where possible select one that has everything you require built-in. It is then likely that there will be no need for any expansion slots during the working life of the computer. However, there will still be at least one slot available to accommodate future developments or changes in your requirements.

ExpressCard

There are alternatives to PC cards, and some manufacturers are now starting to use these instead of PC cards. Whether this is strictly necessary is debatable. Although the PC card system has its origins many years ago and it is getting "a bit long in the tooth", it is nevertheless capable of handling most requirements. It also has the advantage of being well established, which means that it is possible to obtain a wide range of cards that use this technology.

Anyway, it is advisable to check that there is a reasonable range of matching expansion cards available before buying a laptop that has something other than PC card slots. ExpressCard is a new expansion card system that might eventually replace the PC card system. The technology is different, so the two types of card are totally incompatible. Physically, ExpressCards are about half the size of PC cards, and will normally be significantly lighter than PC cards as well. Figure 1.11 shows an ExpressCard slot in a laptop PC.

Sound

Like many other aspects of modern computing, the audio capabilities have grown enormously over the years. The original PCs were fitted with a loudspeaker, but there was no proper hardware to drive it. The purpose of the loudspeaker was to generate simple "beep" sounds. Most modern PCs still have this internal loudspeaker, and it produces a "beep" or two just after the PC has been switched on. This indicates that the built-in test routine has found nothing wrong. If an error occurs, either a different set of "beeps" will be produced, or there will be no sound from the internal loudspeaker.

These days it is the norm for sophisticated audio circuits to be integrated with the main electronics of a PC, although soundcards are still used where even greater sophistication is required. It is unusual for the loudspeakers to be built into a PC. Instead, it is used with stereo headphones or an external multi-channel loudspeaker system.

The situation is rather different with laptop PCs where there are usually built-in stereo loudspeakers. There should still be at least one audio output socket that enables headphones or an external loudspeaker system to be used. There will usually be a microphone input as well, so that the unit can be used with a headset for VoIP, voice recognition, or recording notes.

Do not expect a laptop PC to have the advanced audio facilities that are commonplace with desktop PCs. In particular, any form of surround sound operation is very rare in laptop computers. Having a true surround sound speaker system built into a laptop PC is not really a practical proposition, although a few have extra speakers that give a sort of pseudo surround sound effect. Surprisingly perhaps, very few laptop PCs have built-in audio circuits and output sockets to permit their use with an external surround sound speaker system. This could be a slight drawback for those intending to use a laptop as a home computer.

Ethernet

Networking will probably not be of great importance where a laptop is the only PC you will use, but it is increasingly common for homes to be equipped with more than one computer. It is also increasingly common for some form of broadband Internet connection to be used. The normal method of networking PCs is via an Ethernet port. It is possible to directly link two PCs via their Ethernet ports, but this is a non-standard method that tends to be a bit problematic in practice. The more normal and successful approach is to connect the two PCs, together with any others in the network, via a device called a router.

Many laptop computers are used away from the home or office, and must be synchronised with a PC each time the user gets back to base. In other words, new data on the laptop must be transferred to the desktop PC, and it might also be necessary to transfer new data on the desktop PC to the laptop. There are various ways of copying the data from one PC to another, and using a network is certainly one of the most convenient. It can also be used to provide a way of linking the laptop to other hardware in the system, such as a printer and a modem that provides a broadband Internet connection.

Wi-fi

Wi-fi provides the same basic function as an Ethernet link, but using a radio link rather than connecting wires. It is effectively a wireless Ethernet link, but it is significantly slower than the wired version. This can result in quite long transfer times when dealing with really large amounts of data, but for most purposes the speed of a wi-fi connection is perfectly adequate.

Wi-fi is just about ideal for use with a laptop, since it avoids the need to mess around with any connecting cables when linking and disconnecting the computer from the network. You simply place the laptop anywhere within the operating area of the base unit, switch on the laptop, wait while the operating system boots and makes the connection to the base unit, and then access the network. It depends on the coverage of the base unit, but in most cases the laptop and the base unit do not have to be placed particularly close together. You can probably sit in the garden and still access the network.

Another way of using wi-fi with a laptop is to gain access to the Internet while away from home using so-called wi-fi "hotspots". This is basically just some form of broadband Internet connection and a wi-fi base unit placed in any convenient public place. Anyone having a wi-fi equipped laptop can use the hotspot to obtain an Internet connection. This service is sometimes provided at no charge, but in most cases you have to pay for access and obtain a password before the Internet can be accessed.

The importance of Ethernet ports and wi-fi facilities clearly depends on the way in which the laptop will be used. For many it is essential to have one or the other, but it is obviously pointless if you will never have any need to connect the unit to any form of network, or a broadband Internet connection that requires this type of port. Most laptops are supplied with an Ethernet port as standard, but a wi-fi facility is likely to be an optional extra.

Note that it is possible to add a wi-fi facility to practically any laptop, so there should be no real difficulty if you purchase a laptop that lacks this facility and later on find that you need it. Provided there is a spare expansion slot or USB interface it is just a matter of buying and fitting the appropriate type of wi-fi card. If you buy a laptop that is complete with a wi-fi facility it is possible that it will be provided by an expansion card rather than being genuinely built-into the computer. Having built-in wi-fi circuits is preferable since this method leaves the expansion slot free for other purposes.

Docking station

Many portable devices have some form of docking station as an optional extra. Laptop computers are no exception, but there is not necessarily a dedicated docking station available for every model. There are plenty of these units that are intended for use with practically any laptop PC. Docking stations for laptops are less popular than they were a few years ago, and relatively few users bother with them these days. The basic idea of a docking station is to give some form of expansion to the unit

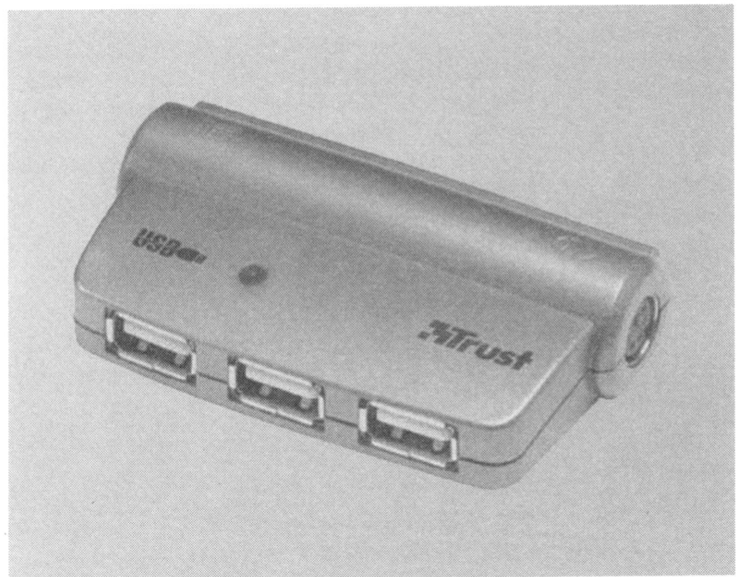

Fig.1.12 A simple docking station is basically just a USB hub

when it is used back at base. The laptop fits into the docking station, which then provides it with additional features.

The main purpose of docking stations with the early laptops was to provide conventional expansion slots. This enabled the laptop to be used more like a desktop PC when it was used back at base, with (say) some extra ports and a special facility of some kind provided by a couple of normal PC expansion cards. The docking station would probably provide a few other facilities as well, such as a standard PC keyboard and mouse.

I suppose that the usefulness of docking stations has decreased as the specifications of laptop PCs have become more impressive. The added expansion potential of a docking station is of little use to most users, since the basic specification of the laptop is perfectly adequate for their requirements. The more simple docking stations are really just powered USB hubs, as in the example of Figure 1.12. With the USB ports of the hub connected to a mouse, keyboard, printer, scanner, or whatever, you simply have to connect the docking station to one USB port of the laptop in order to use it with all the peripheral devices.

Fig.1.13 A more complex docking station provides a range of ports

At the other end of the market there are expensive docking stations that provide a huge range of ports, battery charging facilities, a loudspeaker system, and so on. These are usually dedicated to one particular laptop PC or range or PCs, and are not available for all laptops. The actual facilities provided by these units vary considerably from one to another. In between these two extremes there are general docking stations that connect to the laptop PC via a USB port, and provide it with serial, parallel, and PS/2 ports, and possibly some others as well. Figure 1.13 shows a docking station of this type.

A docking station is certainly very useful where a laptop will be used on the move and at home. It provides a quick and easy means of connecting your laptop to a range of peripherals and disconnecting it again when it is time to go mobile again. However, for most purposes a powered USB hub will be sufficient to facilitate this, and there is no need for a docking station as such. One of the more upmarket docking stations could be a worthwhile proposition provided you really need the extra facilities it provides, such as serial and parallel ports.

Points to remember

In the past, laptop PCs tended to have relatively poor specifications and few of them represented a true alternative to a desktop PC for use at home or in the office. Modern laptops are much more capable, and for most users they now represent a real alternative to desktop PCs. They are not suitable for some of the more specialised applications that require (say) a huge screen, but laptops can handle most types of software.

Laptop PCs used to be extremely expensive, but prices have dropped dramatically in recent years. It is still the case that a laptop PC costs significantly more than an equivalent desktop type. However, the difference is not vast, and the low power consumption of a laptop means that overall it is likely to cost less than a desktop PC in the long term.

They have many advantages, but there are also some drawbacks to laptop PCs. One of these is that they lack the massive potential for internal expansion that is available with a normal desktop PC. This is less important than in the past, since the standard specification is relatively high. Also, there is plenty of scope for external expansion via the USB ports.

When comparing any PCs, laptop or otherwise, it is not safe to assume that one is faster than another because it has a processor that runs at a faster clock rate. A variety of processors are used in PCs, and some require fewer clock cycles per instruction that others. Also, other parts of the computer can have a significant effect on its overall speed. Reviews in magazines and on the Internet are a useful source of information, and often include speed tests.

The built-in pointing devices of laptop PCs offer excellent convenience, but are not to the liking of everyone. An ordinary mouse will usually be offered as an optional extra, or a USB mouse can be connected to one of the computer's USB ports. It is well worthwhile having the option of using a mouse, especially for those who are used to desktop PCs and this method of control.

In a similar vein, it is possible to use an ordinary USB keyboard with most laptop PCs. This is of little practical value for a laptop that will only be used on the move, but it can be useful when using the computer at home if you are not too happy with the built-in keyboard.

There are handheld PCs and other mobile alternatives to laptops. Where one of these alternative devices can handle your applications it will probably represent a much better option than a laptop PC. It will be much smaller, lighter, and probably cheaper as well. It will have no potential as a home PC though.

2

Setting up your laptop

Don't panic

Traditionally, PCs are supplied in one huge box, but on opening that box you find it contains at least three more boxes. Fortunately, things are more straightforward with a laptop PC, which is not in the usual format of three main units plus a mouse. Having the base unit, monitor, keyboard, and mouse merged into one small unit helps to keep the clutter to a minimum, which is why many people opt for a laptop instead of a desktop PC.

Of course, the box will almost certainly be much larger than the laptop itself. Looking at the box you could probably be forgiven for wondering if it really contains a portable computer. Of course, the added bulk is largely padding to protect the computer on its long journey from the factory to your front door. The box should also contain at least a few accessories plus their packaging, which result in further bulk.

As a minimum there should be at least one battery and a charger/mains power supply unit. There should be at least one CD or DVD containing the operating system, and there will often be discs containing various bundled application and utility software. There might be some leads, such as one to connect the laptop's audio output socket to a hi-fi system, or one to connect the laptop's built-in modem to a standard BT telephone socket. What, if anything, you get beyond that depends on the make and model of PC that you have purchased, and whether you bought any optional accessories.

A desktop PC, unless it is primarily intended for business use, is almost certain to be supplied with an amplifier and loudspeakers. A laptop PC is unlikely to be supplied with external loudspeakers as standard, but it will probably have built-in stereo speakers. The small size of the built-in speakers inevitably limits their sound quality. This makes them far from ideal when using the computer to listen to music.

Carrying a decent set of external loudspeakers around with you is not a practical proposition, but any laptop PC should have a socket for stereo headphones. These should provide much better audio quality than the built-in speakers, and are clearly well suited to mobile operation. A set of headphones might be included with the laptop. If not, any headphones intended for use with portable audio players should work well with a laptop PC.

Modern PCs, laptop or otherwise, are often marketed as systems that contain various peripherals that would once have been very expensive optional extras. These usually offer good value for money and make it relatively easy for a complete beginner to buy and set up a computer system. You are unlikely to get a laptop as part of a huge system, but you still have be careful to avoid buying a system that contain expensive items that you are unlikely to find useful.

An inkjet printer is probably the peripheral that is most frequently bundled with laptop PCs, but digital cameras and scanners are sometimes included as well. The so-called "all-in-one" units are also popular as bundled items. These act as a printer, scanner, and photocopier, and sometimes have a fax facility as well. If you need all the facilities provided, I suppose that one of these multifunction devices is a good adjunct for a laptop PC. Like the laptop itself, a multifunction device crams a great deal into a small amount of space.

Although very popular at one time, docking stations for laptop PCs seem to be something of a minority interest these days. This is probably due to the fact that the basic specification of the computers is much higher, which reduces the need for a unit that gives increased expansion potential. Anyway, even if you do obtain a docking station with your laptop, it is a good idea to ignore it initially. Get the laptop set up and working properly on its own first, and then go on to set it up with the docking station.

Discarding

It is tempting to throw away the box and other packaging as soon as the computer has been unpacked. This is not necessarily a good idea though. Retailers and manufacturers generally prefer faulty items to be returned complete with all packaging. Apart from other considerations, this helps to keep everything safe during the journey back to the shop or factory. It is particularly important to keep the packaging if the computer has been purchased via mail order. Using the original packing should ensure that the computer remains undamaged if it should be necessary to return it.

Of course, the packaging is unlikely to be of any further use in cases where the computer is covered by some sort of long term onsite maintenance contract. It should then be safe to discard it all at the earliest opportunity. However, check through all the packing materials very carefully before throwing them away, just in case they contain a small accessory that you have overlooked.

Positioning

With a desktop PC you have to give some thought to the positioning of the computer beforehand, rather than waiting until it arrives. The same thing really applies if you will be using a laptop as a home or small office PC. When using a laptop away from home you generally have to operate it anywhere that provides a reasonable working environment. It is a case of "beggars can not be choosers", and you just have to put up with things like the odd awkward reflection on the screen, or slightly cramped working conditions.

You have to be more particular when using a PC at home, since you will probably spend a fair amount of time sat in front of it. It will be difficult to use the computer if the working conditions are mediocre or poor, and you could soon find yourself suffering from various aches, pains, and strains. This is definitely a case of "prevention is better than cure", and it is something that should be taken seriously.

It is not a good idea to position the computer opposite a window. Although monitors have anti-reflective coatings to reduce reflections from the glass screen, no coating approaches complete effectiveness. The coatings on flat panel monitors are actually quite good, but with the monitor facing a window it is likely that parts of the screen will be very difficult to read during daylight hours. In fact much of the screen could be impossible to read on really bright days.

Also avoid having the PC itself, or any part of the system, close to a radiator or heater. Laptop PCs are designed to have low power consumptions, and they consequently generate less heat than desktop PCs. On the other hand, they still generate a fair amount of heat, and lack the ventilation systems of the type built into desktop PCs. Like desktop PCs, they need to be positioned where they will keep reasonably cool. Feeding them with additional heat is asking for trouble. When the

Fig.2.1 Make sure that you have a multi-way mains adaptor if the computer will be used with peripheral gadgets

system is installed and operational, never cover or in any way hinder the flow of air through any ventilation grilles. Doing so could easily result in costly damage to the equipment and could even be dangerous.

Modern laptop PCs often have plenty of black or dark grey plastic on the exterior, which usually looks very stylish, but does have a practical drawback. With the sun shining on the computer it can get very hot. As far as possible, use a laptop PC that has a black or dark case where it is out of direct sunlight.

A laptop will be powered direct from the mains supply when used as a home computer, making the battery unnecessary unless the computer will sometimes be used in (say) the garden. Ideally the computer system should be positioned reasonably close to a mains outlet. Having the computer and the monitor combined into a single unit means that only a single mains outlet is required in order to supply power to both of them. Of course, further sockets might be needed for major peripheral devices

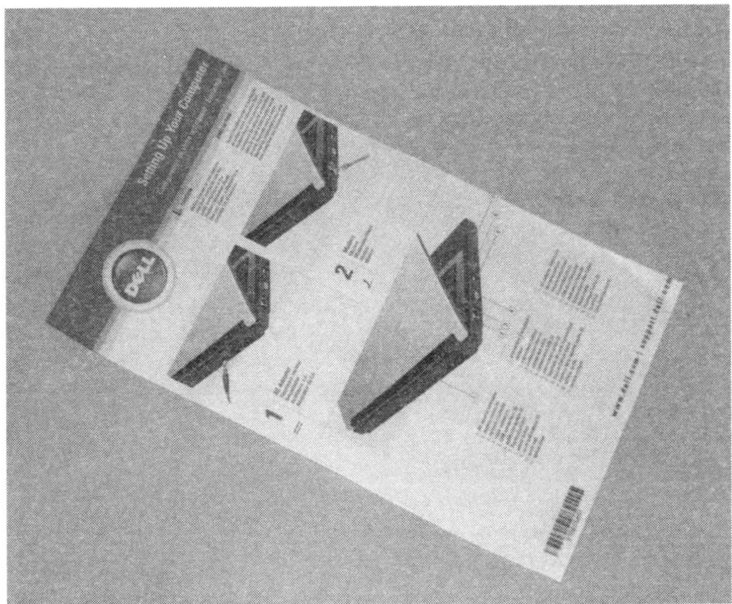

Fig.2.2 Find and read any "Quick Start" leaflet or booklet

such as printers and scanners. If extra mains outlets will be required, make sure that you have a four or six way mains adapter (Figure 2.1) ready when the computer arrives. You can then get straight on with getting everything set up and installed properly.

Unpack carefully

When you first receive any new gadget there is a temptation to rush in and get it unpacked and operational as quickly as possible. With something as complex as a PC this is definitely not a good idea. It needs to be unpacked and set up carefully. Unpacking the PC itself is unlikely to pose many problems, but there are sometimes bits of cardboard that have to be carefully removed from the externally accessible disc drives before they can be used. The screen of the monitor might be covered by a translucent plastic sheet that has to be removed before it is used.

The system should be supplied with an instruction manual that gives details of any obscure bits of packing that must be located and removed.

Fig.2.3 As supplied, the head of a scanner is often locked

These days most computer equipment is supplied complete with a "Getting Started" booklet, "Quick Start" sheet, or whatever, that includes information of this type (Figure 2.2). Always have at least a quick read through with any documentation of this type. A laptop PC is relatively straightforward, so there might not be anything vital in the guide. On the other hand there could be some crucial information, and a quick initial check might avoid unnecessary problems later on. It might even prevent you from making an expensive mistake.

If the system includes a printer or scanner it is virtually certain that these will have some odd bits of packing material that must be removed before trying to use the equipment. Scanners and printers have moving parts that are usually locked in place during transit. They are often held in place by bits of cardboard, plastic, foam material, and the like. These are often hidden somewhere inside the equipment. Some units, and scanners in particular, have a proper locking mechanism that must be released prior to use (Figure 2.3).

It is very important to carefully read the documentation supplied with the system, and to remove any bits of concealed packing material, undo locking mechanisms, or whatever. An attempt to use the equipment without doing so is likely to result in problems such as chewed-up bits of packing material getting into the mechanism, fuses "blowing", etc. The equipment could easily become damaged, and the guarantee is unlikely to cover this type of thing.

Cover up

Most of the packing material will be pretty obvious, but non technical people sometimes have problems with the computers ports and plugs that connect to them. The plugs on computer leads are often supplied with transparent or translucent covers that must be removed before the plugs can be fitted into the connectors on the PCs. Be careful not to overlook the transparent type. Some of these covers tend to be easily missed unless you actually look for them.

The ports on the PC are sometimes hidden behind some form of cover. One purpose of these covers is to protect the ports during transit. They can also help to keep dust out of the ports when they are not in use. The simplest type is just a plastic cover that plugs into a port. These are simply pulled free to reveal the port, but it is advisable to leave them in place until the port is required. It is advisable to keep these covers so that they can be put back in place on a port that will not be used for some time.

The more elaborate covers are built into the case of the computer and typically slide to one side and reveal several ports. It is advisable to slide the cover into the closed position when the laptop is on the move. Unless none of the ports is actually used it will probably be necessary to have the cover in the open position the rest of the time.

Checking the contents

Computer manufacturers have checking procedures which should ensure that you receive everything that you have paid for, right down to the smallest of accessories. Mistakes can occur though, so you need to check that there are no missing items as soon as everything has been unpacked. It is now standard practice for a check list to be included in the box, and this should list the laptop itself plus any items of significance that are supplied with it.

It is unlikely that a major item such as a mains charger/adapter will be omitted, but things such as software discs, leads, adapters, and documentation do get omitted from time to time. Carefully check that each item listed is actually present, including any seemingly minor items. Some of these might not seem to be of great importance, but you might find that somewhere down the line their absence brings things to a halt. Act at once if you are unlucky and something is missing.

Any large accessories purchased with the laptop will almost certainly have their own box and check list. It will therefore be necessary to do separate checks for any items such as printers and scanners. The check list should include a section that tells how to make a claim for missing items. Legally it is the responsibility of the retailer to supply any missing items. You will usually get the speediest result by taking the system back to the shop if you bought the item locally.

Retailers sometimes suggest that you cut out the middle-man and make a claim direct to the relevant manufacturer. Depending on the nature of the problem, this might be quicker than getting the retailer to sort things out. However, you are under no obligation to do so. The retailer has supplied unsatisfactory goods and it is their responsibility to put things right, but use a little common sense here.

Power

Once everything has been unpacked it is time to start connecting everything together. Computer systems usually have quite a number of cables to connect, which can make things a bit confusing at first. Matters are much easier with a laptop PC because the keyboard, monitor, and pointing device are integrated with the main unit. With a charged battery installed it is possible to use the computer without connecting it to anything.

Probably not for long though, because the battery will soon run flat and will have to be recharged. These days, rechargeable batteries mostly seem to be supplied in an almost discharged state. Therefore, the battery will have to be recharged before the computer can be used in earnest. This is something where it is essential to read the instruction manual and follow the manufacturers recharging procedure precisely. Modern rechargeable batteries are much tougher than those of a few years ago, but there will probably be some guidelines that have to be followed in order to ensure a long operating life. Replacement batteries tend to be quite expensive, so you have to treat them with respect and make them last as long as possible.

You might have to install the battery, but it is often supplied already fitted to the computer. In some cases it is not only preinstalled, but is not actually removable by the user. In general, it is better to opt for a laptop where you can replace the battery yourself, and the vast majority of laptops are of this type. With some laptop PCs the battery is recharged by removing it from the PC and then fitting it into the charger unit. The

Fig.2.4 The batteries for laptop PCs are, by necessity, quite large

latter might also be the computer's mains adaptor, or there could be a separate adaptor.

The modern trend is for the battery to be left inside the computer and recharged from a combined charger and mains adapter. This is again something where it is necessary to read the instruction manual, or perhaps consult the "Quick Start" guide, to determine how battery recharging is accomplished with your particular laptop. As is often the case with equipment that uses a rechargeable battery, it is almost certain to take much longer to recharge the battery than it does to run it down. The usual way of working is to recharge the battery overnight. This should provide more than enough time to fully recharge the battery even if it is completely exhausted to start with.

It is possible that the manufacturer will state that the battery is supplied in a fully charged state. In theory, it is then just a matter of installing the battery and using the computer, or simply switching on if the battery is preinstalled. It is unlikely to be as simple as that in practice though. There could have been a gap of weeks or even months between the new laptop leaving the factory and you switching it on. The battery is almost certain to have largely run down during this time. You will then have to recharge it before using the computer, regardless of what the instruction manual may say.

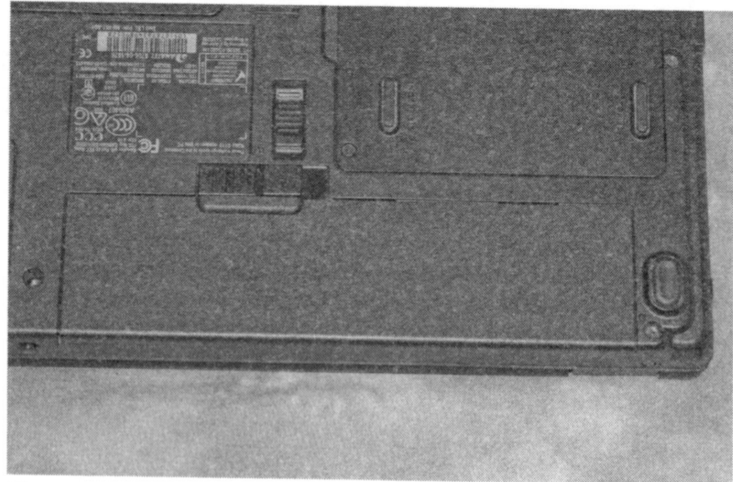

Fig.2.5 The battery compartment door is often secured by a double catch system

Battery changing

There may never be any need to remove the battery from the computer if you only have one battery, it is preinstalled, and it is charged while in the computer. It will otherwise be necessary to remove and reinstall a battery from time to time. Most laptop batteries are quite large, and are rather like elongated digital camera batteries (Figure 2.4).

The battery has to be held firmly in place, but it is unlikely that a screwdriver will be needed in order to remove the cover from the battery compartment. There could well be a double catch mechanism though, as in the example of Figure 2.5. The first catch has to be slid to one side before the second one can be operated and the cover can be removed. Refer to the instruction manual if there are any problems in removing the cover, and do not try the brute force approach.

Make a note of the battery's orientation before removing it from the compartment. It is highly unlikely that it will be possible to fit the battery the wrong way round, but installing a battery is quicker and easier when you know the correct orientation. With the cover out of the way and the battery removed (Figure 2.6), the new battery can be installed. Try to avoid touching the electrical contacts of the battery or the battery compartment. Doing so can lead to corrosion on the contacts and a

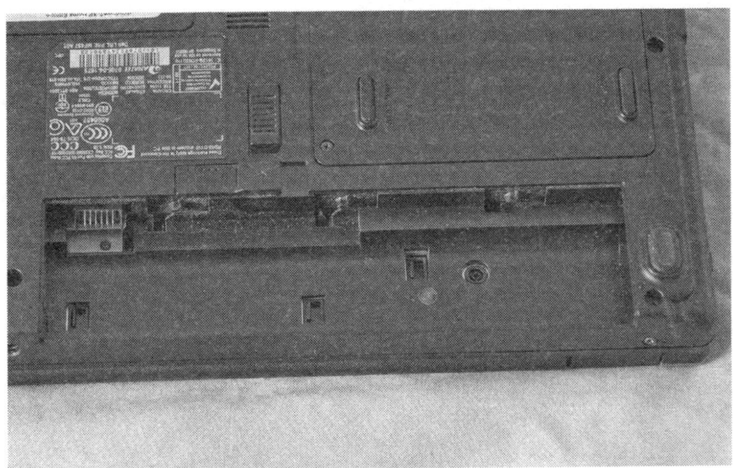

Fig.2.6 The open battery compartment with the battery removed

poor electrical connection. The current drawn from the battery is quite high, which means that a really good electrical connection between the battery and the computer is essential.

Getting connected

In real world computing it is normally necessary to connect a PC to various external devices, even if it is a laptop type. A laptop has a built-in keyboard and pointing device, but as pointed out previously, there are advantages in using an ordinary mouse whenever possible. For the home laptop user an external keyboard could also be worthwhile. Both are offered as optional extras for most laptop PCs.

There is a port that is specifically designed for use with a mouse, but there will not necessarily be a port of this type on a laptop PC. Some mice are designed for use with a USB port, and it is a mouse of this type that is more likely to be supplied with a laptop PC. A keyboard also has its own special port, but once again, some are designed for use with a USB port, and it is more likely to be a USB keyboard that is supplied with a laptop PC.

A USB port is a general-purpose type that can be used with a wide variety of peripherals, including large devices such as printers and scanners. Most modern desktop PCs have several of them. Physical constraints

Fig.2.7 PS/2 connector (left) and the old DIN type (right)

mean that there are likely to be fewer USB ports on a laptop PC, but with a modern type there will probably be at least two of them, and probably more.

It is easy to tell which type of mouse or keyboard you have, since the standard keyboard/mouse connector looks very different to a USB type. The original PC keyboard connector was a large 5-way DIN plug, as on the right in Figure 2.7. This type of connector is intended for use in audio equipment, but it did the job perfectly well. It has now been replaced by a miniature version, as shown on the left in Figure 2.7, and you will only obtain the old type if you buy a pretty old second-hand PC. The new type of connector is usually called a PS/2 type, as it was first used on IBM's PS/2 range of PCs.

The original mice connected to a serial port of the PC, or to a port provided by a special expansion card. Both of these methods are obsolete and have not been used on new PCs for a number of years. As explained previously, modern PCs have a port specifically designed for use with a mouse. Rather unhelpfully perhaps, the mice that are used with this port also have a PS/2 connector. Consequently, there is nothing to prevent

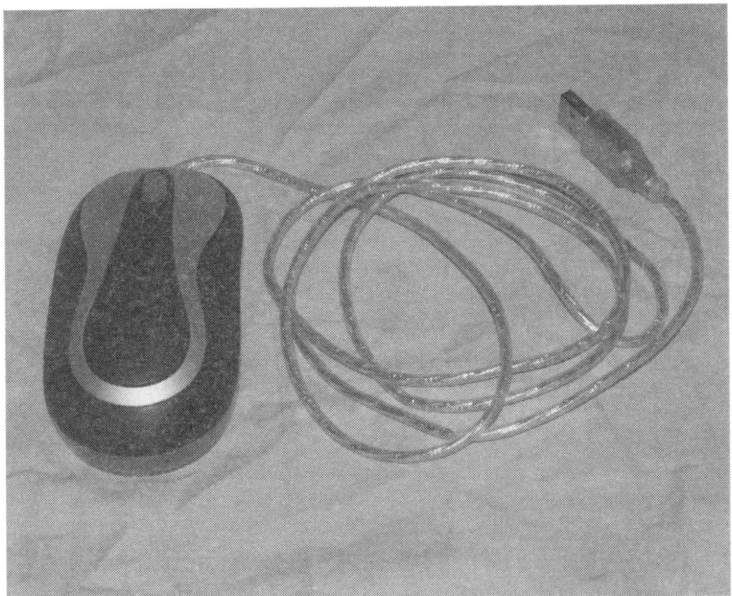

Fig.2.8 Modern mice are mostly of the USB variety, like this one

users from getting the mouse plugged into the keyboard port and the keyboard connected to the mouse port.

Colour coding

Getting the mouse and keyboard connections swapped over is unlikely to cause any problems, but it is best not to put this type of thing to the "acid test". Modern PCs, keyboards, and mice have the connectors colour coded in order to make it obvious which device connects to each of the sockets. In fact a number of the connectors used on modern PCs have this colour coding in an attempt to avoid confusion and errors when installing a new computer system.

In the case of the mouse and keyboard, they are respectively a light green colour and mauve. Consequently, there should be no real danger of getting them swapped over. Just fit the plugs into the sockets of the same colour and everything should be fine.

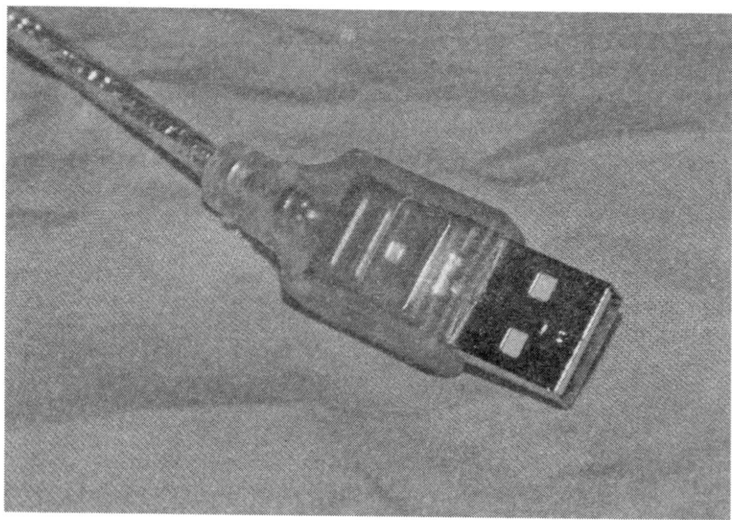

Fig.2.9 A USB connector is much flatter than the PS/2 type

A mouse or external keyboard supplied with a laptop PC is likely to be of the USB variety, and these are easily distinguished from the conventional PS/2 types because the two types of connector are totally different. A typical USB mouse is shown in Figure 2.8, and a close-up of the USB plug is shown in Figure 2.9.

You need to be aware that some keyboards and mice are of the so-called "wireless" variety. Normally the mouse and keyboard are powered from the PC, but this is clearly not possible if there is no connecting cable from the PC to the keyboard or mouse. Wireless peripherals are usually powered by one or two AA or AAA cells. A set of batteries should really be included with the system, but in practice this will not necessarily be the case.

The connection from the computer to the keyboard or mouse is provided by an infrared or radio link. Both methods require a receiver that is connected to the appropriate port or ports of the PC, usually via a short cable. Some receivers connect to a USB port while others connect to one or both of the PS/2 ports. A connection diagram should be supplied with the equipment, but it should be possible to determine which type of port is used by looking at to see what type of plug is used on the receiver. It will almost certainly be a USB type.

Which USB port?

In general, it does not matter which USB port is used for a given peripheral, since all the USB ports of a PC are identical. There are actually two types of USB port, which are the original (USB 1.1) and the new high-speed version (USB 2.0), but it is very unlikely that your PC will have a mixture of the two. Unless you buy a second-hand laptop it will certainly have USB 2.0 ports. These can be used with any USB devices, including USB 1.1 types. Of course, things work at the old USB 1.1 speed if you use a slow peripheral with a high-speed USB port. With anything like this the system is always limited to the speed of the slowest part of the system.

If you are using an older PC that has USB 1.1 ports, it will work with most USB 2.0 devices, but some will not operate at all without the additional speed of a USB 2.0 port. Other units will work with an old USB port, but more slowly and not necessarily in a worthwhile fashion. Neither a keyboard nor a mouse requires high-speed operation, so both should work perfectly well with any USB port.

It is worth bearing in mind that the Windows operating system might get confused if you do not use the same port each time you use a particular USB device. Windows might consider that the device is a new piece of hardware if you connect it to a different port. The "new" hardware will then be installed by Windows. This does not matter too much, but you can end up with each device installed in Windows several times as several different pieces of hardware. This is not generally considered to be a good idea, and it can certainly make troubleshooting difficult if something goes wrong. It is preferable to always use the same port for each USB peripheral.

Finding the ports

Modern PCs are not exactly short of ports, with a number of them on the rear panel, and probably a few more at the front. Laptops are generally less well equipped in this respect, but there should still be plenty of ports scattered around the case. Do not expect the ports to be grouped together in desktop PC fashion. The small size of a laptop means that there is little space available to accommodate the ports. Laptop PC designers do their best to have the ports placed ergonomically, but they are constrained by the practicalities of the situation.

Fig.2.10 This laptop has three USB ports

You should soon get used to things, but initially it will probably be necessary to do a little searching to find the ports you need. The actual ports present vary somewhat from one laptop to another. A typical complement would be something along these lines:

USB ports (Figure 2.10)

As already pointed out, these are the computer's main means of communicating with major peripheral devices such as printers and scanners, and they can also be used with things like keyboards and mice. The flat shape of the connectors means that they are easily distinguished from the other types of connector. There should be at least a couple of USB ports, and there should preferably be three or more. The USB ports of a laptop are entirely standard both physically and electronically. You can therefore make the connections to major peripherals using an ordinary (A – B) USB cable. Smaller peripherals

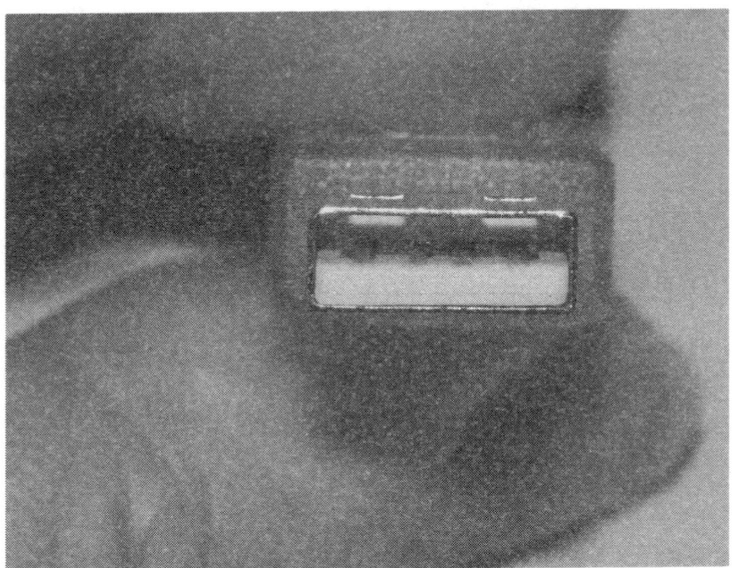

Fig.2.11 A USB plug has one half solid and one half hollow

mostly have a built-in USB plug or lead that connects to a laptop's USB ports in the normal fashion.

"It does not fit" is a common complaint when newcomers to the world of computing try to connect everything together. The computer manufacturers' help lines apparently receive numerous calls from the owners of new PCs who can not get one item or another connected to the base unit. An important point to bear in mind is that the orientation of plugs is often important. There are exceptions, such as the miniature jack plugs that are often used in computer audio systems, but in most cases a plug will not fit if it is upside-down, or even if it is rotated a few degrees from the correct orientation. A USB connector certainly has to be fitted the right way up.

The correct orientation often becomes obvious if you look carefully at both connectors. If you look at a USB plug you will see that it has one half solid and the other half hollow (Figure 2.11). The connector on the PC has a complementary arrangement that makes it impossible to fit the plug upside-down (Figure 2.12).

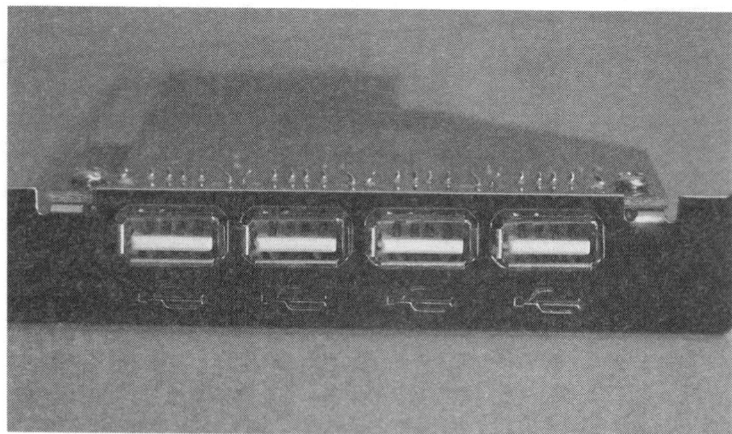

Fig.2.12 USB ports have a complementary hollow and solid arrangement

If it is not possible to see the connector on the PC properly, just try the plug one way, and if that fails, try the opposite orientation. The "hammer and tongs" approach is not the right one with electronic equipment, and attempting to force plugs into sockets is likely to damage something. A plug will fit into a socket once the orientation is correct. It will not fit into a socket properly if the orientation is not correct, and shoving a bit harder will not change that fact. It might damage one of the connectors though, and this type of thing is unlikely to be covered by the guarantee. New connectors are notorious for being a bit reluctant to fit together, but some wiggling and no more than firm pressure is more likely to be successful than using brute force.

Note that there is a potential lack of compatibility between the USB ports of a laptop and some USB peripheral devices. A USB port can supply power to a peripheral gadget, but the amount of power that could reasonably be drawn from a laptop PC is quite low. Consequently, a laptop could be unable to operate with some USB gadgets that draw their power from the PC. There should be no problem with low power devices such as keyboards and mice, but some scanners and other larger devices could fail to work. An error message to that effect will normally be produced on the screen if a USB device tries to draw too much power from the port.

There is a way around this problem in the form of a powered USB hub. The basic function of a USB hub is to enable several peripheral gadgets

Fig.2.13 A modem port. This is for a dial-up connection and not a broadband type

to be used with a single USB port on a computer. A powered hub includes a power supply that enables the hub to provide the full quota of power to each of its USB ports with no power being drawn from the computer.

Modem port (Figure 2.13)

Most laptop PCs have a built-in modem, but note that this is a standard 56k dial-up type and not one for use with a broadband connection. The port on the laptop is usually a miniature telephone type and not a BT telephone connector. Leads to connect this type of port to a UK telephone socket are readily available from computer stores, but a suitable lead will almost certainly be supplied with the computer.

Note that there is a small lever on the plug that connects to this port (Figure 2.14). This is part of a locking mechanism that operates automatically when the plug is inserted into the modem socket. The

Fig.2.14 The plug on the modem lead has a lever that unlocks it from the port

lever must be pressed in order to release the plug so that it can be removed from the socket. Forgetting to press the lever before pulling the plug free is a common way of damaging these plugs, which are mostly of rather lightweight plastic construction.

RJ-45/Ethernet Port (Figure 2.15)

An Ethernet port is sometimes referred to as a RJ-45 port, which I think is a reference to the type of connector used. Anyway, this interface enables the laptop to be connected to a standard PC network. It is also used for some types of broadband Internet connection. RJ-45 connecting cables use the same type of connector at each end, and can be connected either way around. There are two main types of RJ-45 cable, which are the straight and crossover varieties. Straight cables are used for most networking connections. The crossover type is used when two computers are directly linked via their Ethernet ports, rather than being connected via some form of router.

Fig.2.15 An RJ-45 Ethernet port

Fig.2.16 An RJ-45 plug is a locking type with a release lever

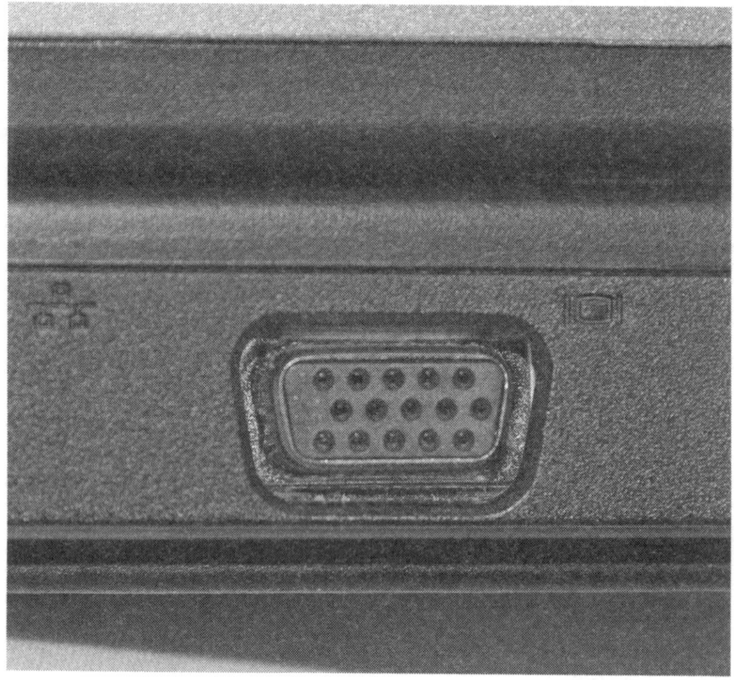

Fig.2.17 Many laptops have a standard 15-pin video output

Like modem plugs, the Ethernet variety have a lever (Figure 2.16) that must be operated before the plug can be disconnected from the socket. Although Ethernet and modem connectors look similar, they are in fact totally different and incompatible. The Ethernet connectors are significantly larger than the modem variety.

Video (Figure 2.17)

Although a laptop PC has a built-in monitor, it seems to be standard practice for a video output socket to be included. This is usually a standard 15-pin (HD15) analogue type that is compatible with any normal PC monitor. The more expensive flat panel monitors also have a digital input that can be used with a DVI video output (Figure 2.18). This type of video connector is becoming more common on desktop PCs and will

Fig.2.18 Few laptop PCs have a DVI video connector

probably replace the HD15 type in due course. It is still relatively rare on laptop PCs, but will probably take over from the HD15 in due course. The digital video signal of a DVI interface can provide better picture quality that the analogue signal of a HD15 interface. Consequently, where the computer and the monitor both have a DVI interface, these should be used to provide the link between the two units.

Firewire/IEEE 1394 (Figure 2.19)

Firewire, which is also known as an IEEE 1394, is a high speed serial port that was originally designed to accommodate the high data rates associated with high quality digital video. It is still in widespread use with digital video cameras and other digital video equipment. In the past it was mainly associated with Mac computers, where it was effectively the Mac equivalent of the USB ports on PCs. Many PCs are now equipped with Firewire ports as standard, or have them available as an optional extra. Firewire is now used as a general purpose port, and it is not restricted to digital video applications.

Firewire ports are only included as standard on some of the more upmarket laptop PCs, and it will not necessarily be available as an optional extra on budget and mid-range units. Consequently, you have to be careful to choose a suitable laptop if you really must have one that is equipped with this type of interface. There are actually two types of

Fig.2.19 4-pin (left) and 6-pin (right) Firewire ports

Firewire port, which are the full six-pin type, and the smaller four-pin variety. Both types are shown in Figure 2.19.

The only difference between the two is that the six-pin type includes a power supply output that enables peripheral devices to be powered from the computer. Four-pin Firewire ports lack the supply outputs, and peripheral devices that use this version must have their own power source. There are Firewire leads that enable four-pin peripherals to be used with a six-pin computer port, or vice versa. However, bear in mind that using a six-pin peripheral with a four-pin computer port will only work if the peripheral does not need to draw power from the computer.

It is a bit unrealistic to expect a laptop PC to supply power to a peripheral device. Accordingly, the Firewire ports on laptop PCs are almost invariably of the four-pin variety and will not work with peripherals that need to draw power from the port. A four-pin port is all that is needed for a digital camcorder and most Firewire devices, but it is best not to take anything for granted and check that any Firewire gadgets you have are compatible with four-pin ports.

Fig.2.20 The power port of a laptop PC

Power port (Figure 2.20)

A laptop PC would in some ways be neater and easier to use if the mains power supply unit was integrated with the main unit. Possibly some laptops do indeed have integrated power supplies, but I have not encountered one of this type. Messing around with external power supplies seems to have become an essential part of modern life, and every household seems to accumulate a fair number of them. I have a drawer containing more than a dozen, and there are several more scattered around the house.

With many types of equipment an external adapter is the only realistic way of handling things, but with a laptop it would probably not be too difficult to integrate the power supply with the main unit. However, this would mean carrying the extra weight of the power supply around with you even if you did not intend to power the computer from the mains supply or recharge the battery. An external power supply is cumbersome and a drawback when using a laptop as a home computer, but only a minor one.

A fair amount of electronic equipment is damaged each year by people accidentally using the wrong adapter. In the likely event that you have a number of these units, make sure that you always use your laptop with the right one. There are probably protection circuits in all laptop PCs, but it is still possible that using the wrong mains adapter could result in a lot of expensive damage.

Legacy ports

These are ports that were once used as the main means for a PC to communicate with peripheral gadgets such as modems and printers. However, these days there are more modern ports available for this type of thing, such as the USB and Firewire types. Consequently, these older ports are now little used and will ultimately be phased-out altogether. Serial, parallel, and game ports are still found on some desktop PCs, but they are not included on modern laptop computers.

There is obviously a problem if you have an old peripheral with a serial or parallel port that you wish to use with your laptop PC. Wherever possible it is probably best to replace the peripheral with a modern device that has a USB port. There is a potential solution in cases where it is not practical to replace the peripheral gadget. It is possible to obtain adapters that enable serial or parallel devices to be used via a USB port. These do not work well in all situations, but in most cases a unit of this type will permit the peripheral to be used with your laptop PC. Some of the more upmarket docking stations provide several legacy ports, and one of these could be the best solution if more than one type of legacy port is needed.

Audio output (Figure 2.21)

This is one respect that a laptop PC is likely to be much more straightforward than a desktop PC. The latter usually has at least three audio sockets, and these days there can be half a dozen or more. A laptop PC is unlikely to have more than three audio sockets, and many have just two. As a minimum there will be an output and an input. The output is likely to be optimised for the types of headphone often used with portable audio devices such as MP3 players, but it should work satisfactorily if connected to active loudspeakers of the type normally used with PCs. Results will probably be acceptable if the audio output is connected to a hi-fi system.

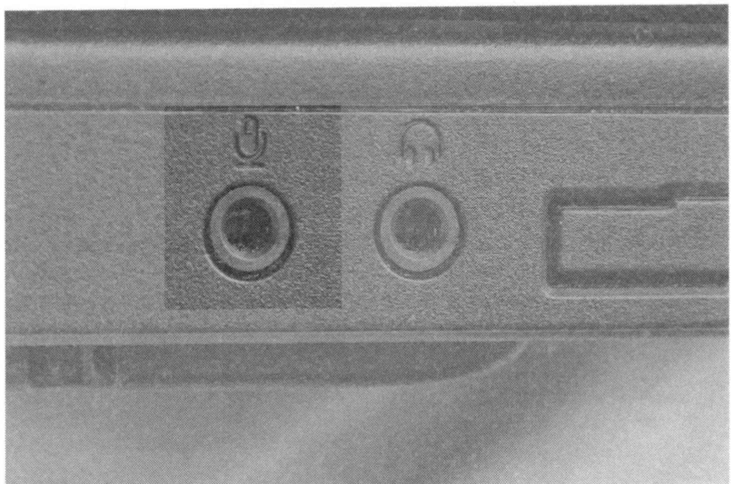

Fig.2.21 The audio input socket will normally work with a microphone

Audio input (Figure 2.22)

The input socket is most likely to be a microphone input. PC microphone inputs tend to be a bit problematic. One reason for this is simply that there are several types of microphone in common use, and an input that is suitable for one type will not necessarily work properly with other types. Another problem is that the original SoundBlaster microphone input was a mono type that included a supply output to power an old-fashioned carbon microphone (as used in old telephone handsets).

Some modern sound systems still have this type of microphone input, although these days it would be used with a modern electret microphone. Some modern PC sound systems have a stereo microphone input and no supply output. These are suitable for dynamic microphones, or for electret types that have a built-in battery. Finding out which type of microphone will work with a given PC is usually a matter of trying the "suck it and see" method.

Fortunately, this is academic for most PC users. Unless you wish to use a voice recognition program or record speech using your PC, it is unlikely that you will need to bother with a microphone. If you obtain a voice recognition program it will probably be supplied complete with a headset

Fig.2.22 The audio output socket is primarily intended for use with headphones

that includes a microphone. With luck, you can just plug this into the appropriate pair of sockets and it will work.

While it is not exactly a standard item of equipment, some laptops are supplied with a headset that includes a microphone, or it is available as an optional extra. Figure 2.23 shows a headset that is intended for use with a PC. Many of the microphones used in these headsets incorporate noise cancelling that is intended to combat general noise in an office, and any noise from the PC.

One can reasonably expect that a headset supplied with a laptop will be properly matched to its audio system, and that the microphone will work without any problems. The plugs on headsets intended for PC use are often colour coded so that they match the corresponding connectors on the rear of the PC. Unfortunately, this colour coding is often absent from laptop PCs. The PC's instruction manuals should indicate the correct method of connecting a headset, but no damage should occur if you adopt a "suck it and see" approach.

Note that some of the more upmarket headsets do not connect to the audio connectors at all. Instead, they connect to the PC via a USB port.

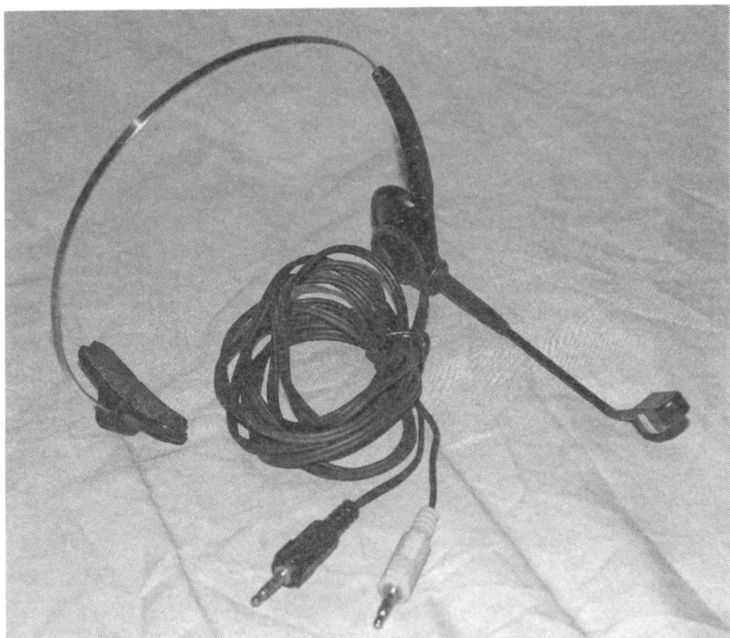

Fig.2.23 A headset for use with audio ports

Headsets of this type (Figure 2.24) often have some integral digital processing that is intended to give better results with speech recognition programs. Anyway, it will be obvious if the PC is supplied with a headset of this type, since it will be fitted with a USB connector, or it will have an adaptor that has a USB connector.

Media PC audio

There are laptop PCs that are designed specifically for media applications, and these often run Windows Media Edition rather than Windows XP. It would seem reasonable to expect a laptop of this type to have the extra audio outputs needed for some form of surround sound speaker system. At the time of writing this anyway, few media laptops do actually have these extra outputs. Some have several built-in loudspeakers that are designed to give a sort of pseudo surround sound effect, but still only have a standard stereo output.

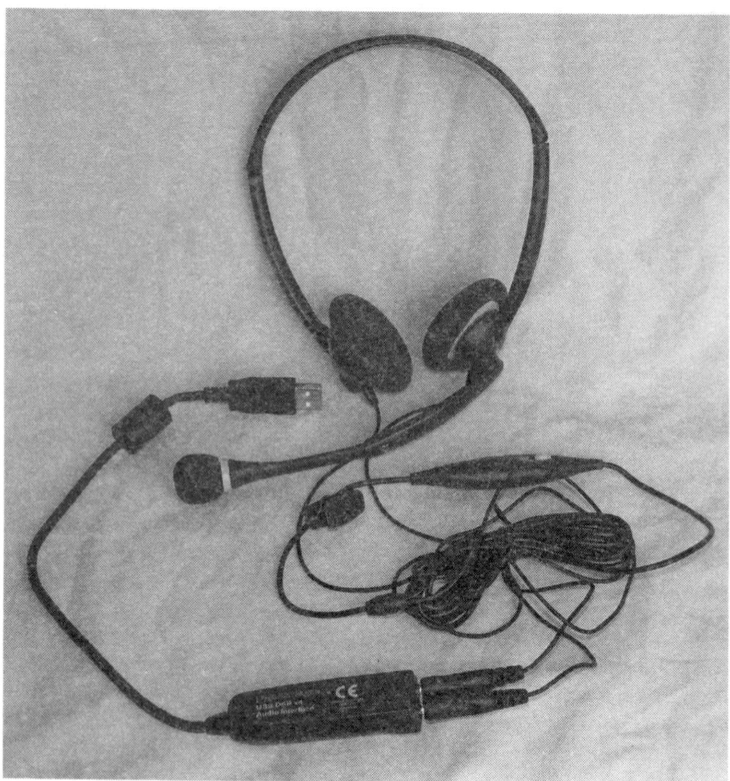

Fig.2.24 A USB headset does not use the audio ports

Possibly this situation will change in the near future, and some current media laptops do indeed have the additional audio outputs needed for operation with a surround sound loudspeaker system. Anyway, the plugs on the speaker system will almost certainly be colour coded. The connectors on a desktop PC are also colour coded, but those on a laptop PC might not be. Knowing the colour coding will at least make it easy to identify the plugs of the speaker system. With luck, both ends of the system will be coded, and it is then just a matter of fitting each plug into the socket on the laptop of the same colour. These are the colour codes used for standard audio connectors in a PC sound system:

Function	Colour
Microphone	Pink
Loudspeaker	Orange
Line output	Lime green
Line input	Light blue

Computers that have some form of surround sound audio system will have some or all of these outputs in addition to or instead of some of those listed above:

Function	Colour
Front loudspeakers	Lime green
Side loudspeakers	Grey
Rear loudspeakers	Black
Central/bass loudspeakers	Orange

For the record, a system of colour coding is used for all the ports of a desktop PC. This is known as the PC 99 system. Although the norm for desktop PCs it seems to be used to a much lesser extent on laptop PCs where it is often a case of black being used for every port. Anyway, these are the PC 99 colour codes for the non-audio ports:

Port	Colour
USB port	Black
PS/2 Mouse port	Green
PS/2 Keyboard port	Purple
Monitor port	Blue
Serial port	Teal/turquoise
Game port	Yellow-orange
Parallel port	Burgundy

Assembly

So far it has been assumed here that the laptop will be supplied fully assembled apart, perhaps, for having to install the battery. It is possible but unlikely that a small amount of assembly will be required before the laptop is ready for use. Any upgrades to the basic specification, such as extra memory for example, will usually be supplied preinstalled. With modern laptops, upgrades such as this usually require the unit to be opened up, and they are not the type of thing with which the average user will ever get involved. In some cases they have to be installed at the factory when the laptop is built.

It is possible that an upgrade that involves an expansion card will be supplied as a card that you have to install yourself. This is not too difficult and it is covered in detail in a later chapter. However, anyone not familiar with simple computer hardware upgrades would probably be well advised to get the retailer to fit the card whenever possible.

There is a slight possibility that some mechanical assembly will be required, but it is far more likely that the laptop itself will be supplied fully assembled with no odd bits of plastic to attach anywhere. The same is not true if you obtain one of the more elaborate docking stations. This may well require a bit of home assembly, but it is unlikely to be any more difficult than other gadgets that arrive as a kit of parts. As always, read the instructions carefully, do not be in any hurry, and assemble the unit in the correct order.

The big moment

With everything connected up correctly, a charged battery installed in the computer or a mains adaptor (Figure 2.25) connected to the power port, you are ready to switch on and boot into the operating system. If there are several peripheral devices connected to the computer it is probably as well to do one final check to ensure that everything is plugged in correctly. Are all the plugs fully pushed into their ports on the laptop and making reliable connections? Even experienced computer professionals have been known to spend quite some time troubleshooting a new PC before they realise that it is not receiving any power. If you are using the mains adaptor, is it plugged into the mains and is the mains outlet switched on?

The system of on/off switching used for laptops is exactly the same as the one normally used with desktop PCs. Switching the computer on is accomplished by operating a pushbutton switch, which is often to be

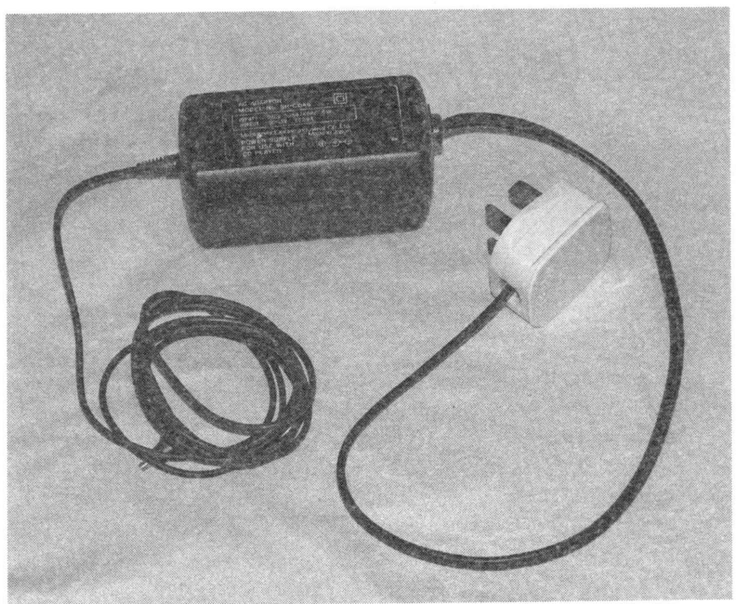

Fig.2.25 Initially, it is probably best to use the mains adaptor. You can take your time with no worries about the battery going flat

found on the keyboard near the function keys. It is not usually too difficult to spot, but if in doubt its position should be indicated in the relevant sections of the instruction manual and the Quick Start Guide.

These days computers are supplied with the operating system preinstalled, and there will usually be some bundled software as well. Therefore, when you switch on the computer it will go through the usual start-up and boot routine and go into Windows. Unfortunately, the first time you boot into Windows it is likely that there will be a certain amount of setting up to do, but this is usually just a matter of answering a few simple questions.

The exact routine varies depending on the make and model of computer, and the software that is bundled with it. Consequently, it is only possible to give some general guidance here rather than precise information. The documentation supplied with the computer should give all the guidance you will need, and there is often an information sheet that goes through the setting up procedure on a screen by screen basis.

Getting Windows running is not usually the main problem. Many new PCs, whether they are desktop or laptop types, are supplied with some preinstalled application software. Some of this software is usually fully functioning, and will prove to be very useful. For example, the ever-popular Microsoft Works office suite is often bundled with new PCs, and no doubt it is found to be extremely useful by many users. Few, if any, would object to having this type of software preinstalled on their PC.

Some other types of software are more contentious. This is something that depends on the make of computer that you buy, but it now seems to be the norm for various trial programs to be preinstalled on new PCs. These are programs that are limited in some way, or "crippled" programs as they are often termed.

A program of this type will typically work in every respect but with inoperative Help and printing facilities. Another ploy is to have a program that runs normally for (say) 30 days after you first run it, but then refuses to run at all. In a similar vein, many PCs seem to be supplied with preinstalled security suites that can be kept up to date without charge, but only for a few weeks or months. The normal subscription fees then apply.

Registering

The main objection to the bundled trial software is that it can make it difficult to get the computer set up and ready for use. You would like to get into the Windows operating system and start computing, but you find that the bundled software tries to get you to go through all sorts of setting up and registering processes. There may be no way of totally bypassing these processes, and it could be necessary to take a certain amount of time going through the setting up procedures. Understandably, this gets many users more than a little narked.

It is worth bearing in mind that the computer manufacturer is paid fees for including this type of bundled software on their PCs. In effect, the cost of you new PC is being subsidised slightly by the producers of the bundled software. Another point to keep in mind is that no manufacturer will preinstall any form of spyware, adware, or anything that hides on your hard disc drive and can not be removed. Any bundled software can be removed if you do not need it. The correct methods of removing unwanted software are covered later in this book.

Therefore, you can simply go through any unavoidable setting up procedures, and then remove the offending software if it is genuinely of no interest to you. It is not actually essential to remove bundled software that you will not use. Removing unwanted software has the advantage of freeing some hard disc space, although the amount that is liberated will not necessarily be that worthwhile.

There is a slight risk that removing software, even if it is done correctly, will mess up the operating system. This is far rarer than it once was, with modern versions of Windows being rather more robust that those of yesteryear. Also, the applications programs and their uninstall programs are more reliable and less likely to damage the operating system.

Windows has a facility know as System Restore which can take the computer back to its previous state if something goes wrong when uninstalling software. There is no guarantee that System Restore will always be able to live up to its name, but it further reduces the risk. However, there is still a slight risk of software removal causing a problem that can not be fixed easily. Those who are not confident at using Windows facilities such as System Restore might prefer to take the safe option of leaving the unwanted software in place.

You will probably not consider this to be an option if a program keeps producing pop-up messages to the effect that you need to renew your subscription, register it, or something of this nature. It might be possible to go into the offending program and disable the messages via an Options or Preferences window, but this is not always possible. Another possibility is to alter the Windows start-up settings so that the program can not run automatically, but it is probably easier and safer to simply uninstall it.

Problems

Modern electronics is generally very reliable, but faults can occur and you might be unlucky. A modern computer is so complex that it is probably that bit more likely to go wrong than something more basic such as an MP3 player or a radio. Anyway, before taking up the matter with the retailer it is a good idea to check that the problem is not due to a minor problem or mistake that can be easily solved.

If the laptop is doing nothing at all, is it actually getting any power? Where the unit is being powered from the mains adaptor, is the latter plugged in properly, is the mains supply switched on, and is the adaptor plugged into the computer properly? The higher wattage mains adaptors, as used with laptop computers, often have an indicator light. Does this switch on when the adaptor is plugged into a mains outlet. Multi-way mains boards can be a bit temperamental. If you are using one of these to provide additional outlets, trying using a different mains socket on the panel or plug the adaptor straight into the wall socket.

There is probably a fault in the computer or the adaptor if power is definitely getting through to the adaptor and then to the computer, but the computer fails to respond properly. Computer help lines tend to receive large numbers of calls from customers who have been unable to switch on their desktop computers. They press the button on the front as per the instruction manual, but nothing happens. The problem is that they have failed to realise that there is a conventional on/off switch at the back of the computer, and that it is set to the "off" position. It is unusual for a laptop computer to have a conventional on/off switch, but it would be as well to check this point in the instruction manual. It might save some embarrassment later on!

If the computer is being run from a mains adaptor, try powering it from the battery instead. It is likely that the mains adaptor is faulty if the computer can be powered from the battery but not the adaptor. Similarly, it is likely that the battery is a dud or is not being charged correctly if it is possible to power the computer from the mains adaptor but not the battery. Did the battery go through the recharging procedure correctly, with the indicator lights switching on and off at the right times, or whatever?

It is possible that a little investigation will find the problem and that there will be a simple solution. There is no point in spending large amounts of time searching for the cause of the problem. You must contact the retailer at once if it proves to be impossible to get the computer to power-up and boot correctly after looking for any obvious problems. It is the responsibility of the retailer to sort out any faults, and not yours.

Assuming the computer will boot into Windows, you should then try to give everything a quick test. For example, will the CD/DVD drive read and write using the appropriate types of disc? Does the sound system work correctly, do any peripherals such as a keyboard and mouse function correctly, and so on? If you can find a way of testing any part of the computer, then do so.

If there are any faults, then you need to find them and get them rectified as soon as possible. You should certainly try to avoid the situation where you do not use (say) a port until you have had the computer for some time. You then find that it does not work properly, but by then the computer is out of warranty.

Any problem found might be of the hardware variety, and very obviously of the hardware variety. For example, a CD/DVD drive door that jams, or a mouse that is mechanically faulty. It is then a matter of returning the faulty item to the retailer.

Bugs

In other cases the cause of the problem might conceivably be in software, such as a faulty driver program or an incorrect setting in Windows. For example, a CD drive that reads data properly but does not play audio discs is probably functioning correctly. The lack of audio is almost certain to be caused by a software problem such as an incorrect setting in Windows or a player program that is not set up correctly.

The retailer will probably have a help line of some sort, and they might be able to provide an easy fix for the problem. If you are having problems with a faulty set-up, then it is likely that everyone else that has bought that make and model of PC will be having the same problem. With anything like this the retailer or manufacturer should soon come up with a solution which should then be available from any relevant help lines.

Note that some of these help lines are not free, or have "strings attached" such as only being free for a limited period. You should not really have to pay for information that helps to get a faulty product working properly. If a computer fails to work properly you are not obliged to use an expensive help line. You can, for example, take it back to the shop and get them to fix the problem. Where the computer is covered by an onsite maintenance contract you should be able to invoke the contract and get someone to fix the problem at your premises, and free of charge.

Turn off

It is not unknown for Windows to boot up correctly, but to give problems when you try to switch off the computer. Sometimes you end up going around in circles and never actually manage to shut down Windows. The more common alternative is that Windows starts to go through its closing down procedure, and it normally gets close to the end, but at some point it stalls and the computer is not switched off. This problem is less common with Windows XP and Vista than it was with some earlier versions of Windows, but it can still happen.

The instruction manual for your computer should include details of how to switch it off if none of the normal methods work. This often involves holding down the On button for a few seconds. Directly switching off the hardware is not usually to be recommended, since it tends to leave a number of temporary files on the hard disc drive. These files are deleted by the operating system when the computer is switched off in the normal way. However, Windows XP is less easily fazed by these files than some of its predecessors, and it should sort things out when it is next booted.

There are several possible causes of Windows failing to shut down properly, but these days it is mainly associated with faulty driver software or other programs. Anyway, if this problem occurs before you start installing any of your own software, the problem is almost certainly due to drivers or other software supplied with the computer. Presumably other users of the same make and model of computer will be experiencing the same problem, and the manufacturer should quickly come up with a solution. The relevant customer support service should be able to supply you with details of this solution.

Points to remember

When you buy any new gadget there is a tendency to get it unpacked as quickly as possible, and start using it without reading the instructions at all. This is never a good idea, and with a major piece of equipment such as a laptop computer it is important to take your time. At the very least, read through any Quick Start Guide supplied with the computer. This should indicate where everything is situated on the laptop and supply any vital snippets of information that you will require.

The Quick Start Guide or instruction manual will usually include a section that lists everything of significance that is included with the computer. Alternatively, there might be a separate sheet that has this information. Carefully check the contents of the box to ensure that everything that should be included has been supplied.

Once you are ready to switch on the computer, the process for switching it on and off is the same as for a desktop PC. There will be an "on" button somewhere on the laptop, and most likely somewhere close to the keyboard. Pressing this button switches on the computer and sends it through the usual start-up and booting routine. The computer is switched off using the normal Start - Turn Off Computer - Turn Off routine.

The operating system is normally supplied preinstalled on the computer's hard disc drive. Any bundled application software will usually be preinstalled as well. This means that, in theory anyway, you just have to switch on the computer, wait for it to boot into Windows, and then start using it. In practice there will probably be a certain amount of setting up to do before you can get started, but this should all be very straightforward.

Some of the bundled software might be of the trial variety. This can be uninstalled, as can any application or utility programs that are preinstalled. In many cases it is not worth bothering to uninstall unwanted programs, but it is probably best to do so if the programs take up large amounts of hard disc space or keep flashing onscreen messages at you.

Although a laptop computer is self contained, in practice it will usually have to be connected to peripheral gadgets and to the Internet. There will probably be a substantial number of ports liberally scattered around the edges of the computer. Study the computer itself and the instruction manual to determine where each port is situated. The ports you are most likely to need are the USB and audio types, so make sure that you know where they are, and which audio socket is which.

Do not start messing around with the computer if it is clearly faulty. You will probably do more harm than good, and you will almost certainly invalidate the warranty if your handiwork causes further damage to the computer. Get in touch with the manufacturer's or retailer's customer support service, or take it back to the shop if you purchased it locally.

Customising and updating

Screen resolution

Having ascertained that your new laptop PC will boot into Windows properly and it can then be shut down without any problems, it is then ready for use. At least, in theory it is ready for use. In the real world it is usually necessary to do a certain amount of customising and install some software before a new PC is ready to be used in earnest.

As supplied, the computer should have video settings that give good results with Windows itself, and with most application programs. The screen settings will usually have the monitor operating at its native resolution, which is the resolution that will give optimum results in most situations. However, under certain circumstances it can be advantageous to alter the video settings, including the resolution used.

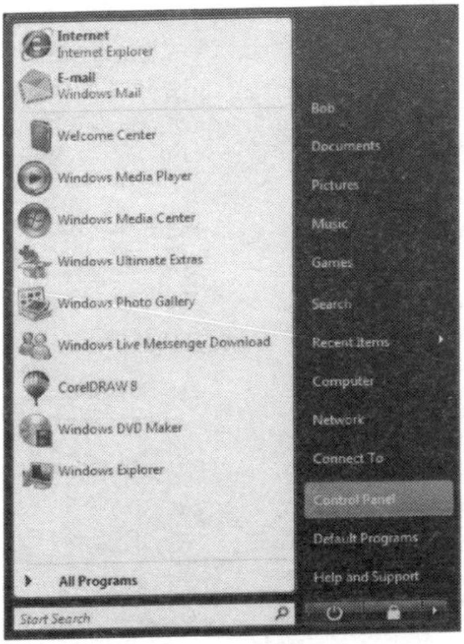

Fig.3.1 The Control Panel has an entry in the Start menu

For example, some games might not work very well with default settings. Changing to lower resolution and fewer colours will often give faster and smoother action, albeit with lower quality graphics. There are other occasions when a change in the video settings could be advantageous, such as when using the computer with an external monitor.

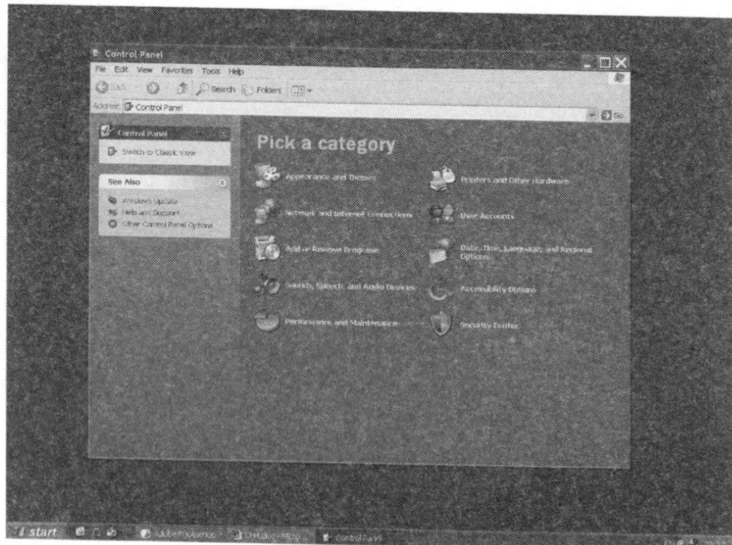

Fig.3.2 The Windows Control Panel

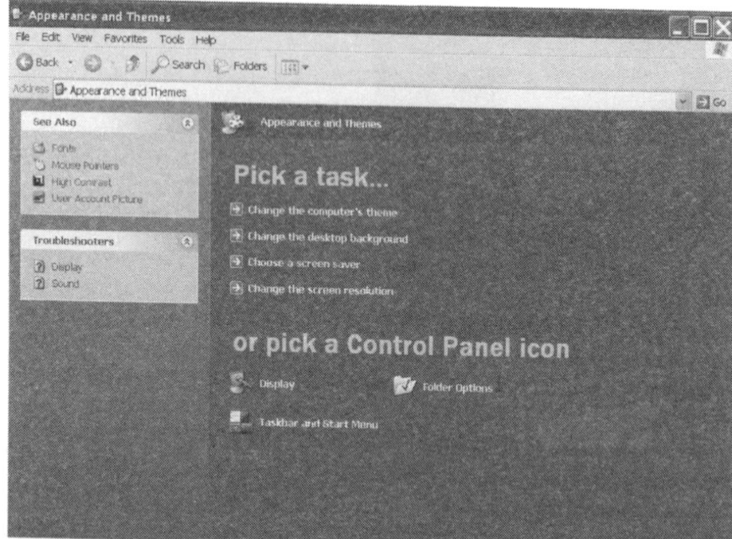

Fig.3.3 Here the Display link is activated

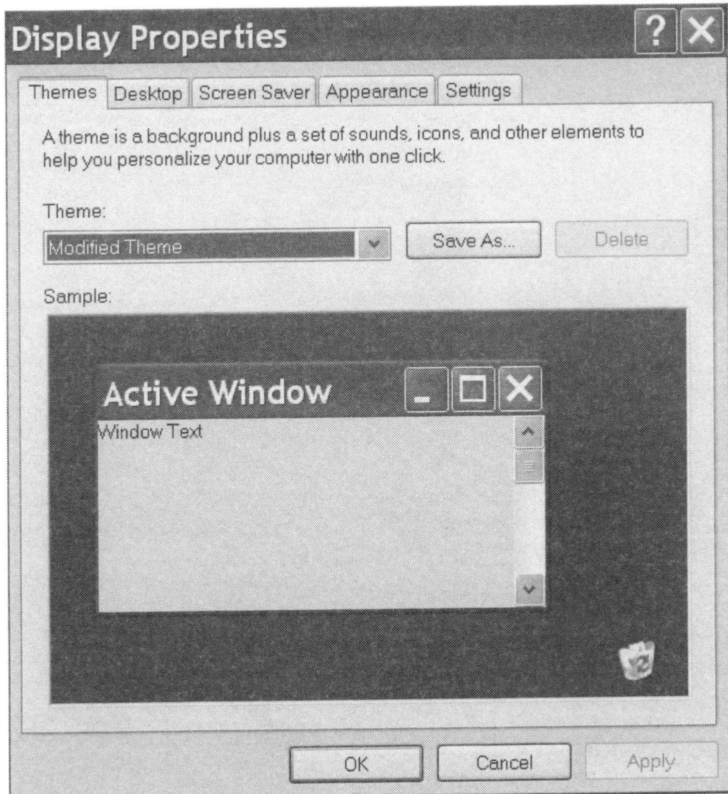

Fig.3.4 The Themes section of the Display Properties window

When you need to change the video settings, the first task is to launch the Windows Control Panel. The available routes to this built-in Windows program depend on how Windows is set up, but with a new installation there should be a menu entry for it in the Start menu (Figure 3.1). Left-click the Start button in the bottom left-hand corner of the Windows Desktop, and then left-click the Control Panel entry. A new window containing the Control Panel should then appear (Figure 3.2).

Next, left-click the Appearance and Themes link at the top left-hand corner of the main panel, or the Appearance and Personalization link in Vista. This will change the Control Panel to look like Figure 3.3. Here you must left-click the Display link in the bottom section of the main panel, and this will launch a small window (Figure 3.4). The Display Properties

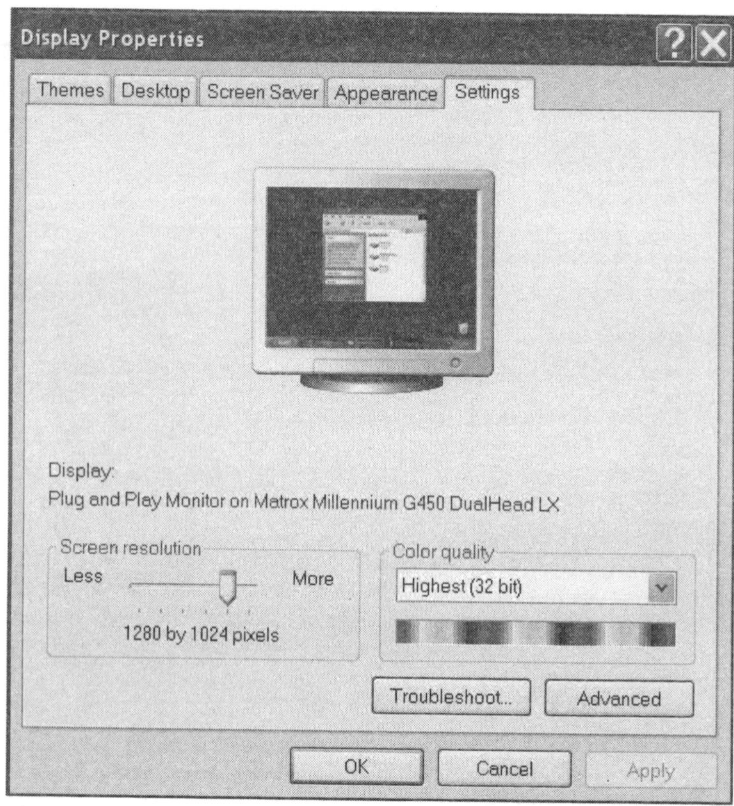

Fig.3.5 The Settings section of the Display Properties window

window is extremely useful, and it provides tremendous control over the appearance of Windows. Since many application programs have their appearance based on the colour schemes, etc., of Windows, this utility also governs the appearance of most of the programs that you will be using.

The Display Properties window has five sections, and the Themes section is selected by default. Note that in Windows Vista there are five separate windows that are accessed via the links in the Personalization section. The controls that we require are obtained by left-clicking the Settings tab near the top right-hand corner of the window, or the "Adjust screen resolution link" in Vista. This changes the window to look something like

Figure 3.5. The Screen Resolution slider control can be used to adjust the horizontal and vertical resolution of the screen, and there will typically be about half a dozen combinations on offer.

A computer's display is produced from thousands of tiny dots, or pixels as they are called. It is a sort of high-tech mosaic. Screen resolution is specified in terms of the number of pixels used. With a screen resolution of (say) 1024 by 768, there are 1024 pixels in each row, and 768 rows. This gives 786,432 pixels in total, which might sound a lot, but this is about the minimum that will give good results with much of the software in use today.

Opinions differ about the ideal screen resolution, but it is dependent on the type of software you will be running and the characteristics of the monitor you are using. In general, higher resolution is better, but only if your monitor can handle it properly. In the case of a laptop, its LCD screen should give good results at its highest resolution. However, high resolution requires a large monitor so that you can see everything clearly. Even for those with good eyesight, a small but highly detailed screen is difficult to use. Using a PC is likely to be very tiring if you have to strain your eyesight in order to see the screen properly. It could be harmful to your eyesight as well. A laptop that has a small screen which normally runs at a high resolution might be easier to use if a lower resolution is selected. This is really a subjective matter, and you have to choose whatever resolution suits you best.

The scan rate used by the monitor is also an important factor. The picture on the monitor is updated at a rate that is usually between about 50 and 100 times per second. This is normally called something like the "scan rate" or "refresh rate", and is given as a frequency in hertz. A scan rate of 75 hertz (75Hz) for example, means that the picture is updated 75 times per second. You will probably find other frequencies mentioned in monitor specifications, but the scan rate is the only one that is of importance to most users.

In the past it was quite common for monitors to have impressive maximum resolutions, but these could only be achieved by resorting to quite low scan rates. This usually gave a picture that had a noticeable flickering making these monitors difficult to use for anything other than short periods. Modern monitors are generally better, and it should not be a problem using the built-in LCD monitor of a laptop PC. It could be a significant factor if the laptop is connected to an external monitor.

A slight problem with some flat panel monitors is that they do not handle fast movement very well. For example, an onscreen object moving quickly

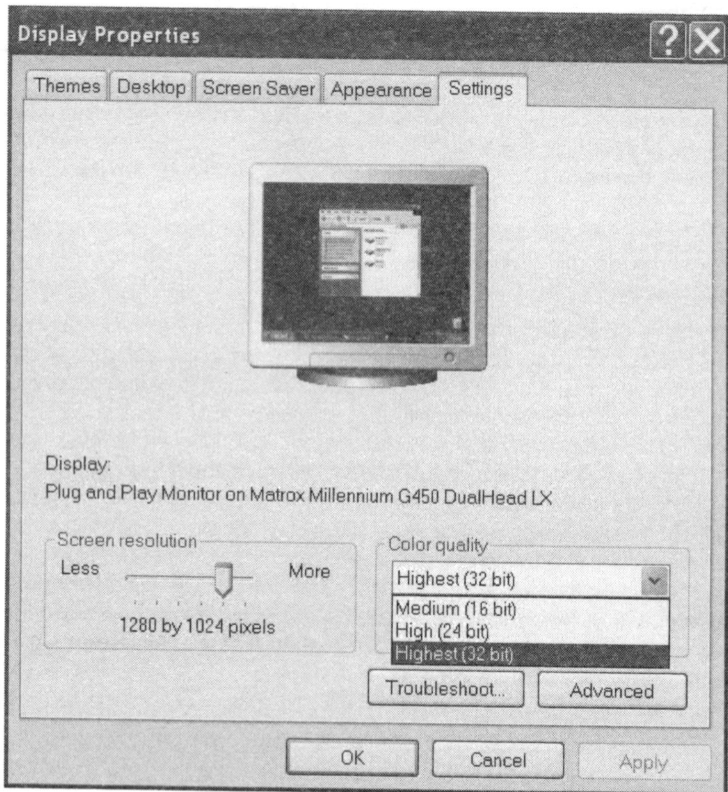

Fig.3.6 The Color quality menu offers various colour depths

across the screen can tend to leave a slight and brief trail. With many types of software this is not particularly noticeable, but it can be very apparent with some games or when playing videos on a PC. This is just a characteristic of some monitors and there is nothing that can be done about it by adjusting the video settings.

Colour depth

Colour depth is just a fancy term for the number of colours that can be displayed. This is a factor that is governed by the display adaptor in the PC rather than the monitor, although with flat-panel screens the monitor might be the limiting factor. There is usually a choice of three colour

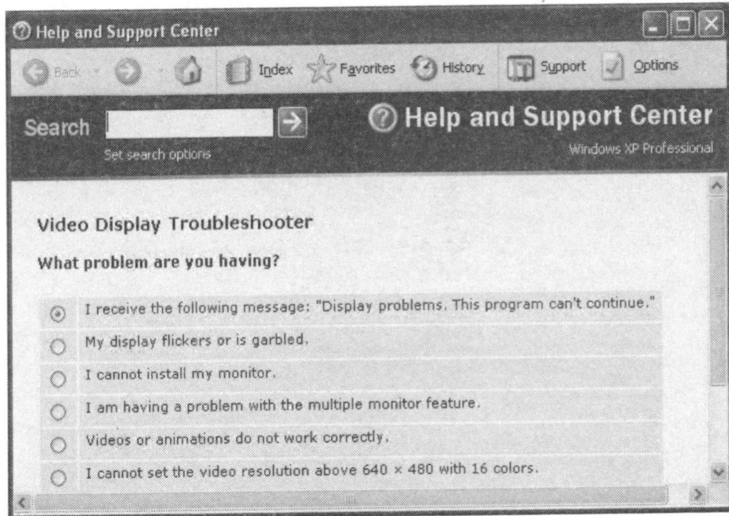

Fig.3.7 The Video Display Troubleshooter

depths on offer from the Colour quality menu near the bottom right-hand corner of the Display Properties window (Figure 3.6). These are 16, 24, and 32 bits, bit there could be some lower options as well. This table shows the correlation between the number of bits and the number of colours provided:

Bits	Colours
4	16
8	256
16	65536
24	16.777 million
32	About 4,300 million

In general, higher colour depth settings give better looking results, especially when photographic images are displayed. On the other hand, the results obtained using 16-bit resolution are very good, and there is probably no point in going beyond 24-bit resolution. Bear in mind that greater colour depth tends to slow things down, and that some programs

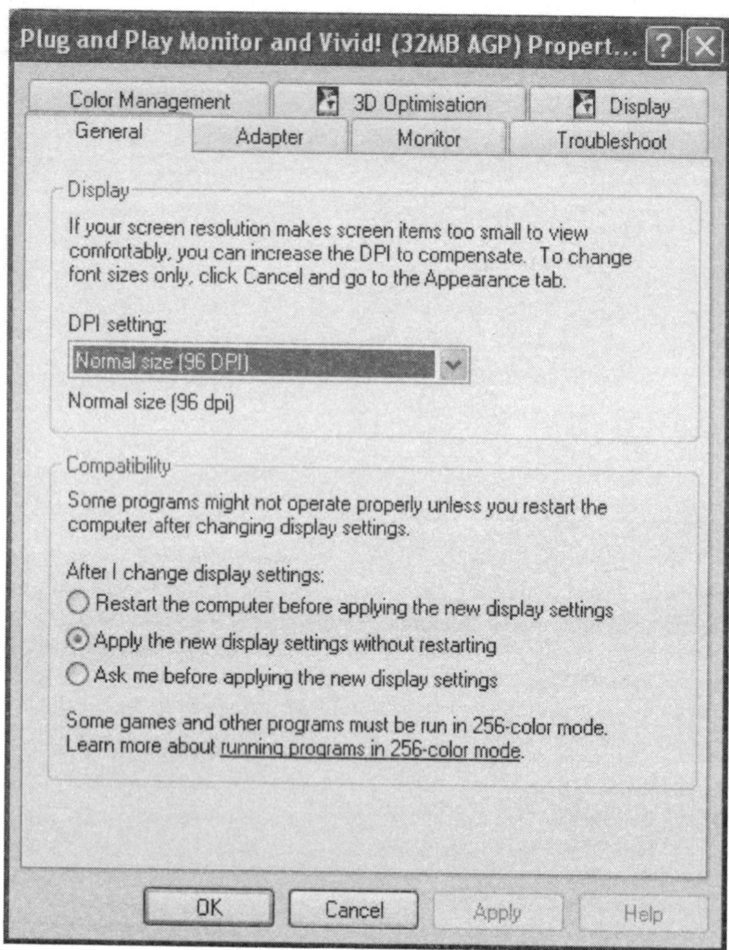

Fig.3.8 Operating the Advanced button produces this window

might not operate at a usable speed unless a fairly low colour depth is used. The optimum colour depth is the lowest one which gives a display quality that you find acceptable.

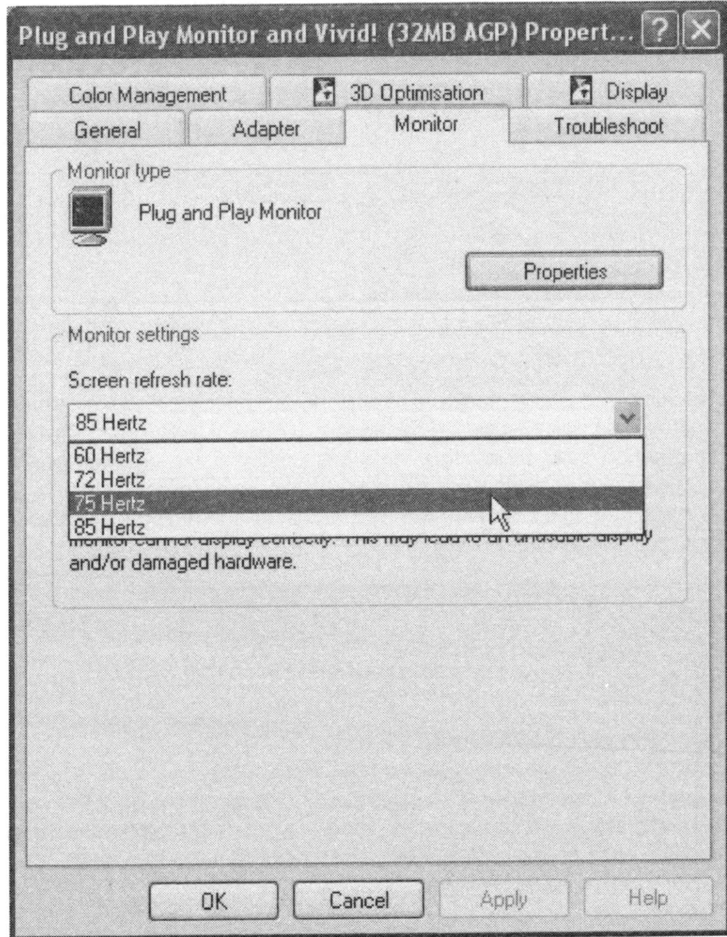

Fig.3.9 A range of scan frequencies is available here

In practice

Having set the required screen resolution and colour depth, operate the Apply button. It is likely that Windows is overestimating the abilities of the monitor if the screen goes blank or produces an unstable image. The screen should return to normal in a few seconds though. One way

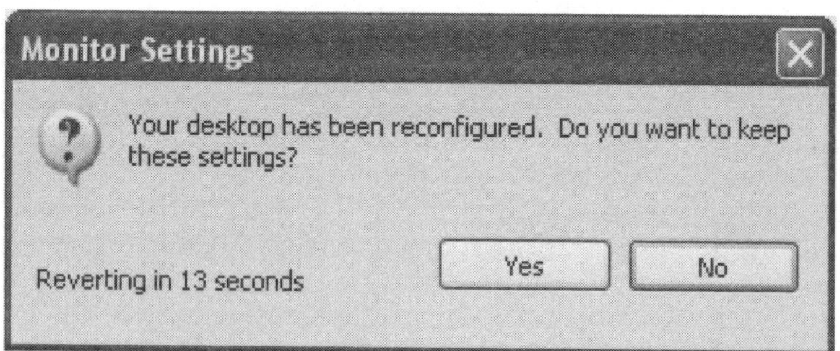

Fig.3.10 Operate the Yes button if this window is displayed properly

of tackling the problem is to operate the Troubleshoot button, which launches the Video Display Troubleshooter (Figure 3.7). By going through the questions and suggested cures it is likely that the problem would soon be solved. However, the most likely cause of the problem is Windows setting a scan rate that is too high for the monitor, and this is easily corrected.

First set the required screen resolution again, and then left-click the Advanced button to bring up a window like the one in Figure 3.8. Next, operate the Monitor tab to switch the window to one like Figure 3.9. Activate the Screen refresh rate menu, and choose a lower rate than the one currently in use. In this example the rate was reduced from 85 hertz to 75 hertz. Left-click the Apply button and observe the screen.

With luck, this time a small window like the one shown in Figure 3.10 will be visible on the screen. If so, operate the Yes button to keep the new scan rate. If not, wait for a proper display to return and then repeat this process using an even lower scan rate. Note that the maximum scan rate for a monitor generally reduces as the screen resolution is increased. Consequently, the higher the screen resolution used, the lower the scan rate that will have to be set.

Deleting

As pointed out previously, it is likely that the new computer will have been supplied with some preinstalled software that is of no interest to you, and which might actually be a bit of a nuisance. Removing unwanted software from a PC is not usually too difficult, but it is important to go about things in the right fashion. Simply deleting the files and folders associated with programs you wish to remove is definitely going about

Fig.3.11 The Apple QuickTime submenu

things in the wrong fashion. It will certainly free some hard disc space, but deleting program files and folders is also likely to produce a few problems.

Most programs are installed onto the computer using an installation program, and this program does not simply make folders on the hard disc and copy files into them from the CD-ROM. It will also make changes to the Windows configuration files so that the program is properly integrated with the operating system. If you simply delete the program's directory structure to get rid of it, Windows will not be aware that the program has been removed. During the boot-up process the operating system will probably look for files associated with the deleted program, and will produce error messages when it fails to find them.

Matters are actually more involved than this, and there is another potential problem in that Windows utilizes shared files. This is where one file, such as a DLL type, is shared by two or more programs. In deleting a program and the other files in its directory structure you could also be deleting files needed by other programs. This could prevent other programs from working properly, or even from starting up at all.

If a program is loaded onto the hard disc using an installation program, the only safe way of removing it is to use an uninstaller program. There are three possible ways of handling this.

Custom uninstaller

Some programs load an uninstaller program onto the hard disc as part of the installation process. This program is then available via the Start menu if you choose All Programs, and then the name of the program concerned. When you choose this option there will be the program

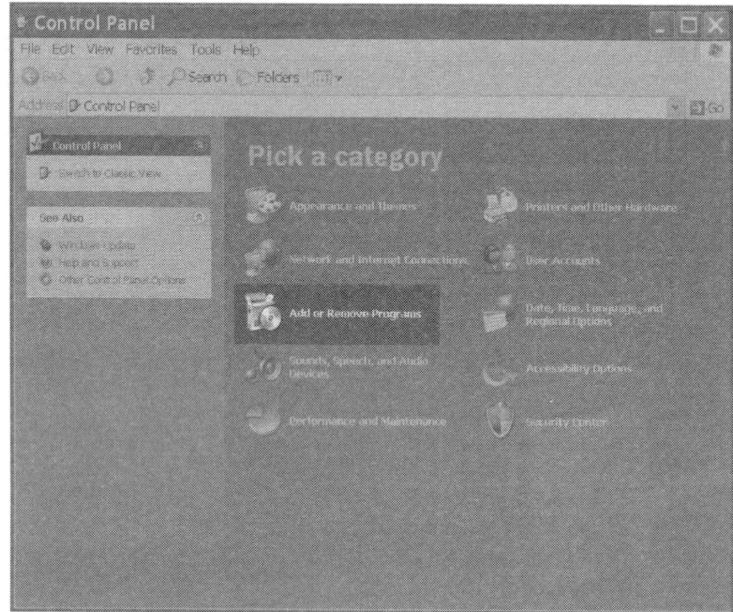

Fig.3.12 Activate the Add or Remove Programs icon or text

itself, plus at least one additional option in the sub-menu that appears. If there is no uninstall option here, no custom uninstaller has been installed for that program. The example of Figure 3.11 shows the submenu for the Apple QuickTime program, and this one does include an option to uninstall the program. Uninstaller programs of this type are almost invariably automatic in operation, so you have to do little more than instruct it to go ahead with the removal of the program.

With any uninstaller software you may be asked if certain files should be removed. This mostly occurs where the program finds shared files that no longer appear to be shared. In days gone by it did not seem to matter whether you opted to remove or leave these files, with Windows failing to work properly thereafter! These days things seem to be more reliable, and it is reasonably safe to accept either option. To leave the files in place is certainly the safest option, but it also results in files and possibly folders being left on the disc unnecessarily.

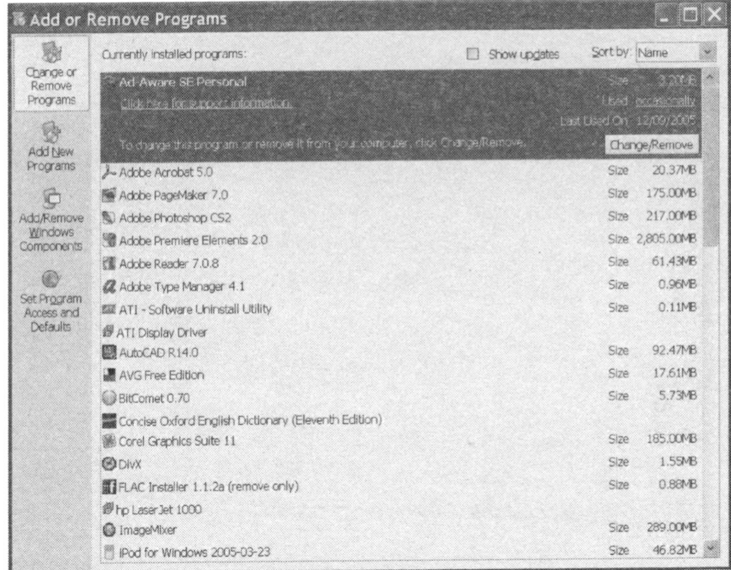

Fig.3.13 A list of installed programs is provided

Windows uninstaller

Windows has a built-in uninstaller that can be accessed via the control panel. In Windows XP, from the Start menu select Control Panel, and in the Control Panel (Figure 3.12) left-click the Add or Remove Programs icon. In Windows Vista, go to the Control Panel and select the "Uninstall programs" link in the Programs section. By default this takes you to the uninstaller, and the main section of the screen shows a list of the programs that can be uninstalled via this route (Figure 3.13). Removing a program is just a matter of selecting it from the list and then operating the Remove button. Confirm that you wish to remove the program when prompted in the new window that appears, and the removal process will then begin.

In theory the list should include all programs that have been added to the hard disc using an installation program. In practice there may be one or two that have not been installed "by the book" and can not be removed using this method. Some programs can only be removed using their own uninstaller program, while others have no means of removal at all. It is mainly older software that falls into the non-removable category, particularly programs that were written for Windows 3.1 and not one of

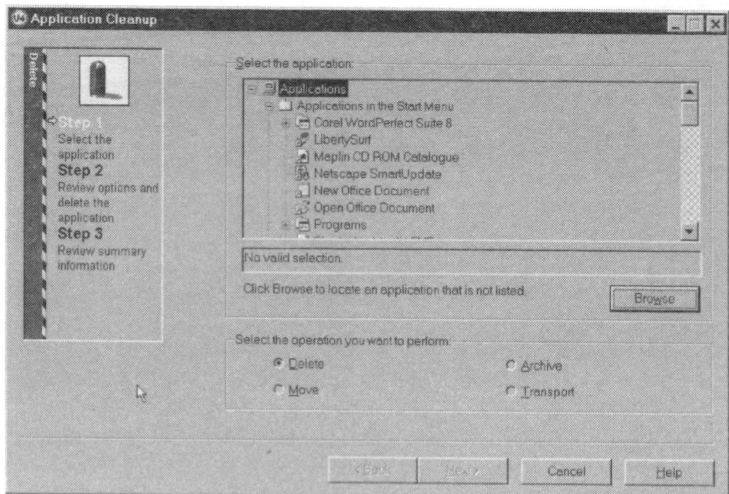

Fig.3.14 The CyberMedia Uninstaller program in action

the 32-bit versions of Windows. In fact it is very unusual for old Windows 3.1 software to have any means of removal. Fortunately, there is very little software of this vintage that is still in use.

Third party

There are uninstaller programs available that can be used to monitor an installation and then uninstall the software at some later time. As this feature is built into any modern version of Windows, and the vast majority of applications programs now either utilize the built-in facility or have their own uninstaller software, these programs are perhaps less useful than they once were.

Most will also assist in the removal of programs that they have not been used to install, and this is perhaps the more useful role. Most will also help with the removal of things like unwanted entries in the Start menu and act as general cleanup software, although Windows itself provides means of clearing some of this software debris. Figure 3.14 shows the CyberMedia Uninstaller program in action, but there are numerous programs of this type to choose from.

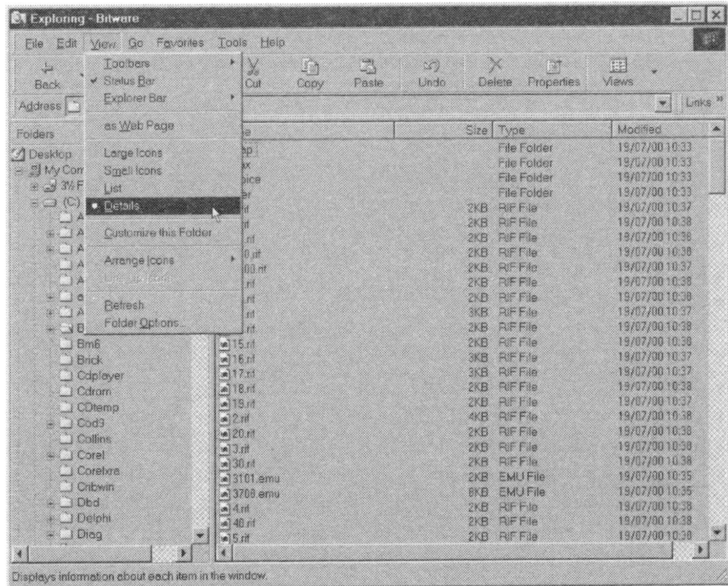

Fig.3.15 Select the Details option from the View menu

Leftovers

Having removed a program by whatever means, you will sometimes find that there are still some files and folders associated with the program remaining on the hard disc. In some cases the remaining files are simply data or configuration files that have been generated while you were trying out or setting up the program. There should obviously be nothing of any importance here when deleting unused software from a new computer. Accordingly, there should be no problems if these files are deleted using Windows Explorer. In other cases the files could be system files that the uninstaller has decided not to remove in case they are needed by other applications. Removing files of this type is more risky and it is probably better to leave them in place.

Sometimes the folders may seem to be empty, but it is best to check carefully before removing them. An important point to bear in mind here is that not all files are shown when using the default settings of Windows Explorer. Using the default settings hidden files will live up to their name and files having certain extensions are not shown either. In normal use this can be helpful because it results in files that are likely to be of interest

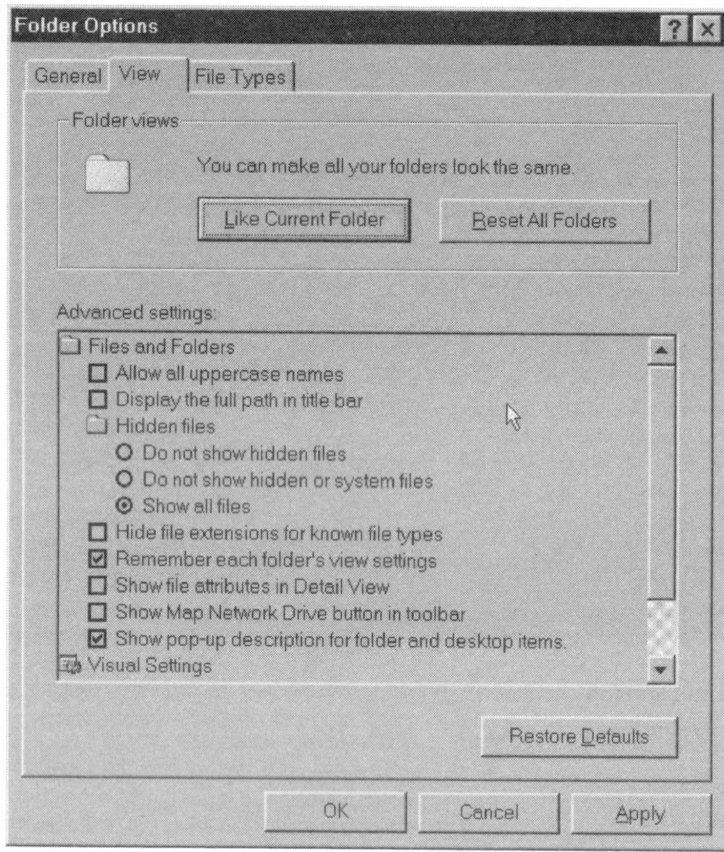

Fig.3.16 Operate the View tab in the Folder Options window

being shown, while those that are of no interest are hidden. This makes it much easier to find the files you require in a folder that contains large numbers of files.

It is clearly unhelpful when looking inside folders to see if they contain any files, as it could give the impression that a folder is empty when it does in fact contain files. Windows Explorer should be set to show as much detail about the files as possible. First go to the View menu and select the Details option (Figure 3.15). This will result in the size, type, and date of each file being shown. Then go to the View menu again, select Folder Options (Organise - Folder and Search options in Vista), and then left-click on the View tab in the new Window that appears (Figure 3.16).

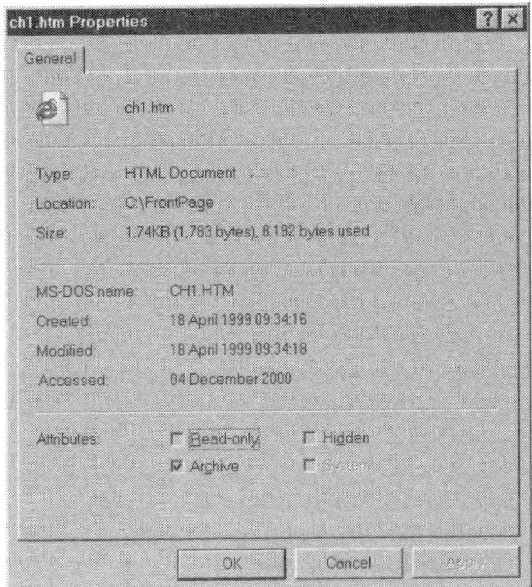

Fig.3.17 The properties window for a file

Under the Hidden Files entry in the main section of the window select the "Show all files" option. The hidden files are certain critical system files, such as those associated with the Windows Registry, that are not normally displayed by Windows Explorer so that they can not be accidentally altered or erased by the user. I would recommend ticking the checkbox for "Display full path in title bar". This way you can always see exactly what folder you are investigating, even if it is one that is buried deep in a complex directory structure.

Remove the tick in the checkbox next to "Hide the extension for known file types". The extension should then be shown for all file types, which makes it easy to see which one is which when several files have the same main file name. When viewing the contents of directories you can use either the List or Details options under the View menu, but the Details option provides a little more information. It provides the file type if it is a recognised type, the date that the file was created or last altered. If the "Show attributes in Detail view" checkbox is ticked, it will also show the attribute of the file. These are the letters used for each of the four attributes:

A Archive

H Hidden

R Read-only

S System

Thus a file that has "R" as its attribute letter it is a read-only type, and one that has "HA" in the attribute column is a hidden archive file. Choose the List option if you prefer to have as many files as possible listed on the screen. Details of any file listed can be obtained by right-clicking on its entry in Windows Explorer and then choosing the Properties option from the pop-up menu. This will bring up a screen of the type shown in Figure 3.17, which shows the type of file, the creation date, when it was last modified, size, etc. The Windows Vista version is more elaborate, but still provides the same basic information.

Make sure that the checkbox for the "Remember each folder's view settings" is not ticked. Placing a tick in this box gives each folder its own settings, making it necessary to alter the settings for individual folders rather than altering them globally.

If any folders are definitely empty, there should be no problem if they are removed. The same is true of data and configuration files that are no longer needed. With other files it may not be clear what their exact purpose is, and it is a bit risky removing files of unknown function.

Softly, softly

Unfortunately, it is not uncommon for uninstallers to leave large numbers of files on the hard disc. The uninstaller seems to go through its routine in standard fashion, and reports that the program has been fully removed, but an inspection of the hard disc reveals that a vast directory structure remains. I have encountered uninstallers that have left more than 50 megabytes of files on the disc, removing only about 10% of those initially installed.

Other uninstallers report that some files and folders could not be removed, and that they must be dealt with manually. Some uninstallers seem to concentrate on extricating the program from the operating system by removing references to the program in the Windows registry, etc., rather than trying to remove all trace of it from the hard disc.

If you are simply trying to remove a troublesome program that produces annoying pop-up messages, uninstalling it should have the desired result and prevent the messages from appearing. If you are trying to free hard disc space, an uninstaller that leaves many megabytes of files in place is not very helpful. Try to keep things in perspective though. The hard disc drives used in laptop PCs generally have lower capacities than those used in desktop PCs, but the actual capacity is still likely to be quite high at around 40 gigabytes or more. Will removing (say) 100 megabytes (0.1 gigabytes) of files really make that much difference?

Removing leftover files is a bit risky, so due care needs to be taken if you do decide to go ahead. Most modern PCs are supplied with a disc that can be used to quickly restore the hard disc to its original state. Since no data will have been placed on the hard disc drive at this stage, there is not a lot to lose by taking things back to the beginning again. It is still better to avoid problems though, and take a softly, softly approach.

A safe way of handling things is to leave the directory structure and files intact, but change some file or folder names. If only a few files have been left behind, try adding a letter at the front of each filename. For example, a file called "drawprog.dll" could be renamed "zdrawprog.dll". This will prevent Windows from finding the file if it should be needed for some reason, but it is an easy matter for you to correct things by removing the "z" from the filename if problems occur.

If there are numerous files in a complex directory structure to deal with it is not practical to rename all the individual files. Instead, the name of the highest folder in the directory structure should be renamed. This should make it impossible for Windows to find the file unless it does a complete search of the hard disc, and the change is easily reversed if problems should occur. Provided the computer runs for a few days with no problems it should then be safe to go ahead and remove the files and folders.

User accounts

At least one user account is produced when Windows XP is installed. There will often be two accounts, which are the Administrator account , and one for the user of the PC. Both accounts are normally assigned the same password. The idea is for the Administrator account to be used by the person that looks after the computers in an office. Each user of a PC has a separate account, with Windows set up the way that each user likes it when they use their account. As far as possible, each user effectively has their own PC, but obviously only one user at a time can login and utilise each PC.

Some computer retailers supply their PCs fully set up and ready for use, sometimes complete with several user accounts installed. However, things do not normally operate this way if you buy an "off the shelf" PC, although it is often offered as a fairly pricey option. Any additional accounts you require normally have to be set up manually yourself.

Of course, user accounts can be irrelevant, especially in a home or small business environment. They may offer no advantages when there is

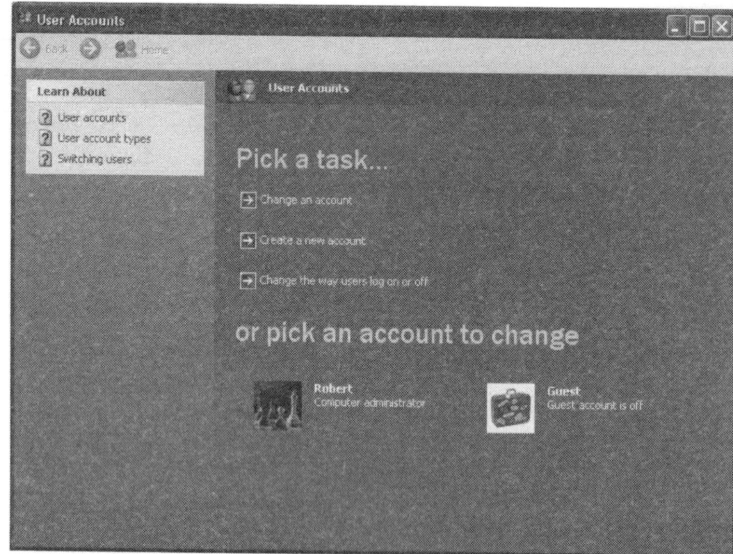

Fig.3.18 The User Accounts window

only a single user for each PC. Even with two or three users per PC, they might prefer not to bother with the complication of separate accounts. On the other hand, some individual users do actually have several accounts, with Windows set up in a different fashion for each type of use. It is really a matter of personal preference.

Administrator

The Administrator account is usually reserved for making changes to the system or troubleshooting, since it gives full control over the system. As a minimum, there should be at least one additional account for normal use. As pointed out previously, this will often be installed by default. It might be necessary to add it yourself, and you will probably wish to add one or two extra accounts if the PC is for family use.

The first step in adding a new account is to go to the Control Panel and left-click the User Accounts icon, or the "Add or remove user account" link in Vista. This launches a window like the one in Figure 3.18. Left-click the link for "Create a new account", which switches the window to the one shown in Figure 3.19. Type a name for the account into the textbox and then operate the Next button.

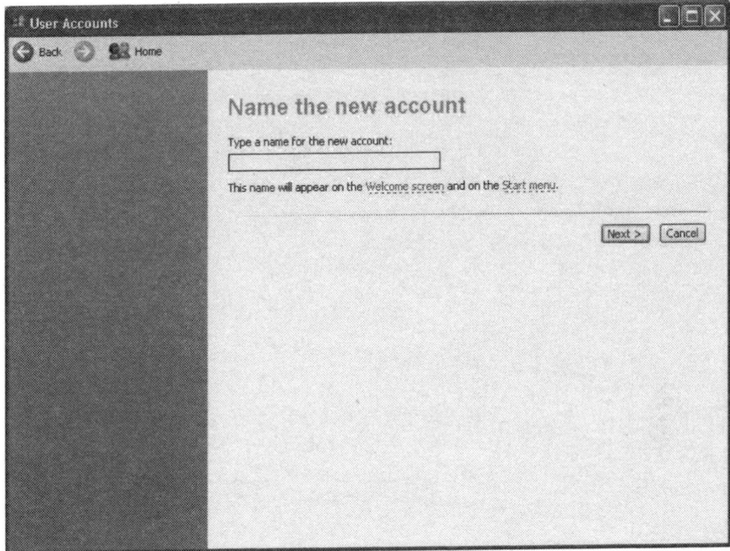

Fig.3.19 Here is name is provided for the new account

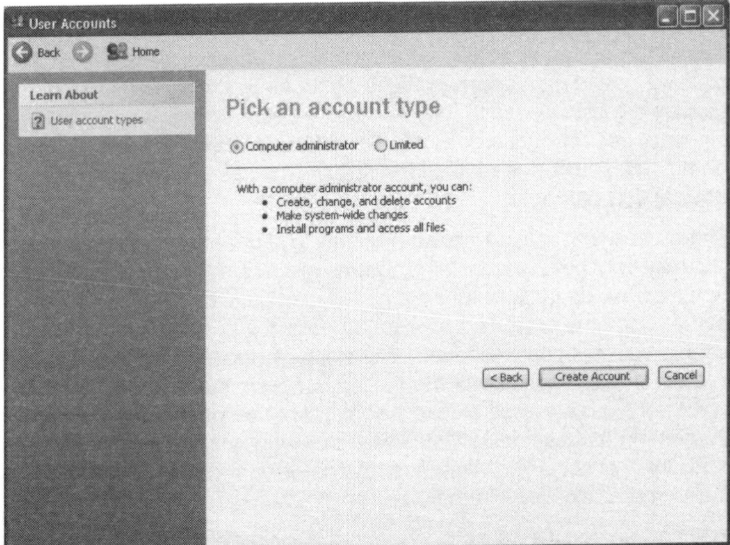

Fig.3.20 This window is used to choose the type of account

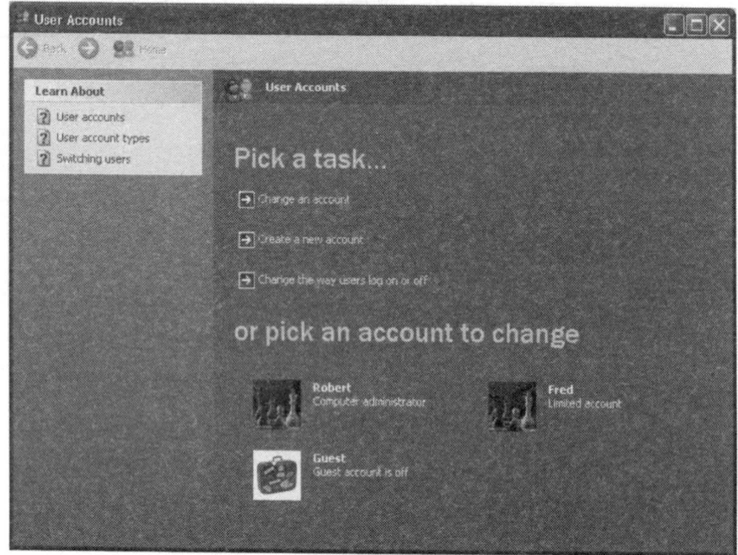

Fig.3.21 The User Accounts window shows an icon for the new account

The type of account is selected at the next window (Figure 3.20). Note that with Windows Vista this is done in the first window. An administrator account provides freedom to make changes to the system, but these abilities are not needed for day to day use of the computer. A limited or standard use account is generally considered to be the better choice for normal use, since the restrictions reduce the risk of the system being accidentally damaged.

There are a few points to bear in mind if you opt for a limited account. You might not be able to install programs when using this type of account. Any that you do install might not be fully available to other users. Also, some programs produced prior to Windows 2000 and XP might not be usable with a limited account. It is possible to make changes to the system that will only affect the limited account, but any wider ranging changes are likely to be blocked. It might not be possible to undertake something as basic as uninstalling a program when using this type of account. Consequently, there is no alternative to an administrator account if maximum flexibility is required.

Having selected the type of account using the radio buttons, operate the Create Account button. The original User Accounts window then returns,

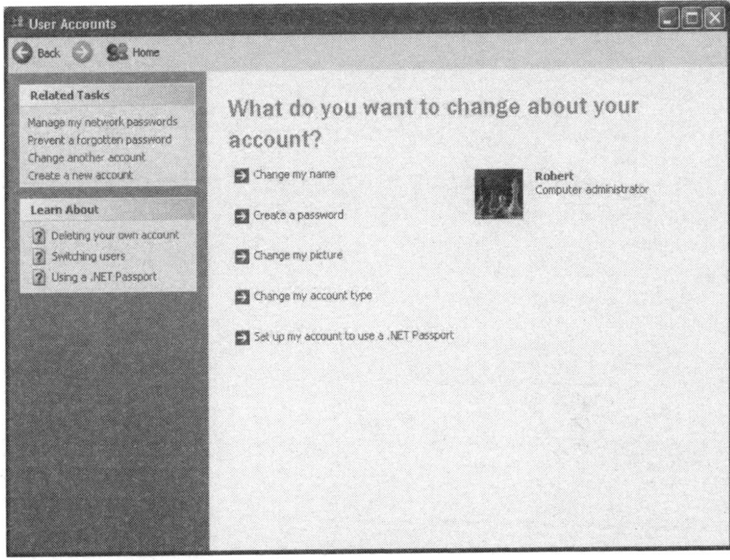

Fig.3.22 Operate the Create password link

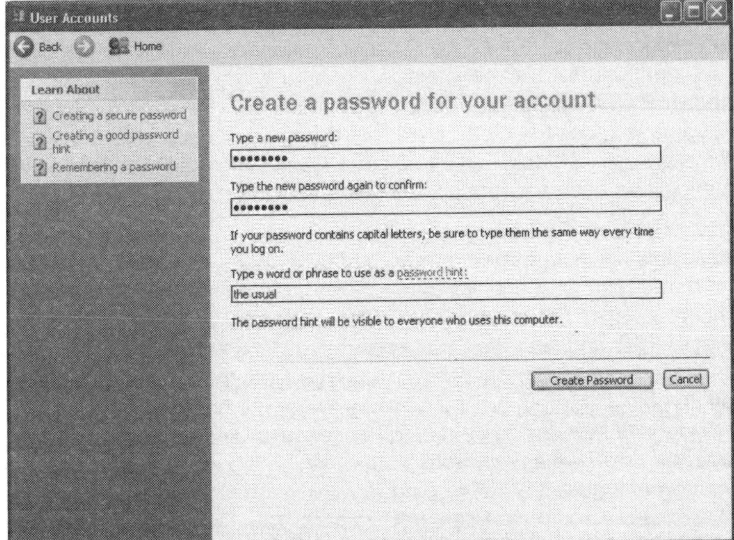

Fig.3.23 In this window the password is entered twice

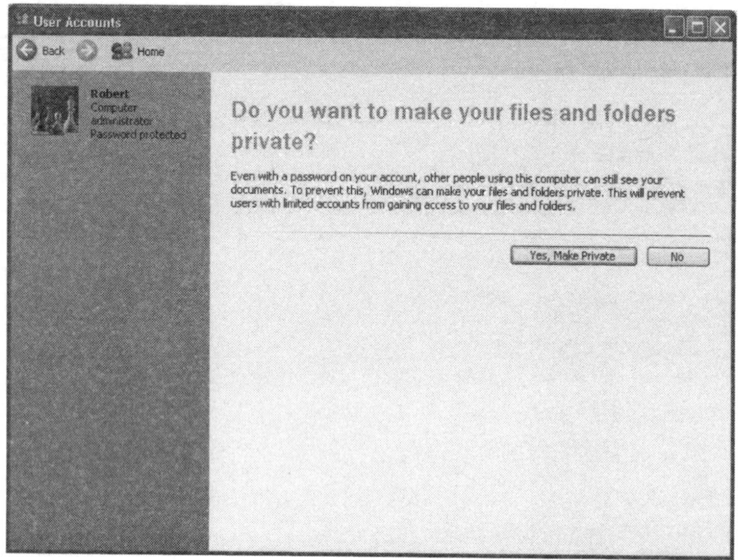

Fig.3.24 This window provides the option of making the user's files private

but it should now contain the newly created account (Figure 3.21). There are other facilities in the User Accounts window that enable the login and logoff settings to be altered. By default, the Welcome screen is shown at start-up, and you simply have to left-click the entry for the new account in order to use it. Note that the new account will start with a largely blank desktop. Each account has its own desktop and other settings, so each account can be customised with the best settings for its particular user.

Accounts are not password protected by default. To add a password, go to the User Accounts window and left-click the entry for the account that you wish to password protect. This switches the window to look like Figure 3.22, and here the Create password link is activated. At the next window (Figure 3.23) the password is typed into the top two textboxes, and a hint is entered into the other textbox. The hint is something that will jog your memory if you should happen to forget the password. Next operate the Create Password button, which moves things on to the window of Figure 3.24. This window explains that password protection does not prevent other users from reading your files. Operate the Yes Make Private button if you would like to prevent other users from accessing your files. Note that this window does not appear when using

Fig.3.25 The Classic version of the Windows Control Panel

Windows Vista. This completes the process, and the password will be needed the next time you login to that account.

On button

The button that is used to switch on the computer might have an additional function, or it might do nothing at all while the computer is switched on. The safe option is to have it do nothing at all, since there is a risk that it will be operated by mistake. This is the likely default setting, but it might have an alternative function. Windows enables the function of the On button to be altered by the user, but only a few options are available.

Start by going to the Control Panel, and then left-click the Switch to Classic View link near the top left-hand corner of the window. The Control Panel will then change to look something like Figure 3.25, but the exact icons present depends to some extent on the installed software and the computer's hardware configuration. However, there should always be a Power Options icon, and double-clicking it will produce the Power Options Properties window (Figure 3.26).

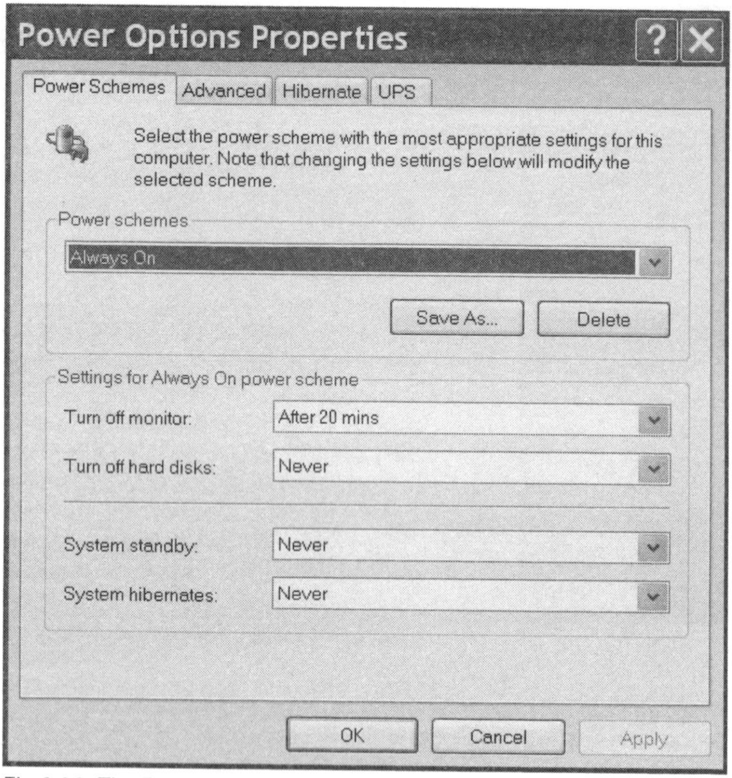

Fig.3.26 The Power Options Properties window

It is the Advanced section of the properties window that is of interest in this case, and it is selected by left-clicking the Advanced tab near the top of the window. The Power Options Properties window then changes to look like Figure 3.27. There are two menus near the bottom of the window, and Figure 3.28 shows the options available from the power button menu. Note that with Vista you have to operate the "Change advanced power settings" link, and then go to the "Power button and lid folder", followed by the "power button action" folder.

The options available via the sleep button menu are exactly the same. Note though, that by no means all PCs, whether laptop or desktop, actually have a Sleep button. If there is one on your laptop it will probably have a crescent shaped icon that resembles a new moon. In the likely

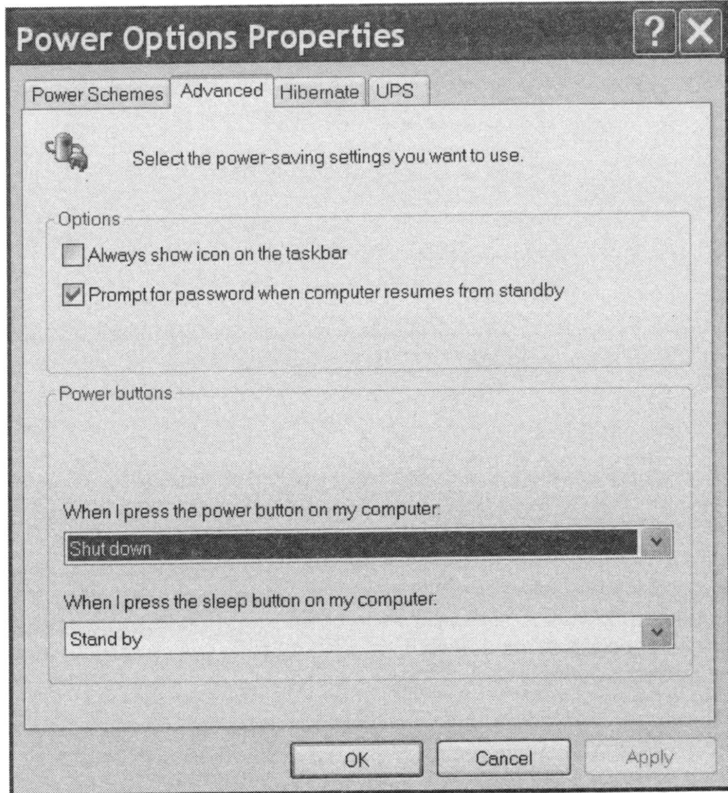

Fig.3.27 The advanced section of the Power Options Properties window

event that there is no Sleep button on you computer, the settings in the menu for this button will be of no practical importance.

These are the functions provided by each menu option:

Do Nothing

As it says, with this option selected the On button will be totally inoperative once the computer is running. While this limits the usefulness of the button, it does ensure that there is no danger of accidentally operating it and switching off the computer. Bear in mind that any accidental shutting down of the computer is not just a minor inconvenience. It is likely to result in a certain amount of work being lost, so it is best avoided!

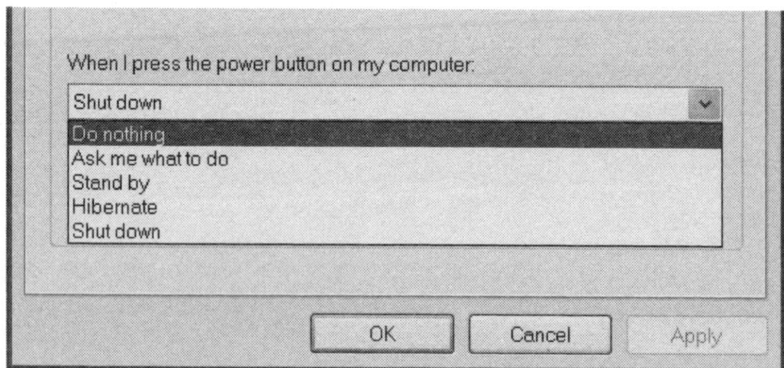

Fig.3.28 A menu provides five On button options

Ask me what to do

Pressing the On button with this option selected produces the same small window (Figure 3.29) that appears when shutting down the computer in the normal way. This is a useful option since it does not render the On button useless when the computer is running, but accidentally operating the button will not immediately shut down the computer. Instead, you have the usual options, which include shutting down the computer, restarting it, or cancelling the operation and carry on with your computing.

Standby

If your PC has a Sleep button, then it is this option that the button will usually provide. In this context "sleep" and "standby" are alternative terms for the same thing. When a computer is set into the standby mode it might appear to be switched off, or there could still be a few obvious signs of activity. This depends on the particular computer concerned and the way in which it is set up. Typically, the monitor will switch off, as will the hard disc drive or drives.

The point of the Standby mode is to take the computer into a state where it consumes relatively little power. The main point of this when using a desktop PC is to save electricity and reduce the running costs. With a laptop it is more a matter of reducing the drain on the battery if the computer will not be used for a while, but you wish to avoid shutting it down and starting up again. You can place the computer into the Standby mode via the Start menu, so it is not essential to have a button set up to access this feature. On the other hand, having the On button or a Sleep button to access the standby mode is a convenient way of handling things.

When using the standby mode you should bear in mind that any work that has not been saved to the hard disc drive will not be saved automatically by the operating system when the computer enters the standby mode. Therefore, some work is likely to be lost if the power fails while the computer is in this mode. The risk is probably very small when using a desktop PC, but is clearly much higher when working with a laptop PC where the battery might be nearing exhaustion. When you use standby mode it is advisable to make sure that all work is saved to the hard disc first.

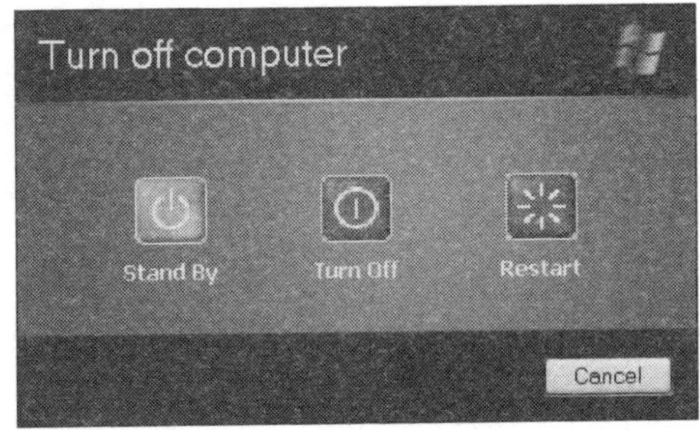

Fig.3.29 The usual closing down options are provided

Hibernate

The hibernate mode is similar to the standby type, but it copies the contents of the computer's memory to the hard disc drive. This means that, in theory at any rate, it is possible for the system to switch off more of the hardware in this mode and it can recover from a power failure with all data intact. The price that is paid for this is that it takes much longer for the computer to enter this state and exit from it again. Also, the hibernate mode uses up hard disc space, so there must be enough free disc space for this mode work.

Although fine in theory, the hibernate mode does sometimes give problems in practice. Having entered this mode, you might find that the computer crashes or behaves erratically when you try to return it to normal operation. I would certainly recommend trying it a few times to check that it works reliably with your computer before making it a normal part of the way you work. This mode seems to be little used in practice.

Probably most PC users settle for the standby mode if they will not be using their laptop for relatively brief periods. In this mode it can be brought back to normal operation very quickly. If it will not be used for some time, probably the best approach is to make sure that everything is safely

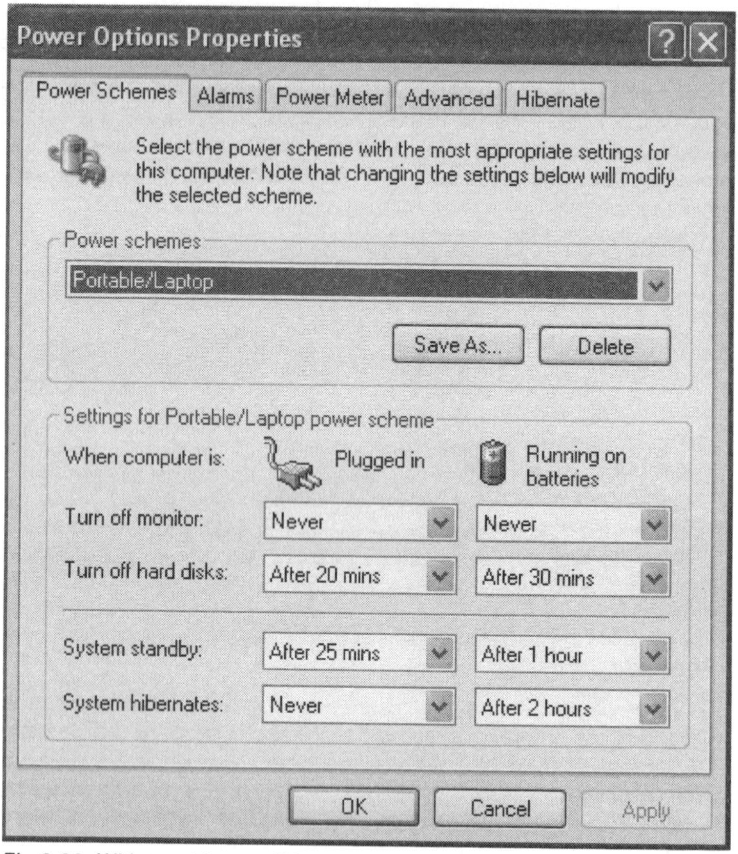

Fig.3.30 With most laptop PCs there are more power options

saved to disc and then shutdown the computer. Reboot the computer when you are ready to resume work. After all, the computer is in the ultimate power saving mode when it is switched off.

Shutdown

In this mode the computer shuts down when the button is operated, but without the usual window that gives you other options (Figure 3.29). Having pressed the button, the computer will shut down and there is no opportunity to change your mind. This has to be regarded as a bit risky and probably not an option that is worth using.

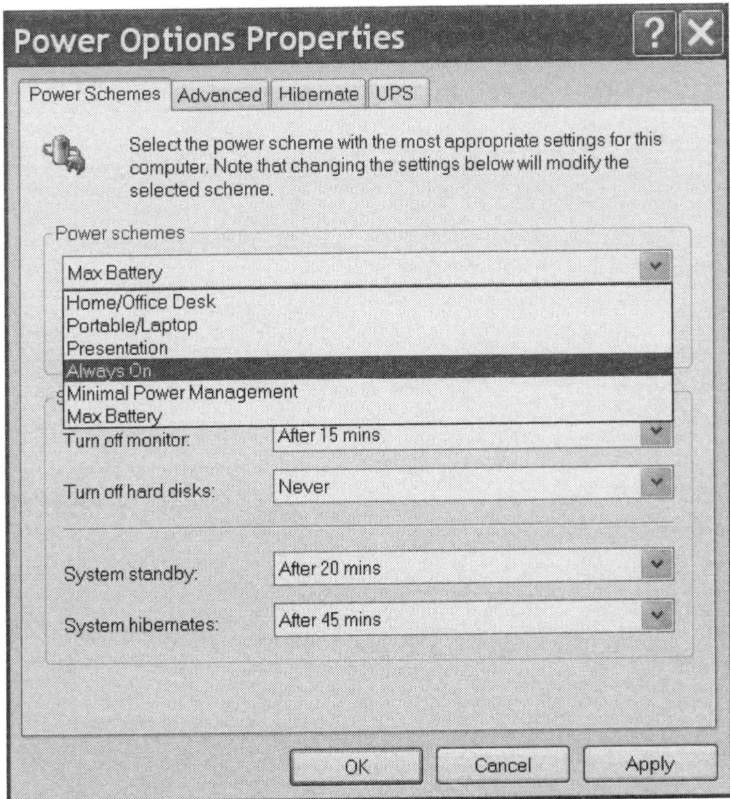

Fig.3.31 Several power management options are available

Open and shut

With most modern laptop PCs there will some extra features available from the Power Options Properties window. Figure 3.30 shows the initial Power Options Properties window for a modern Dell laptop PC. This section allows various parts of the hardware to be automatically switched off when a specified condition has been met. You might like to change something here, but it is probably best to leave these settings unless there is good reason to do otherwise. There are other power management options available from the menu (Figure 3.31), including an Always On option that effectively removes any power management.

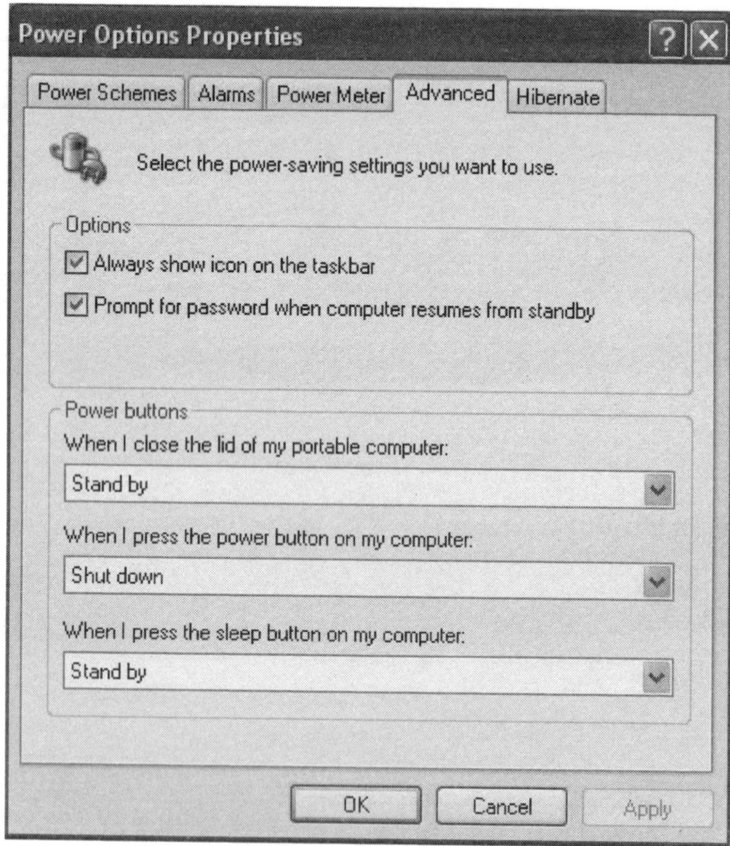

Fig.3.32 There is an additional menu for the lid of the computer

Fig.3.33 The menu for the lid has three options

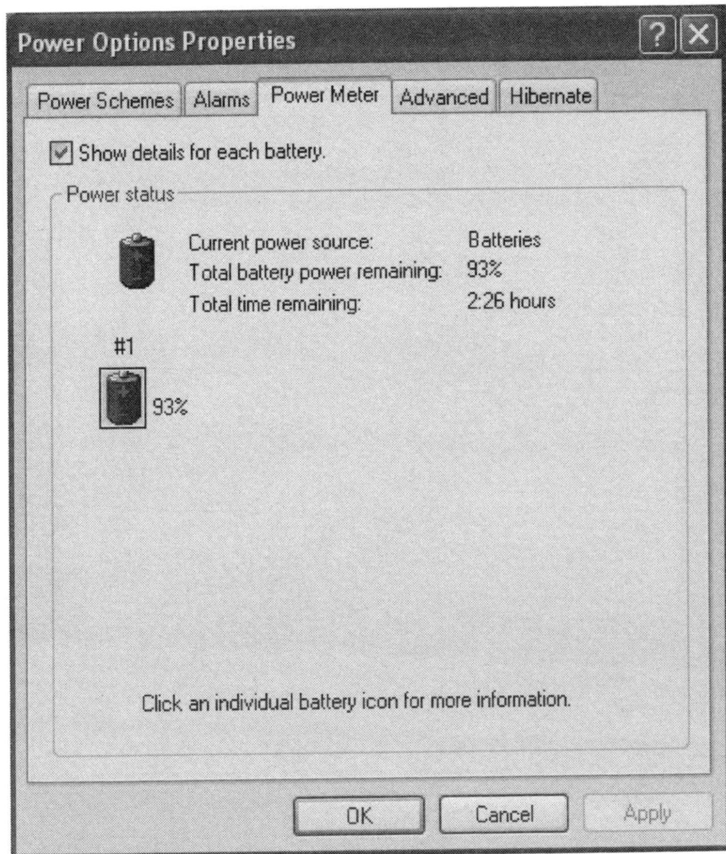

Fig.3.34 The Power Meter shows the state of the battery

In the Advanced section (Figure 3.32) there are three menus in the lower part of the screen. The extra one is for the lid of the computer, which in most laptop computers operates a switch when the lid is closed. Note that there are only three options in this menu (Figure 3.33). It is not generally considered to be a good idea to have the computer switched on when the lid is closed, since this can lead to a build-up of heat in the case.

While it is unlikely that there would be any risk of a fire occurring, it is possible that the high temperature in the case could result in some of the components failing. Therefore, it is probably not a good idea to have

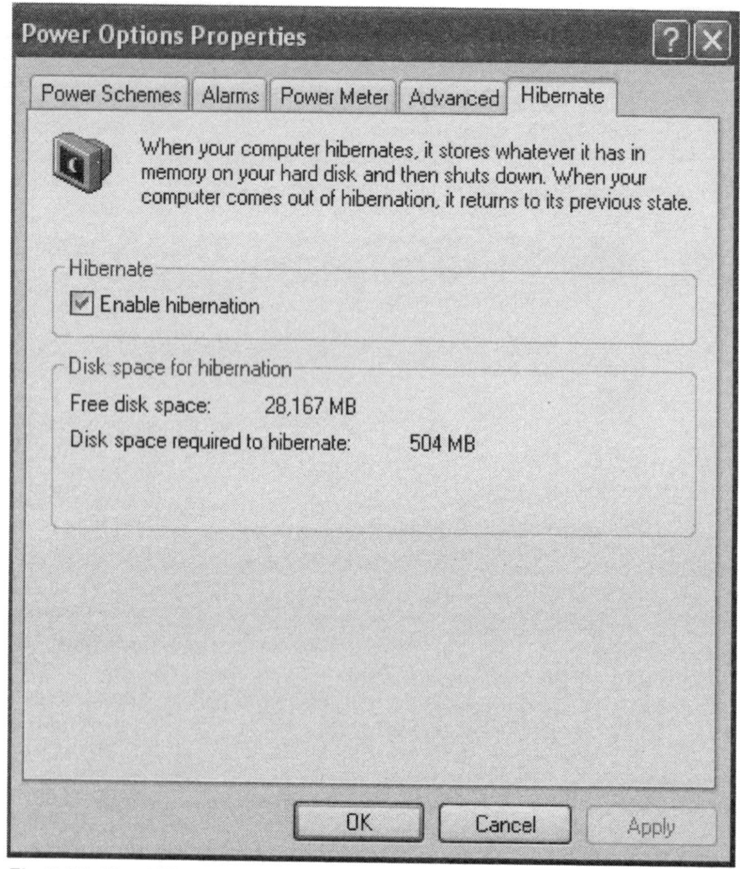

Fig.3.35 The Hibernate section of the Power Option Properties window

the Do nothing option selected here. Either of the other two will ensure that the monitor is switched off when the lid of the case is closed, which should in turn ensure that overheating does not occur.

In this version of the Power Options Properties window there is a Power Meter section (Figure 3.34). This section gives information about the amount of charge left in the battery, and the approximate operating time left before the battery has to be swapped or recharged. Note that this type of thing can only be an approximation, and that the power drawn from the battery depends on the task being undertaken by the computer.

For example, something like playing a DVD will result in higher than average power consumption due to the DVD drive running continuously, and also because of the fairly intensive use of the processor and graphics card that is require by this type of thing. The figures provided by any sort of power meter facility therefore have to be regarded as nothing more than a rough guide. Nevertheless, any facility of this type is very useful and it is well worth checking the Power Options Properties window to see if a laptop has anything of this type.

While in the Power Options Properties window it is worth taking a look at the Hibernate section (Figure 3.35). Unless the checkbox is ticked it will not be possible to place the computer into the Hibernate mode. The section beneath this shows the amount of free hard disc space that is available and the amount needed in order to take the computer into the Hibernate mode. In this example there should be no problem if the computer is sent into hibernation. Only about half a gigabyte of hard disc space is required, while the there is over 28 gigabytes of storage space available on the hard disc drive.

Reset

It is normal for desktop PCs to have a reset switch that can be used to restart the computer if it hangs up so badly that there is no other way of restarting it. This switch is usually small and recessed into the case so that it is virtually impossible to operate it by accident. These days there are some desktop computers that do not have a reset switch, and it seems to be something of a rarity of laptop PCs.

With a desktop PC it is possible to reset the computer by switching it off, waiting a few seconds, and then turning it on again. This option is not a practical proposition with a laptop PC, since it is unlikely to have a conventional on/off switch. Even if a laptop PC is being run from its mains adapter, "pulling the plug" on it will not necessarily switch it off. If there is a charged battery installed, it will continue to run for some time under battery power.

I suppose that as a last resort it would be possible to remove the battery for a few seconds, and then replace it. This is probably not a good idea though, and it is certainly not a course of action that I would recommend. If you delve into the computer's instruction manual you should find a means of switching it off if none of the usual routes is successful. Many laptops can be switched off by holding down the On switch for several seconds, but no doubt there are other methods in use.

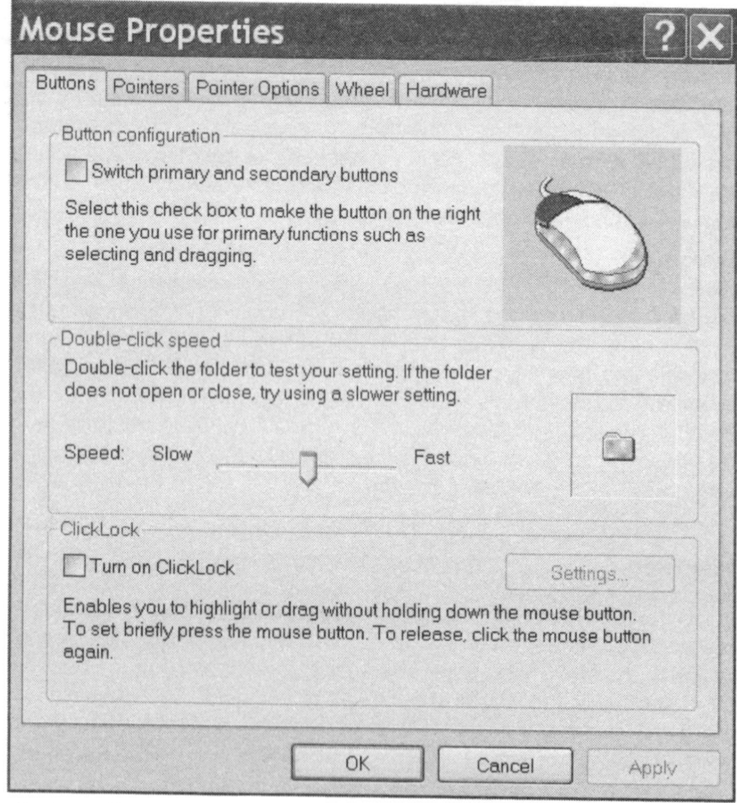

Fig.3.36 The Buttons section of the Mouse Properties window

Mouse

These days all laptop computers have a built-in pointing device of some kind, but many people still use a mouse when the computer is being used at home or in the office. Some even prefer to take a mouse when using a laptop on the move. The built-in pointing devices are ingenious and have improved over the years, but few users find them genuinely easy to use. A mouse generally provides a much quicker and easier means of controlling the pointer.

The mouse is often problematic when first using a PC. Either the pointer goes flying across the screen with the slightest of mouse movements, or

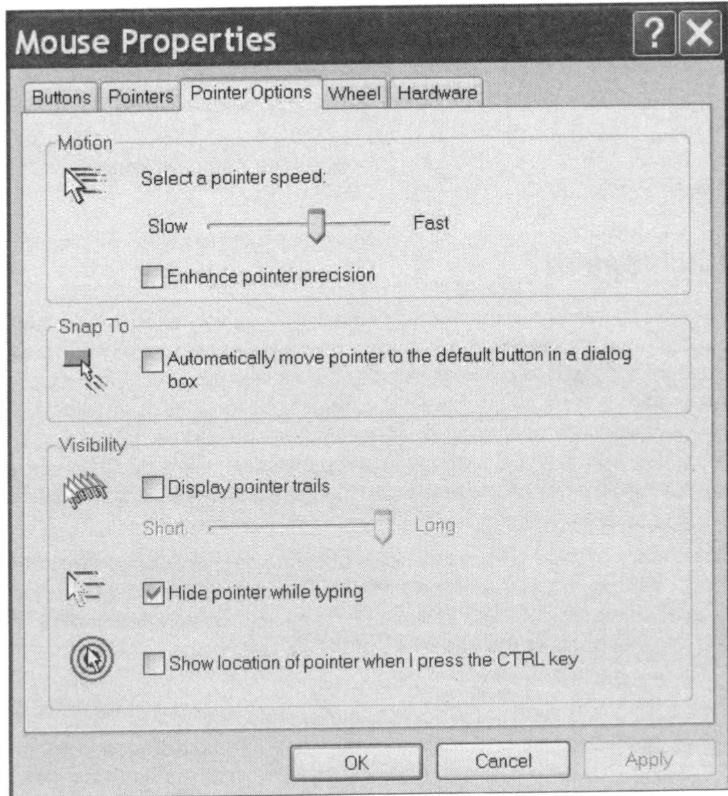

Fig.3.37 The Pointer Options section of the Mouse Properties window

a huge amount of movement is needed in order to make it move a significant distance. The ideal mouse sensitivity is very much a matter of personal preference, and it also depends to some extent on the type of software in use. High sensitivity is suitable for most programs where the pointer will only be used to make menu selections. Low sensitivity is better in situations where very precise control of the pointer is needed, which mainly means graphics applications such as photo editing and technical drawing.

Windows enables the sensitivity of the mouse to be adjusted to suit each user's requirements. The first step is to go to the Windows Control Panel. If the Control Panel is not already in the Classic View, left-click the "Switch to Classic View" link, which is near the top left-hand corner of the window. There will be either a straightforward Mouse icon, or one that mentions a specific make and (or) model of mouse. This depends on whether the PC is equipped with a Microsoft mouse, a generic type, or one of the more upmarket mice. In this case the mouse is a Microsoft type and double-clicking the Mouse icon produces the standard version of the Mouse Properties window (Figure 3.36).

Click speed

The slider control near the middle of the window is very useful. It enables you to adjust the maximum time that can be used between the two mouse clicks of a double-click. It is likely that a slower double-click speed is required if you find that double-clicks tend to be ignored by Windows. If double-clicks are still ignored, either you are not releasing the button properly after the first mouse click, or the mouse is of low quality and it is not opening the switch contacts even though you are releasing the button sufficiently.

The control for the mouse sensitivity is obtained by left-clicking the Pointer Options tab near the top of the window. The Mouse Properties window then changes to look like Figure 3.37. The slider control near the top is the one that controls the sensitivity of the mouse, or the "mouse speed" in Microsoft's terminology.

If the control is moved to the right, a smaller amount of mouse movement will be needed in order to move the pointer a certain distance. Moving the slider to the left has the opposite effect, with greater mouse movement being needed in order to move the pointer a certain distance. Note that you can move the slider control by placing the pointer over it and then dragging it to a new position. Alternatively, left-clicking to one side of the control results in it moving one step in that direction.

Finding the optimum setting is really a matter of trial and error. You have to be practical about things, and using a low speed setting is not very practical if you have only a very limited amount of space for the mouse. The mouse keeps running over the edge of its allotted area, making it necessary to keep picking it up so it can be repositioned near the middle of its operating area. Lack of space is likely to be a common problem if you use a mouse with your laptop while working away from home or the office.

Windows provides a possible solution for those requiring precise control without having a large area for the mouse. In order to activate this facility it is merely necessary to tick the "Enhance pointer precision" checkbox.

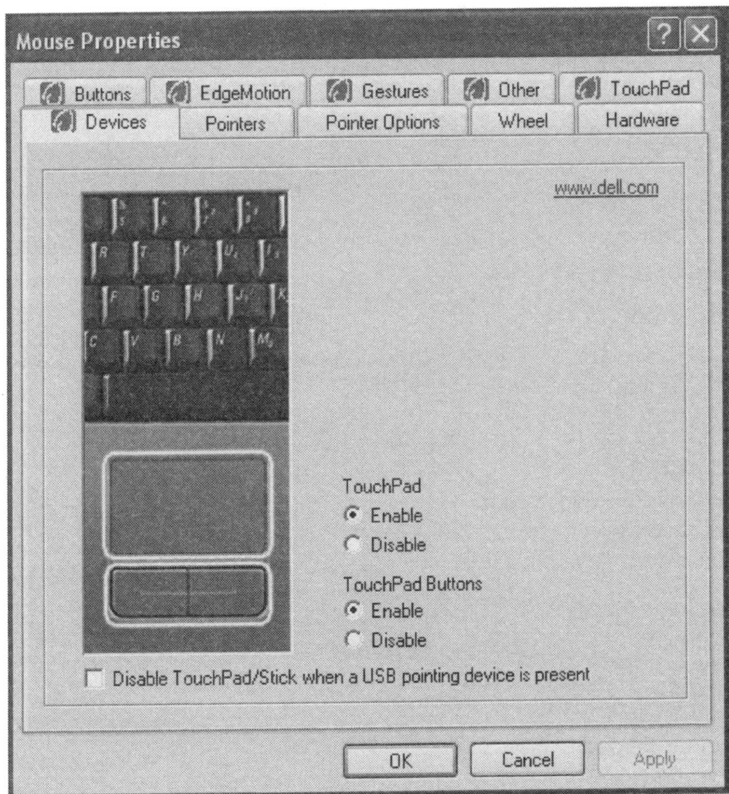

Fig.3.38 The properties window for a built-in pointing device. This has more sections than a normal Mouse Properties window

This is just below the speed control. The way this system works is very simple. When the pointer is moved quickly, the mouse has its normal degree of sensitivity. This is made quite high so that relatively little mouse movement is needed in order to move the pointer around the screen.

When the pointer is moved slowly, the sensitivity is automatically reduced so that precise positioning of the pointer is much easier. This system relies on the fact that users tend to go much more slowly and carefully when trying to position the pointer very accurately, and it can be very effective. Having two mouse sensitivities is sometimes called "mouse acceleration" incidentally. There will be other differences if you are using a mouse that has its own property window rather than the standard

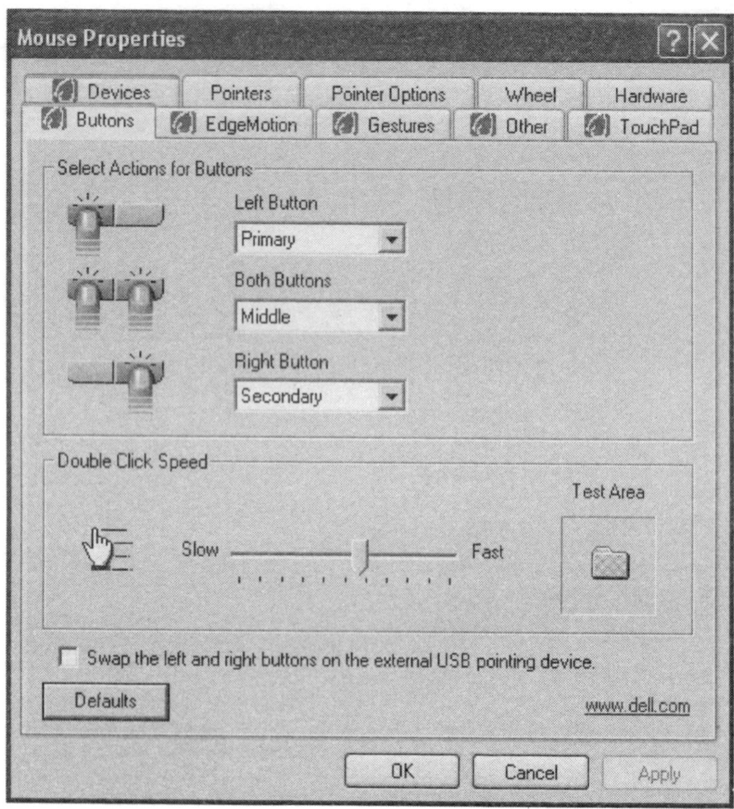

Fig.3.39 The Buttons section has the usual facilities

Windows type. Essentially the same controls are always present though, and it should not be too difficult to find the ones you need.

Built-in

Various types of built-in pointing device have been used over the years, but these days the vast majority of laptops use a small touchpad where the pointer is controlled by simply moving your finger over the pad. A variation on this scheme of things is essentially the same, but with a stylus being used instead of a finger, or there might be the option of using either. These touchpads seem to become ever more sophisticated, and they are more than basic pointing devices. Consequently, compared

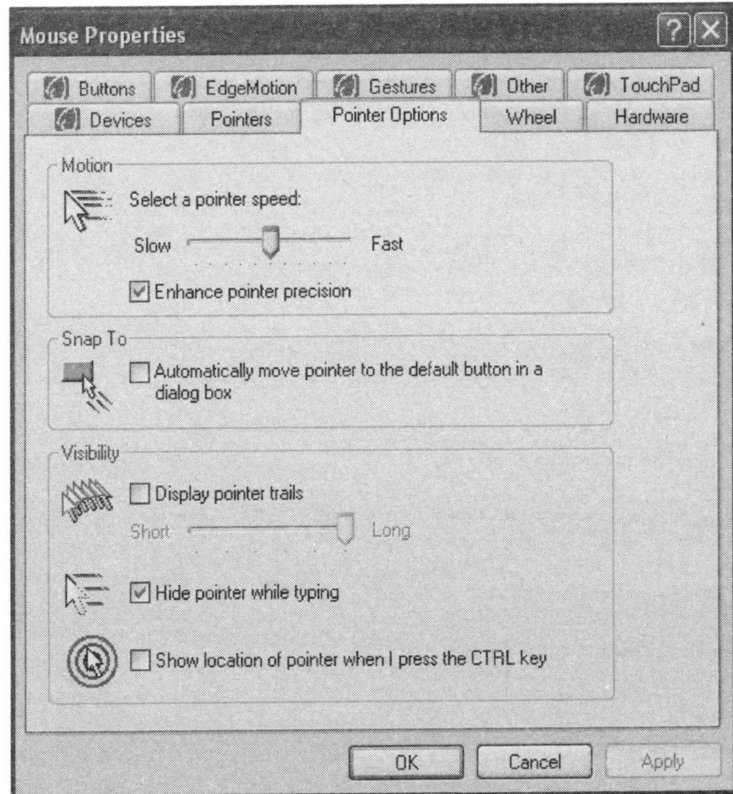

Fig.3.40 The Pointer Options section includes a speed control

to an ordinary mouse they often have several more options available in the Mouse Properties window.

This is demonstrated by Figure 3.38, which shows the Mouse Properties window for the touchpad of a Dell laptop PC. This has some ten sections, which compares to about five or six for a typical mouse. Note that the touchpad will probably appear in the control panel as a mouse rather than as a touchpad or some other more apt description. This can be a little confusing, especially if the computer also has an ordinary mouse installed. However, there is no real danger of making adjustments in the wrong properties window, since the one for the touchpad will have many more settings than the one for the mouse.

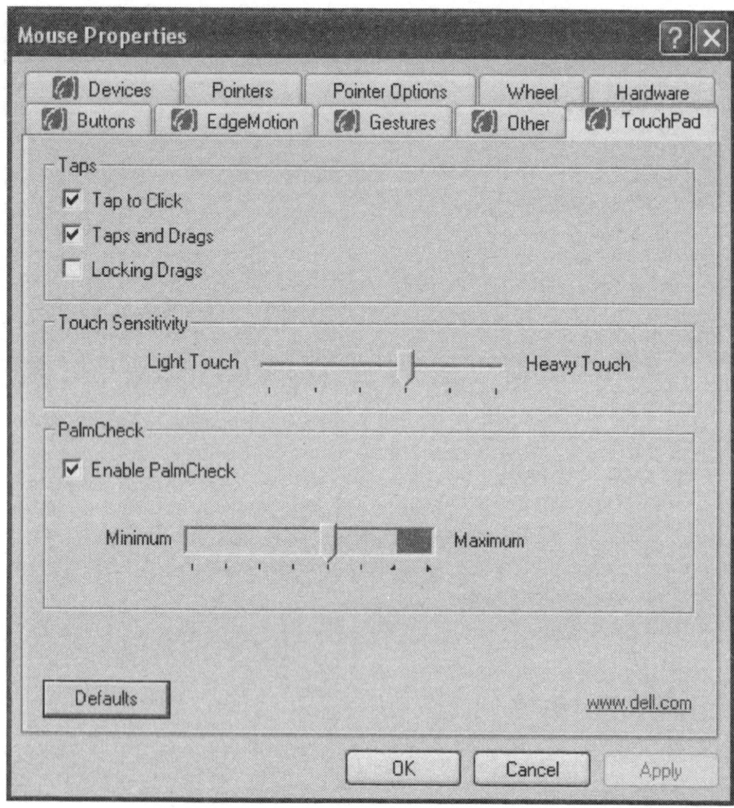

Fig.3.41 The TouchPad section has settings that have no mouse equivalents

Figure 3.38 shows the Devices section of the Mouse Properties window, and this has some useful options. The two sets or radio buttons enable the touchpad and its buttons to be switched on or disabled. It can be useful to disable both of these when a laptop will only be used as a home or office PC with a mouse acting as a pointing device. Switching off the touchpad and its buttons ensures that neither of them can give problems with accidental operations. The checkbox near the bottom of the window can be very useful when the computer is often used on the move with the touchpad as the pointing device, but when back at base a mouse is used instead. With the checkbox ticked, the touchpad is automatically switched off when a USB mouse is in use.

Some of the parameters that can be adjusted are the usual ones that are available for a mouse. The Buttons section (Figure 3.39) has the usual facilities for setting the functions of the buttons and adjusting the double-click speed. As explained previously, the double-click speed controls the maximum time that can elapse between clicks before they are interpreted as two separate events. The buttons on a laptop can be a little more awkward to operate than those on a mouse, so a slightly longer time (slower click speed) might be needed. If you find that double-clicks often fail to have the desired effect, then a slower double-click setting should certainly be tried.

The Pointer Options section (Figure 3.40) has the usual slider control that can be used to adjust the pointer's speed. There are some other options available here, but the speed control is definitely the most important one. As one would expect, the TouchPad section (Figure 3.41) has parameters that have no mouse equivalents. For example, there is an option that enables double-taps on the pad to be interpreted as double-clicks of the left button.

There is also a pressure sensitivity control. Pressure sensitivity is where the pressure on a touchpad or a graphics tablet is used to control some aspect of an application program. In paint and photo editing programs for instance, the pressure information is often used to control the width of lines produced with certain of the program's drawing and painting tools. The pressure control determines the amount of force you need to use in order to utilize a facility of this type.

The EdgeMotion options (Figure 3.42) control the way in which the system operates when your finger reaches an edge of the touchpad. By necessity, the touchpad has to be quite small. It is still possible to move the pointer from one side of the screen to the other, but only if a high pointer sped is set. The problem with this approach is that it makes precise control of the pointer very difficult. Moving your finger a few millimetres produces a large amount of onscreen movement by the pointer.

Setting a much lower pointer speed gives much more precise control, but you tend to run out of space on the touchpad when moving the pointer over a large distance. Of course, you merely have to remove your finger from the pad and reposition it somewhere near the opposite edge so that you can continue moving the pointer. This is a bit slow and cumbersome though.

If you use the EdgeMotion feature, the pointer will continue to move even though your finger has reached the edge of the touchpad. This enables a relatively low pointer speed to be used, and accurate control

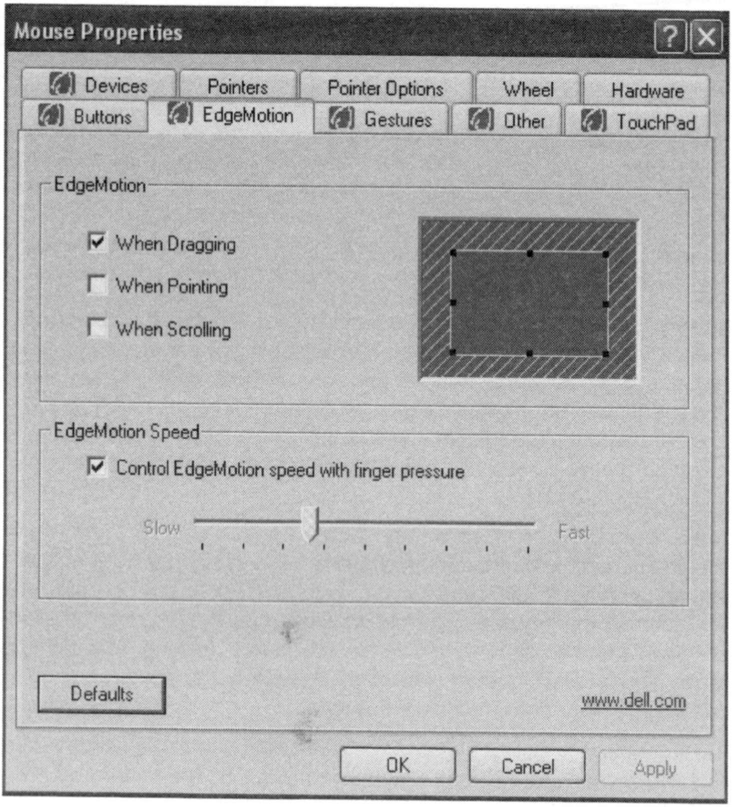

Fig.3.42 The EdgeMotion facility aids large pointer movements

to be obtained, but large movements of the pointer are still relatively easy. How well any clever features of this type work in practice is something that you have to determine for yourself. A feature that is a godsend for one user may well be completely unusable by another user.

The exact features available tend to vary slightly from one touchpad to another, so it is a matter of reading the instruction manual to determine what special facilities are provided. It should also include details of how to control them via the Windows Control Panel. If you will be using the touchpad a great deal, it makes sense to spend some time investigating its features, trying them for yourself, and "fine tuning" any that prove to be genuinely useful. A little time spent on this type of thing can make using a laptop computer a much easier and more pleasant experience for the next few years.

Updating

When you buy a new computer it would seem reasonable to expect that all the software, including the operating system, will be fully up to date. In practice it is not as simple as that, and things tend to change quite quickly in the world of computing. Operating systems tend to be updated quite frequently as minor bugs are fixed, security "holes" are "plugged", existing features are updated, and new features are added. The same is true of most other types of software, although to a lesser degree in most cases.

Driver programs are probably the type of software that is most frequently updated. These are needed in order to make practically any piece of hardware operate properly under Windows. Driver software has a reputation for poor reliability, and some manufacturers have been known to rush new items of hardware onto the market. This has sometimes resulted in hardware being sold to the general public even though the drivers had not been properly tested and debugged. I have had one or two items of new hardware where the driver software was so bug ridden that it was not even possible to install it!

The drivers and other software supplied with a new PC should work reasonably well, but there could be minor problems. Even where everything works well, there could still be updates that would provide better security, added features, or whatever. Whether it is worthwhile bothering with updated software is debatable. Clearly it is worthwhile seeking and installing new software if you need to sort out a problem of some kind, or the update is needed to fix a security problem.

The situation is different with new drivers or other software that provides better functionality rather than bug or security fixes. Most computer users have tales of new and improved software that has actually been much less use than the previous version. Driver software is certainly not immune from this phenomenon. For inexperienced computer users it is probably best to heed the advice of the old adage "if it ain't broke, don't fix it".

In recognition of the fact that new drivers are not always quite as good as they are supposed to be, Windows now has a facility that makes it easy to go back to the previous driver. Consequently, there should be a way back to normal operation if you should happen to install a driver that turns out to be a bit of a disaster. Even so, inexperienced users might prefer not to get this deeply into the workings of the operating

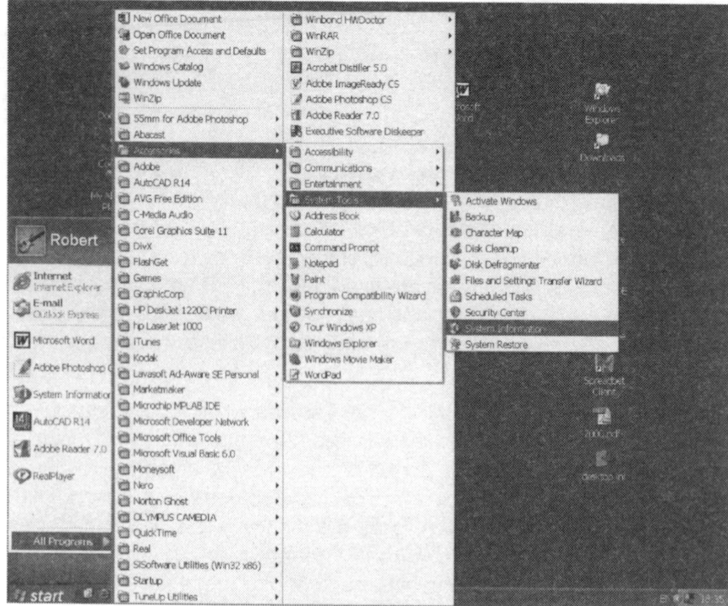

Fig.3.43 Launching the System Information program

system. If you are happy with the way your computer is working, there is probably not a great deal to be gained from installing any updates that are not crucial.

Finding drivers

The appropriate customer support service for your PC should be able to supply any updated drivers that are required to get the PC into full working order. In the real world, you can often save yourself some telephone calls and a fair amount of hassle by searching for them yourself. Computer manufacturers often have a Support or Download section on their web sites where you can download the latest drivers for the hardware used in their PCs. In fact there is usually a facility of this type for any computer related device, including such things as printers, scanners, and digital cameras.

There is inevitably a delay between manufacturers of the hardware coming up with new drivers, and these drivers finding their way onto the web

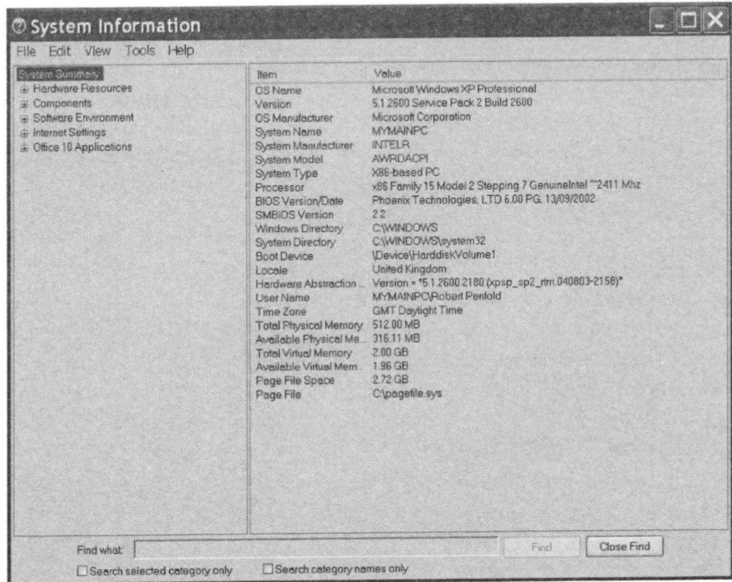

Fig.3.44 The initial window of the System Information program

sites of PC manufacturers. A point you have to bear in mind here is that many PC manufacturers actually build relatively few of the components used in their PCs. In fact many PCs are actually assembled entirely from "off the shelf" components, with the manufacturer just doing an assembly job.

Consequently, it is often possible to obtain drivers earlier by going to the web sites of the companies that produced the individual components. Unfortunately, determining which hardware is used in a given PC can be a bit difficult, and tends to be even more problematic with laptop PCs. Your PC should really be supplied with a specification sheet that lists all the components that it uses, including the exact model of graphics card, soundcard, modem, etc. The problem with a laptop PC is that most or all of the hardware is integrated with the main board rather than being in the form of expansion cards. This means that it might not be quite the same as any "off the shelf" expansion card, and finding the right driver can be difficult.

There is actually a useful facility built into Windows that can provide many details about the operating system and hardware used in your PC. It is accessed by going to the Start menu and selecting All Programs –

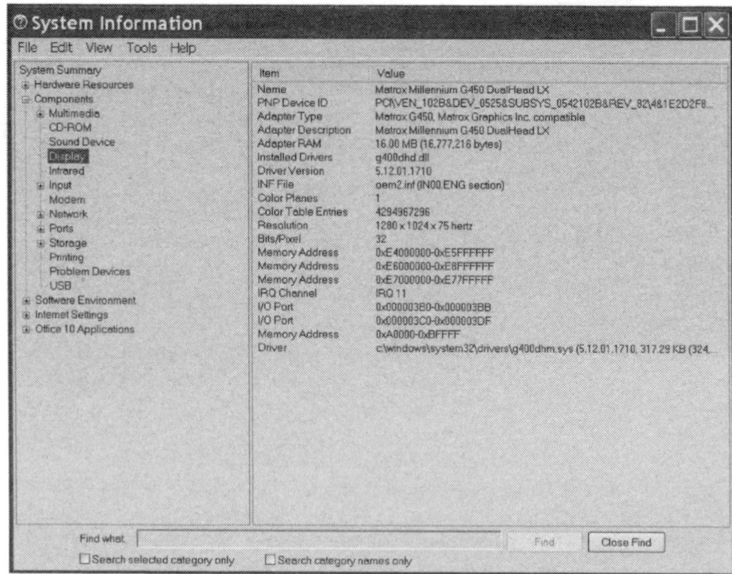

Fig.3.45 Here the Components category has been expanded

Accessories – System Tools – System Information (Figure 3.43). The initial window will look something like Figure 3.44, and it provides some basic details about the operating system, processor, and amount of memory fitted to the computer.

If you are concerned that you might have been "short changed", and the PC might not have the right processor or amount of memory installed, this section of the System Information utility will provide the answers. In this example the PC is equipped with an Intel 2411MHz (2.41GHz) processor and 512 megabytes of memory. The genuine memory is referred to as Total Physical Memory by the System Information program. The virtual memory is actually space reserved on the computer's hard disc drive, and this is used when there is insufficient physical memory. Things generally slow down a bit when a PC starts using virtual memory.

The processor is actually a 2.4GHz type. There is often a small discrepancy between the processor's specified speed and the one reported by the System Information program. It does not really matter whether the processor is running slightly faster or slower than its stated speed, or the program has made a minor error when calculating its speed. A small difference is of no practical consequence. A large error could

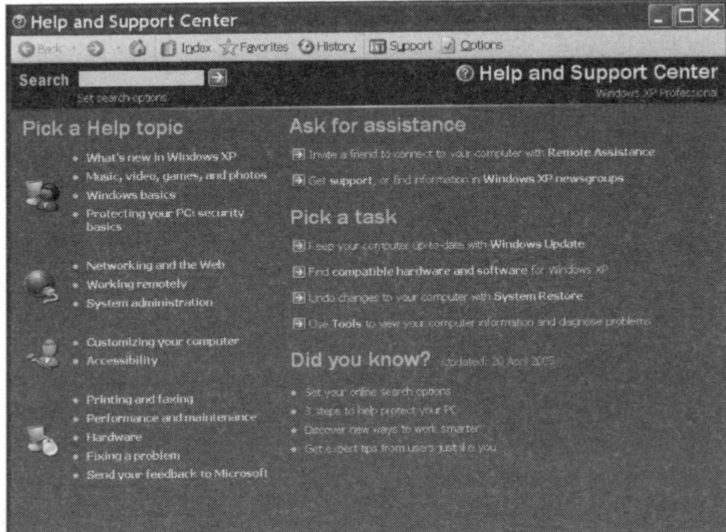

Fig.3.46 Left-click the Windows Update link

be due to the PC being set up incorrectly, but it is more likely to be due to the processor having an equivalent speed rating. In other words, it runs at (say) 2.5GHz, but it is equivalent to an Intel chip running at 3GHz. The manufacturer therefore decides to call it a 3.0GHz processor rather than a 2.5GHz for marketing reasons.

The System Information program has various categories listed down the left-hand side of the window, and left-clicking the little button to the left of each category results in it being expanded (Figure 3.45). In this example the Components category has been expanded, and then the Display section has been left-clicked to select it. Details of the display hardware are listed in the right-hand section of the window. This shows that the display adapter is a Matrox Millennium G450, and it even gives the exact version of it (Dual Head LX). An entry lower down the list shows that the display adapter is fitted with 16 megabytes of video memory.

Anyway, if you are sure that you have correctly identified the hardware and located the correct drivers, it is safe to go ahead an install them. Trying to install the wrong drivers will not necessarily be a disaster, because it is likely that the operating system or the driver program will detect the error and halt the installation. It is still something that is best avoided though, so do not try to install any driver software if there is even the slightest doubt about its legitimacy.

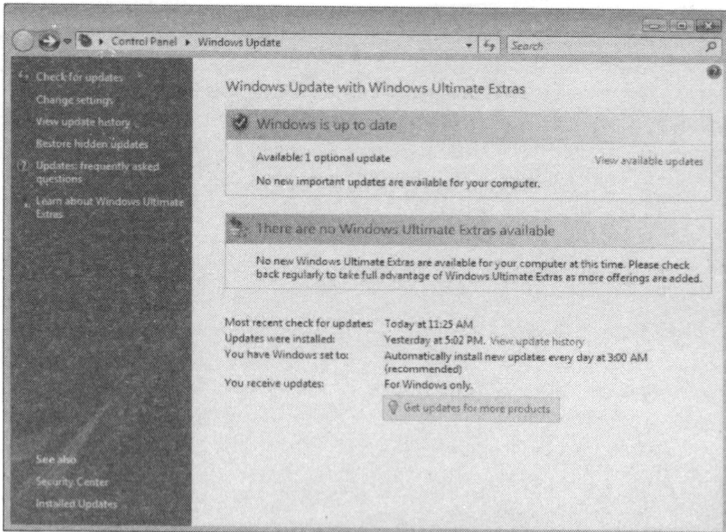

Fig.3.47 The Windows Vista Automatic Update window

Windows has facilities for updating driver software, but many of the driver programs downloaded from the Internet and supplied with new hardware do not actually use these facilities. You therefore have to carefully read through the documentation supplied with the driver software to determine the correct method of installing it. In the case of software downloaded from the Internet, the source web site will often provide instructions, or they may be contained in a file that forms part of the download. The software is often installed by running an installation program and then restarting the program. Windows completes the installation process during the boot-up procedure.

Windows update

If you do not fancy trawling the Internet in search of better drivers, there is a simpler alternative that you can try first. Windows has an automatic update feature, which will sometimes find and install more up-to-date drivers. This is not its primary purpose though, and it is mainly aimed at fixing any odd problems that users encounter with Windows. These days an equally important reason for having this feature is that it provides security updates.

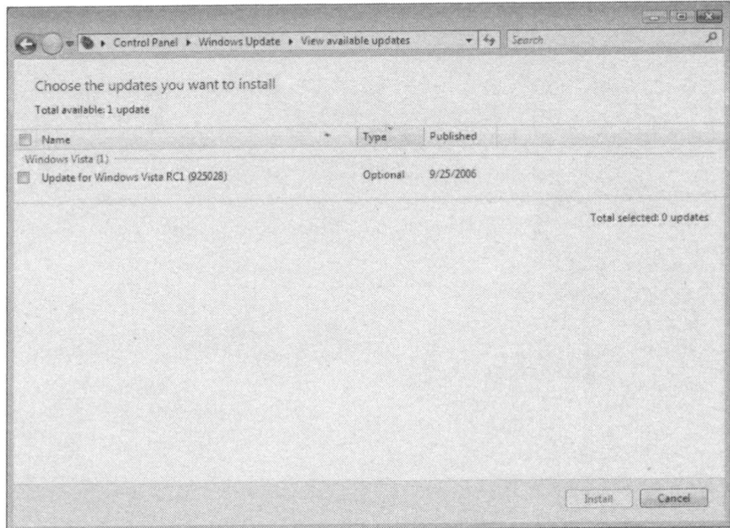

Fig.3.48 The optional updates in Windows Vista

Many viruses and worms are designed to exploit a security flaw in an applications program or the operating system itself. Sometimes these flaws have already been covered by software updates, but not everyone has bothered to update their PCs and the infection has been able to spread. In fairness to amateur PC users, there have been worms that have exploited old security "holes" in the operating systems of servers. The professionals maintaining the affected servers had not bothered to routinely update their systems. Some worms and viruses exploit previously unknown security flaws, but patches to fix the problem are soon made available when this sort of thing occurs.

Anyway, the fact that you have a new PC with the Windows operating system newly installed does not mean that it is fully up-to-date. This depends on factors such as the age of the disc used to install Windows, and whether any updates were installed via the Internet as part of the installation process. In most cases the newly installed operating system will not have the latest updates, so it is worthwhile using the automatic update feature even if there are no apparent problems with the PC. This is especially important if you will be using the PC to access the Internet.

Depending on the version of Windows in use and the setup of your PC, it might be possible to launch the Windows automatic update facility via

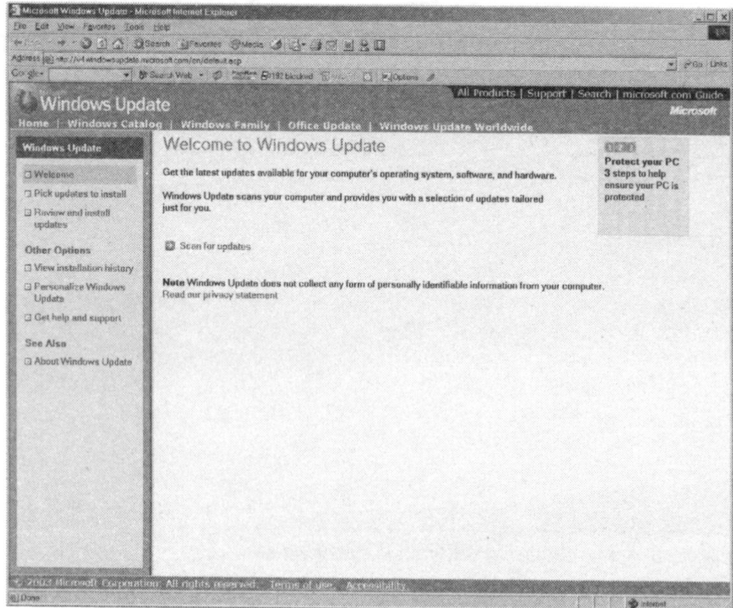

Fig.3.49 The Welcome screen of the update system

the Windows Ultimate Extras option (Vista) or Windows Update option (XP) in the start menu. With Windows XP you might have to select Help and Support from the Start menu), and then left-click the Windows Update link in the new Window that is launched (Figure 3.46). This is the first option in the "Pick a task" section. Of course, the PC must have an active Internet connection in order to use any form of online update system.

The Windows Vista update facility (Figure 3.47) is largely automatic. Optional updates are not installed automatically, and a list of those that are available can be obtained by activating the "View available updates" link. In the example of Figure 3.48 there is just one optional update available. An update can be installed by ticking its checkbox and operating the Install button.

The Windows XP update system produces the Welcome screen of Figure 3.49, and the first step is to operate the Scan for Updates link near the middle of the page. The scanning process is usually quite quick and produces a list of available updates in the left-hand section of the screen (Figure 3.50). Left-clicking an entry brings up a list of available updates

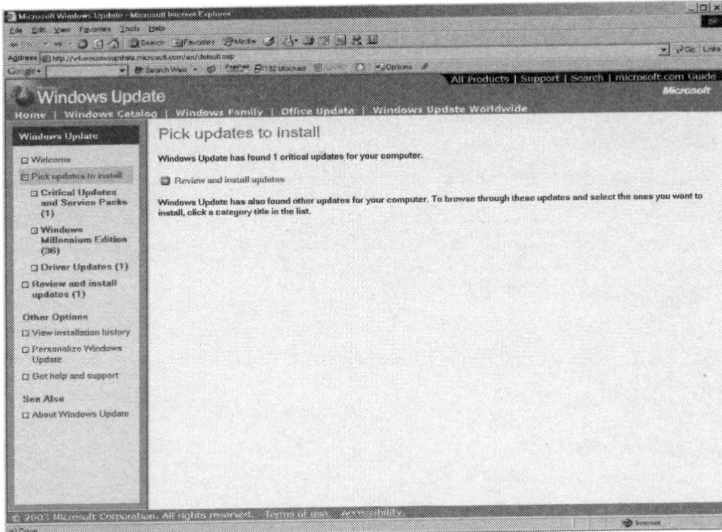

Fig.3.50 A list of available updates is produced

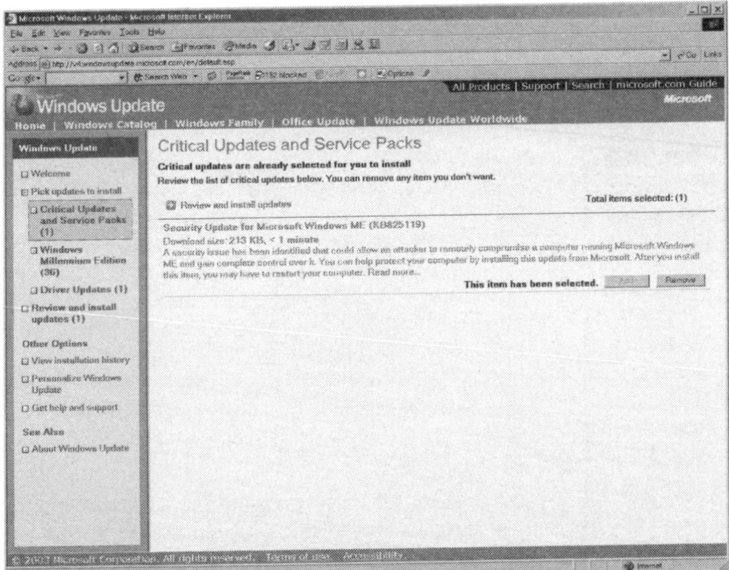

Fig.3.51 Details of updates can be displayed in the main panel

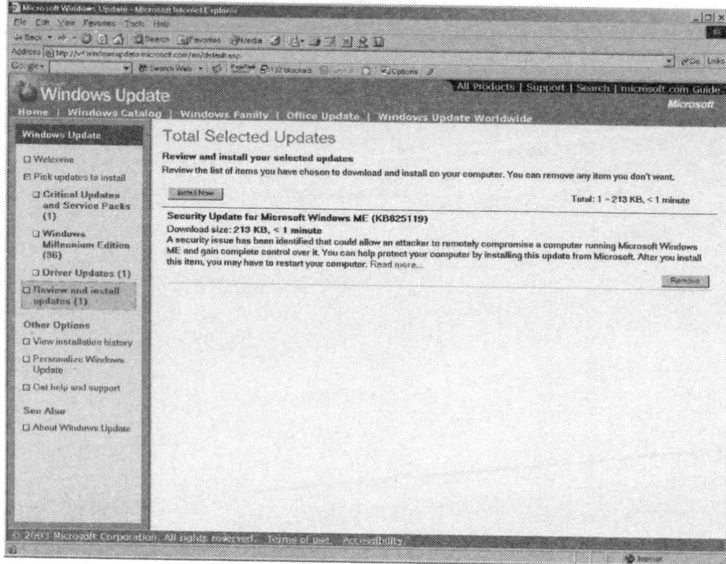

Fig.3.52 Operate the install button in the main panel

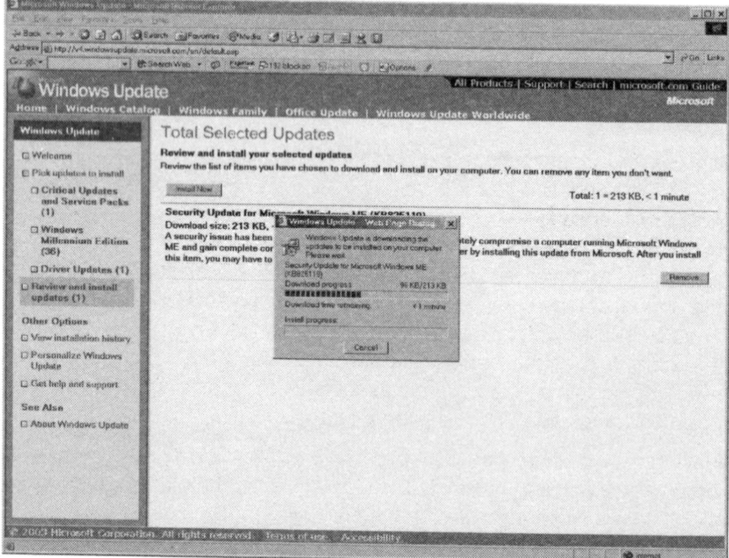

Fig.3.53 The small window shows how things are progressing

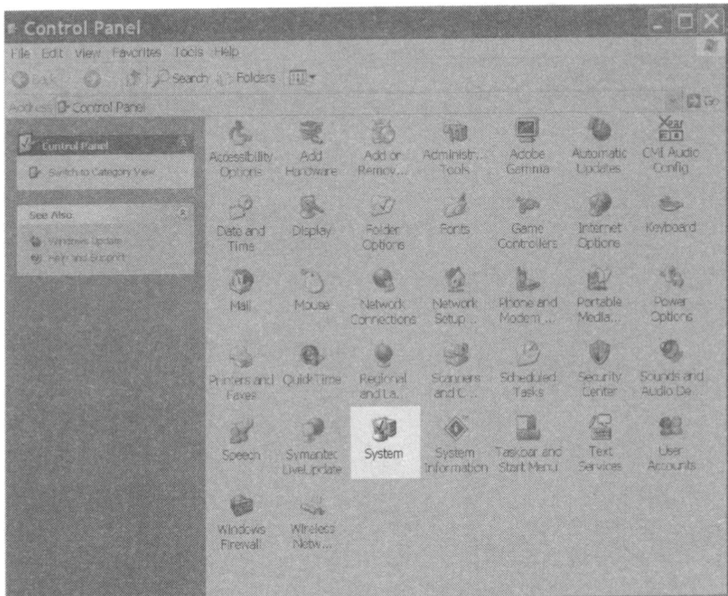

Fig.3.54 Double-click the System or System Properties icon

in that category. The list, together with details of each update, is displayed in the main section of the window, as in Figure 3.51. In this example only one update is listed, but this is a security type that needs to be installed.

It is as well to look through the other categories to see if there is anything worth installing, but you will probably find that many of the updates are not of relevance to the Windows installation you are using. There might be foreign language updates for example. In the current context, if there are hardware driver updates you will presumably wish to select them. In the normal course of events though, you might prefer to leave well alone and not bother with hardware updates. This depends on whether you feel confident about dealing with any problems that might arise as a result of updating the drivers. The situation is different with security updates, which should always be installed.

Having selected the required updates via the Add and Remove buttons, activate the Review and Install Updates link in the left-hand section of the window. Then operate the Install button in the main section of the window (Figure 3.52). The updates will then be installed and a small window will show how the process is progressing (Figure 3.53). Once

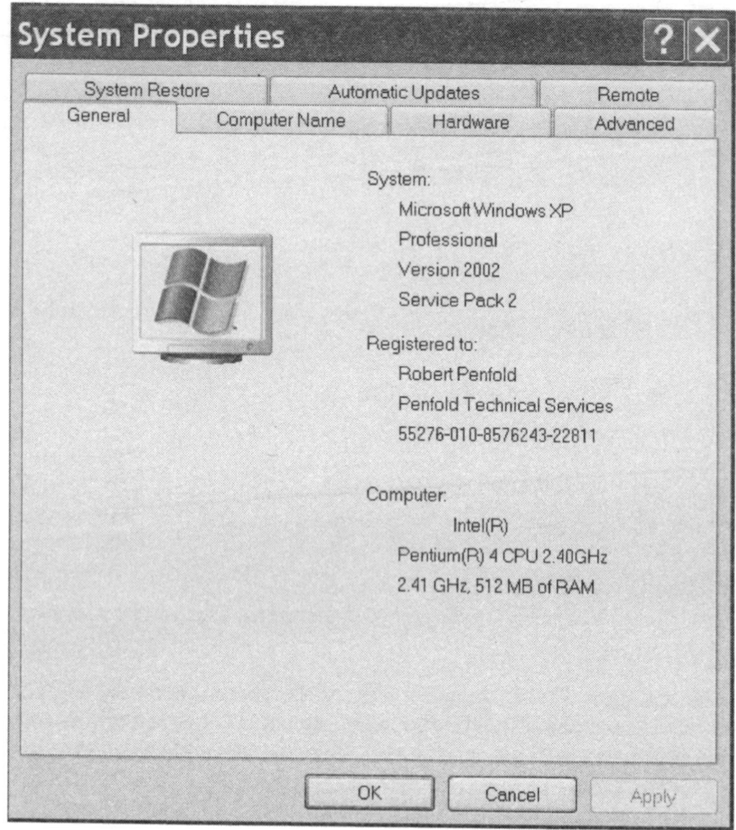

Fig.3.55 The General section of the System Properties window

the updates have been installed you will be asked if you would like to reboot the computer. It is not essential to do so, but the updates will not take effect until the computer has been rebooted.

Automatic update

The method used to update application software depends on the particular program in question. Some programs have an automatic update feature, and a facility of this type is available for Windows XP. It might be turned on by default, but if not it is very easy to turn on the

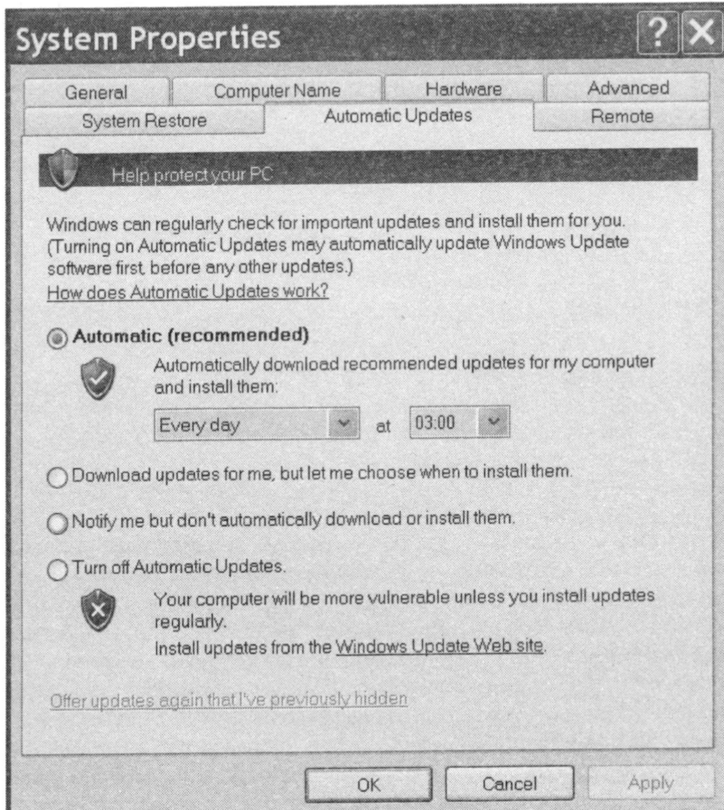

Fig.3.56 Left-click the Automatic radio button

Automatic Update feature. However, you must be logged in as the Administrator or be using an account that has administrator privileges. Note that with Windows Vista the default is for updating to be automatic, but it can be switched off.

Start by going to the Control Panel, and if necessary, left-click the Switch to Classic View link near the top left-hand corner of the window so that the Classic version of the Control Panel is obtained (Figure 3.54). Launch the System Properties window (Figure 3.55) by double-clicking the System icon, and operate the Automatic Update tab near the top of this window. In Windows Vista, go to the update window and operate the Change settings link.

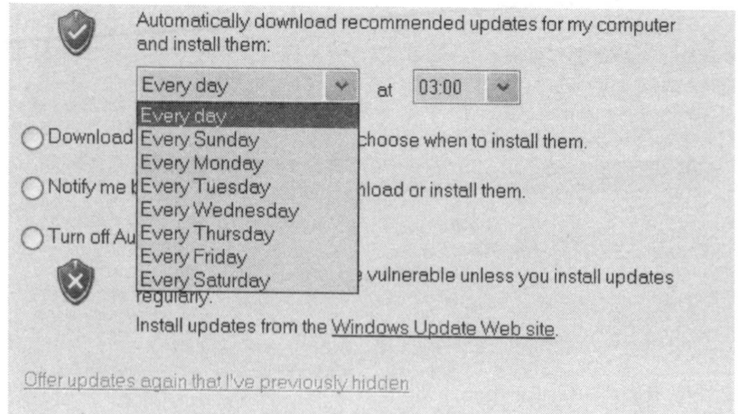

Fig.3.57 You can choose the day of the week that the automatic updating will take place

The window will change to look like Figure 3.56, and automatic updating is activated by left-clicking the Automatic radio button. By default the computer will look for updates every day. The drop-down menu on the left (Figure 3.57) gives the option of having the update performed once a week on the selected day. The menu on the right gives a choice of 24 times in the day when the search for updates will be performed. It is important to select a time when the computer is likely to be switched on. Choosing a time such as 3-00 AM when the computer will always be switched off effectively disables the automatic updating. Having made the required changes, operate the Apply and OK buttons to make the changes take effect and close the System Properties window.

Of course, any automatic update facility is dependent on the PC having an active Internet connection when the search for updates takes place. This is not a problem when using some form of broadband connection, since it will be active whenever the PC is switched on. Automatic updating works less well with a dialup connection, where there is a good chance that the connection will not be active when the searches take place. Also, any large downloads that are required should not be a problem when using a broadband connection. Large downloads might not be a practical proposition when using a dialup Internet connection.

You need to be aware that the Automatic Update facility does not install every available update. It installs only those that Microsoft deems to be high priority or critical updates. This seems to mean any updates that fix potential security weaknesses, and those that fix serious bugs. Lower priority updates such as newer drivers and added features or improvements to Windows are unlikely to be installed automatically. Therefore, it is still necessary to use the normal updating facility from time to time so that you can select and install useful but non-critical updates.

Software update

Updating application programs can sometimes be done automatically, but this is by no means a feature of all programs. Where this feature is available it will probably handle nothing more than minor bug fixes. Minor version upgrades such as from version 7.0 to 7.1 are unlikely to be covered by an automatic update facility, and will have to be handled manually.

Major upgrades from (say) version 7.21 to version 8.0 are not usually made available as free upgrades. For this type of thing it is normally necessary to purchase the upgrade version of the program, which could be pretty expensive. In general, it is best not to habitually buy program upgrades. The cost can start to mount up, eventually dwarfing the original purchase price of the programs. Only buy upgrades if they provide new features that are genuinely useful to you, and they represent reasonable value for money.

As explained previously, the application software bundled with PCs is sometimes a sort of second class version. Even where a bundled program is a fully featured version, it might not be possible to upgrade it when a new version comes along. I suppose that this is reasonable, given that you have probably paid very little for the bundled software. On the other hand, one might have expected the software companies to gleefully accept all the upgrade business they could get. Apparently, selling version upgrades is the way in which they obtain most of their income.

An automatic update facility is still very useful even if it only handles a few bug fixes. The way in which automatic updates are handled varies from one program to another, and it is something that is often enabled or disabled when the software is installed. It should be possible to alter the automatic update settings once the program is installed. For manual updates it is a matter of going to the web site of the software company and looking for any updates in the Support or Download section of the site. If you find a likely looking update, it should be accompanied by detailed download and installation instructions.

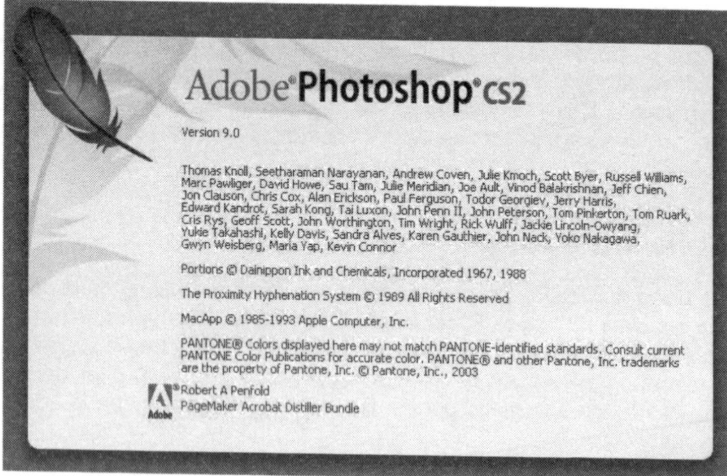

Fig.3.58 The Welcome window of Adobe Photoshop CS2

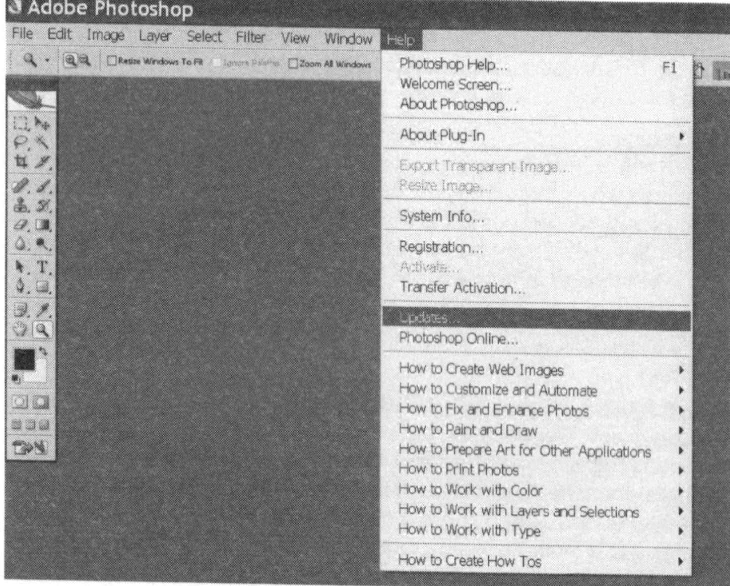

Fig.3.59 There is an Update facility in the Help menu

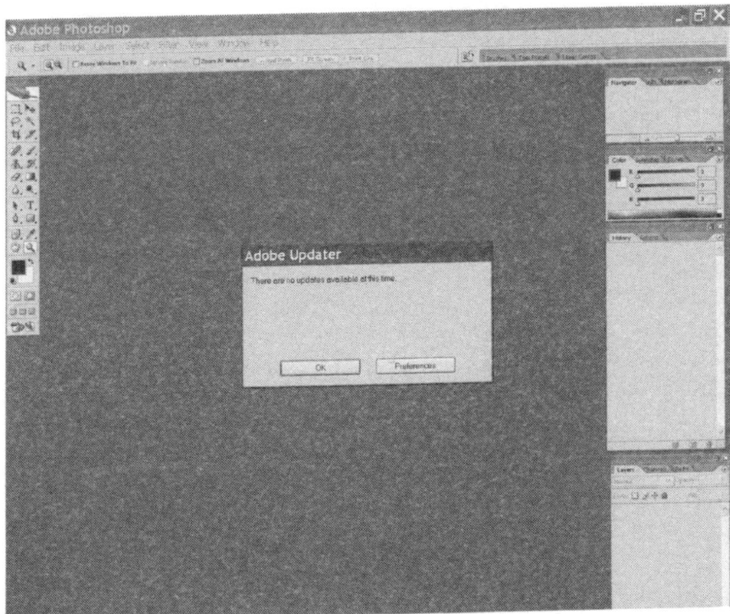

Fig.3.60 In this case no new updates were found

Before looking for updates it is more than a little helpful to know the exact version of the program that you are currently using. This will often be displayed on the welcome window that is displayed while the program loads, and this window can usually be brought onto the screen via the Help menu. There will usually be an "About" menu entry, or a menu entry called something like "About" followed by the name of the program.

Figure 3.58 shows the Welcome window for Adobe Photoshop CS2, and in this case it states near the top of the window that it is version 9.0 of the program.

Some programs have a built-in Update facility, and this is usually accessed via the Help menu. As can be seen from Figure 3.59, Photoshop CS2 has an Updates option in its Help menu. Selection of this option results in the program searching the Adobe web site for updates. With a facility of this type it is normal for any suitable updates to be installed automatically, but in this case no new updates were found (Figure 3.60).

Operating the right-hand button in Figure 3.60 opens the Preferences window that is used to control the automatic updating facility (Figure

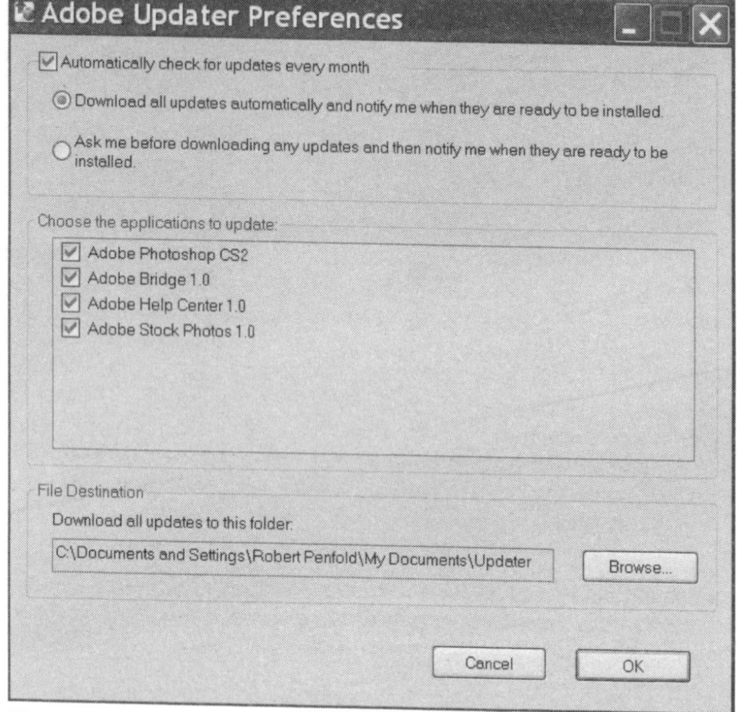

Fig.3.61 This window enables automatic updating to be switched on or off

3.61). This is the same window that appears during the program's installation process. It enables this feature to be enabled or disabled, and you can opt to have updates installed automatically or only if you give permission. Photoshop CS2 is supplied complete with three additional programs, and you can select which of the programs utilise the updating facility.

Software manual

There are numerous references to instruction manuals in this book, but this all-important publication is something that will probably be conspicuously absent when you unpack your new laptop PC. It is likely that it will also be missing when you look down the checklist of items that should be included with the computer. The modern way of doing

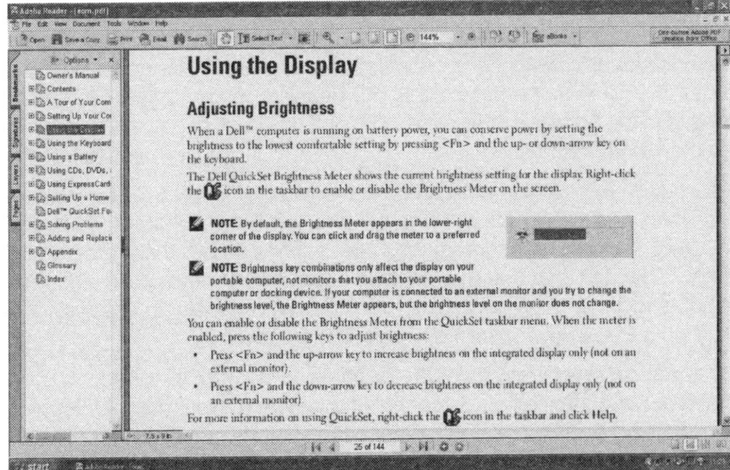

Fig.3.62 This software user manual uses the Adobe Acrobat Reader program

things is to have the instruction manual in software form, which usually means a PDF file. It will either be on a CD-ROM/DVD, or it will be preinstalled on the computer's hard disc.

There will be some printed instructions such as a Quick Start guide that will enable you to get the computer "up and running", but after that you have to refer to the software instruction manual. The printed documentation should include details of how to access the full manual. In many cases it is just a matter of selecting the appropriate option from the start menu, or double-clicking the manual's icon on the Windows desktop. Where the instruction manual is on a CD-ROM or DVD it is usually just a matter of inserting the disc into the computer's CD/DVD drive. The disc will then run automatically and the manual will appear on the screen.

In the example of Figure 3.62 the manual for a Dell laptop PC has been run by double-clicking its icon on the Windows desktop. The manual is actually a file in PDF format, which is the one that is most commonly used for documentation stored on a disc. This format requires the Adobe Acrobat Reader program, which will almost certainly be supplied preinstalled on a modern laptop PC. It should certainly be preinstalled in cases where the computer has a manual that uses this format. This is a program that you will probably need sooner rather than later, so it is worth going to the Adobe web site (www.adobe.com) and downloading it if it is not already installed on your new laptop PC. There is no charge for downloading, using, and installing this program. It has no restrictions, but it is only a file reader, so it is not possible to use it for editing PDF files. On the other hand, you can print out individual pages, page ranges, or the whole manual.

Most large PDF documents, like the example in Figure 3.62, have a sort of folder and file structure shown in the left-hand column. What it is actually showing is chapters and subsections rather than folders and files. The idea is to find the required section in this structure, and then double-click its entry to display it in the main panel. In this way it is possible to quickly jump to any part of the document.

The main alternative to the PDF format is some form of HTML, as used for web pages and sites. A manual of this type runs in Internet Explorer, or whatever Browser program is set as the default for HTML files. In use, things are usually much the same as using a PDF file in Adobe Acrobat Reader. A menu structure down the left-hand side of the screen provides rapid access to any part of the document.

Points to remember

As supplied, a laptop will almost certainly operate at its highest screen resolution. For most purposes and for most users, this is the resolution that will provide the best results. However, a lower resolution can be used if you need to make games run faster, a program needs a specific screen resolution, or something of this ilk. Do not change the screen resolution unless there is a good reason for doing so.

By default there will be an Administrator account, and probably one ordinary user account as well. Any others you require must be added by going to the User Accounts window, which is accessed via the Control Panel.

In order to make most changes to the system it is necessary to use the Administrator account, or an account that has administrator privileges. It is generally considered safer if most user accounts do not have Administrator privileges, since this reduces the risk of users making inadvertent changes to the system.

The Windows Control Panel can be used to alter the function that the On button provides after the computer has been switched on. The safest option is to have it do nothing at all, which ensures that the computer can not be accidentally switched off by leaning on the button. Other options include placing the computer into standby (Sleep) mode or Hibernate mode.

Some PCs have a Sleep button that can be used as a quick means of placing the computer into the Standby mode. If present, this button will usually be labelled with a crescent icon that looks like a new moon. It is not essential to have buttons in order to place the computer into the Standby or Hibernate modes. Both of these can be entered via the options in the Start menu.

A laptop PC often lacks a reset button, which can make it difficult to switch off if the computer should happen to crash so badly that the normal methods of resetting and shutting it down do not work. Most laptops do not have a conventional on/off switch, but still have a means of switching off in an emergency. This often takes the form of holding down the On button for several seconds.

If a conventional mouse is used with a laptop computer, the parameters of the mouse can be adjusted via the Windows Control Panel and the appropriate properties window. It is often necessary to make changes to the speed and double-click settings in order to get things working to your satisfaction.

Any modern laptop computer should have a built-in pointing device of some kind. This is almost invariably some sort of touchpad, although it might be called a mouse in the Windows Control Panel. A touchpad has the usual parameters associated with a mouse, but it is likely to have a number of additional parameters as well. It is worth spending some time investigating any extra facilities and their associated parameters. The computer will be much easier to use if you understand the touchpad and get it set up for maximum ease of use.

Windows has a facility for automatically updating itself via an Internet connection. This only covers the updates that Microsoft considers to be "critical", which generally means security updates and fixes for serious bugs. There is also a manual updating facility, and this can be used to install various updates including improved hardware drivers.

Those with limited experience of dealing with PCs should think twice before installing an update that provide new facilities rather than fixing problems. In fact all PC users need to carefully consider whether this type of update is worthwhile. If your PC is working well and doing everything you need, there is a lot to be said for leaving it that way. In this context, "new" and "improved" do not necessarily mean that your PC will be more reliable.

4

Transferring settings

Out with the old

Matters are relatively simple if you buy a new laptop PC and it is the first PC that you have owned. You do not have an existing PC that is loaded with all your data and programs, and that has been set up just the way you like it. It is a matter of gradually buying and installing any additional software that you need, and making changes to the set-up of the computer to make it easier for you to use.

Life is much more difficult for existing PC users that have an old PC that has all their programs installed, all their data loaded, and the settings just the way that they like them. You buy a new computer that is much better than the original, but as supplied it is difficult to use because it does not have the right programs installed, it has none of your data loaded, and it has the default settings instead of the ones that you prefer.

The easy way

I suppose that in an ideal world it would be easy to set up a new PC so that it had all the programs and settings of your old PC. You would simply link the two PCs via some form of network connection, and then tell Windows to make one PC operate just like the other. Windows would then copy programs from one PC to the other, and make the necessary changes to the Registry. The support files needed by any customisation of the programs would be copied to the appropriate folders on the new PC's hard drive. Perhaps all your data files would also be copied to the new PC. Unfortunately, Windows has no built-in facility of this type. However, as explained later in this chapter, it can provide some help in setting up one PC to mimic another.

There are actually third-party programs available that can copy programs, data, and settings from one PC to another. There are numerous programs that will just transfer settings from one PC to another. Unfortunately, many of these programs are difficult or impossible to obtain in the UK, and the ones that try to fully clone your old PC seem to be especially difficult to obtain. One would probably expect this type of software to be in big demand, since it is potentially useful for anyone upgrading from one PC to another. This does not seem to be the case though, and it can be difficult to track down any program migration software.

One possible reason for the scarcity of this software is that much of it has a reputation for being something less than user-friendly. A more likely reason is that many users take the opportunity to start afresh with a clean and uncluttered PC when they upgrade to a new one. However, as PCs become more heavily customised, the "clean sweep" approach becomes more difficult and time consuming. With a heavily customised PC it is possible that you would never get the new one set up in exactly the same way as your old PC. Finding out how to implement every little tweak could take too long, and you might never remember how some of the changes were originally implemented.

Anyway, if you have a heavily customised PC it might be worthwhile tracking down some program migration software if the alternative methods do not meet your requirements. The expense is probably not justified if your old PC has not been subjected to a fair amount of customisation. Installing everything from scratch is almost certainly the best approach where your old PC has little or no customisation. The time taken to install all the software should not be too great, and the "clean" installation should ensure that the new PC operates at the peak of efficiency.

Transfer Wizard

Even when installing everything from scratch, most Windows users would probably like a quick and easy means of transferring some basic settings from the old PC to the new one. Using special software to transfer some settings should not have any significant affect on the performance of the new PC, even if the old computer is not running at maximum efficiency. The types of setting that are normally transferred are very basic things such as screen colours, and the homepage used by Internet Explorer. Most settings transfer programs do not handle things that could have a major effect on the new PC's performance. Transferring settings of this type would be risky and could easily bring the new PC to a standstill.

Users of Windows XP do not need to buy any software in order to transfer files and some basic settings from one PC to another. It has an integral facility of this type in the form of the Files and Settings Transfer Wizard. This facility was introduced with Windows XP, and it is not available when using earlier versions of the Windows operating system. However, as will be explained in more detail later, there is a way of using it with computers that run under Windows ME.

Various means of file transfer are supported, including a direct cable connection, copying to a home network drive, and removable media such as floppy discs or Flash cards and a card reader. The method recommended by Microsoft is to use a home network, as this is likely to be the quickest and easiest. The wizard automatically detects a suitable direct cable connection and configures itself accordingly, so this method should also work quite well. Although floppy discs might seem to be impractical in an application of this type, the amount of data transferred to the new PC will often be quite modest. The number of discs required to complete the transfer is typically about half a dozen to a dozen.

Even so, using floppy discs is relatively slow and inconvenient, so it is probably best not to use this method if an alternative is available. For laptop users there is the complication that few modern laptops actually have a built-in floppy disc drive. There is a possible solution in the form of external USB floppy drives, and these are very good where it is necessary to read data from old floppy discs into your new laptop PC. It is probably not worthwhile buying an external floppy drive specifically to transfer Windows settings. There are other methods that cost about the same but are easier and quicker.

Speed gain

Since little settings data is being transferred by using this wizard, it might not seem to be a worthwhile proposition. However, it can still save a large amount of time since transferring files and settings via the wizard should be quite fast. Having to manually set up dialup connections, various Windows settings, etc., would almost certainly take much longer. The amount of time saved depends on how many settings have been altered on your old PC. Clearly there will be relatively little to gain by using this wizard if few settings have changed from their defaults. A great deal of time can be saved if you like changing anything that can be customised.

What types of setting will the wizard transfer to your new PC? Anything concerned with the appearance of Windows will almost certainly find its way onto the new PC. In addition to the obvious things such as the colour scheme and wallpaper, changes in the Windows sounds will also be copied to the new PC, as will mouse and keyboard settings. Most Internet settings will be transferred, including the ones that govern the way your PC connects to the Internet. Settings associated with Internet Explorer will also be copied, such as your homepage, security settings, and favourites. Cookies will also be transferred. Most PCs accumulate huge numbers of cookies over a period of time, so it might be advisable to clear unwanted cookies from the old PC prior to using the wizard.

Email settings will be transferred to the new PC, but only if you use Outlook or Outlook Express. On the face of it, users of popular Email services such as Yahoo! and Hotmail will have to make other arrangements. However, the settings for these web-based Email services are stored on the server, and not on the users' PCs. You should therefore find that an Email service of this type is exactly the same, regardless of which PC is used to access it. Some facilities might be dependent on cookies stored on the user's PC, but these cookies should be transferred by the wizard.

The biggest weakness of this wizard is that it does not transfer the settings for most application programs. Windows itself will operate much as it did on your old PC, but the same might not be true for the word processor, image editor, accounting program, etc. As one would expect, the popular Microsoft programs such as Word, Access, and Excel are catered for.

Some of the very popular programs from other software companies will also have their settings transferred. The Real Player program, for example, will have its settings moved to the new PC. However, few other non-Microsoft applications are supported. Note that it is only the settings for these programs that are transferred, and not the programs themselves. The programs must be installed on the new PC in the usual way before the settings are transferred.

Getting started

The Windows Easy Transfer program of Windows Vista is run by going to the Start menu and selecting All Programs, Accessories, System Tools, and Windows Easy Transfer. The initial window of Figure 4.1 eill then appear. The Files and Settings Transfer Wizard of Windows XP is run by going to the Start menu and then choosing Programs (or All Programs), Accessories, System Tools, and finally Files and Settings Transfer Wizard. This will launch the initial window of Figure 4.2. The initial windows are just the usual Welcome screens, but operating the Next button moves things on to where the process starts in earnest. Figure 4.3 shows the second screen of the Files and Settings Transfer Wizard of Windows XP.

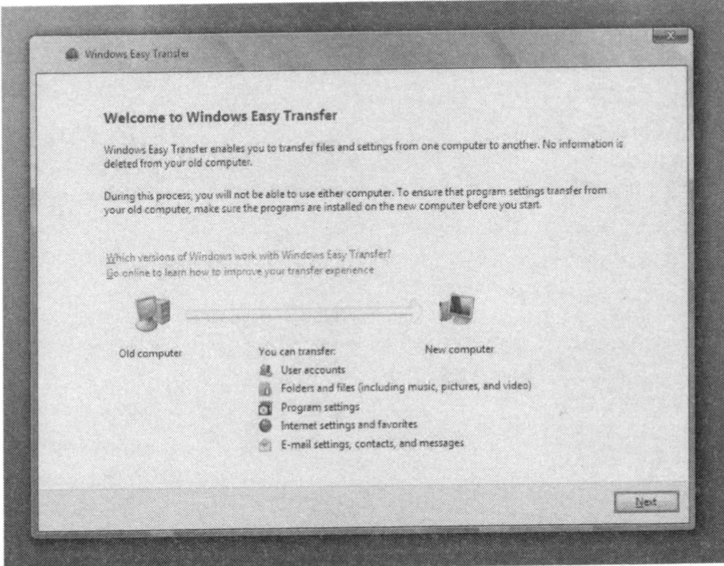

Fig.4.1 The Windows Easy Transfer program of Windows Vista

How you proceed from here depends on what you are trying to achieve, and the exact method to be used.

For the sake of this example we will assume that you are running the Files and Settings Transfer Wizard on a new PC that has Windows XP as its operating system. You therefore need to transfer the files from your old PC to this new one. On the face of it, the transfer is not possible if your old PC is running under an earlier version of Windows, such as Windows ME, since earlier versions of Windows do not have the Files and Settings Transfer Wizard. This would render the settings transfer facility completely useless to many users. Fortunately, there is a way around the problem. Windows XP can make a program disc that will run under earlier versions of Windows, enabling the transfer to be made.

At the window of Figure 4.3, make sure that the New Computer radio button is selected, and then operate the Next button. When running Windows XP with Service Pack 2, it is likely that the warning window of Figure 4.4 will appear on the screen, even though the wizard is a Microsoft program. Operate the Unblock button so that the wizard can continue to run properly. This should move things on to the window of Figure 4.5. It is not essential to make a program disc if you have the proper Windows

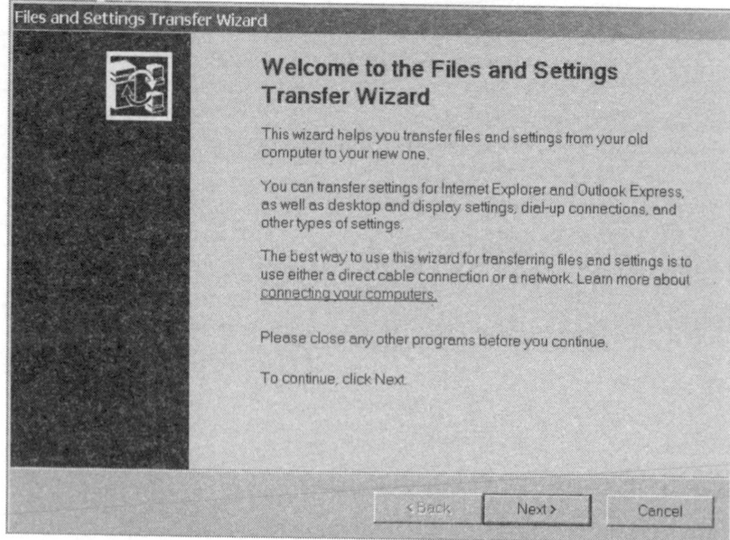

Fig.4.2 The Wizard starts with the usual Welcome screen

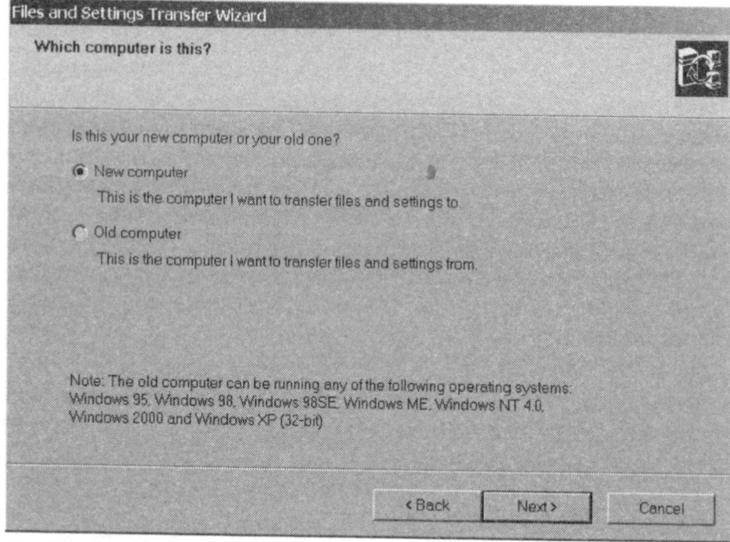

Fig.4.3 At this screen you indicate whether you are running the wizard on the old computer or the new one

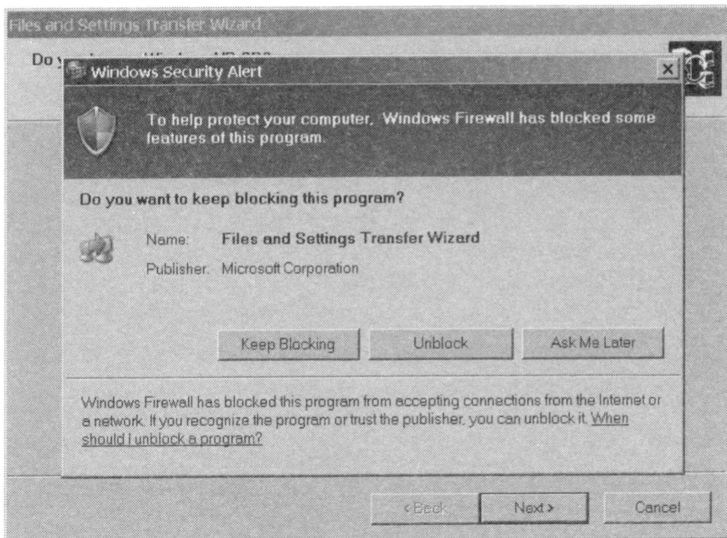

Fig.4.4 This warning message will probably appear if you are running Windows XP SP2

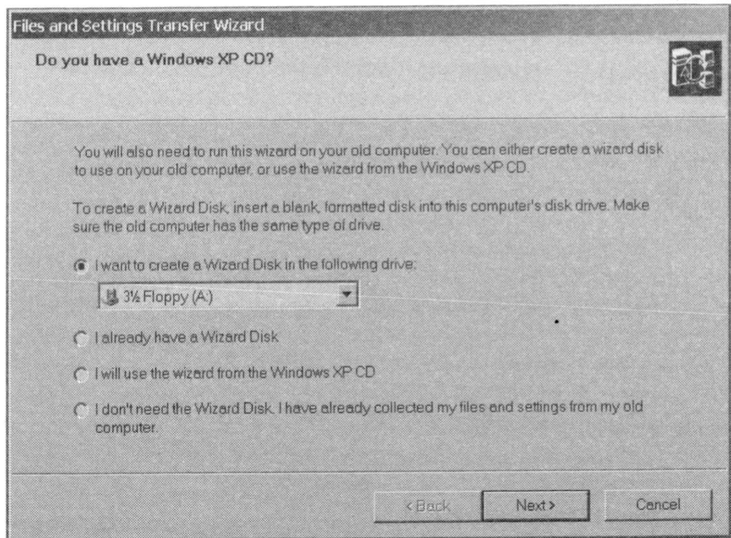

Fig.4.5 A program disc enables the wizard to be run on another PC

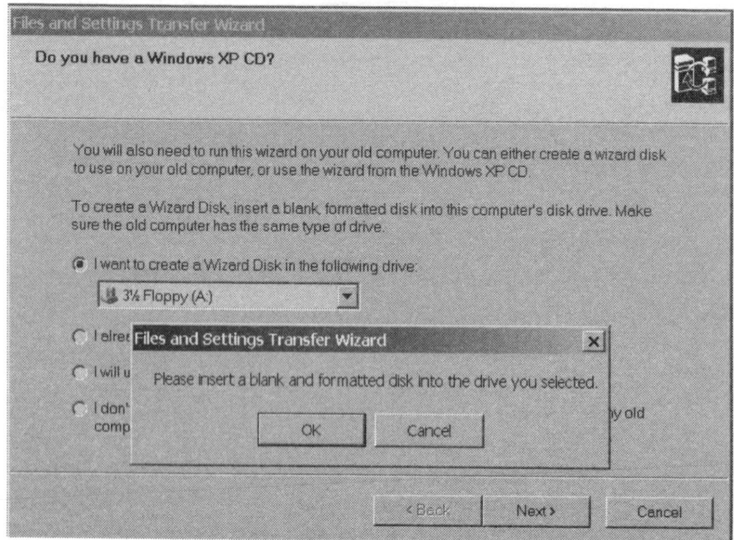

Fig.4.6 Insert a disc into the floppy drive when prompted

XP installation disc, as this disc contains the wizard program. However, many PCs have Windows preinstalled and are not supplied with a Windows installation disc. Even if you do have a Windows installation disc, it might still be easier to make the program disc. Doing so will avoid the need to go through drawers and cupboards searching for the Windows disc!

To make a wizard program disc, first make sure that the top radio button is selected. Use the menu immediately below this to select the appropriate drive, which in most cases will be drive A (the floppy disc drive). Operate the Next button to move on to the next stage, and insert a floppy disc into drive A when prompted (Figure 4.6). Note that the program is too large to fit onto a single 1.44-megabyte floppy disc, so it is better to use a higher capacity disc such as a Flash type wherever possible. Since a laptop PC is unlikely to have a floppy disc drive anyway, a Flash type is the obvious choice in the present context. I used a Compact Flash card and a card reader for this example. The window of Figure 4.7 will appear when the program has been copied to the disc or discs.

The next step is to run the wizard program on the old PC, and collect the files that will be transferred to the new PC. In order to run the program, select Run from the Start menu, and then type the path to the program

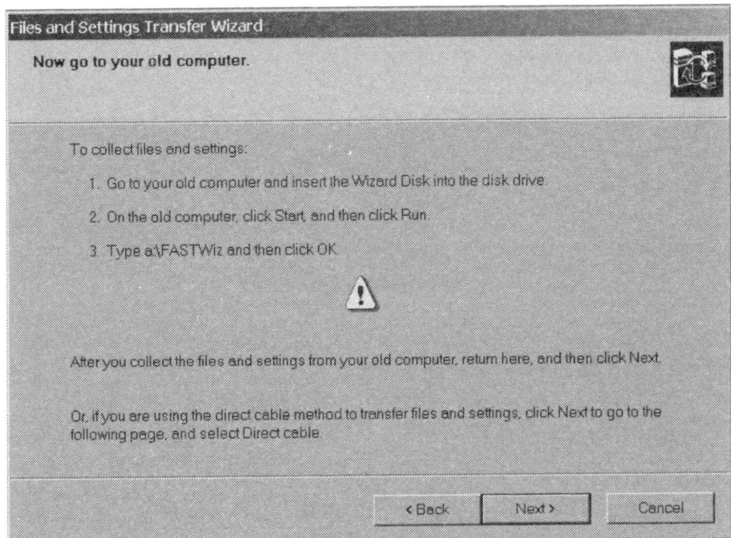

Fig.4.7 This screen appears once the program disc or discs have been completed

and its name. Alternatively, operate the Browse button and then use the file browser to locate the program. Once the textbox has the correct path and filename (Figure 4.8), operate the Run button. You will then get a feeling of déjà vu, with the Welcome page for the Files and Settings Transfer Wizard appearing again. As before, operate the Next button to move on to the first "real" window of the wizard, but this time select the Old Computer radio button (Figure 4.9).

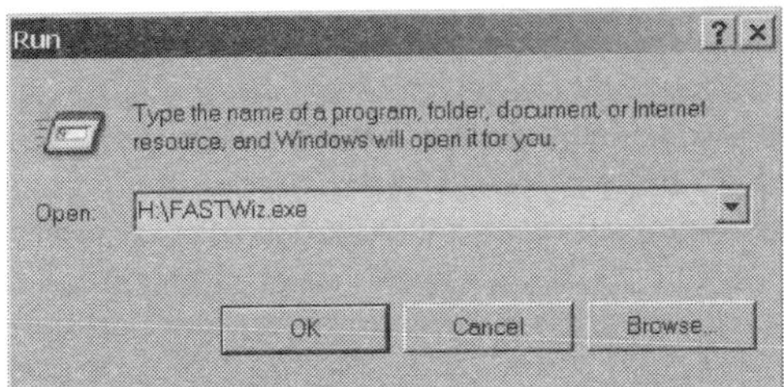

Fig.4.8 Enter the path and filename for the wizard program

There will probably be a brief wait, during which the window shown in Figure 4.10 will be displayed. Eventually the window shown in Figure 4.11 should appear on the screen, and it is then a matter of selecting the method that will be used to collect the files. In this example it is removable media that is being used, and it is therefore the third radio button from

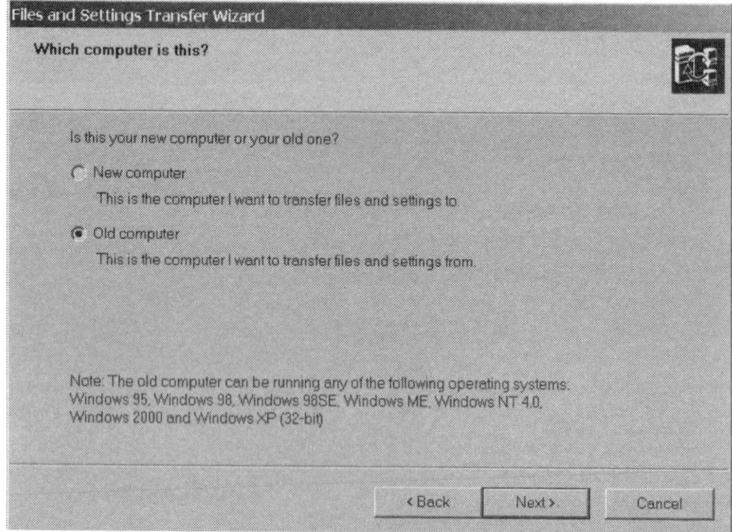

Fig.4.9 This time it is the "Old computer" radio button that is selected

the top that is selected. The appropriate drive is chosen from the drop-down menu, and then the Next button is operated.

Decisions

You then have to select which files and settings will be copied to the disc or discs (Figure 4.12). The default is for settings and files to be transferred to the new PC, but the radio buttons enable only one or other of these to be selected. Ticking the checkbox enables the user to select which files and settings will be transferred to the new system. The scrollable list in the right-hand section shows the files and settings that will be selected by default. There will usually be little or nothing to be gained by using anything other than the default selection.

One possible exception is where a large number of files are selected by default. This is unlikely to be a problem when using a network or direct connection to transfer the files, but it could be awkward when using some types of removable disc. Transferring large amounts of data via this route might be very time consuming, and could require a large number of discs. If you opt to select the files and settings manually, the

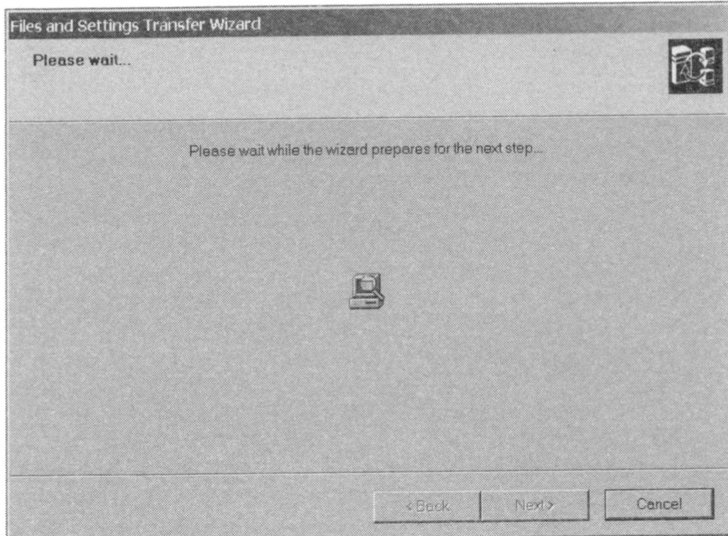

Fig.4.10 There will be a short wait, during which this window will be displayed

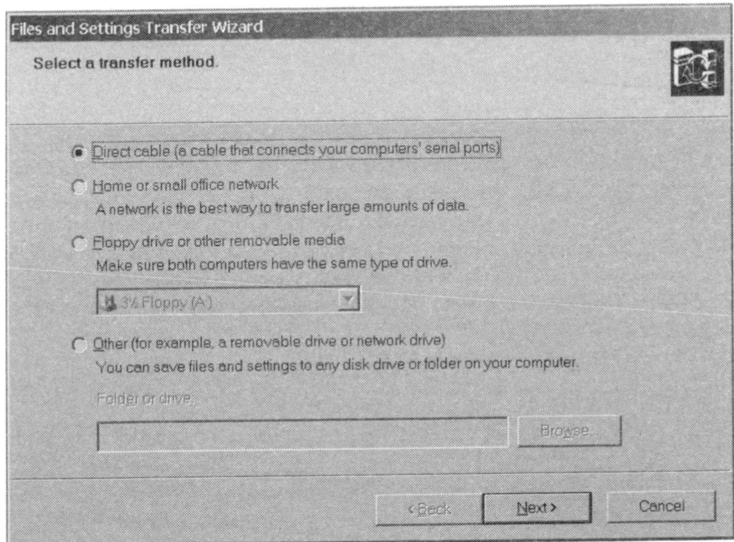

Fig.4.11 Select the method that will be used to collect the files

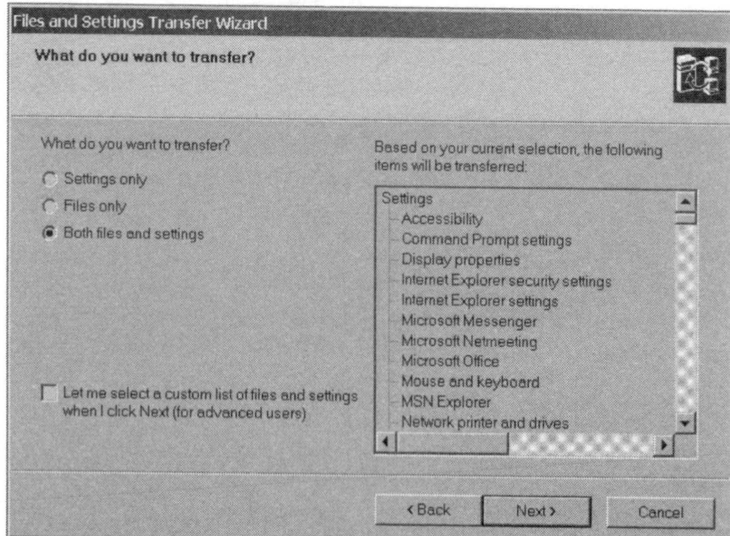

Fig.4.12 Here you have the option of selecting the files and settings that will be transferred

window of Figure 4.13 is obtained at the next stage. This enables files or settings to be deleted from the list, new files to be added via a file browser, and so on.

In this case it is only the settings that have to be transferred. Any files that are needed on the new PC will be manually selected and copied to a CD, and then copied from there to the hard disc of the new PC. Accordingly, the Settings Only radio button was selected and the Next button was operated. A warning was provided at the next window (Figure 4.14), but this will only be produced if settings for non-Microsoft software will be transferred. As one would probably expect, the relevant software must be installed on the new PC prior to transferring the settings from the old PC.

After moving on from any warning screen, the familiar bargraph will appear (Figure 4.15) while the files are collected and copied to disc. There may be pop-up windows that provide information about the amount of data that has been gathered, the number of discs required, and this sort of thing. Simply follow any onscreen instructions that are provided. The window of Figure 4.16 is displayed once the files have been copied

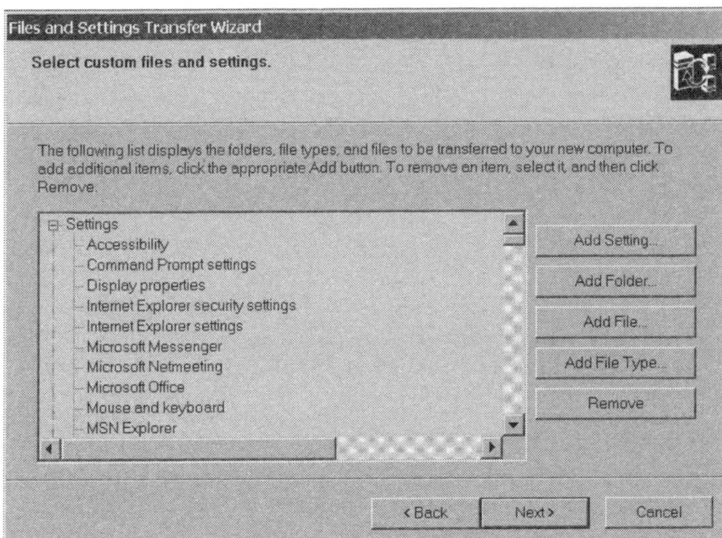

Fig.4.13 This window is used to select the required files and settings

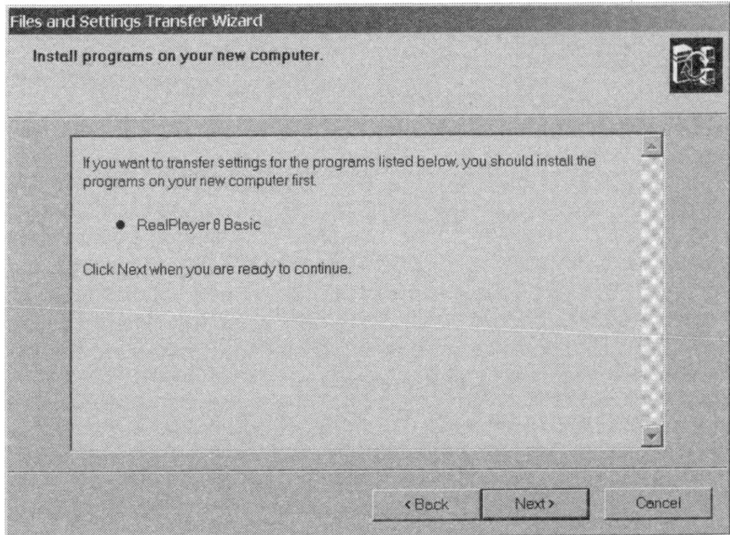

Fig.4.14 This screen warns that the relevant software must be installed on the new PC before the settings can be transferred

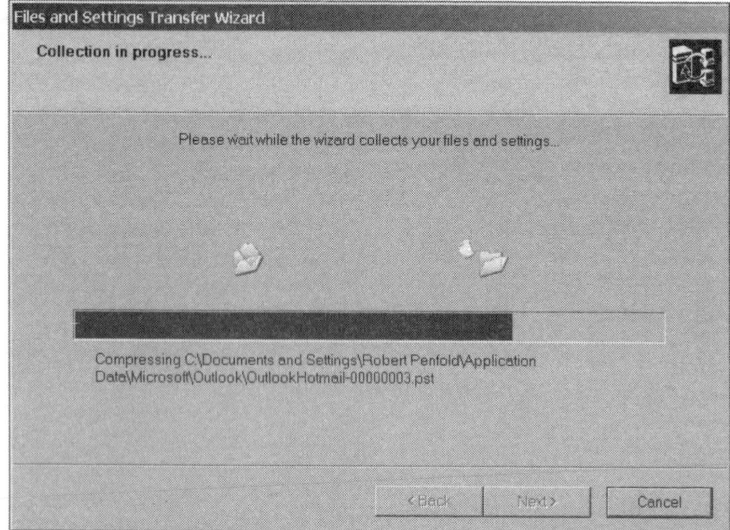

Fig.4.15 This screen shows how the copying process is progressing

successfully. Operate the Finish button to close the window, and then return to the new PC.

Making the transfer

Now it is time to return to the new computer. Note that it is not essential to leave the wizard running while you gather the files and settings data from the old PC. You can close the wizard and then run it again when you are ready to transfer the data to the new PC. When you get to the screen of Figure 4.17, make sure that the bottom radio button is selected and then operate the Next button. This takes you to the screen of Figure 4.18. The same screen should be obtained if the wizard is left running and the Next button is operated.

The radio buttons are used to select the appropriate method of transferring the files to the new computer, and in this case the removable media option is required. The middle radio button is therefore selected, and then the appropriate drive is selected from the menu. A message like the one in Figure 4.19 will appear, and this prompts you to insert the first disc into the drive. Note that this message will appear even if the files are stored on a single "disc" such as a Flash card. Where

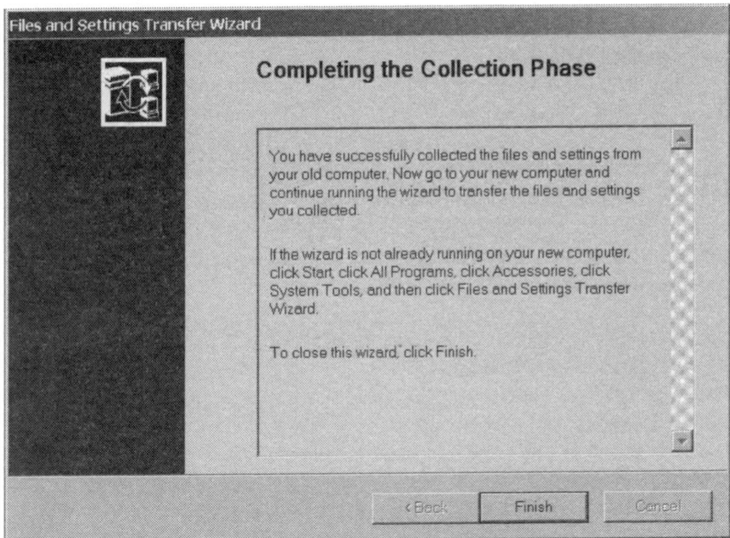

Fig.4.16 Everything has been copied successfully

appropriate, in due course you will be prompted to insert discs two, three, four, etc. Once again, a status window will show how far the process has progressed (Figure 4.20).

Eventually the process will be completed, but this can take a few minutes even if relatively small amounts of data are involved. This is presumably due to the large number of changes that have to be made to various Windows configuration files. In this case the window of Figure 4.21 informed me that the transfer had been completed, but it also indicated that there was a problem with one of the settings. Any settings that have not been transferred correctly must be sorted out manually. In this case there was a problem with a network printer, and it was due to the printer being connected direct to the new PC and not via the network. There was actually nothing to sort out and everything worked fine.

The wizard will produce a final message such as the one in Figure 4.22, indicating that the changes will not take effect until you log off or reboot the computer. It is advisable to log off and on again or reboot the computer so that the system can be checked. As a quick check, try going on to the Internet to see if the homepage of the new computer matches that of the old PC. In this example the two pages matched correctly (Figure 4.23 and 4.24), and the list of favourites had also been transferred correctly.

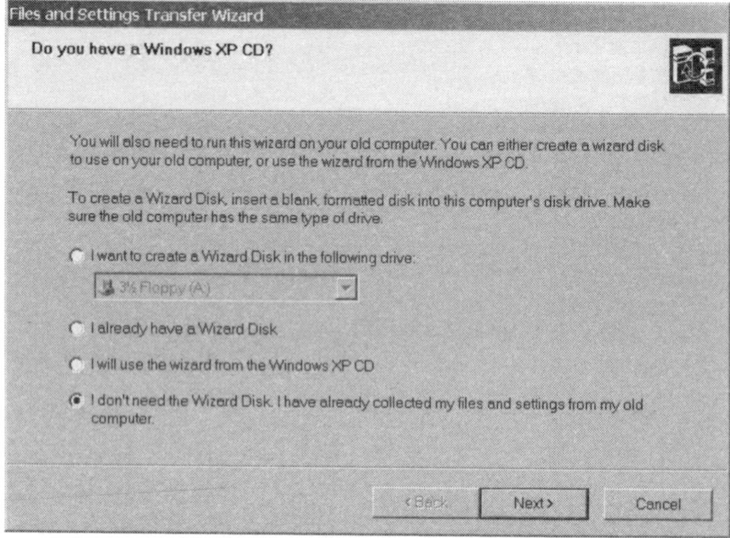

Fig.4.17 At this screen the bottom radio button is selected

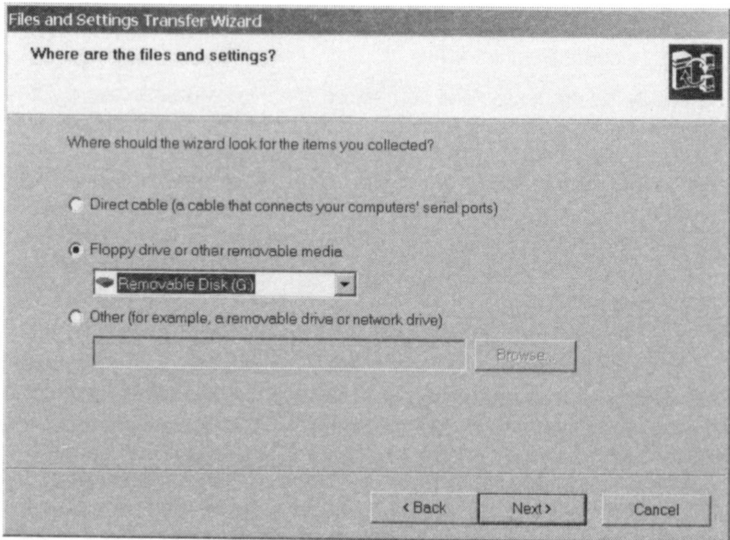

Fig.4.18 Select the appropriate method of file transfer

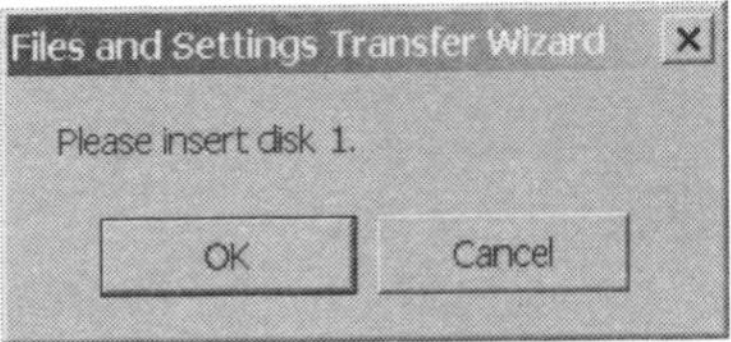

Fig.4.19 Insert a disc when prompted by this pop-up

Some things, such as the customisation of the toolbars in Microsoft Office applications, will not be transferred. Consequently, there will still be some manual changes to make, but using the Settings and Files Transfer Wizard should substantially reduce the amount of manual changes required. It can potentially save a great deal of time and effort. There is little to be lost by trying this little known feature of Windows XP. In the unlikely event that it all goes horribly wrong, it should be possible to return the PC to its former state using the System Restore function.

Easy Transfer

The Windows Easy Transfer facility of Windows Vista is used in essentially the same fashion as the XP transfer wizard. However, it is only usable with PCs that run Windows Vista or Windows XP. It will operate in a restricted fashion with PCs that have Windows 2000 as their operating

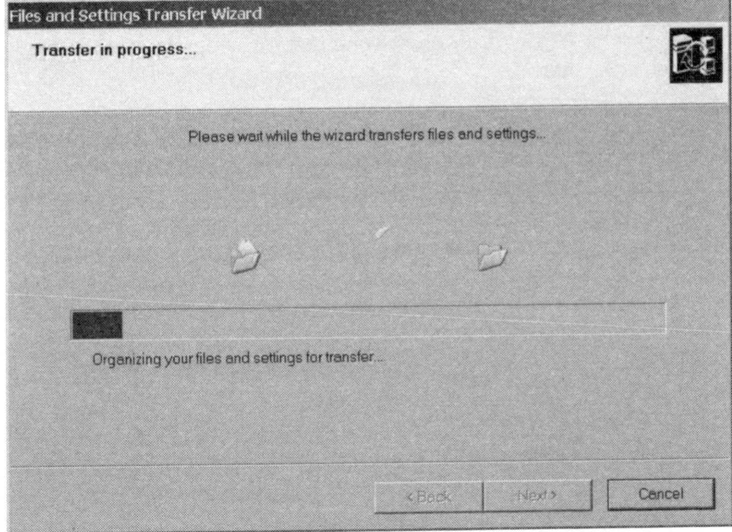

Fig.4.20 A status window shows how far the transfer process has progressed

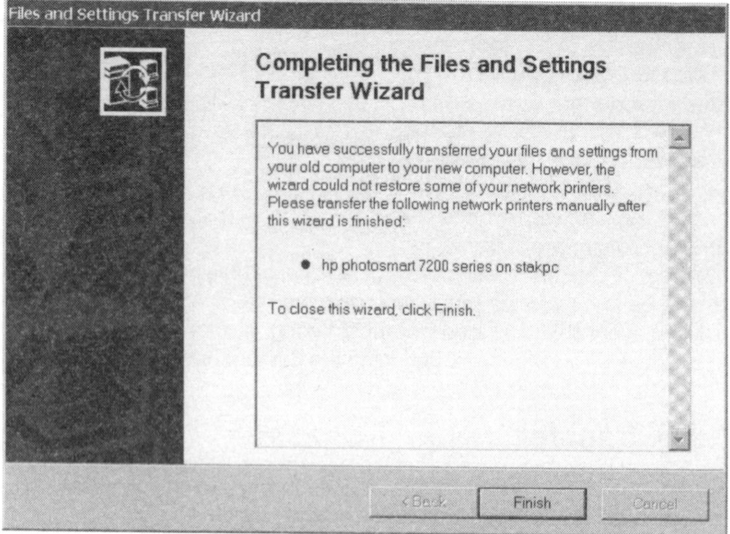

Fig.4.21 The transfer has been completed, but there is a minor problem

system. The program is transferred to and run on the source computer if it runs under Windows XP or 2000, so that the necessary files settings data can be gathered.

Address backup

Some programs have built-in facilities that enable some types of setting to be transferred from one PC to another. With Windows XP you are probably better off using the Settings and Files Transfer Wizard, where this will have the desired effect. Where the Settings and Files Transfer

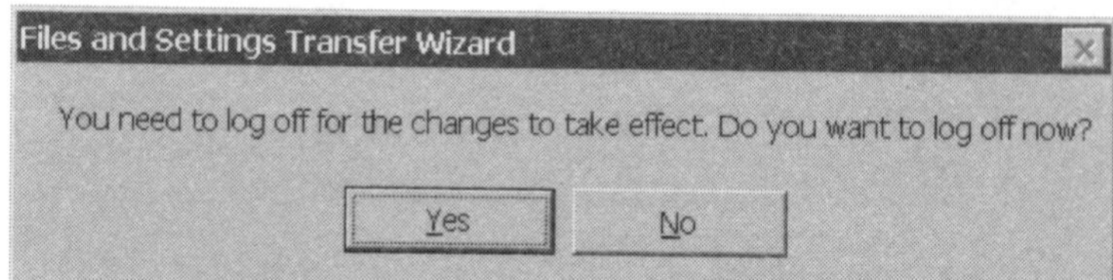

Fig.4.22 The changes will not take effect until you log off or reboot the PC

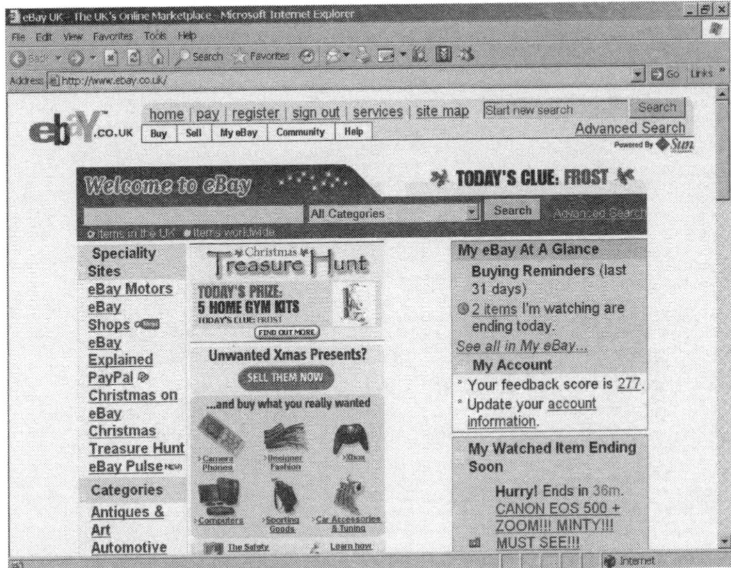

Fig.4.23 The homepage of the old PC

Wizard does not have the desired effect, there is probably no alternative to any built-in transfer facilities of your applications programs. The obvious drawback of this method is that the transfers have to be done one-by-one, which could be quite time consuming. Also, you are likely to be using some of the more obscure facilities of your application programs. Finding out whether the required facility exists, and how to use it if it does, could require a lot of time consuming research.

Email address books are a common problem when moving on to a new computer. Many users have the problem of getting their existing Outlook Express address book transferred to the new PC. With only a few addresses it would not take too long to enter the data manually, but even with a few entries things are quicker and more reliable if the address book is exported from one PC to the other. It is actually possible to import and export an address book, and it is not a bad idea to make a backup copy of the data. If your PC crashes and the data on the hard disc is lost, you can restore your backup copy of the address book which should be stored on a floppy disc, CD-RW, etc., and not on the hard disc.

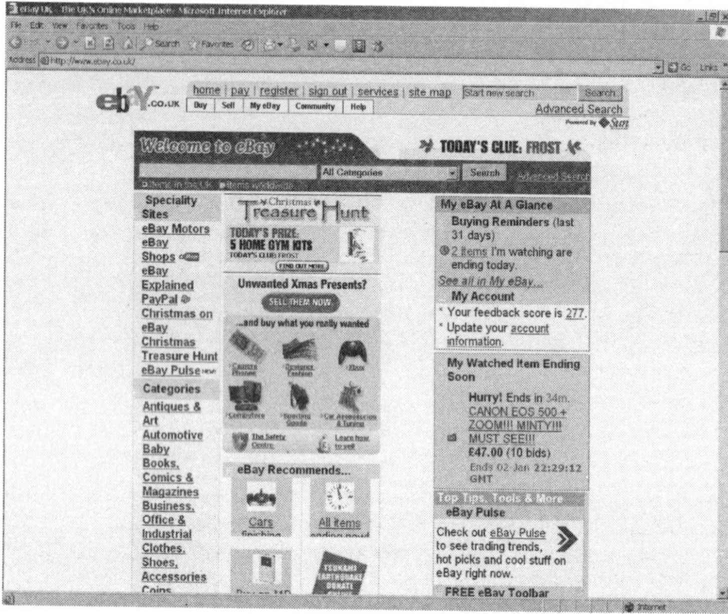

Fig.4.24 The new PC now has the same homepage

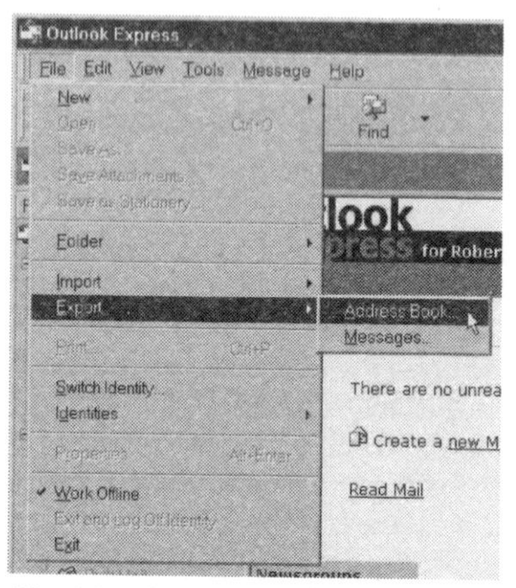

Fig.4.25 Select Address Book from the submenu

To export the address book go to the File menu and select Export followed by Address Book from the submenu (Figure 4.25). A window like the one in Figure 4.26 should then appear. Two types of file are available, and the lower option (the plain text file) should be selected. This produces another window (Figure 4.27) where a filename for the backup copy can be entered into the textbox. However, I would suggest using the Browse button and the file browser that this brings up (Figure 4.28). Choose the folder where you wish to save the file, type a suitable filename for the file, and choose the "csv" option for the file type. Then operate the Save button to return to the previous window. Operate the Next button, which brings up a window like the one of Figure 4.29, where you can select the fields that will be exported. If in doubt select everything! Operate the Finish button and the backup copy will be saved to disc.

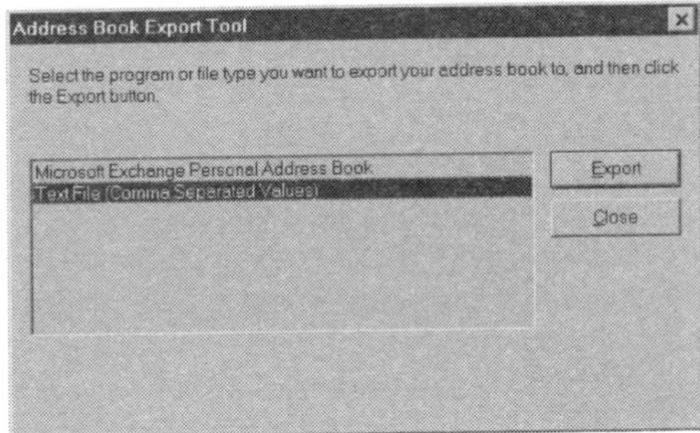

Fig.4.26 Select the Plain Text File option

The importing process is the same whether you are restoring a backup copy after a system crash or putting an existing address book on a new computer. Go to the File menu and select Import, followed by the Other Address Book option. In the new window that appears (Figure 4.30) select Text File from the list of importable file types. Then operate the

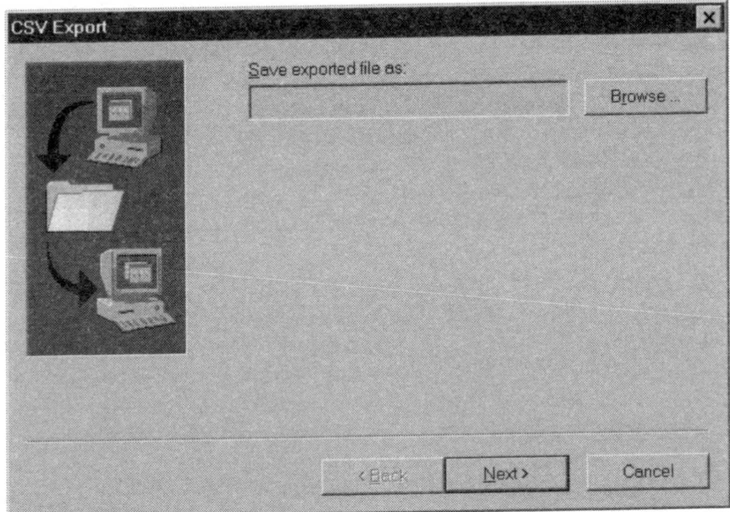

Fig.4.27 It is best to use the Browse option when you reach this window

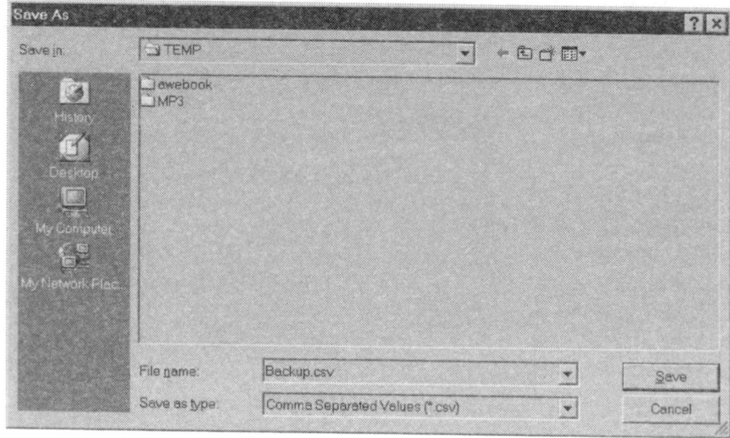

Fig.4.28 Choose csv as the file type

Import button, which brings up a window like the one shown in Figure 4.31. Either type in the full name of the backup file including the path and extension, or use the browser to locate and select it. Operate the Next button to bring up a window like the one of Figure 4.32, where you

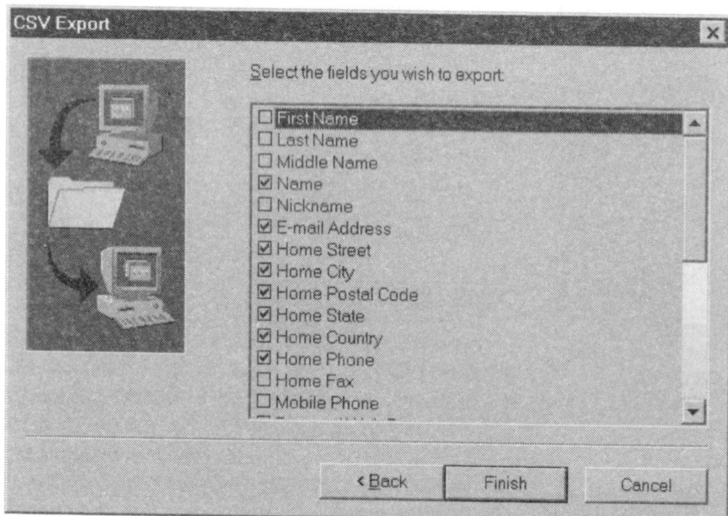

Fig.4.29 You can save selected fields or all of them

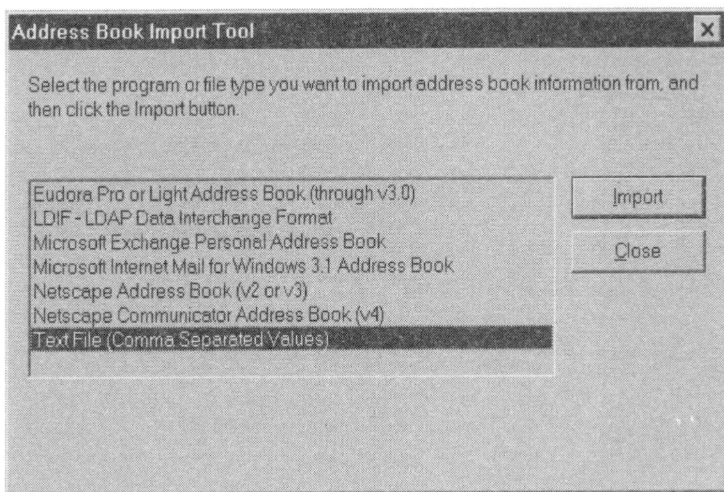

Fig.4.30 Select the correct file type, which is a text file in this case

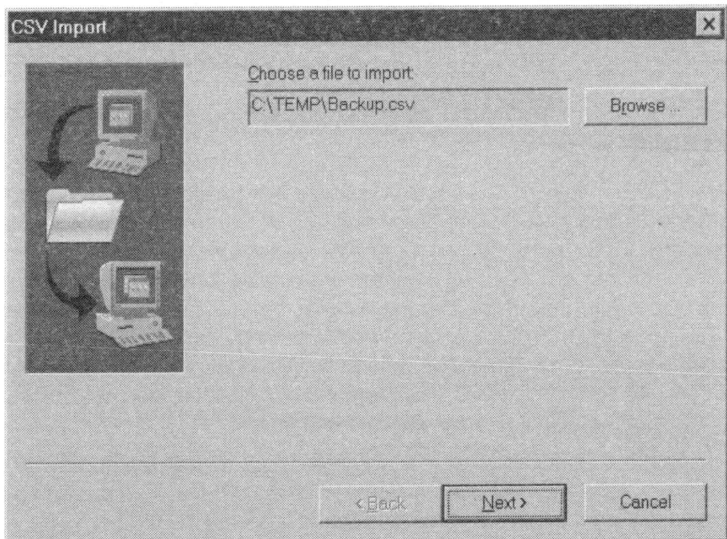

Fig.4.31 Type the full filename or use the browse feature to locate the correct file

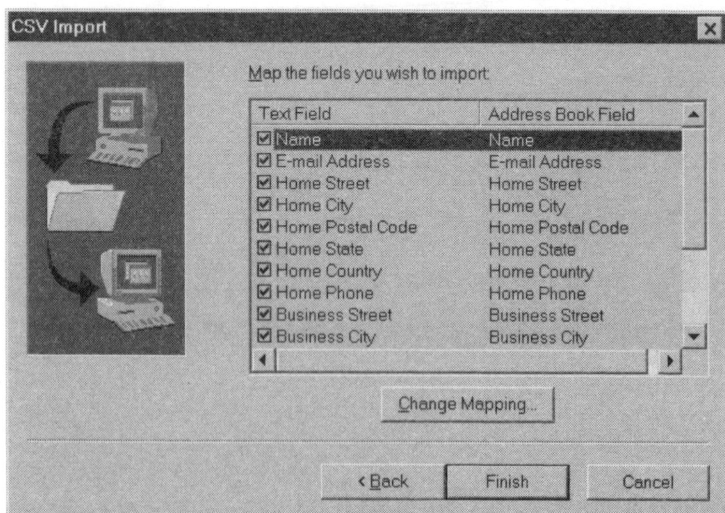

Fig.4.32 Select the fields that you wish to import. The default is for all available fields to be imported

can select the fields that will be imported. Left-click the Finish button to complete the process and import the address book.

Finally

Any facilities that can be used to transfer settings, etc., from one PC to another will obviously vary from program to program. With a voice recognition program for example, it might be possible to save the speech profiles to disc and then transfer them to the new PC. This avoids having each user go through the training process before the program can be used properly. With some programs it might be necessary to use a little ingenuity, as in the previous Outlook Express example. Facilities for backing up settings or customised features can often be used as a means of transferring them from one PC to another.

A ploy that often used to work in the past was to install the application program on the new PC, and then overwrite the program's folder with its equivalent on the old PC. It was important to install the program on the new PC so that the appropriate changes were made to the Windows Registry. Without having the program properly installed in Windows there was little chance of it running properly. Overwriting the new installation with the old one transferred any customisation of the program to the new PC.

Unfortunately, this method is unlikely to work with a modern version of Windows. It used to be normal for programs to use configuration files to control their settings and customised features. However, this way of handling things has now been largely phased out, and most or all of the settings are now stored in the Windows Registry. For this reason, overwriting the program's folder with a copy of the old one is unlikely to have the desired effect. There will probably be no configuration files in the folder for the old installation, so no configuration information will be copied to the new computer. The most likely result is that the program will not have any settings transferred, but it will become unstable and produce error messages!

Points to remember

It is possible to buy programs that will transfer settings from one PC to another, but some of these programs do not seem to offer anything more than the facilities that are built into Windows XP. The more advanced migration programs will copy programs, settings, and even data from the old PC to the new one. Unfortunately, these programs seem to be very difficult to obtain in the UK.

The Files and Settings Transfer Wizard is a little known facility of Windows XP that can be used to transfer Windows settings and files from one PC to another. The equivalent facility in Windows Vista is provided by the Windows Easy Transfer program. The settings of some application programs can also be transferred, but few non-Microsoft programs are catered for.

The transfer can use a network, a direct connection link, or removable media such as floppy discs or a Flash card in a reader. In most cases the amount of data transferred to the new PC is quite small, so using something as basic as a few floppy discs is a practical proposition.

On the face of it, the Files and Settings Transfer Wizard is only usable if the old PC is running under Windows XP. This is not the case though, because the Wizard can produce a program disc that will run under earlier versions of Windows. Running the wizard on the old PC and gathering the files to be transferred is therefore a straightforward task.

In general, any settings that affect the appearance of Windows will be transferred by the Files and Settings Transfer Wizard. This includes things such as the screen colours, and even the sounds that Windows uses. Things such as dial-up connections will also be transferred, as will the Favourites list and homepage of Internet Explorer. Some changes will have to be made manually though, including customised toolbars in Office applications.

Where appropriate, application programs often have facilities for transferring settings from one PC to another. It can be necessary to use a little ingenuity though. For example, a facility that is primarily intended as a means of backing up and restoring settings is likely to be usable as a means of transferring them from one PC to another.

When using a modern version of Windows it is unlikely that simply copying a program's folder from one PC to another will transfer any settings. These days the settings and customisation information are normally stored in the Windows Registry, not in configuration files. This copying method could easily result in the program becoming unstable and generating error messages.

5

Troubleshooting

Problems, problems

There can be software problems with a PC at any time, but there is a higher level of risk with a new PC when a number of programs are being installed. I think it is fair to say that modern software is written to higher standards than much of the software that was available in the past. Also, modern versions of Windows such as Windows Vista are more robust than the earlier versions. Consequently, the likelihood of problems occurring is lower now than in the past. Whereas it used to be regarded as inevitable, these days you probably stand at least an evens chance of avoiding any significant problems. Fortunately, Windows has a facility that should enable things to be corrected fairly rapidly if a major difficulty should arise.

More minor problems are a different matter. Most of these stem from the fact that your idea of how the computer should be set up will not necessarily be matched by the software companies. Having installed some new software you might find that something does not work in quite the way it did previously. This could genuinely provide an improvement, or you might consider that things were better prior to the change. Some of these problems can be avoided by carefully selecting the correct options during installation, while most of the others are easily changed back again via the normal Windows facilities.

Disaster recovery

Modern PCs are usually supplied with a recovery disc or discs that can be used to take the computer back to its original state, as supplied from the factory. These days it is unusual for ordinary Windows installation discs to be supplied as standard, but they are usually available as an optional extra. Being realistic about matters, if the operating system becomes so badly damaged that the computer will not run or even boot properly, the recovery discs provide a more convenient option than the normal installation discs. The operating system and any bundled software can be quickly reinstalled and you can then try again at getting everything set up correctly, and your application programs installed.

The exact method used varies from one manufacturer to another, but in general the recovery discs are very easy to use. It is just a matter of booting from the first recovery disc instead of the hard disc drive, and then following a few simple on-screen instructions. However, you need to carefully read through the documentation for the recovery disc before getting started, since some preliminary setting up might be required before they can be used.

Bear in mind that any recovery system that takes things "back to square one" will result in the loss of any data on the hard disc drive. This will probably be of no practical consequence when you are dealing with a problem that occurred when initially setting up the computer. It is likely that there will be no data stored on the computer at this stage, or that any you have installed will already be fully backed up. However, where appropriate you must make a backup copy of data stored on the PC before using the recovery discs.

System Restore

A useful facility called System Restore was introduced in Windows ME, and essentially the same feature is present in Windows XP and Vista. It has to be emphasised that this is not a conventional backup program, and it can not be used to make a set of backup discs for use in the event of a hard disc failure. This is simply because it uses the main hard disc to store the backup files, and if the hard disc fails, the backup files are inaccessible. System Restore is designed specifically to deal with problems in the operating system. On the face of it you should be able to restore a hacked system if your PC has been attacked by a virus, or a system that has been damaged by a rogue program during installation.

Unfortunately, the System Restore facility has its limitations, and it is possible that it will have been targeted by the virus, or accidentally disabled by a poorly written installation program. However, it is still well worthwhile trying it as a quick fix before reinstalling everything from scratch. After all, you will have lost nothing other than a small amount of wasted time if it fails to work. If it should work, a great deal of time reinstalling everything will have been saved. The chances of success are probably very good where the problem is due to some newly installed software going awry.

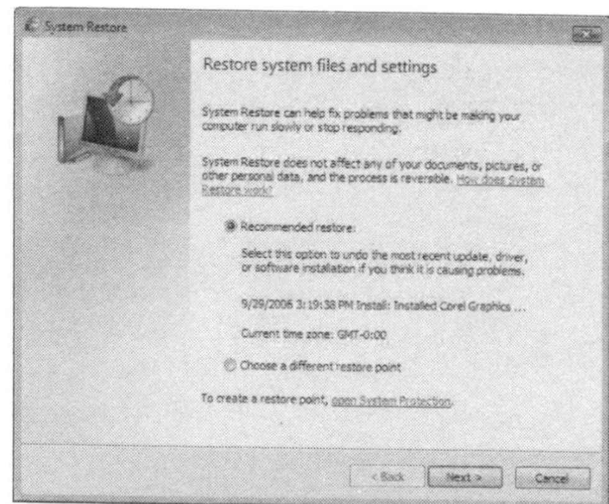

Fig.5.1 The initial System Restore screen in Windows Vista

The purpose of the System Restore facility is to take the system back to a previous configuration. In the current context the idea is to take the PC back to a state prior to the problem software being installed. Ideally you should periodically add new restore points so that if something should subsequently go wrong with the operating system, it can be taken back to a recent restore point. However, Windows adds restoration points periodically, so it is not essential to routinely add your own.

The main reason for adding your own restoration points is that you feel there is increased likelihood of problems occurring. The most common example of this is adding a restore point prior to installing new software, which clearly applies in the current context. If anything should go horribly wrong during the installation process, going back to the restoration point should remove the rogue program and fix the problem with the operating system. You can then contact the software publisher to find a cure to the problem, and in the mean time your PC should still be functioning properly.

When going back to a restoration point the program should remove any recently added programs, but it should leave recently produced data files intact. Of course, with any valuable data that has not been backed up already, it would be prudent to make backup copies before using System Restore, just in case things do not go according to plan. The program fitself does provide a way around this sort of problem in that it does permit a restoration to be undone. If a valuable data file should vanish "into thin air" it should be possible to return the PC to its original configuration, backup the restored data, and then go back to the restoration point again. Any programs lost during the restoration have to be reinstalled from scratch.

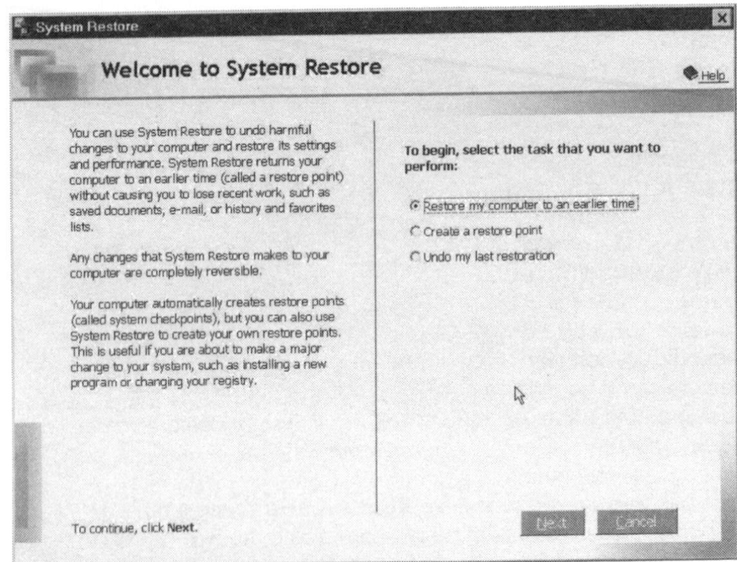

Fig.5.2 The Welcome screen of the System Restore program

In use

The System Restore program is buried deep in the menu structure, but it can be started by going to the Start menu and then selecting Programs, Accessories, System Tools, and System Restore. The program is controlled via a Wizard, so when it is run you get the screen of Figure 5.1 (Vista) or Figure 5.2 (XP) and not a conventional Windows style interface. The radio buttons in the XP version give three options, which are to go back to a restoration point, create a new one, or undo the last restoration. When the program is run for the first time there is no restoration to undo, so this option will not be present. The Vista version is simpler, and you only have the options of restoring

As pointed out previously the system will automatically create restoration points from time to time, but you will probably wish to create your own before doing anything risky or that will make large changes to the system. With XP, start by selecting the "Create a restore point" option and then operate the Next button. The next screen (Figure 5.3) asks the user to provide a name for the restore point, and it is helpful if the name is something that will be meaningful. There is no need to bother about

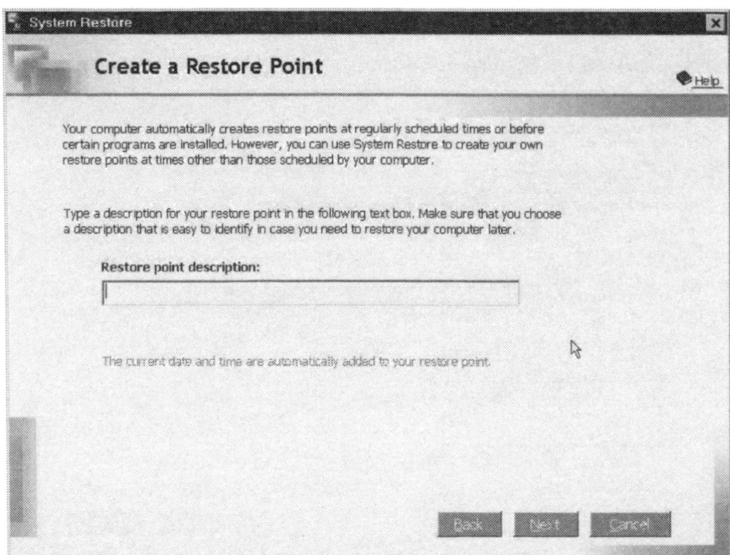

Fig.5.3 The system creates restore points, but you can add your own

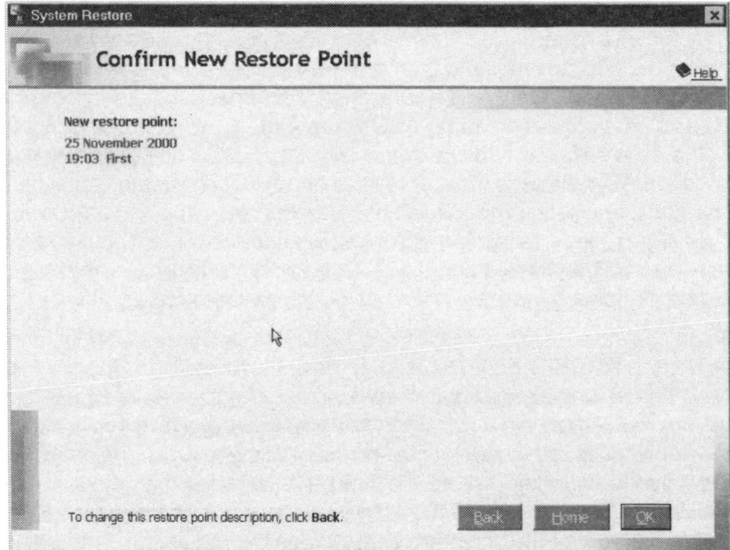

Fig.5.4 You can check things before creating a restoration point

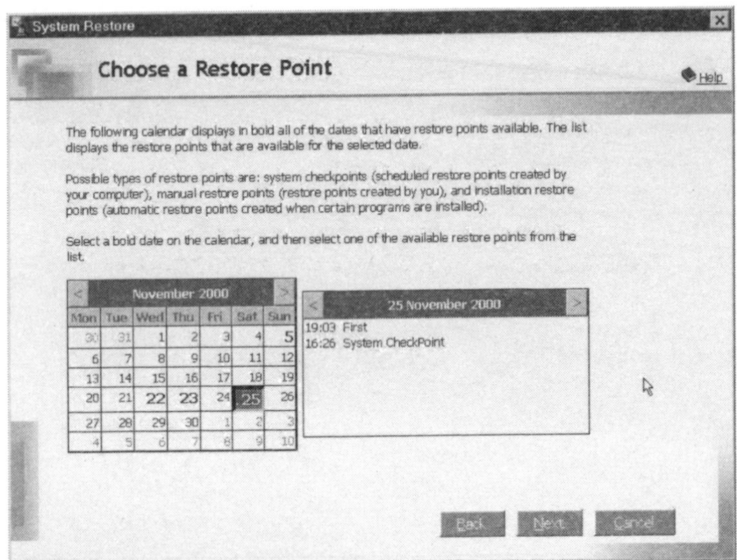

Fig.5.5 Choosing a restoration point

including a date, as the program automatically records the date and time for you. There will be a delay of at least several seconds when the Next button is pressed, and then a screen like the one shown in Figure 5.4 will appear. This gives you a chance to check that everything is correct before the restoration point is created. If everything is all right, operate the OK button to create the restoration point and terminate the program. With Vista it is a matter of operating the Open System Protection link, and then operating the Create button in the new window that appears. Type a name for the restore point in the small window that appears, and then operate the Create button. After a short delay an onscreen message will confirm that the restore point has been created successfully.

To go back to a restoration point with XP, run the program as before, and select the Return my computer to an earlier time option. Operate the Next button, and after a short delay a screen like the one of Figure 5.5 will appear. If there are a number of restore points available you can use the arrowheads in the calendar to find the one you require. The dates on the calendar in larger text are the ones that have restore points. Left-clicking on one of these will show the available points in the screen area just to the right of the calendar. Left-click on the required restore point and then operate the Next button. This brings up a screen and warning

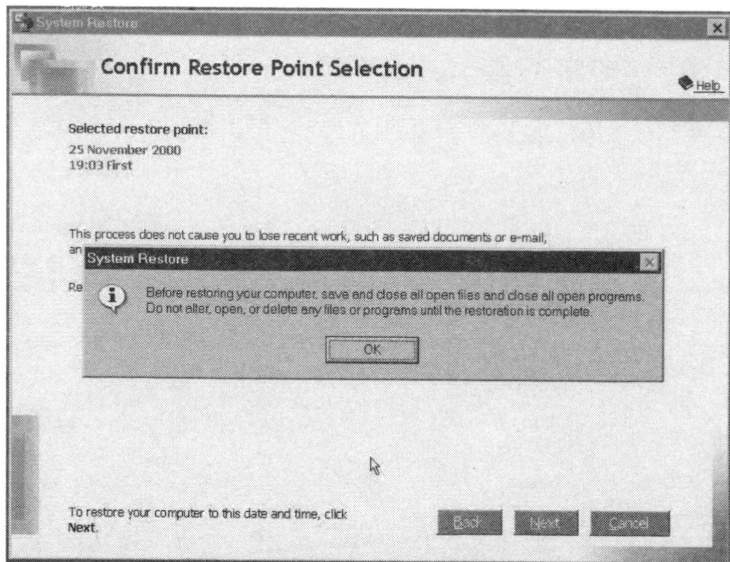

Fig.5.6 A warning message gives you the chance to change your mind

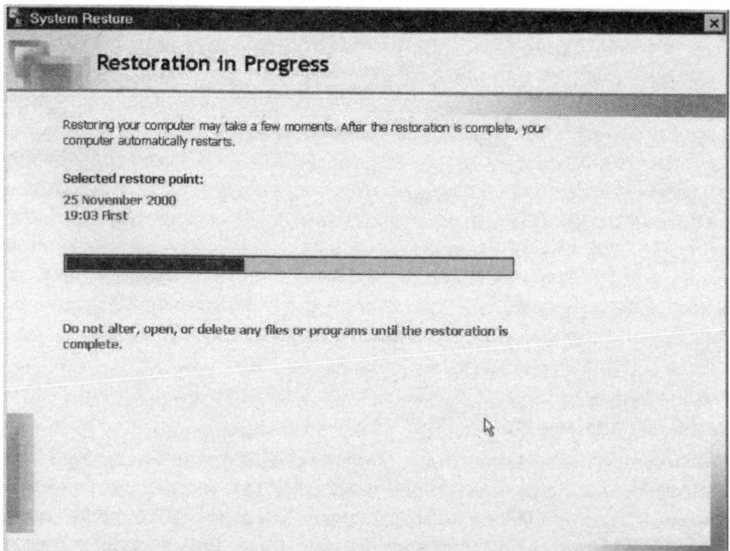

Fig.5.7 You can see how the restoration process is proceeding

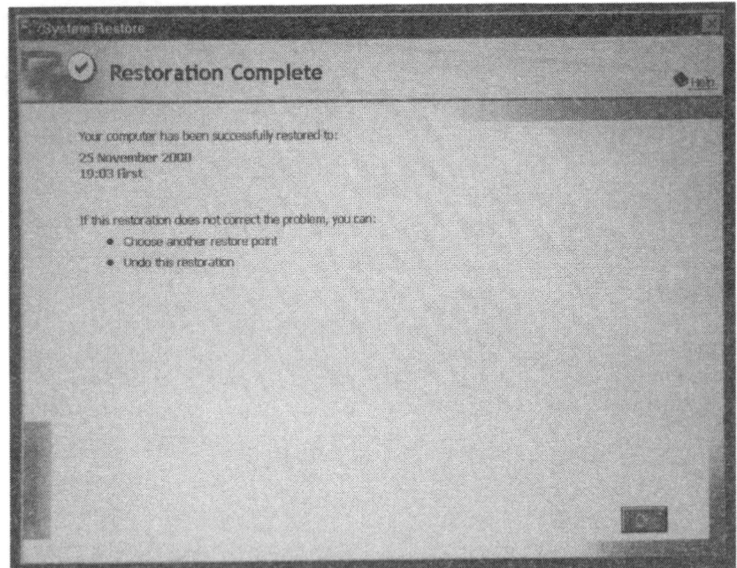

Fig.5.8 This message appears once the computer has rebooted

message, like Figure 5.6. Left-click the OK button to remove the warning message, and close any programs that are running. If you are satisfied that the correct restore point has been selected, operate the Next button and the program will begin the restoration process. A screen showing how things are progressing will appear (Figure 5.7). Heed the warning on this screen, and do not do anything that will alter, open or delete any files while the program is running. Just sit back and do not touch the computer until the program has finished its task. Once the restoration has been completed the computer will reboot, and a message will appear on the screen (Figure 5.8). This confirms the point to which the computer has been returned, and indicates the options if the PC fails to operate properly using this restore point. Left-click the OK button to finish the boot process, and the computer should then have shifted back in time to the appropriate restoration point.

With Vista it is just a matter of accepting the default option (Recommended restore) in order to undo the most recent changes. In the current context this is the one that will normally be used. The other option produces a list of restore points so that you can choose one. Either way, it is then a matter of going through the usual process until the restoration is finished.

There is never any guarantee that the System Restore facility will work, and an error message stating that it can not restore the selected point will sometimes be obtained. You can try a different restoration point, but it is quite likely that none will be available if one of them fails. In my experience it works properly in the majority of cases, but a seriously damaged system is quite likely to result in System Restore failing. As already pointed out, there is not a great deal to lose by trying it in cases where the only alternative is to wipe the hard disc and reinstall everything.

Backup

There is a fairly basic backup and restoration program built into Windows XP, and a more advanced one in Vista. Various third-party backup programs that offer more advanced facilities are available. As with any PC, it is important to have a full and recent backup copy of you laptop PC's hard disc drive. If a catastrophic failure should occur, this enables the computer to be taken back to its state at the time the backup was made. In other word, it takes it back to a state where all your application programs are installed, everything is set up just as you like it, and most of your data is installed on the hard disc drive as well. In order to get things right up to date it is just a matter of installing any recent data from the backup source.

The alternative is to start from scratch, with the recovery discs being used to take the computer back to its factory setup. Then all your programs have to be installed, any customisation of the settings has to be done one by one, and all your data has to be installed. This could take a considerable amount of time. A proper backup and restoration strategy should save a great deal of time and effort.

File association

Most data files are easily opened under the Windows operating system. It is just a matter of locating the file in (say) Windows Explorer, and then double-clicking its entry or icon. Windows then runs the appropriate program and loads the file into it. So how does Windows know which program to use for a given file? The system used by Windows relies on file extensions and file associations.

Extensions are letters that are added to the end of a filename, although they are not necessarily shown in Windows Explorer and other file browsers. This depends on how the program is set to operate. The extension usually consists of three letters, and it is separated from the

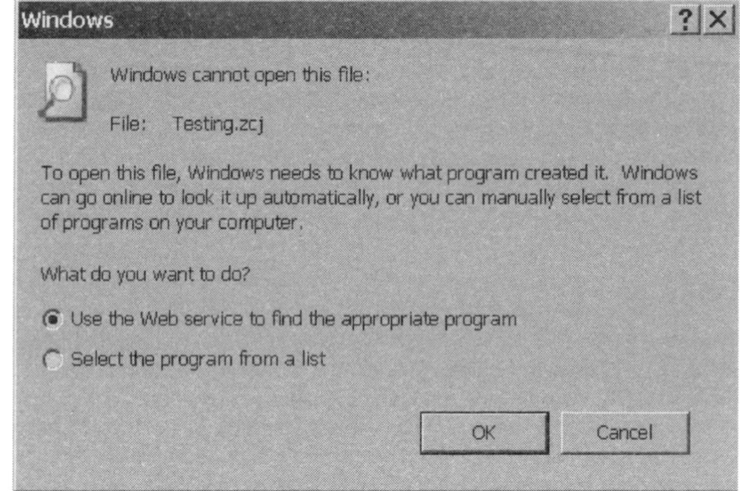

Fig.5.9 Windows responds with this screen if no suitable file association is found

main filename by a full stop. The file I am generating while writing this piece is called "CH5", but the full name including extension is "CH5.doc". The "doc" extension indicates that it is a file generated using Microsoft's Word word processor program.

File associations is basically just a list of file types that Windows stores on the hard disc drive, and for each entry there is a corresponding program. When you double-click on a file, Windows refers to this list if the extension is not one that can be handled by its integral facilities. It then runs the corresponding program and opens the file that you activated.

This system should always work properly provided the file is one that originated on your PC. When you install a new program on your PC, where appropriate it will add its data type or types to the list of file type associations. Windows will then know what to do if you activate a file that was produced by that program, or any file of the same type. This system works quite well, but I suppose it is inevitable that problems occur from time to time.

Probably the most common problem is that you double-click a file and it does indeed open, but in the wrong program! In most cases the file is opened using a program that can handle the file type in question, rather than just causing the program to produce an error message when it is

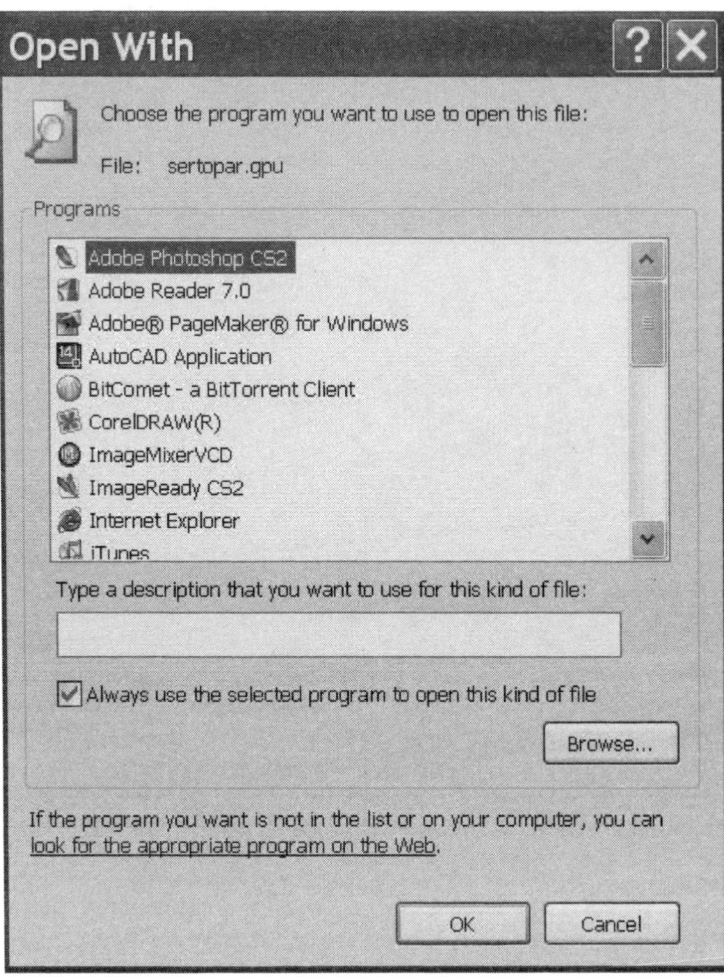

Fig.5.10 Select the correct program from the list

unable to load the file. The usual cause of this problem is that the original file association has been hijacked by a program that you have subsequently installed on your PC. The new program has made itself the default program for that particular type of file, and it has deleted the original association for that file type.

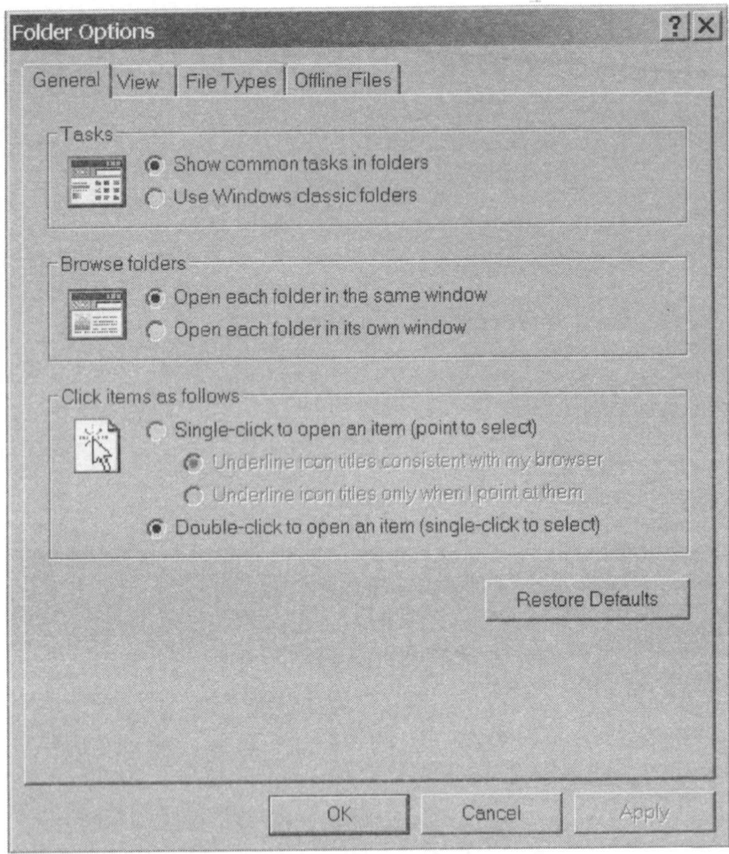

Fig.5.11 The General section of the Folder Options window

Alternatively, a badly written installation program might have accidentally obliterated or altered some of the file associations. Windows produces a response like the one shown in Figure 5.9 if you double-click a file but Windows does not have a program associated with that type of file. There are two options here, and the default option is to let Windows search databases on the Internet in an effort to find the correct program for the file you are trying to open. Note that this option requires an active Internet connection. In most cases you will simply need to select the other option, and then select the appropriate program from the list provided (Figure 5.10).

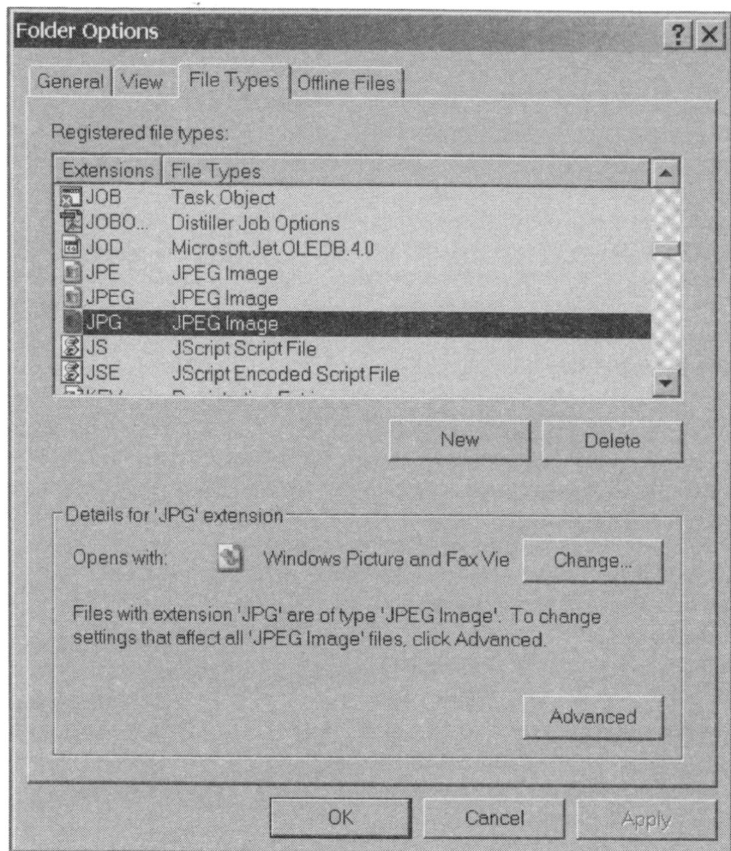

Fig.5.12 A scrollable list of file associations is provided

Associations list

In XP you can obtain a list of the file associations by going to the "classic" version of the Windows Control Panel and double-clicking the Folder Options icon. The equivalent facility of Vista is obtained by locating the file in Windows Explorer, right-clicking its entry, selecting Open With from the pop-up menu, followed by Choose Default Program from the submenu that appears. With XP a new window will be launched (Figure 5.11), and the next step is to operate the File Types tab near the top of

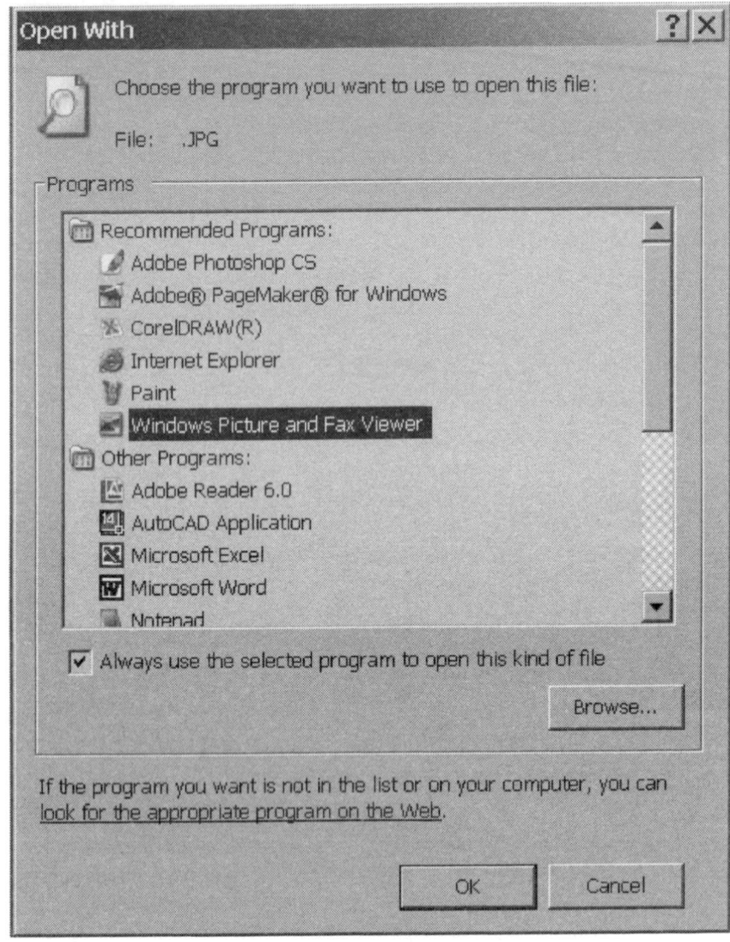

Fig.5.13 A list of the installed programs is provided

the window. This changes the window, and in the upper section it will show a scrollable list of the associated file types. Left-clicking an entry in the list will highlight it, and the program associated with it will then be named in the lower part of the window. In the example of Figure 5.12, the "JPG" entry has been highlighted, and the lower part of the window indicates that this is associated with the Windows Picture and Fax Viewer program. This is one of the built-in programs of Windows.

If an association is not as required, it can be changed by highlighting the appropriate entry in the list and operating the Change button. A new window is then launched, and this shows a list of the installed programs (Figure 5.13). Left-click the correct program to select it, and then operate the OK button to close the window. In this example the "JPG" extension had become associated with the built-in file viewer instead of the Photoshop CS program. I therefore selected the Photoshop CS entry, operated the OK button, and back in the Folder Options window the correct association had been restored.

Things operate slightly differently in Windows Vista. With Vista you are taken straight to a window that provides a list of compatible programs. Double-clicking the entry for the program you wish to use results in the file being opened in that program, which then becomes the default for that file type.

There is a possible complication when changing file associations, and this is caused by some very simple programs not being installed in Windows in the normal way. In most cases these programs are not installed in Windows at all, but due to their basic nature they will still manage to work properly when run. Since these programs are not installed in Windows, they do not appear in the list of installed programs, and there is no easy way to associate a file type with one them.

It can be done by operating the Browse button, which launches the standard Windows file browser. This is then used to locate and select the correct program file. This is easy enough for those with plenty of computing experience, but it can not be recommended for beginners. Fortunately, these days the vast majority of programs are installed in Windows, and this problem is unlikely to occur. Remember that it should be possible to run the appropriate program and then load a data file. Therefore, it is not essential to have a file association in order to open a data file.

Battery

Problems with laptop batteries used to be quite common, but improvements in the technology have helped to make them less problematic. Even so, you would be well advised to read through the section of the full instruction manual that deals with recharging the battery and keeping it in good condition. Some general points can be made here, but with battery technology advancing all the time it is advisable to seek specific information for the battery used in your particular laptop PC.

A common complaint with a new laptop is that the battery runs down much more quickly than expected. Laptop PCs use clever techniques to keep the power consumption to a minimum, but the amount of power required to keep one operating normally is still quite high. The drain on the battery will be even higher if you undertake tasks that involve things like intensive use of the processor or continuous operation of a CD-ROM or DVD drive. The quoted operating life of the battery is typically only two or three hours, but it will be less than this if the computer is used for activities that involve relatively high levels of power consumption.

Another point to bear in mind is that some rechargeable batteries need to go through several charge/discharge cycles before they achieve full capacity. Therefore, you may need to fully charge and run down the battery a few times before it becomes fully up to standard and its operating life per charge can be assessed properly. The instruction manual should always give this recommendation in cases where the battery is a type that needs to be "exercised" before it reaches full capacity.

I generally try to take rechargeable batteries through a few charge/ recharge cycles before using them in earnest regardless of whether this point is addressed by the instruction manual. In practice few rechargeable batteries seem to work really well until they have been used for a while. Another point to bear in mind is that most rechargeable batteries work best if they are run down and recharged on a regular basis. It is likely that the battery will not perform well if it is left unused for a few weeks or more. Fortunately, in most cases it can be restored to full capacity by taking it through a full charge and discharge cycles.

Memory effect

You tend to hear a great deal about the so-called "memory effect" when rechargeable batteries are discussed. The basic premise of this is that a rechargeable battery does not provide full capacity unless it is fully discharged before it is recharged. Supposedly, recharging a 50 percent discharged battery gives you a battery of half the normal fully charged capacity. In other words, the battery "remembers" how long it was used and its state prior to being recharged, and this becomes its new capacity.

While it is true that the original nickel-cadmium (Ni-Cad) batteries work best when taken through full charge and discharge cycles, problems with the "memory effect" have perhaps been a little exaggerated at times. Fortunately, the batteries used in modern laptop PCs are not of the nickel-cadmium variety. They are mostly based on some form of lithium-iron technology, which gives higher capacities from smaller and lighter batteries.

This type of battery is also totally free from any "memory effect", so there is no problem if a partially discharged battery is topped-up. Note though, that some manufacturers do recommend that the battery should occasionally be fully discharged and recharged. This will supposedly keep it in optimum condition.

No charge

Modern rechargeable batteries have quite long operating lives, but they do not last forever. In some instances the battery will outlast the rest of the computer, but most laptop PCs require at least one new battery during their operating life. Sometimes it is pretty obvious when the battery has failed. It does not take a significant charge and the computer either fails to switch on at all or it only does so for a few seconds before powering down again.

There will usually be some warning signs before this stage is reached. There will often be a noticeable reduction in the computing time obtained between charges. Probably the clearest sign of the impending demise of the battery is when it will not hold a charge for more than a day or two. In general, rechargeable batteries do not hold their charge as well as primary cells. Even so, they normally take a few weeks or more to fully discharge when left unused. The battery will soon need replacement if you find that it has almost fully discharged even though the computer has not been used for a few days.

Leave it in

Of course, the battery is likely to be of little interest when a laptop is used as a normal home or office PC. The computer will always be powered from the mains supply via the adaptor, rendering the battery of no use. One battery is normally part of the standard equipment supplied with the computer, so buying the computer without a battery is unlikely to be an option.

This is perhaps a little unfortunate; since it means that you are paying for an expensive battery that is of little practical value to you. On the other hand, it is handy to have the option of using battery power. It leaves your options open, and you can use the computer in the garden or on the move if the need should arise.

If you will not be using the battery, should it be left in the PC or removed? There are a couple of good reasons for leaving the battery in the computer. One is simply that if you should decide to use the computer away from a mains outlet, you simply do so. The battery in the computer will be fully charged and ready for use whenever you need it. When stored outside the computer the battery will gradually lose its charge, and it will probably have to be fully recharged overnight before it can be used.

The other advantage of having the battery in the computer is that it effectively provides you with a UPS (uninterruptible power supply). The idea of a normal UPS is that it powers the computer in the event of the mains power failing. Provided everything works as it should, the batteries in the UPS take over when the mains supply fails, and the computer carries on working as if nothing had happened. Some units do not go on powering the computer for very long, but you still have plenty of time to save your data and close down the computer normally.

With other units the power is maintained for a few hours. With luck, the mains supply will have been restored before the backup battery runs down. The battery in a laptop PC effectively gives you a UPS of this type, because the battery immediately takes over if the mains supply fails, or you accidentally knock the power plug from its socket in the computer! The battery will usually provide two or three hours of computing, by which time normal operation will usually have been restored.

If you do decide to keep the battery in the computer, it is probably as well to periodically run the battery down and recharge it again, so that it is kept in good working order. It is important to store the battery sensibly if you decide not to keep it in the computer. It should be stored in a cold dry place where there is nothing metal. Do not underestimate the amount of power that a modern laptop battery can provide. If any metal short-circuits the battery terminals it is likely that a great deal of heat will be generated. This clearly represents a fire hazard, and it will not do the battery a lot of good either.

As pointed out previously, the battery will tend to run down over a period of time even if it is not used. This means that it will have to be fully recharged before it can be used in earnest. It is a good idea to occasionally charge the battery, run it down, and recharge it again so that it is kept in good condition. If you simply leave the battery in a drawer for a few years and then try to use it, do not be surprised if it has a very limited capacity or does not work at all.

Quick change

The virtues of an extra battery for computing on the move were mentioned in an earlier chapter. The rather limited operating time available from a single battery means that any serious computing while away from home is likely to be dependent on at least one extra battery. You are otherwise reliant on there being a convenient power point that can be used with the computer's mains adaptor, but in practice there will seldom be a power point that you can use.

A few laptop PCs have some form of quick battery changing facility that enables the battery to be changed without switching off the computer first. This usually operates by having a battery or capacitor in the computer that briefly provides power while the batteries are swapped. However, with most laptop PCs it is necessary to switch off the PC prior to changing the batteries. It might be possible to put the computer into "hibernation" instead, although this might not be a great deal quicker than switching it off and rebooting once the battery has been changed.

Low power

It is important to avoid the situation where the battery runs down completely and the computer cuts off. These days there is little risk of the abrupt shutdown giving Windows any problems when it reboots, but you could find that some of your data has not been saved to disc and has been lost. Ideally you should save all you data to the hard disc drive and shut down the computer just before the battery becomes completely exhausted.

As explained in a previous chapter, there is a battery gauge built into Windows, and this gives an indication of the charge left on the battery. Many laptop computers are supplied with utilities that can be brought up on the screen by pressing a couple of keys, and these often represent a more convenient means of gauging the charge left in the battery. You have to read through the documentation for your computer in order to determine whether it has a utility program of this type, and if so, how it is accessed.

Some very clever technology is used to gauge the charge remaining in the battery, but bear in mind that it is only giving a rough estimate. It is gauging rather than making an accurate measurement, so it is advisable to be conservative and assume that the remaining charge is actually a little less than that indicated. It is quite likely that the charge left on the

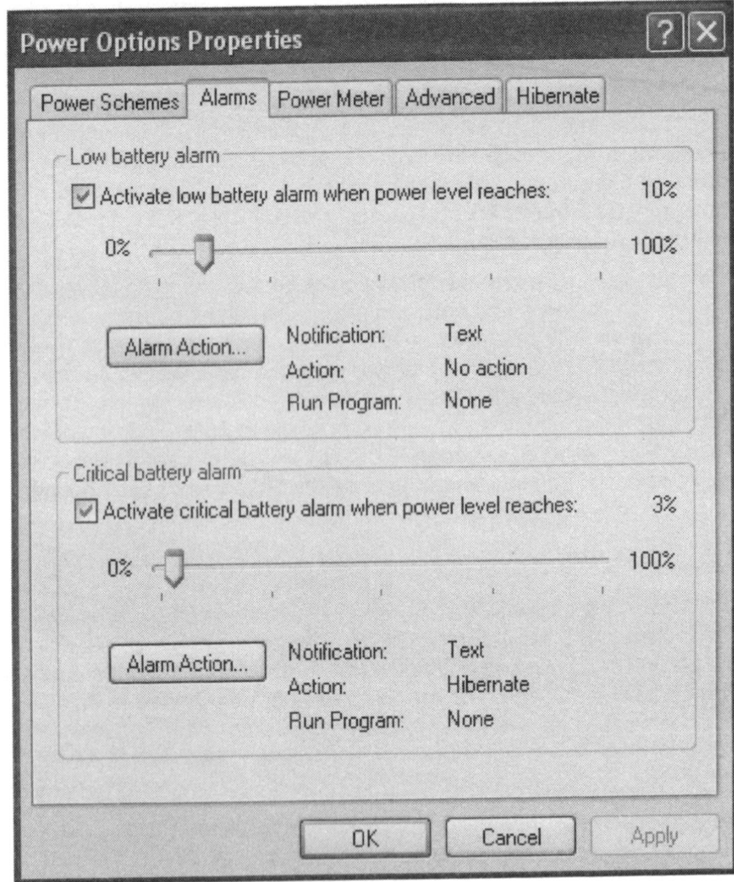

Fig.5.14 The Alarms section of the Power Options Properties window

battery is indeed somewhat less than that indicated by the battery gauge software.

If you do not bother to check the state of the battery there should still be no risk of the computer suddenly switching off with no warning because the battery has become completely exhausted. Windows will provide a warning message when the battery has about 10 percent of its charge left, and again when the battery is down to three percent of full charge. This is the last warning you will get though, and the computer will shut

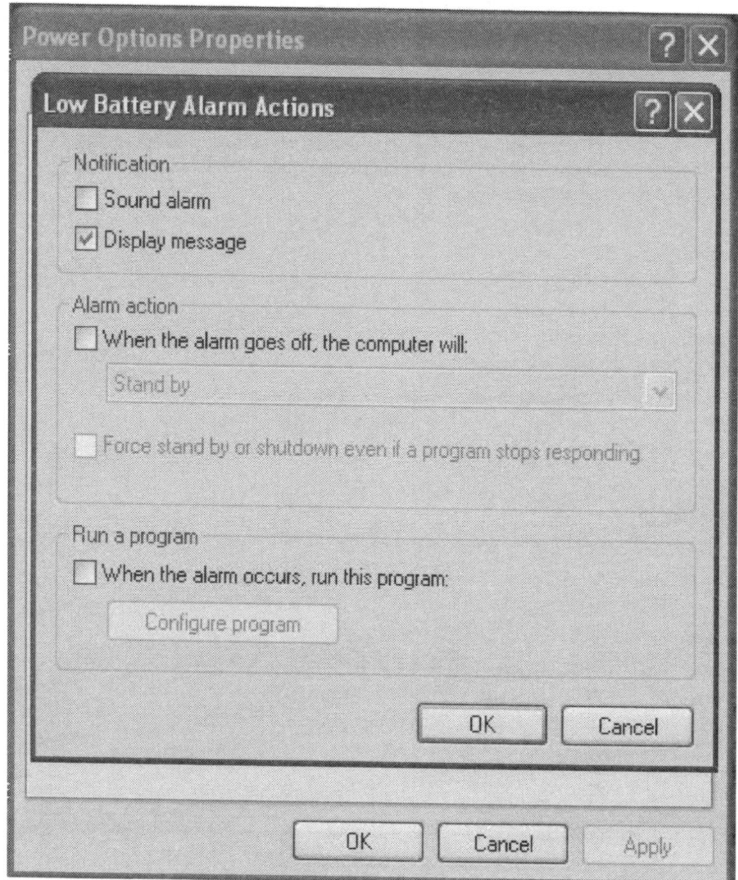

Fig.5.15 You can choose the action or actions provided when the alarm is activated

down in what will usually be a very few minutes later. There should be time to save your data and close Windows normally, but there will probably not be sufficient power for anything more than that.

It is possible to alter the levels at which the warnings are issued. This will not usually be necessary, but it could be advantageous to do so if you find that there is too little operating time left after the final warning. The settings are altered by first launching the Control Panel from the

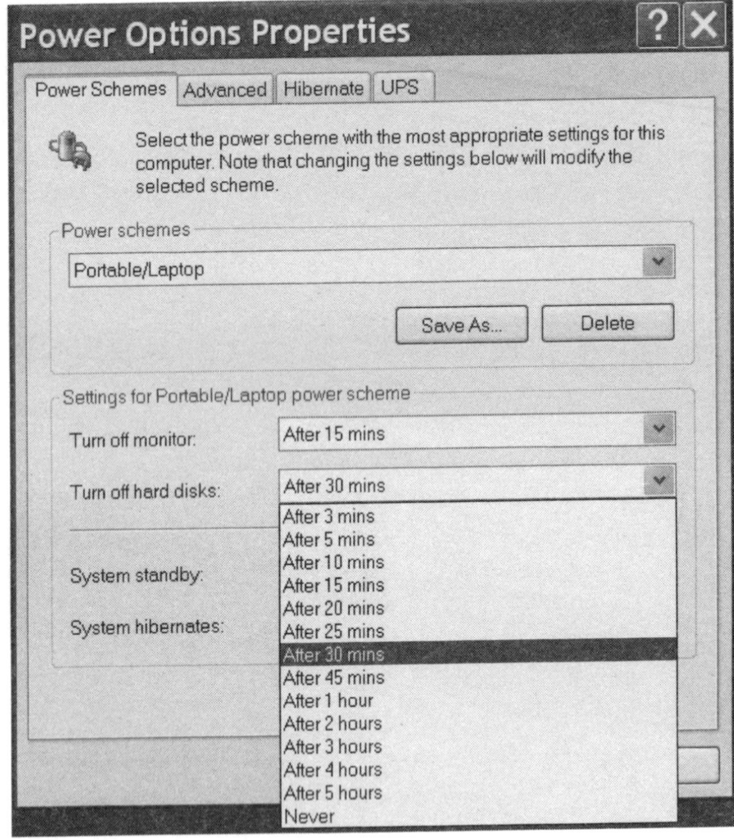

Fig.5.16 This menu provides a choice of delays

Start menu. With the Control Panel in the "classic" view, double-click the Power Options icon, and then operate the Alarms tab in the Power Options Properties window (Figure 5.14).

There are two slider controls that enable the alarms to be activated at the appropriate battery levels. The upper slider sets the point at which the initial warning is produced, and the lower control sets the point at which the second warning is obtained. It is possible to disable an alarm by removing the tick from its checkbox, but I would definitely advise against doing so.

There is an Alarm Action button for each of the alarms. Operating this produces a new window, as in Figure 5.15. Only the onscreen message is produced by default, but there is the option of having an audible alarm as well as or instead of this message. As usual, having a tick in its checkbox enables the feature, and removing the tick disables it. Further options are available from the lower section of the window, such as having the computer placed in Standby mode or having a selected program run, but these facilities are not normally needed.

Saving power

There are ways of saving power and extending the battery life, but do not expect miracles from this type of thing. Also, there is generally a price to be paid for the reduced power consumption. This price is normally a reduction in speed at some stage of the proceedings. For example, some laptop PCs have a system that enables the computer to run at reduced power consumption, but this involves slowing down the computer for all or part of the time. The reduced speed is unlikely to be a major drawback when undertaking an undemanding task such as word processing, but it could slow down the computer to an unacceptable degree when running an application that requires a large amount of processing power.

The Power Schemes section of the Power Options Properties window enables the monitor and or hard disc drive to be switched off after a period of inactivity. The default settings provide quite long delays before the switch-off occurs, but shorter times are available from the drop-down menus (Figure 5.16). As an LCD monitor switches on almost immediately, having it shut down after a few minutes of inactivity is quite a good idea.

This approach tends to be slightly less satisfactory with the hard disc drive. With the drive motor has stopped, it takes a few seconds for it to get back up to full speed so that the drive can operate normally again. This can introduce noticeable delays when using the computer.

Probably the most effective way of reducing the power consumption of the computer is to make sure that the brightness of the monitor is no higher than it really needs to be. It would be a mistake to set the brightness so low that viewing the screen is difficult. On the other hand, setting the brightness any higher than the minimum needed for comfortable viewing is just wasting power.

With some laptop computers the screen brightness is automatically reduced when the battery is used as the power source. With any laptop PC there should be a control or controls specifically for setting the screen's

Fig.5.17 The keyboard of a Dell laptop PC

brightness. Alternatively the keyboard and certain key combinations will give control of the screen brightness, and probably the contrast as well.

Power utility

Some laptop PCs are supplied complete with a power management utility program. This might be in addition to the built-in facilities of Windows, or in place of them. Where such a utility is provided, it should provide facilities that go beyond the standard ones built into Windows. With this type of thing it is necessary to carefully read through the documentation for the program to determine what features are available, and how they are controlled.

Keyboard

Those used to a standard PC keyboard could be forgiven for thinking that a laptop keyboard has little in common with the standard layout. A closer inspection shows that most of the familiar keys are there, but there is an obvious omission in that there is no numeric keypad. Where the laptop is not used on the move you might prefer to "throw in the towel" and not bother about getting to grips with the built-in keyboard. An ordinary USB PC keyboard can be connected to the computer, which can then be used instead of the built-in unit.

It is probably worthwhile giving the built-in keyboard an extended trial rather than simply ignoring it. Of course, there is probably no real

Fig.5.18 This is the keyboard of a Sony laptop PC

alternative to using the built-in keyboard if the laptop will be used on the move. You have to learn to use it effectively, which should not really take too long.

If you look at a few laptop keyboards you will probably notice straight away that there are a number of differences from one to another. This is demonstrated by the two examples in Figures 5.17 and 5.18. These are respectively the keyboards of Dell and Sony laptop PCs. I suppose that this is not too different to the situation with standard PC keyboards. There is the basic 105-key layout, but many real-world keyboards have a number

Fig.5.19 A block of 16 keys can act as a numeric keypad

of additional keys. Manufacturers perhaps take a few more liberties with laptop keyboards, but the layout is usually based on a well tried basic arrangement.

Numeric keypad

Although there is no separate numeric keypad on a laptop keyboard, it has not been omitted altogether. When Num Lock (Numbers Lock) is off, a cluster of 16 keys at the right-hand end of the keyboard operate normally. Switching on Num Lock results in these keys operating as a something approximating to a normal PC numeric keypad. The alternative functions are marked on the keys themselves (Figure 5.19).

In order to switch Num Lock on it is just a matter of pressing the Num Lock (Num Lk) key once. There will usually be an indicator light that switches on to confirm that the keyboard is in the Num Lock mode. In order to switch the Num Lock function off again it is just a matter of pressing the Num Lock key again. The indicator light should switch off again to confirm that the keyboard has been returned to normal operation.

Fn key

The Fn key was originally an extra key of the Shift/Control/Alt variety, and it was used to help make up for the lack of keys on the early laptop keyboards. Modern laptop PCs tend to have more keys than the early types, and the need for the Fn key has diminished. This is not to say that it is no longer needed. These days it is often used in conjunction with other keys to controls special functions. The exact functions available and the key combinations used to access them vary from one laptop PC to another. It is a matter of studying the instruction manual to find details of the available controls. These are typical uses for the Fn key:

Raise and lower the volume of the internal sound system

Mute and reactivate the internal sound system

Increase and decrease the brightness of the built-in monitor

Activate the Hibernate and (or) Standby mode

Lock and unlock the built-in keyboard

Switch on or disable an external monitor

Launch power management or other software utility

Fig.5.20 This is the touch pad on a Dell laptop PC

Custom keys

Practically every laptop has one or more custom keys. In other words, keys that are only found on that particular make of laptop, or even keys that are unique to a laptop of a particular make and model. These keys are usually to be found above the main keyboard, but they are occasionally found elsewhere. In most cases the custom keys are linked to a utility program of some kind that runs automatically when the key is operated. The non-standard nature of these keys means that you must delve into the instruction manual in order to determine their functions.

Touch pad

These days every laptop PC seems to have a built-in touch pad (Figure 5.20), or mouse pad as it is also known. This is a very effective way of controlling the pointer, and it is also a very neat solution as it is built into the computer itself. An ordinary mouse is probably a better means of controlling the pointer when the laptop is used back at base, but a mouse tends to be very inconvenient when computing on the move. The touch pad is a more practical means of handling things.

When people use a laptop computer for the first time it seems to be quite normal for the touch pad to be problematic. This is not usually due to any major shortcomings in the design of the touch pad. It stems more from the fact that computer users are used to controlling the pointer via a mouse, and that they have difficulty adjusting to a new method It is probably best to accept that you will not learn to use the touch pad proficiently in a couple of minutes. It will take a while to get used to a new way of working, and it might never be quite as quick and easy as using a mouse.

The basic technique for using a normal touch pad is to use your forefinger to operate the pad and move the pointer, and your thumb to operate the two buttons. Only a very light touch is needed in order to move the pointer. Using a lot of pressure will simply wear out the pad and the end of your finger! It will not provide better control of the pointer. Dragging objects tends to be a bit awkward since you have to hold down the left button with your thumb while moving the pointer with your forefinger. It is a good idea to practise this until you become reasonably proficient at it.

Initially you might find that unexpected menus tend to keep popping up on the screen. This is caused by accidentally operating the right mouse button instead of the left one. Again, some practice should help you to get things right and avoid the problem. If the pointer tends to jump all over the place it is likely that you are touching the pad in two places at once. Learn to control the pointer with you forefinger while keeping your other fingers well clear of the pad.

A common problem when first using a touch pad is that menu items are selected even though you have not operated the left mouse button. This occurs with touch pads that enable a tap on the pad to simulate clicking the left button. This is a very useful feature, but it can produce confusing results if you do not realise that it is active. It can also produce erratic results if the sensitivity is too high. Although you consider that your finger is hovering over the pad, the driver software might interpret any slight twitching as mouse clicks.

It might be best to disable it if this feature produces frequent problems. Alternatively, try tweaking the settings for the touch pad to see if an improvement can be made. There might be a utility program that can be used to control the touch pad settings. In most cases though, it is controlled via the appropriate section of the Windows Control Panel (refer to chapter 3).

Some laptops have a trackball rather than a touchpad. This is effectively an upside-down mechanical mouse where the mouse remains stationary and your hand rolls the ball. Although trackball controllers were once the norm for laptops, they now seems to be have been largely replaced by touchpads. Anyway, a pointing device of this type has what are essentially the standard mouse settings, and it should therefore be fairly easy to set up satisfactorily.

Points to remember

These days it is normal for PCs to be supplied with a disc or discs that can be used to take the operating system back to its original state. This provides an easy way of “going back to square one” if the operating system becomes seriously damaged and is no longer usable. Any bundled software is normally reinstalled as well. However, bear in mind that any data on the hard disc drive will be erased by reinstalling Windows. Any important data must therefore be copied from the hard disc drive prior to reinstalling Windows.

System Restore is very useful when there are problems with the operating system. It effectively winds back time and takes the operating system back to an earlier date. The general idea is to take the operating system back to a date when it worked properly, undoing any recent changes that have caused problems. There is no guarantee that System Restore will always work, but in most cases it will have the desired effect. Recently installed software will be removed by System Restore, but data on the hard disc drive will not be erased.

By default, Windows provides two warnings before the battery becomes completely exhausted and the computer is forced to shut down. When you see the second warning it is time to save any unsaved data and shut down Windows. Windows provides a battery gauge feature, and many laptops are supplied with a utility program that provides a similar feature. Bear in mind that any battery gauge only gives an estimate of the power left in the battery, and not an exact measurement.

There are various ways of reducing the current consumption of a laptop computer so that the battery life is extended. Many of these involve compromises that will impact on the performance of the computer in some way. Probably the most effective way of conserving the battery is to make sure that the brightness setting of the monitor is no higher than is absolutely necessary.

There is a problem with the File Associations feature if double-clicking a file results in the wrong program being launched. It is possible to obtain a list of file associations and make changes to it, so this problem is easily corrected.

By necessity, the keyboard of a laptop PC is substantially different to that of a desktop PC. There is no separate numeric keypad, but a cluster of 16 keys perform this function when Num Lock is on. The Fn key of a laptop keyboard has no equivalent on the standard PC keyboard. These days it is normally used in conjunction with other keys in order to control things like the volume of the internal sound system and the brightness of the monitor.

The touch pad often provides difficulties for those who are new to laptop computers. Light pressure is all that is needed when using your forefinger to control the pointer. The two buttons are operated using your thumb. If you keep choosing menu options by accident, it is likely that the pad is a type which can use a tap on the pad to simulate a mouse click. The options window for the touch pad should enable the sensitivity setting of this feature to be reduced. If it still produces problems it might be necessary to disable it altogether.

6

Expansion

Internal expansion

One of the reasons for the success of the early PCs was undoubtedly their potential for internal expansion. If you needed more memory, a bigger hard disc drive, additional ports, or some sort of specialised interface, it was usually possible to achieve the required upgrade without too much difficulty. In many cases it was just a matter of adding a suitable expansion card or fitting a new card in place of the original. Some upgrades were more difficult, but in most cases they could be undertaken by the user.

Modern desktop PCs probably rely less on internal expansion than the early PCs, but with few exceptions they still have massive potential for this type of expansion. Things like memory, disc drives, and specialised interface cards can still be added. It might even be possible to upgrade the microprocessor. When a desktop PC starts to become a bit "long in the tooth" it is even possible to fit a new main board complete with a faster processor and the latest type of memory.

Unfortunately, internal expansion is one aspect of laptop PCs that does not really compete with the desktop variety. In an extreme case, there will be no realistic possibility of any internal expansion at all. You are out of luck if (say) you buy the laptop and then decide that you need more memory. Most laptop PCs are a bit more accommodating than this, but not very.

With a desktop PC it is possible for the user to undertake most types of upgrading. A knowledgeable user can perform any type of upgrading. The situation is very different with laptop PCs. Getting a laptop PC open so that you have access to the interior is usually quite difficult, and there is a strong risk of damaging the hardware if you do not get it quite right. Once the case is open, the parts required for the upgrade could be difficult to fit, if you can actually obtain suitable parts.

In general, it is advisable not to attempt any form of internal upgrade yourself. It is probably best not to attempt any internal work on a laptop

PC even if you have plenty of experience at upgrading and repairing desktop PCs. It is sometimes possible to return the computer to the manufacturer or a service centre for an upgrade, such as having a larger hard disc drive or more memory fitted, but the total cost of this type of thing is usually very high.

You should aim to obtain a laptop that has an initial specification that is high enough to meet your needs during its lifetime. Computer technology tended to move on quite quickly in the past. When you bought a new and up-to-date PC it seemed as though it was already out of date by the time you had taken it home and set it up. Things no longer progress at such a rate, and a computer that has a good specification now should still be capable of running most software in a few years time. On the other hand, it would be prudent to choose one that has a specification slightly in advance of your current needs. This will involve additional expense initially, but it could work out cheaper in the long term.

External expansion

A modern laptop PC might have little scope for internal expansion, but there seems to be an almost endless list of gadgets that can be used to provide external expansion. The obvious drawback of this approach is that it is not very convenient with a computer that will be used on the move. Being realistic about matters, most users will probably not be prepared to take large amounts of additional gear with them when out and about with their laptop PC. This means that some external upgrades will only be available when working back at base. Depending on the nature of the external units, and the way in which you use the computer, this may or may not be acceptable. Of course, external expansion should pose few problems when a laptop is used as an ordinary home or office PC. This method should be perfectly all right provided you can find a small amount of additional space to accommodate everything.

External expansion enables the capabilities of a laptop PC to be greatly enhanced, but this approach has its limitations. There are some types of enhancement that can not be provided by external units. These are some of the things that can not be accommodated using this method:

Normal memory (RAM)

Faster processor

Better video card

On the other hand, there are plenty of things that can be handled via external expansion, including these:

Floppy disc drive

Hard disc drive

Flash drive or Flash card adaptor

Sound system

Wi-fi adaptor

Addition ports

Television/radio adaptor

Video capture

External drives

A modern laptop will have a built-in hard disc drive of reasonable capacity, but the drives fitted to laptop PCs generally have much smaller capacities than those found in desktop PCs. One likely reason for this is that it is difficult to get very high capacities into the relatively small amount of space available in the drive bay of a laptop. Another possible reason is that very high capacity drives tend to have relatively high power consumptions, which makes them an unattractive proposition for a battery powered computer.

Although the typical capacity of a laptop's hard disc drive is not very great by the standards of desktop PCs, in absolute terms it is still likely to be quite high. At 40 gigabytes or more, the hard disc drive should be capable of accommodating all your programs and large amounts of data as well. Of course, over a period of time the amount of data on the hard disc drive could accumulate to the point where storage space starts to run out. One solution is to backup some of the data onto CDs or DVDs and then clear it from the hard disc drive.

Another approach is to use an external hard disc drive to store the older data. This is in some ways a neater solution, and it certainly has the advantage of enabling large amounts of data to be stored in one place. This is likely to be more convenient than having it spread across what could well be dozens of CDs or DVDs. Also, if there are very large data files such as video types, using CDs will not be an option, and even the

Fig.6.1 A 120-gigabyte external hard disc drive

higher capacity of DVDs could be inadequate from time to time. Large files should present no problems when using a hard disc drive.

Another advantage of a hard disc is that it gives very quick access to your data. This is likely to be an important factor with any files, but is especially important when dealing with files that are hundreds of megabytes or more in size. Provided it uses a USB 2.0 or Firewire interface, an external hard disc drive should be able to transfer data at a comparable rate to an internal type. The main route to external expansion with a laptop or a desktop PC is usually the computer's USB ports, although Firewire ports should be at least as effective, if fitted. Any form of external drive will normally be connected to the computer via one or other of these routes.

External hard disc drives tend to look rather nondescript due to the lack of controls. They are basically just boxes containing a hard disc drive and a USB/Firewire interface. There are usually power and disc activity indicator lights, and possibly an on/off switch, but there is unlikely to be anything more than that. The example shown in Figure 6.1 is a Lacie 120 gigabyte external drive. External drives are very easy to use, since it is basically just a matter of connecting it to a suitable port on the computer

Fig.6.2 This is a disc enclosure and interface. You supply your own hard disc drive

and then waiting for Windows to recognise the disc and add it to the drive list. It can then be used just like an internal drive.

Drive enclosures

You have to make sure that you know exactly what you are buying when dealing with external hard disc drives. Some units are enclosures (Figure 6.2) rather than disc drives. In other words, you are buying a case that has a built-in interface that can connect an ordinary ATA or SATA hard disc drive to a USB port. The enclosure normally comes complete with any additional equipment that will be needed, such as cables and a power supply unit.

These enclosures are primarily aimed at people who have a spare hard disc drive, perhaps after upgrading a desktop PC. The drive can be added into a low-cost enclosure to produce a neat external drive. Of course, you can buy a hard disc drive specifically for use with one of these enclosures, and it in terms of cost it might be competitive with a normal external hard disc drive. This method certainly gives a huge

Fig.6.3 A USB floppy disc drive is probably the only way of handling this type of media using a modern laptop

choice of drive units. However, you have to be careful to buy an enclosure having an interface that matches that of the hard disc drive, and this method is probably best for those who have some experience at dealing with computer hardware.

Other drives

Any current type of drive seems to be available as an external USB or Firewire device, which means that they can be added to a laptop PC. One of the most popular types of external drive is the humble 3.5-inch floppy type (Figure 6.3). Although it was once common for laptop PCs to have a built-in drive of this type, it is something that does not seem to feature in modern PCs of any type.

It is not really worthwhile adding a floppy drive if you simply need a means of backing up small amounts of data, or a way of swapping small amounts of data with another PC. There are better ways of doing this, such as using CDR discs, CD-RW discs, and Flash cards. A floppy disc drive is normally added because the laptop PC must be able to deal with existing data that is on 3.5-inch floppy discs. Even where this is the case, transferring the data onto some other type of disc such as a CDR

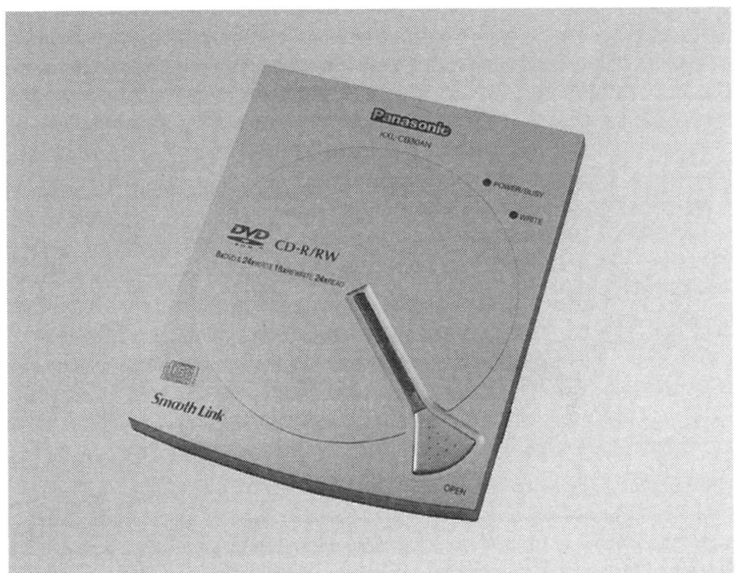

Fig.6.4 This external drive is a combined DVD reader and CD writer

or CD-RW type might be a better option. Anyway, there should be plenty of suitable drives available if it should be necessary to add a 3.5-inch floppy disc drive.

Any normal type of CD and DVD drive is available as an external unit. The example shown in Figure 6.4 is a Panasonic combination CD-RW and DVD reader. Most modern laptop PCs have some form of CD or DVD as standard. The most likely reason for adding an external unit is that the built-in drive is a CD type whereas you need to read or write some form of DVD. External DVD readers and reader/writer drives are readily available.

Power source

Some external hard disc drives require their own battery supply or mains adaptor while others can be powered from the host PC. Most seem to have their own power source rather than relying on the host PC for power. Bear in mind that there will probably be only a limited amount of power available from the USB port of a laptop computer. This means that it can

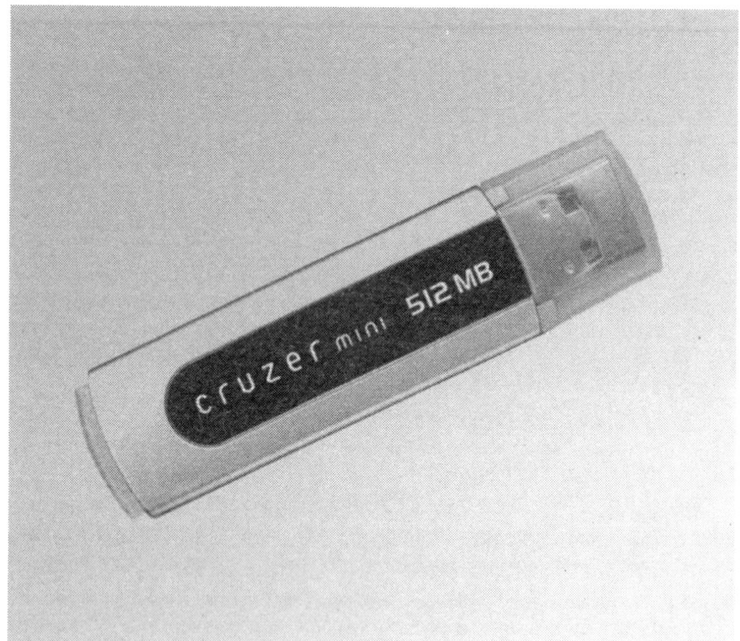

Fig.6.5 This pen drive provides 512 megabytes of storage, which is modest by current standards

power small peripherals such as mice, but anything more substantial is unlikely to work unless it has its own power source.

Firewire ports on laptop computers are usually of the 4-pin variety, which means that no power output is available from these ports. Consequently, they can only be used with peripherals that have their own power source. Using a 4-pin to 6-pin adaptor lead will not work in such cases. The lead will provide the required data coupling between the computer and the peripheral, but no power will be supplied to the peripheral device.

Flash memory

As pointed out previously, these days there are plenty of alternatives to floppy discs, and they all offer far higher capacities. In some cases the capacities on offer are equivalent to hundreds or even thousands of 1.44-megabyte floppy discs. Probably the most popular of these alternatives

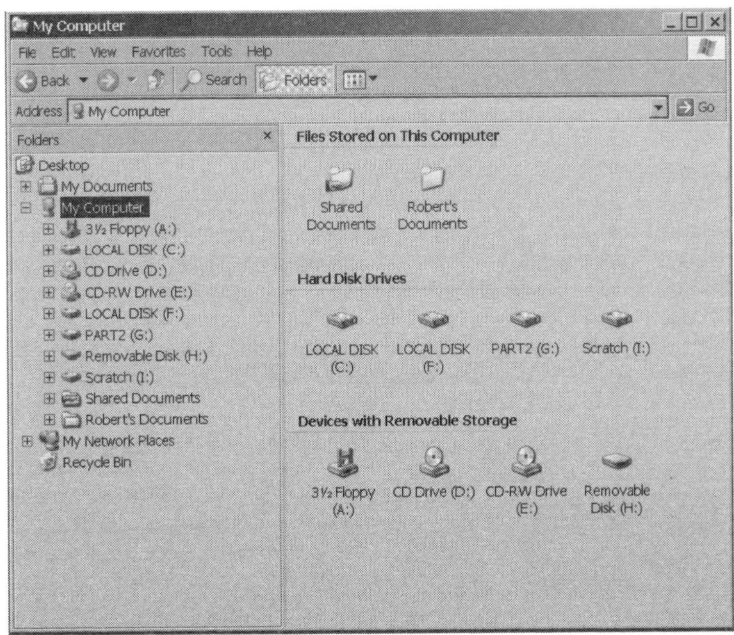

Fig.6.6 An external drive is given a drive letter by the operating system

at present is Flash memory, which is sometimes in the form of a so-called "pen drive". This is a gadget that looks rather like a large pen, but removing the top reveals a USB connector (Figure 6.5).

It is not really a drive in the conventional sense, since the data is not stored on some form of disc or tape. There are no moving parts, and a device of this type is purely electronic. These devices are also known as "Flash drives", which is a bit more accurate but is still a little misleading. The "drive" part of these names is derived from the fact that the gadget is accessed as a drive in the operating system and when using application software.

The data is stored on Flash memory, which is the same type of memory that is used in digital cameras and various portable electronic devices. Unlike the main memory of a PC, Flash memory does not get a severe case of amnesia when the power is switched off. You may sometimes encounter references to "non-volatile" or just "NV" memory, and this name is used to describe any form of memory that retains its contents when the power is switched off. Flash memory is of the non-volatile variety, which makes is suitable for backing up data or transferring it from one PC to another.

In addition to the Flash memory itself, a pen drive includes a USB interface and some electronics. Together with the driver software built into modern versions of Windows, this makes the unit appear as a normal drive to the operating system. Note that versions of Windows prior to XP and ME will require suitable drivers to be installed in order to make a pen drive usable. The necessary software is normally supplied with the drive, but it is advisable to check this point if you are not using a current version of Windows. The Plug and Play feature of Windows ME and XP will recognise a pen drive and automatically install the software to support it. However, with Windows ME you might need the Windows installation disc in order to complete the installation.

The pen drive will normally be added to the end of the existing series of drive letters. For example, if the PC already has drives from A to F, the newly added pen drive will be drive G. In the example of Figure 6.6, Windows Explorer has found the Flash drive and it is listed as drive H. Windows usually refers to Flash drive as a "Removable Disk", which means that it is effectively an outsize floppy disc as far as the operating system is concerned. The practical importance of this is that removing the drive will not have dire consequences for the smooth operation of the PC.

Note though, that it might be necessary to switch off the drive via software control before it is removed. In fact this will almost certainly be necessary. There is otherwise a risk of an error message being produced, and the operating system could become confused. The deactivation process usually requires little more than operating a button in the Windows taskbar. The instructions provided with the drive should explain how to switch the drive on and off.

The small size of pen drives makes them ideal for use with a portable PC. You can take two or three of these drives with you when computing on the move, and the increase in the size and bulk of the equipment will be so small that it is unlikely to be noticeable. Pen drives are widely used as a means of swapping data between a laptop PC and a desktop computer.

The capacities of early pen drives were often quite low, with something in the region of 16 to 32 megabytes being typical. This is equivalent to about one or two dozen floppy discs, and is sufficient for many purposes. Flash memory technology has moved on quite fast in recent years,

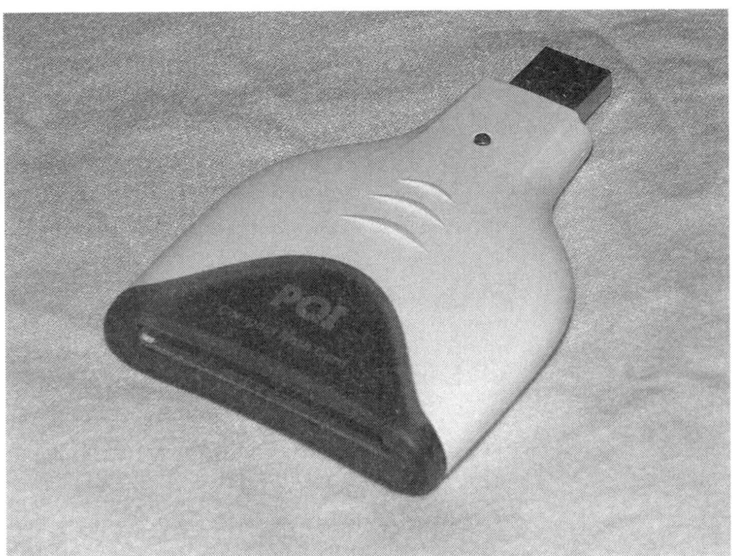

Fig.6.7 This card reader is for use with Compact Flash cards

resulting in much higher capacities and massive price reductions. Capacities of around 512 megabytes to 4 gigabytes are now commonplace, making it possible to transfer large amounts of data via these drives. Real-world pen drives often incorporate other features, such as MP3 players or some form of wireless adaptor. Of course, the extra features substantially increase the cost, so it is better to opt for a basic drive unless you really need the extra facilities.

Card reader

Pen drives are useful gadgets, but they have an obvious limitation in that it is not possible to change the "disc". In other words, you really have something more like an external hard disc drive than a floppy disc drive. You can unplug one drive and fit another, but it is not possible to leave the drive in place and change the "disc". For many purposes it would be better if the drive could be left connected, with some interchangeable Flash memory cards being used rather like very high capacity floppy discs. Provided all your PCs were equipped with a suitable drive, data could be written to a memory card on one PC and then read on any of the others. Where a large amount of data has to be backed up to Flash

Fig.6.8 Some printers have card readers that can be used with several different types of Flash card

memory, you would simply need a few high capacity Flash cards, which would be used in the drive, one after the other until all the data had been saved.

A big advantage of this method is that it would not involve switching off a drive before removing the "disc". Unplugging a memory card would leave the drive connected to the USB port, so there would be no vanishing hardware to confuse the operating system. The "discs" would appear and disappear as they were moved from one PC to another, but Windows is not fazed by simple disc changing of this type. The memory cards could therefore be freely exchanged between PCs, just like floppy discs.

There is a device called a "card reader" that is the flash memory equivalent of a floppy disc drive. The card reader connects to a USB port, and like a pen-drive, and it is used by the operating system as a "Removable Disk". The difference is that there is no built-in memory. Some card readers are designed for use with a single type of memory card, such as the one shown in Figure 6.7. This accepts type 1 Compact Flash cards.

Other card readers can be used with half a dozen or more different types of memory card. Some printers have a built-in card reader (Figure 6.8), and these usually have slots for all the popular types of memory card. The card reader in a printer is primarily included so that prints can be made direct from the files on memory cards. However, it will usually act as a normal card reader when the printer is connected to a PC.

Some PCs have a built-in card reader, but this feature is still something of a rarity for anything other than media PCs. Whatever "flavour" cards the reader accepts, they are the equivalent of the floppy discs. One card can be removed and another one can be fitted in its place.

Disc swapping

Swapping discs other than the floppy variety has sometimes caused problems in the past. The usual snag was that on changing the disc the operating system refused to acknowledge that a change had been made. It still showed the contents of the original disc in file browsers, and attempts to access any of these files obviously failed and produced an error message. Fortunately, this does not happen with card readers, which are treated by the operating system as a truly removable disc drive. If you remove one card and fit another, file browsers should show the files on the second card, and there should be no difficulty in accessing them.

Although the cards are used like high-capacity floppy discs, they have high capacities and are formatted more like hard disc drives. They are mostly formatted using the old FAT16 system, but with large cards the more recent FAT32 system is sometimes used. In fact the very high capacity cards must use FAT32 formatting, since the FAT16 system can not handle capacities of more than two gigabytes.

FAT16 and FAT32 drives can be read by any version of Windows, including Windows XP and Vista systems where the hard disc drive uses the NTFS file system. Consequently, there should be no difficulty in reading a card produced using a PC running Windows ME even if the card reader is connected to a PC running Windows 2000 or XP. A transfer in the opposite direction should be equally successful. In fact many gadgets that use memory cards also use the FAT16 or FAT32 file systems. Memory cards from many digital cameras, for instance, can be read on a PC that is equipped with a suitable card reader. Note though, that some devices use their own system of formatting, and that cards from older digital cameras are often unreadable via an ordinary card reader.

Several different types of memory card are available, but it is a good idea to use one of the most popular types unless there is a good reason to do otherwise. The more popular types of card are available in high capacity versions and are relatively cheap. The maximum capacities of the less common types are sometimes quite low, and they can easily

Fig.6.9 Compact Flash, Secure Digital, and XD memory cards

cost more than twice as much as an equivalent card in a more popular format.

The two most popular types of Flash card are Type 1 Compact Flash (CF) and Secure Digital (SD) cards. Type 1 Compact Flash cards are the most widely used, and almost certainly represent the best choice for PC data transfer and storage. Secure Digital cards are also very popular though, and they also represent a good choice. Compact Flash and Secure Digital cards having capacities of up to a few gigabytes are now readily available. Figure 6.9 shows Compact Flash, Secure Digital, and XD Flash cards.

Speed

The "Flash" name tends to give the impression that this type of memory is extremely fast. Unfortunately, the name refers to the process used when writing data to the card, and it is not meant to imply super-fast operation. The reading and writing speeds of Flash memory are actually quite slow by current standards, and they are not even very fast when compared to various types of true disc storage. Most Flash memory manufacturers use a speed rating that is essentially the same as the one used for CD-ROM drives. There is a slight difference in that the rating used for a CD-ROM drive is the maximum it can achieve, and the actual speed obtained near the middle of the disc is usually much lower. There is no Flash memory equivalent to this, and the quoted speed should be obtained when writing to any part of the disc.

A speed rating of X1 is equivalent to about 150k per second. Most memory cards are not actually marked with a speed rating, although this information is usually included in the manufacturer's data. A card that has no marked rating usually has a speed of about X4 to x12, and can read or write data at about one megabyte or so per second. Note that there is no point in using a faster card with a reader that has a USB 1.1 interface, or is connected to a USB 1.1 port. A "bog standard" memory card can transfer data at a rate that is about double that of a single device on a USB 1.1 port.

At the time or writing this it is possible to obtain memory cards that have speed ratings of up to about X133, although it seems likely that significantly faster cards will be developed. These cards are mainly intended for use with electronic gadgets that handle large amounts of data, such as digital video cameras and the more upmarket digital cameras. However, they also offer the potential for moving large amounts of data from one PC to another in a reasonably short time, or for backing up data. A card having a rating of x60 for example, can read and write data at up to nine megabytes per second. In theory at any rate, a gigabyte of data could be written to the card in less than two minutes, and then copied onto another PC in a similar amount of time.

Of course, transfer speeds of this order requires a reader that supports a high speed interface such as USB 2.0 or Firewire. Using either type of interface and a matching card reader should enable data to be read and written at something very close to the maximum speed rating of the card. Where high-speed operation is needed it is important to check that a USB card reader is a genuine USB 2.0 type. Some are described as "USB 2.0 compatible", which means that they are actually USB 1.1 devices that can operate at USB 1.1 speeds with a USB 2.0 interface.

Note that some manufacturers do not use speed ratings such as X20 and X40. Instead they simply state the maximum rate at which data can be read from and written to the card. In order to compare the speeds of various cards it might be necessary to do a conversion from one type of

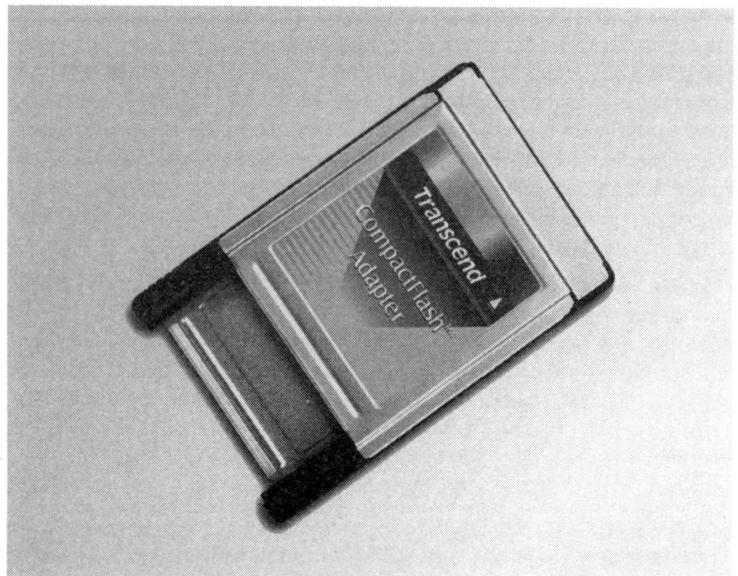

Fig.6.10 This PCMCIA card is a reader for Compact Flash cards

speed rating to the other. I have a SanDisk Ultra II card that has quoted read and write rates of 9 and 10 megabytes per second respectively. Dividing these figures by 0.15 gives their equivalent ratings in the Xn system.

This gives read and write speeds of X60 and X67 respectively. The read speed of a Flash card is usually a little faster than the write speed. In the Xn system it is the slower rate that is used, so my SanDisk Ultra II card is an X60 type and not an X67 card. To convert a Xn rating into its equivalent in megabytes per second, multiply its speed rating by 0.15. An X80 card, for example, can transfer data at up to 12 megabytes per second.

PCMCIA FLASH

It is perhaps worth mentioning that there is an alternative to using a USB or Firewire card reader if your laptop has a spare PCMCIA slot. It is possible to obtain PCMCIA cards that are complete with some FLASH memory, and PCMCIA card readers for use with FLASH cards (Figure 6.10). The latter are the more practical proposition. A PCMCIA card reader has the advantage of providing a reader that is largely built into

Fig.6.11 Flash cards are normally supplied in a plastic case

the computer, which makes it a neater solution for computing on the move. The only real drawback is that this type of card reader seems to be significantly more expensive than the USB or Firewire variety.

Precautions

Flash cards are well suited to use with laptop computers, and they are now utilized by a substantial proportion of laptop users. However, there is one slight drawback of using memory cards, and this is that they are not the toughest of components. In fairness, they are probably a lot tougher than some of the alternatives. Even so, when using any Flash memory cards it is essential to observe a few simple rules in order to ensure that the cards do not become damaged.

Memory cards are reasonably safe when inside a gadget such as a MP3 player, camera, or card reader, but they need to be treated with due care when not tucked away inside a device. They should be kept away from direct sunlight, moisture, and high temperatures. It is best not to touch any exposed metal on connectors as this could give poor electrical connections. Due to their small size and thinness it is inevitable that

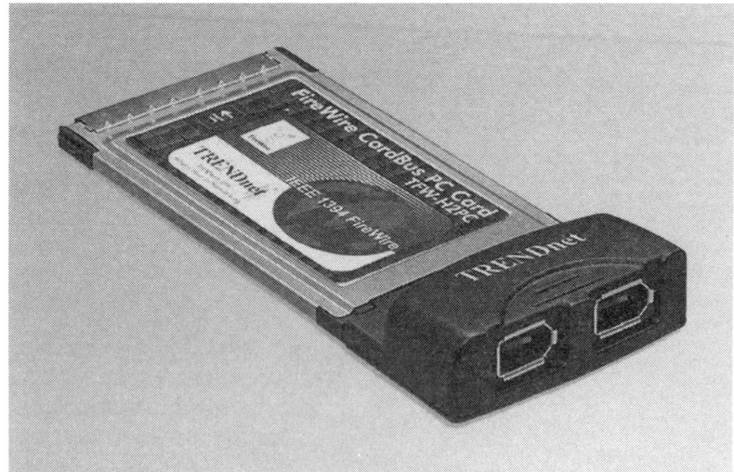

Fig.6.12 This PCMCIA card provides two Firewire ports

memory cards are not very tough, and care must be taken to avoid physical damage. Flash cards are normally supplied with a plastic case (Figure 6.11), and it is best to keep them in this when they are not installed in a player or other gadget.

Ports

While the average laptop has a fair sprinkling of ports, this is one respect in which desktop PCs are generally superior. The lack of ports will probably not matter when a laptop is primarily needed for computing on the move, but it can be a drawback in cases where the computer will be used as a home of business type. Adding extra ports is unlikely to pose any problems. As pointed out in a previous chapter, a powered USB hub can be used to convert a single USB port on the computer into what is typically about half a dozen USB ports. If there is a spare PCMCIA slot, in conjunction with a suitable card this can be used to add USB or Firewire ports. The example shown in Figure 6.12 provides two Firewire ports.

Laptop PCs do not usually have legacy ports (serial and parallel ports), but these can be added via adaptors that connect to a USB port. Many of the more elaborate docking stations also have legacy ports. This subject was covered in a previous chapter and will not be considered in more detail here.

Fig.6.13 An upmarket sound adaptor from Creative

Sound

The sound systems of laptop computers tend to be rather basic by the standards of desktop PCs. I suppose that this is reasonable given that few users would be prepared to take multi-way speaker systems on their travels, but it can be a bit limiting where a laptop will be used as a home computer. There are soundcards for PCMCIA slots, but a greater range of USB sound systems is available. These range from relatively simple devices that look like pen drives through to upmarket gadgets for the real sound enthusiast (Figure 6.13). Even the simplest USB sound adapters seem to offer 5.1 or 5.2 surround sound, which should be sufficient for most users.

Points to remember

The scope for internal expansion is largely absent with modern laptop PCs. It might be possible to get the manufacturer or a service centre to add more memory or provide a hard disc upgrade, but the do-it-yourself approach is not a good idea. An upgrade such as a better video card is not usually a practical proposition, since the video circuits are part of the main board. Laptop PCs can not use ordinary PC expansion cards.

External drives that are actually based on Flash memory are now quite cheap. They are available in the form of pen drives that have the memory and electronics in a single unit, or as a card reader that can be used with standard memory cards such as Compact Flash and Secure Digital cards. Both types provide a reasonably low-cost method of backing up or transferring several hundred megabytes of data, or even a few gigabytes.

Flash memory has a speed rating that is based on the one used for CD-ROM drives. A speed of X1 is about 150 kilobytes (0.15 megabytes) or so per second. It is normally only the faster cards that are marked with a speed rating. The speed of unmarked cards is usually between about X4 and X12.

With any external drive that uses a USB port it is as well to bear in mind that a USB 1.1 port only supports speeds of up to about 0.6 megabytes per second. This is adequate for many purposes, but will give long read and write times when gigabytes of data are involved. USB 2.0 and Firewire interfaces are much faster, and should not hinder the performance of any external storage device.

Any external drive should be properly integrated with the operating system so that it has its own drive letter, just like an internal drive. With most types of drive, whether fitted externally or internally, it is possible to use the standard Windows Cut, Copy, Paste, and Delete functions.

Additional USB ports can be provided by a powered USB hub connected to one of the existing USB ports. Firewire ports can be provided by a PCMCIA card. Few laptops have legacy ports, but serial and parallel ports can be obtained via USB adaptors and some USB docking stations.

Surround sound can be provided by using an adaptor that connects to a USB port or fits into a PCMCIA slot. The USB option is better in that it provides a much wider choice. Few PCMCIA soundcards are available. One of the more simple USB adaptors will be adequate for most users, but there are upmarket adaptors for those that need them.

7

Synchronising

File transfer

Synchronisation is something that is unlikely to be of much interest if you use a laptop PC as a home computer. On the other hand, it is crucial if you use a laptop PC for computing on the move but have a desktop PC back at base. Synchronisation is the process of keeping files on the laptop up-to-date with those on the desktop PC, and vice versa. In other words, if you work on a file using one computer, you need the equivalent file on the other computer to be updated as well. It will then be of no consequence which PC you use, with the data being kept up to date on both of them. Whichever PC you use, you know that it will have the latest version of each data file.

In the current context it is only certain data files that are of interest. The idea is not to have the system on one PC as an exact clone of the other. This would ensure that the data files on the two PCs were kept in perfect synchronisation, but it would also mean that the system on one would be copied to another and very different computer. The one with the cloned system would be unlikely to work properly after synchronisation! This means that the system can not be fully automated, and the user has to select the files that will be synchronised.

Linking

In order to synchronise two computers it is necessary to have a link between them to facilitate the data transfers. There does not actually have to be a link as such, and one approach is to copy files to a disc, transfer the disc to the second computer, and then copy the files from the disc to that computer. Flash memory cards and card readers are well suited to this type of thing, but it is advisable to use fast cards and a suitable reader if large files will be transferred.

Windows actually has a built-in facility for linking two computers. It is called Windows Direct Connection, but it is little used in practice. One problem is that it relies on a connection between the serial or parallel ports of the two computers. Since most laptop PCs and many desktop PCs no longer have serial or parallel ports this is no longer possible in many cases. Even where both PCs are suitably equipped, using the Windows Direct Connection facility tends to be problematic, and by current standards the connection is quite slow. It is not a subject that will be considered further here.

At one time IrDA (Infrared Data Association) links looked as though they would become very popular for use when synchronising laptop and desktop PCs. This method has the advantage of using a form of wireless link, but it probably fell from favour as it can be difficult to implement in practice. It is also relatively slow and only operates at short ranges. This type of link has now been superseded by other types of wireless link, and it is not a topic that will be considered any further here.

Bluetooth adaptors plus suitable software can provide a wireless data link between two PCs, but this is another method that has its drawbacks. The link has the advantage of being wireless, and it is provided by radio transmitters and receivers that provide a reasonable operating range. However, the maximum rate at which data can be transferred is quite slow by current standards, and this type of link can be a bit awkward to use in practice.

USB link

USB was not really designed as a means of linking two PCs, but some manufacturers have produced leads that enable USB interfaces to be used in this role. Actually, these leads include some electronics that "fool" each computer into thinking it is connected to another computer rather than a peripheral of some kind. The main problem with the original USB links was a lack of speed due to the use of USB 1.1 interfaces. It is a system that should work much better with USB 2.0 interfaces, and the modern USB 2.0 versions of these cables presumably provide much higher transfer rates. The USB approach to linking PCs seems to have fallen from favour though, and it will not be pursued further here.

The best type of link is a standard network type, or a wi-fi wireless type. Networking is covered in chapter 9, so it will not be considered in detail here. A normal network connection operates at 100 megabits per second, which equates to a maximum transfer rate of over 10 megabytes per second. The actual rate obtained when using two real-world PCs is likely to be somewhat less than this, but it still represents an impressive transfer

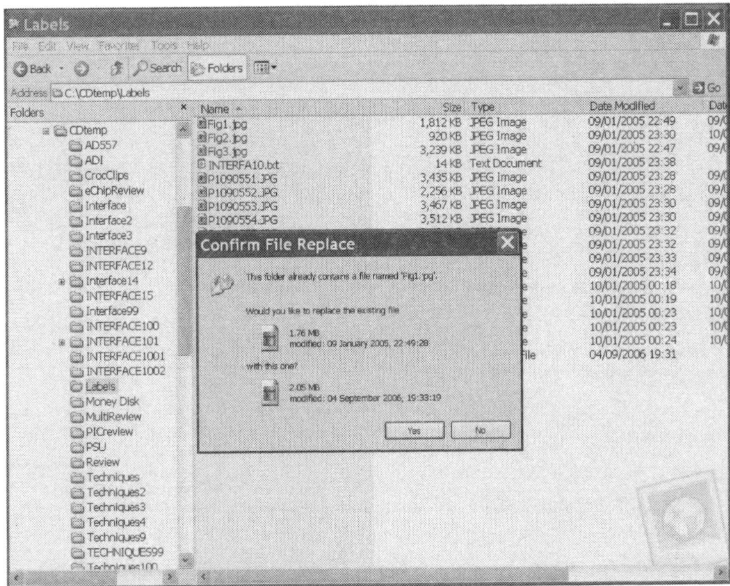

Fig.7.1 Windows provides a warning message if you try to overwrite a file with one of the same name

rate. These days many PCs have high-speed network interfaces that, in conjunction with suitable equipment, can operate at even higher speeds.

A wi-fi link is essentially a wireless version of a standard Ethernet network. In fact normal Ethernet equipment and wi-fi units can be used in the same network, and often are. The operating range of a wi-fi system is quite good, but the data transfer rates are a bit slower than those obtained from a wired Ethernet network. However, rates of a few megabytes per second can be obtained, which is more than adequate for most purposes.

A big advantage with any form of Ethernet network is that it is properly supported by Windows XP and Vista, which makes it reasonably straightforward to use. It is also well tried and tested technology that should give relatively few problems. Although Ethernet equipment was quite expensive at one time, it has gradually come down in price along with most other hi-tech products. A simple Ethernet network should certainly be quite cheap these days, aided by the fact that most laptop and desktop PCs have Ethernet interfaces as part of their standard equipment.

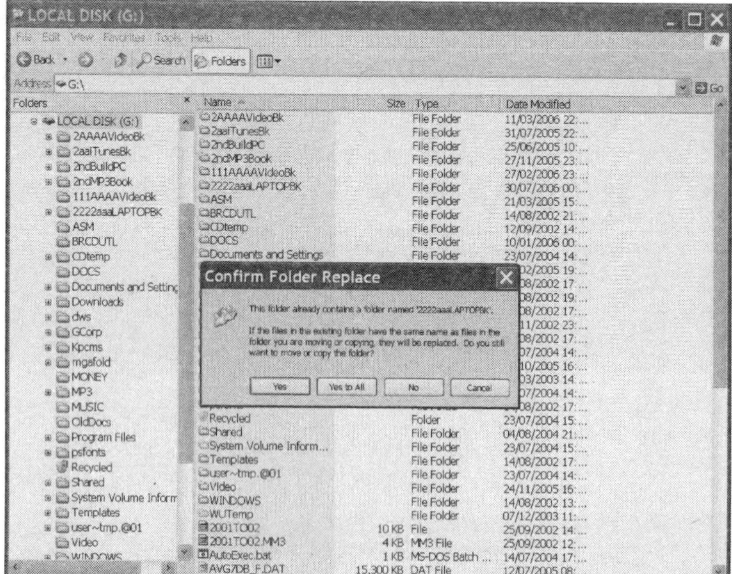

Fig.7.2 You can opt to overwrite any files with duplicate names

Direct approach

Windows has built-in facilities for keeping data on two computers properly synchronised, but you do not have to use these facilities. Whatever type of link is used, or if some form of disc is used to make the transfers, you can simply copy files from one computer to another. This is safe enough when copying files to a computer for the first time, but it involves a certain amount of risk when it involves overwriting files. You have to make sure that no mistakes are made, and that you do not accidentally overwrite a new file with an older version of itself.

Windows will provide a warning message when you try to overwrite a file with one of the same name (Figure 7.1). In the upper section this shows the size of the existing file and the date that it was last modified. The lower section shows the same information for the file you are trying to copy to the folder. It should be safe to go ahead if the upper file has an earlier date than the lower file. You are about to overwrite the more up to date version of the file if the lower file has the earlier date. It is then essential to left-click the No button to abort the operation and avoid destroying some of your hard work.

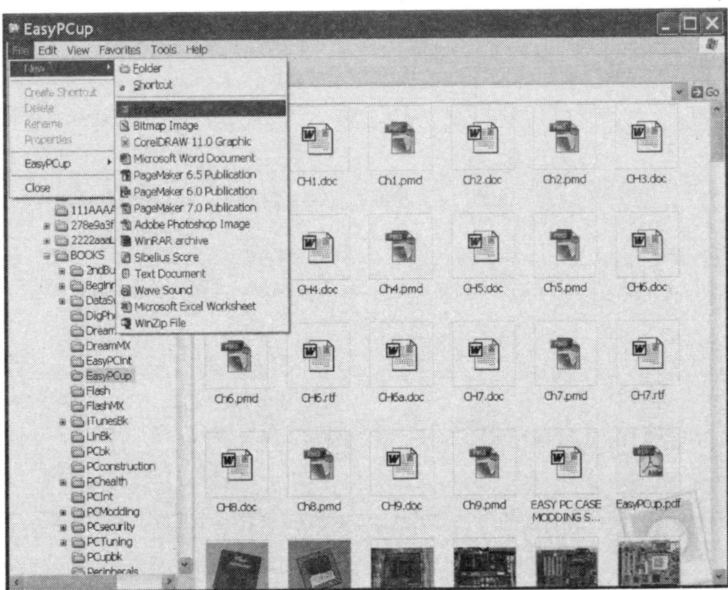

Fig.7.3 Select Briefcase from the submenu

The warning message is different when a number of files are being copied to a folder and Windows finds there is a file with the same name as the one that is about to be copied. This version of the message (Figure 7.2) has four buttons, one of which is marked “Yes to All”. Operating this button results in an existing file being overwritten in cases where one of the source files has the same name. This is a quick way of handling things in that you do not have to provide manual confirmation each time an existing file is overwritten. On the other hand, it is very risky in that it does not provide an opportunity for errors to be spotted and corrected. Get it wrong and you could obliterate a lot of hard work.

Briefcase

The Windows Briefcase facility provides help with synchronising data and can help to avoid accidentally overwriting new files with older versions. The Briefcase is basically just a folder, but it is a type that has some special features. In earlier versions of Windows it was a standard folder that had its icon on the Windows desktop, but it is handled a little differently in Windows XP and Vista. There is no Briefcase icon and

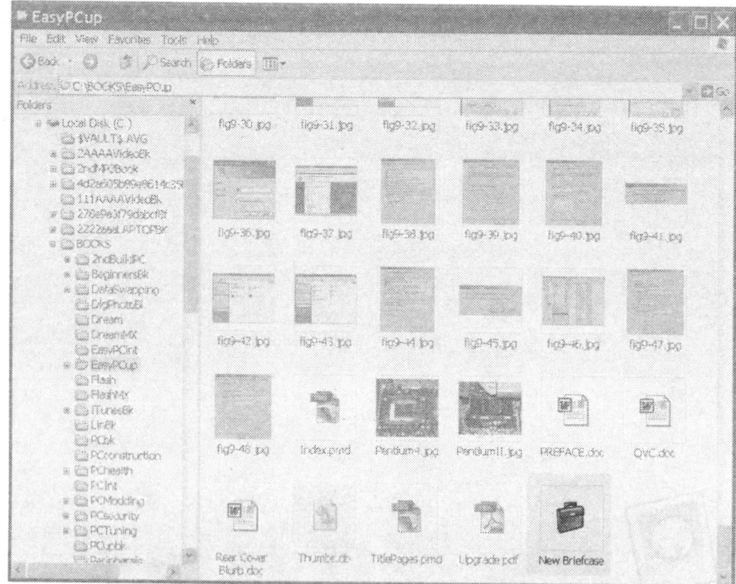

Fig.7.4 An icon for the New Briefcase folder has been added

folder by default, and you have to produce them yourself. An advantage of the current system is that there is no requirement to have the Briefcase on the Windows desktop. It can be placed in any folder.

In order to produce a Briefcase in Windows XP, first use Windows Explorer (Start – All Programs – Accessories – Windows Explorer) to open the folder that will be used to contain the Briefcase. Then select New from the File menu, followed by Briefcase from the submenu that appears (Figure 7.3). With Windows XP or Vista a Briefcase can be produced by right clicking a blank area of a folder, and then selecting New from the pop-up menu followed by Briefcase from the submenu. An icon labelled New Briefcase will then be added to the contents of the folder (Figure 7.4). Double-clicking the icon to open the New Briefcase folder produces a welcome message (Figure 7.5). This provides some basic information about the folder and the way it is used. Operate the Finish button to remove the message, which only appears the first time the folder is accessed.

As with a normal folder, the New Briefcase name can be changed. Any change in name will not affect the way in which the folder operates, and it will remain a Briefcase type. If you have two or more computers with

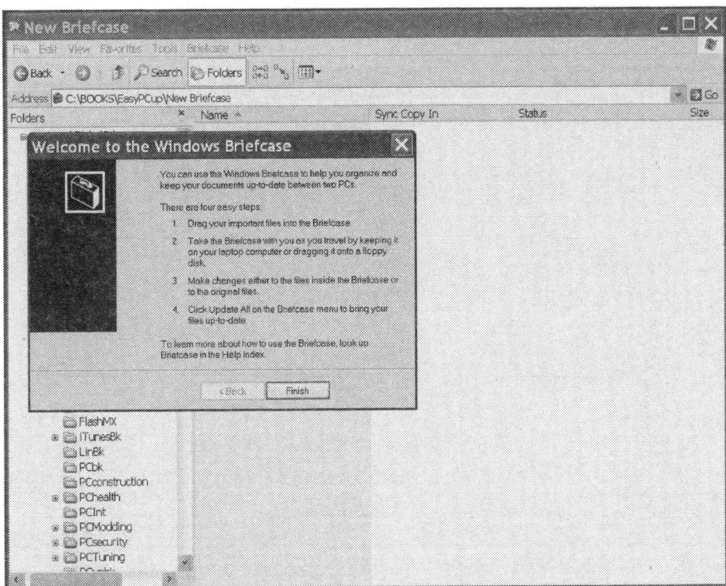

Fig.7.5 Operate the Finish button to remove this message

Briefcase folders, then it is definitely a good idea to avoid possible confusion by giving them different names, such as "Briefcase 1", "Briefcase 2", etc. In order to change the name, right-click on the folders icon and then select Rename from the pop-up menu that appears. The new name is then typed into the textbox beneath the icon. If necessary, a Briefcase folder can be deleted in the normal fashion.

It is worth noting that you are not restricted to one Briefcase folder per PC. It is possible to have any number of them, and they do not even have to be in different folders. If more than one Briefcase is added to a folder, the additional folders will be called New Briefcase (2), New Briefcase (3), and so on. The fact that you can do this does not necessarily mean that it is a good idea. I suppose that it might be helpful to have separate Briefcase folders for different types of file, but it is probably best to use no more of these folders than is really necessary.

Files are copied to the Briefcase in the normal way, such as using the Copy and Paste features of Windows, or dragging them to the Briefcase folder. In Figure 7.6 some files have been copied to the Briefcase folder and the Details option has been selected (View – Details). The Status field shows that the files are "Up-to-date". When files are copied to a

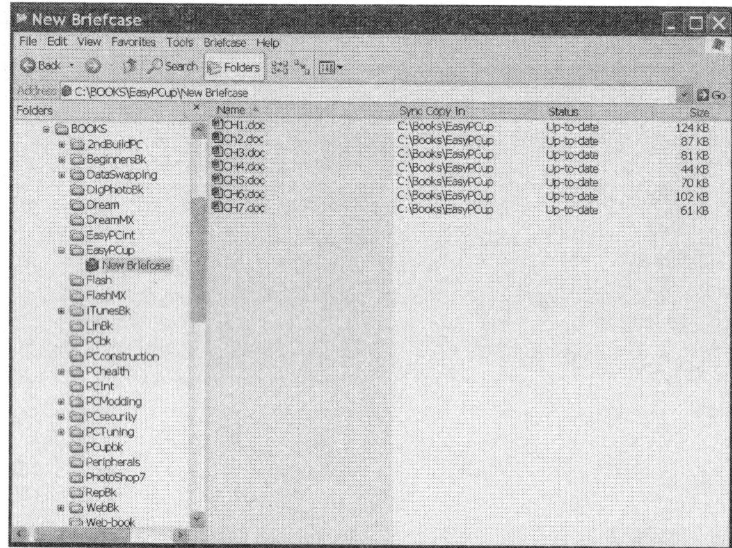

Fig.7.6 As one would expect, the files are up-to-date at this stage

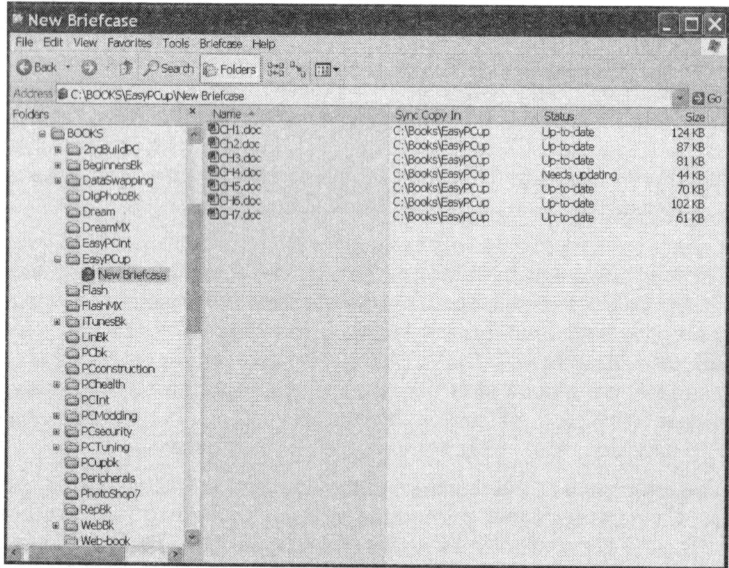

Fig.7.7 The status of one file is "Needs updating"

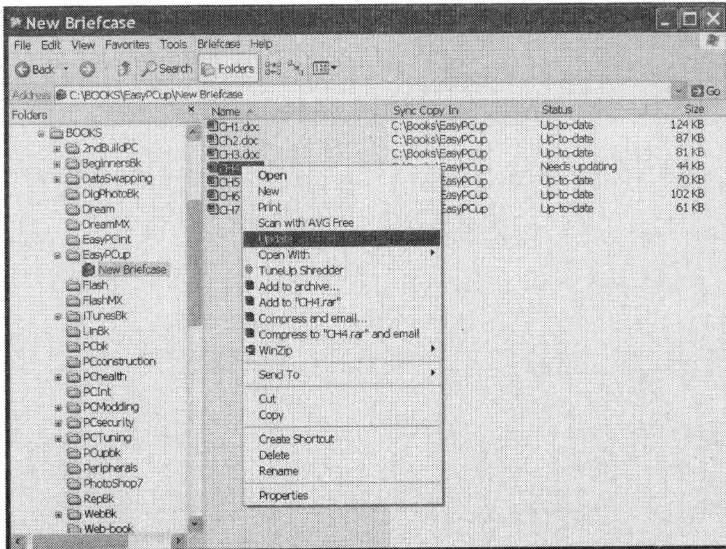

Fig.7.8 Select the Update option from this pop-up menu

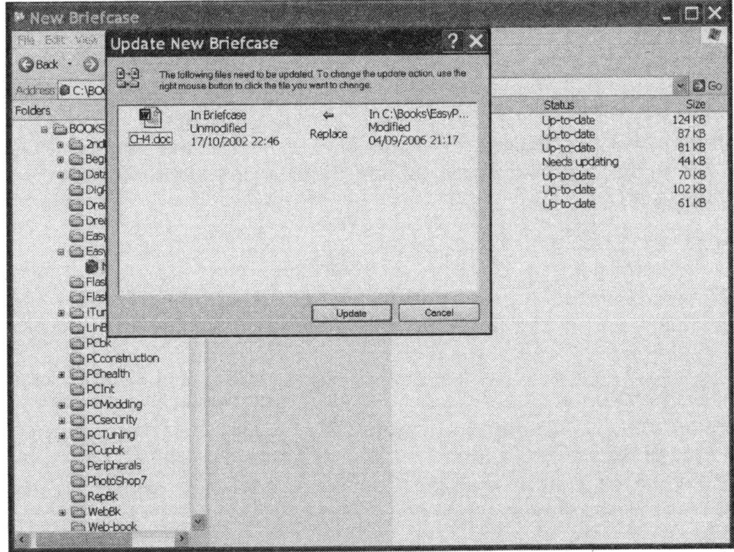

Fig.7.9 Operate the Update button to overwrite the old file

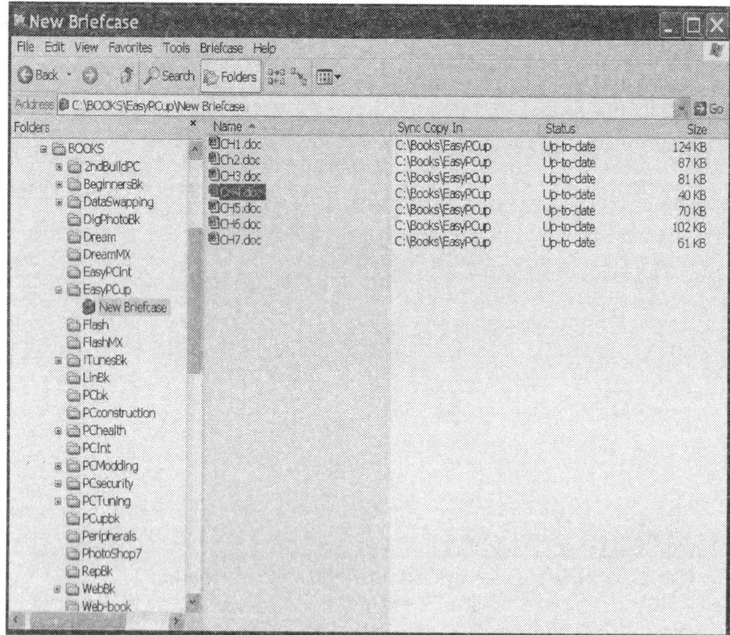

Fig.7.10 The status of the file is "Up-to-date" once again

Briefcase folder they are genuinely copied to the folder, rather than shortcuts to the originals being used. This means that any changes made to the original files will not result in changes to the copies in the Briefcase folder.

However, Windows monitors the two sets of files. A warning will be given in the Status field if a copy is found to be different to the original. This is demonstrated in Figure 7.7, where one of the original files has been modified, and the entry in its Status field has changed to "Needs updating".

A file can be updated by right-clicking its entry and selecting the Update option from the pop-up menu (Figure 7.8). A small pop-up window gives details of the source file and the one that will be overwritten, and gives you a chance to abort the operation Figure 7.9). Operate the Update button if you wish to go ahead and update the file in the Briefcase folder. The Status field for the file will then show that it is up-to-date again (Figure 7.10).

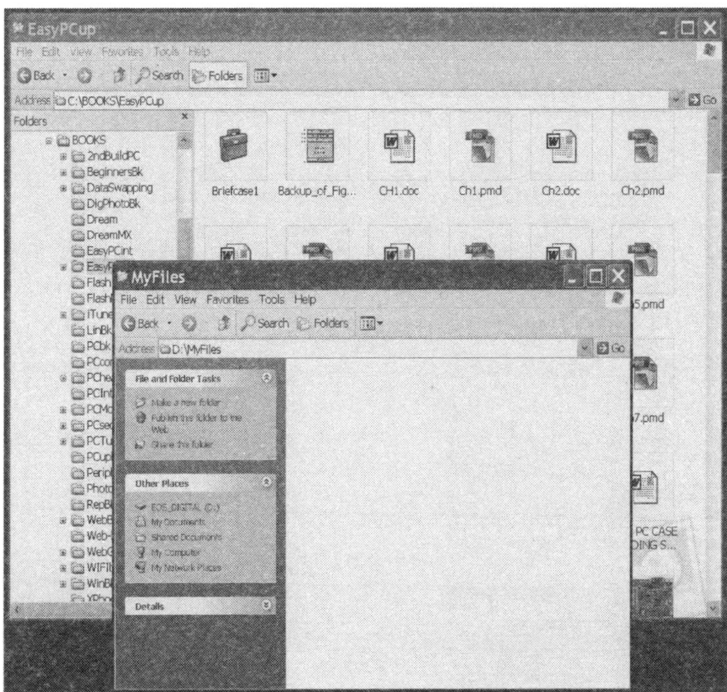

Fig.7.11 The Briefcase folder will be dragged from the large window to the smaller one

Moving

Having created a Briefcase, populated it with files, and checked that everything is up-to-date, the next step is to move it to the other computer. In the current context the Briefcase will usually have been produced on a desktop PC, and it will be copied to a laptop PC. However, it can be used in precisely the same fashion with any two PCs. Note that there is no need to produce a Briefcase folder on the second PC. The general idea is to have one Briefcase that is moved to and fro between the two PCs.

With some sort of network link between the two computers it should be possible to get the Briefcase folder on the desktop PC in one window and the destination folder on the remote computer in another window. It is probably best to make a folder on the remote computer that is specifically for holding the Briefcase folder. In the example of Figure

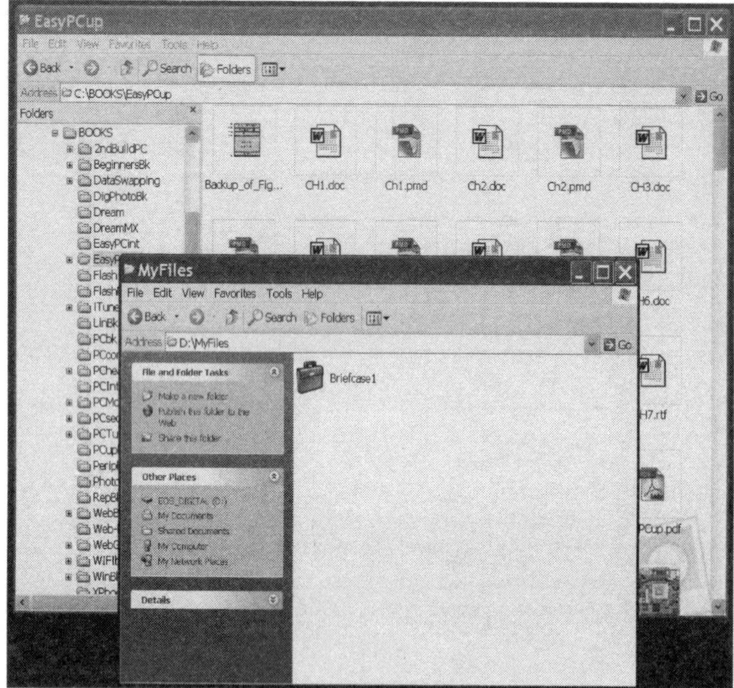

Fig.7.12 The Briefcase has been moved rather than copied

7.11 the transfer is being made via a Flash card and card readers. The larger window is for the folder that contains the Briefcase, and the smaller one is for the destination folder on the Flash card. Dragging the Briefcase from the large window to the smaller one produces the result shown in Figure 7.12. This type of operation would normally result in the folder being copied to the destination, with the original being left in place. It does not work this way with a Briefcase folder, and it is really a move, or cut and paste operation that has been provided. The original Briefcase folder has been deleted from the large window and a copy has been placed in the small window.

This is basically all you have to do when using some form of network link. With the Briefcase folder on the remote computer, which will usually be the laptop PC, its contents can then be modified using this PC. There is an extra step in the process when the transfer is made by way of a

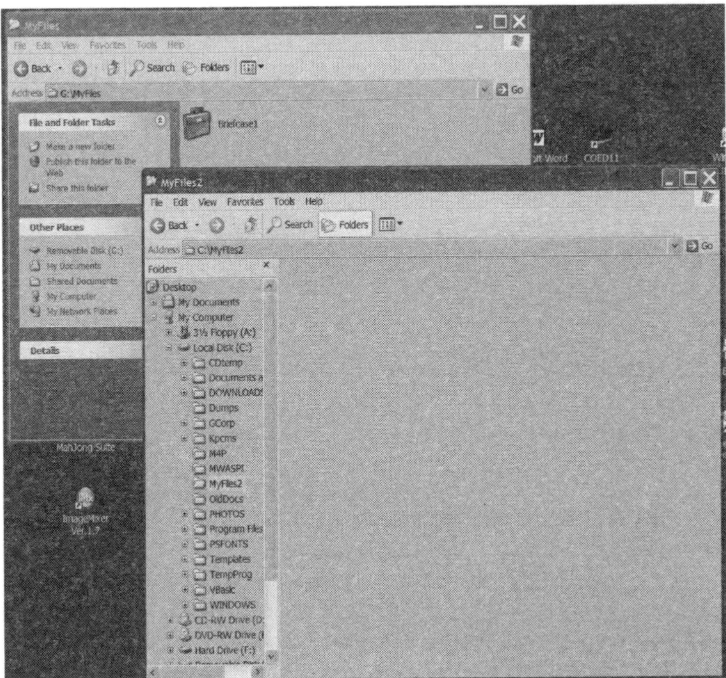

Fig.7.13 The Briefcase will be copied from the card to the remote PC

Flash card or other form of removable disc. It is just a matter of copying the Briefcase from the disc or card to the appropriate folder on the remote PC. Figure 7.13 and 7.14 show "before" and "after" views, and once again, the Briefcase has been moved from one folder to the other rather than being copied.

In reverse

Having made some changes to the files in the Briefcase, it is then a matter of reversing the moving process to put the Briefcase back in the appropriate folder on the Desktop PC. The Status field should then reflect any changes that have been made, and in the example of Figure 7.15 there are two files marked as "Needs updating". This time it is the files in the Briefcase that are more up to date, and the originals that need updating.

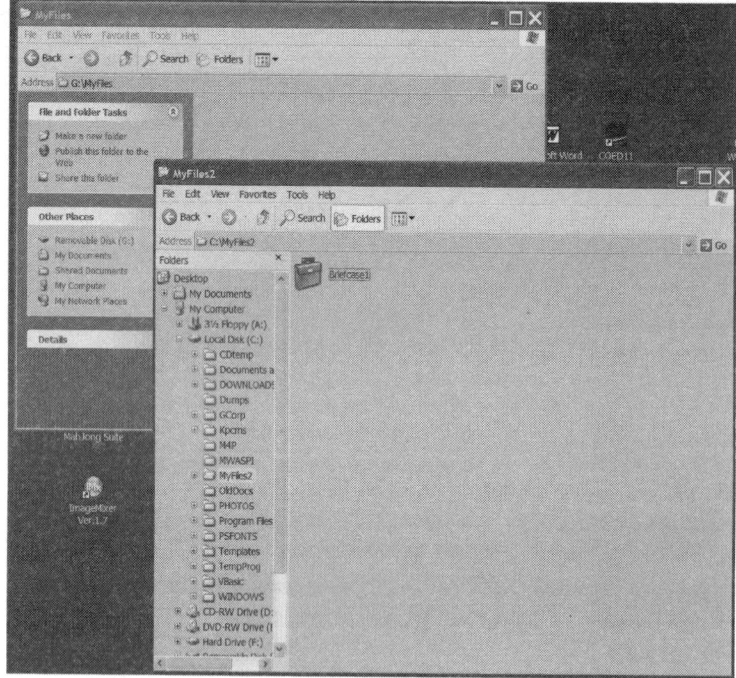

Fig.7.14 Once again, the Briefcase has been moved rather than copied

Right-clicking the entry for a file produces a pop-up menu where the Update option is selected. A small window then appears (Figure 7.16), and this shows which file will be overwritten. Windows has correctly determined that the file in the Briefcase must overwrite the original one. This is not difficult, because Windows can look at the time and date that each file was last modified. It quite reasonably assumes that the last one to be modified is the most up-to-date. Assuming all is well, it is just a matter of operating the Update button to overwrite the old file with the new version. This process is repeated for each file that needs to be updated, and everything will then be properly synchronised again (Figure 7.17).

Of course, things are likely to become confused if you work on a file using the laptop computer, do some work on the file on the desktop PC, and then try to synchronise them. Neither of the files contains all the latest modifications, and some work will be lost whichever file is

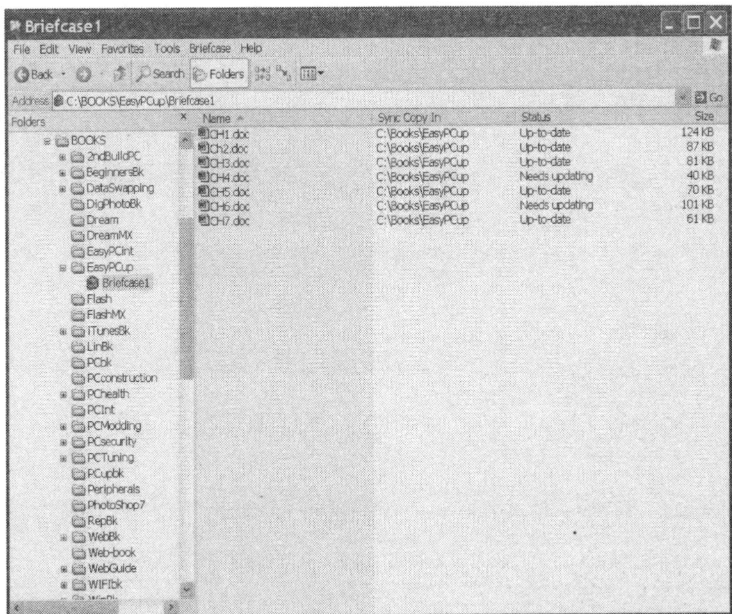

Fig.7.15 Windows has detected changes to two files that now require synchronisation

overwritten. Therefore, it is important to work in a sensible fashion, with no modifications being made using the desktop PC while a file is on the laptop.

Eventually you will probably wish to get rid of the Briefcase folder, or perhaps just its contents with the folder being left in place for use with a new set of files. It is perfectly all right to erase a Briefcase folder or any of its contents using the normal Windows facilities. The source files will be left in place and will not be modified in any way.

Third-party

The built-in synchronisation facilities of Windows are adequate for most purposes, but there are third-party synchronisation programs available that offer more facilities. These are probably not worthwhile if you will only be working with a few files at any one time. They are more worthwhile if you will be working with numerous files, and most of these programs will to some extent automate the synchronisation process.

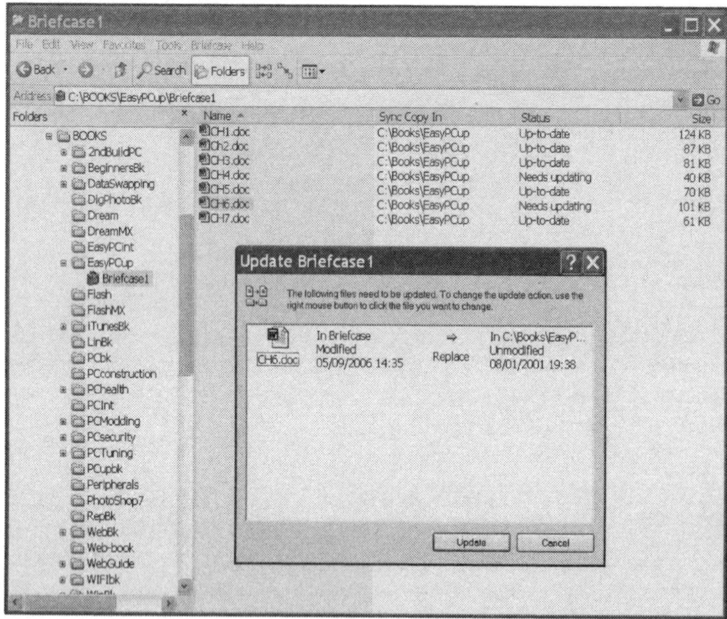

Fig.7.16 Operate the Update button to overwrite the old file

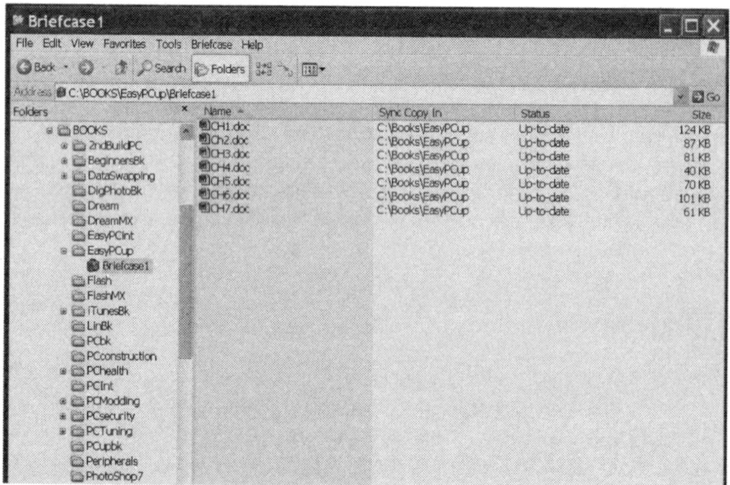

Fig.7.17 The files are now properly synchronised again

Points to remember

If you work with a desktop PC and a laptop type, you will probably wish to transfer files to the laptop, work on them, and then copy them back to the desktop PC. Keeping the files on the two PCs up-to-date is a process known as "synchronisation".

Windows has a simple but effective file synchronisation facility in the form of Briefcase folders. This system makes it easy to keep files on two computers properly synchronised. In use it is easier if the files are synchronised via some form of network connection, but the Windows synchronisation system works properly if files are swapped via Flash cards or some form of removable disc.

There are various methods for linking two PCs so that file transfers can be achieved. Unfortunately, some of these methods are now obsolete and can not be easily implemented using modern PCs. Others can still be implemented but are likely to be impractically slow unless quite small amounts of data are involved. A simple Ethernet network system is very fast and represents a good choice where large amounts of data must be transferred. Wi-fi is ideal for use with laptop PCs, but is not quite as fast as a wired Ethernet network.

The files to be synchronised are copied into a special type of folder, which in Windows terminology is a "Briefcase". The files in this folder are copies of the originals, but Windows will detect any change in the copies or the originals. Its synchronisation facilities can then be used to update the older versions of the files concerned.

A Briefcase folder can be renamed just like any normal Windows folder, and it will still operate as a Briefcase folder once it has been renamed. The contents of a Briefcase folder can be deleted using the normal methods, as can the folder itself. This erases the files that were in the Briefcase, but it does not affect the source files in any way.

You do not have to use the built-in synchronisation facility of Windows. The files can be copied from one PC to the other using the standard copying and transferring techniques, but it is then up to you to ensure that a newer version of a file is not overwritten by an older version of itself. There are third-party synchronisation programs that can be used if it is necessary to keep large numbers of files properly synchronised.

8

Security

Be prepared

Many computer users take the view that they do not need antivirus software until and unless a virus attacks their PC. This is a rather short-sighted attitude and one that is asking for trouble. By the time that you know a virus has infected your PC it is likely that a substantial amount of damage will have already been done to the system files and (or) your own data files. Using antivirus software to help sort out the mess after a virus has struck is "shutting the stable door after the horse has bolted". The virus may indeed be removed by the antivirus software, but there may be no way of correcting all the damage that has been done.

Another point to bear in mind is that your PC could be rendered unbootable by the virus. Many viruses attack the operating system and will try to make the system unbootable. If the system is not bootable, you can not install antivirus software. Also bear in mind that most antivirus programs do some basic checks as part of the installation process. The program will not be installed if any hint of a virus is detected. The reason for this is that the installation process involves copying numerous files onto the hard disc and making changes to some of the Windows system files. This can provide an opportunity for the virus to spread and do further damage.

Many antivirus programs can be used once a virus has attacked a PC, and even if the PC can not be booted into Windows. One approach is to either have a set of boot floppy discs supplied as part of the package, or for these rescue discs to be produced during installation. If the PC becomes unbootable at some later date and a virus is thought to be the cause, the PC is booted from the first disc in the set. A series of checks are then performed, with the other discs being used as and when required.

A more modern alternative to this method is for the installation disc to be a boot type. The basic facilities provided are generally much the same as when using a set of boot discs, but there is no need to keep changing discs. Also, the high capacity of a CD-ROM means that more facilities are easily included in the program suite, if required. The drawback of both methods is that the discs will be something less than fully up-to-date, and may not be able to handle some of the more recent viruses.

Supplied software

The importance of antivirus software is such that many PCs are now supplied with an antivirus program as part of the preinstalled bundle of software. Unfortunately, this is not quite as good as it may seem at first. The antivirus software is usually fully functioning, but it normally comes with quite a short subscription to the manufacturer's update service. There is not usually any limit to the length of time that the software can be used, but the virus definition database starts to become out of date once the update subscription has expired. This means that the program will be very good at finding old viruses, but its ability to detect new ones soon becomes non-existent.

There is no problem here if you are satisfied with the program and you are prepared to pay the subscription charge for the update service. It is important to realise that the degree of protection offered by the program will effectively diminish with the passage of time if you continue to use it without bothering with updates. The program will still provide some protection, but it will also start to leave your computer open to attack by an ever increasing range of viruses.

Free protection

There are better ways of handling things than continuing to use a commercial antivirus program that is relying on out of date virus definitions. There are online virus checking facilities that can be used to periodically scan your PC, but the drawback of this method is that there is no real-time protection for your PC. By the time you do a virus scan it is possible that a virus could have been spreading across your files for some time. By the time it is detected and removed it is likely that a significant amount of damage would already have been done.

An antivirus program running on your PC will usually provide real-time protection. In other words, it monitors disc drive activity, Internet activity, or anything that might involve a virus or other malicious program. If any suspicious files are detected, there is an attempt to alter system files, or any dubious activity is detected, the user is warned. In most cases the

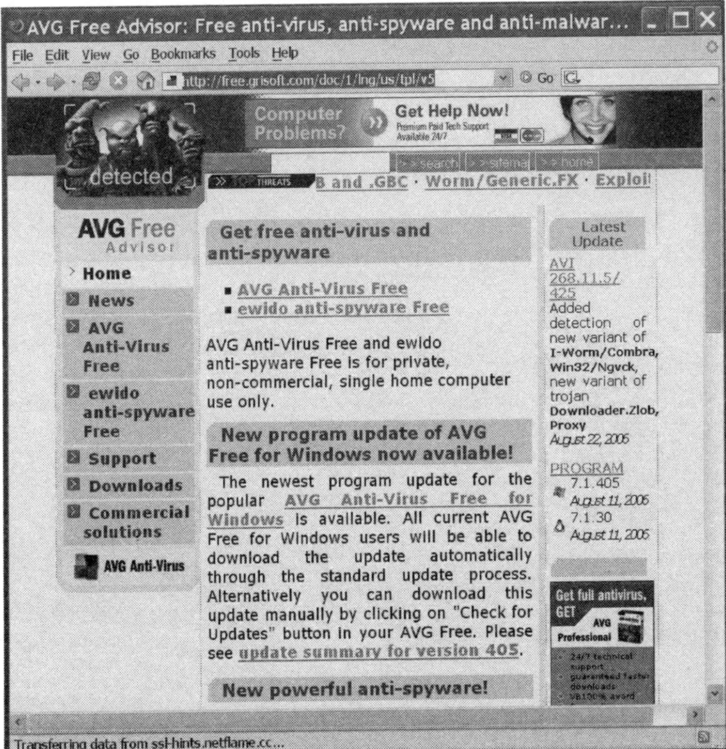

Fig.8.1 The home page for AVG's free software

virus or other malicious program is blocked or removed from the system before it has a chance to do any harm.

The alternative to using online virus scanning is to download and install a free antivirus program. There are one or two totally free antivirus programs available on the Internet, where you do not even have to pay for any online updates to the database. The free version of AVG 7.0 from Grisoft is one that is certainly worth trying. The Grisoft site is at:

www.grisoft.com

On the home page there might be a link to the free version of the program, but it does not seem to feature quite as prominently in the home page as

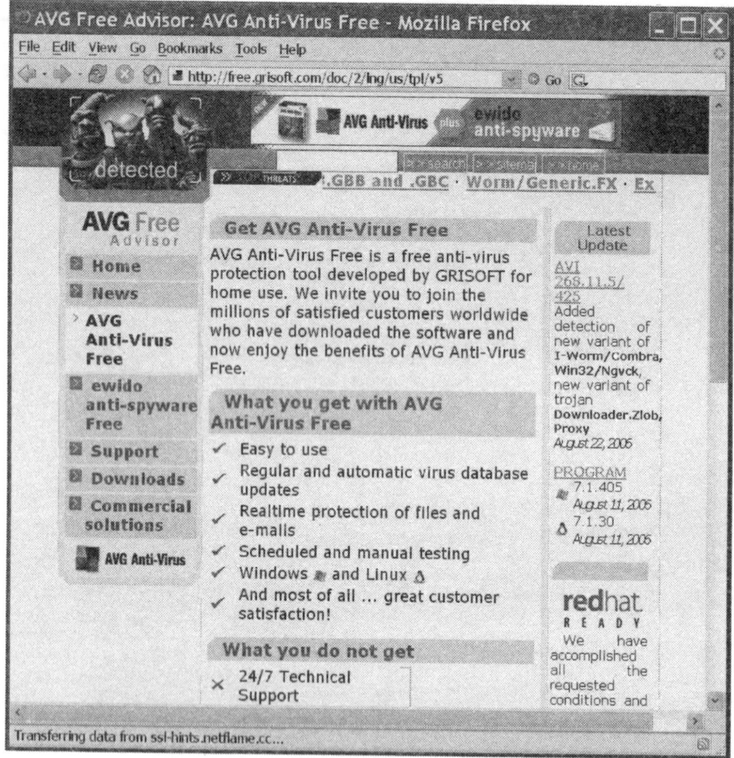

Fig.8.2 This is the page that deals specifically with AVG Free

it did in the past. At the time of writing this, the web address for Grisoft's free software is:

http://free.grisoft.com/doc/1/lng/us/tpl/v5

If there is any difficulty in finding the home page for the free edition, try using "AVG", "free", and "edition" in any good search engine. Having found the right page, it will look something like the web page of Figure 8.1. This gives some information about the free software available from Grisoft, including their antivirus program. Operating the AVG Anti-Virus Free link in the left-hand column brings up the page that deals specifically

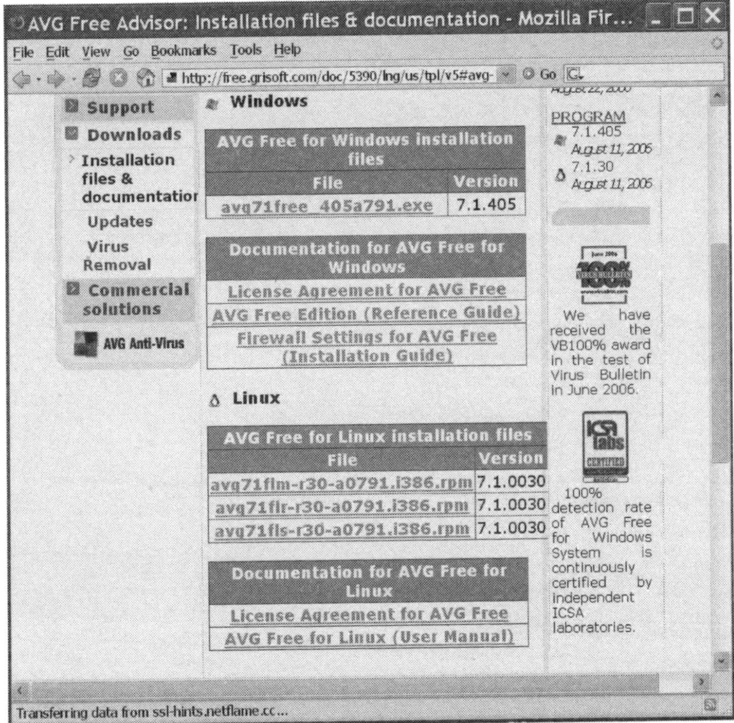

Fig.8.3 A number of files are availablle for download

with this software (Figure 8.2). This page includes a link that enables the program file to be downloaded. In fact there are a number of links (Figure 8.3), but it is the one for the Windows installation files that is needed in this case. It is actually just a single file that is downloaded, but this is an archive that contains all the installation files.

There are also some documentation files available, and it is possible to read these online (Figure 8.4) provided your PC has the Adobe Acrobat Reader program installed. However, it is definitely a good idea to download them and store them on the hard disc drive in case they are needed for future reference. It is a good idea to at least take a quick look through the Reference Guide which, amongst other things, provides installation instructions.

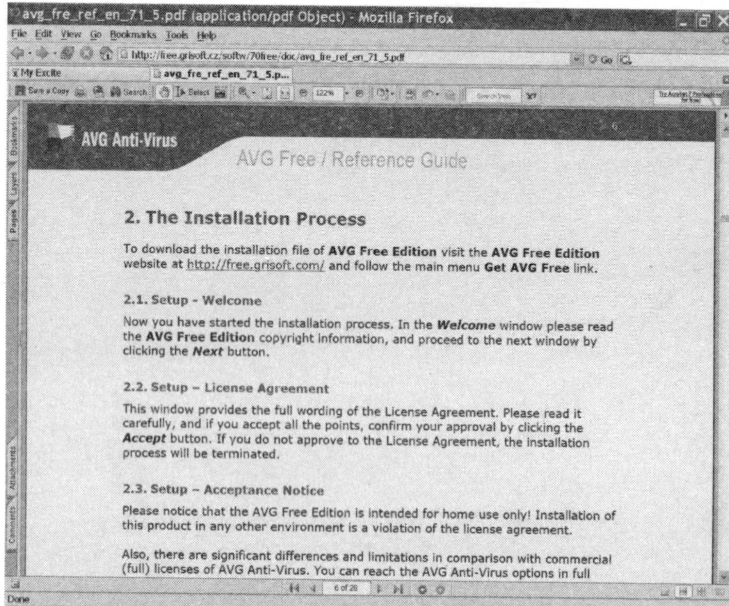

Fig.8.4 The documentation can be read online

Daily updates to AVG are available free of charge, so although free, it should always be reasonably up-to-date. This program has a reputation for being very efficient, and it did once detect a couple of backdoor Trojan programs on my system that a certain well known commercial program had failed to detect. It is certainly one of the best freebies on the Internet, and it generally performs very well in comparison to commercial equivalents.

Earlier versions of the free AVG program had one major limitation, which was the lack of a rescue mode of the type provided by Norton Antivirus and some other programs. In the current version there is a basic facility that enables a rescue disc to be produced. This can be used to backup important system files so that they can be restored if the originals become damaged by a virus. There is still no facility to boot from a floppy disc or a CD-ROM drive and then run virus checks.

Note that the rescue disc only works with hard disc drives that use the FAT 32 format. Windows XP can operate under this format, but it is normally used with the NTFS format. If in doubt about the file system

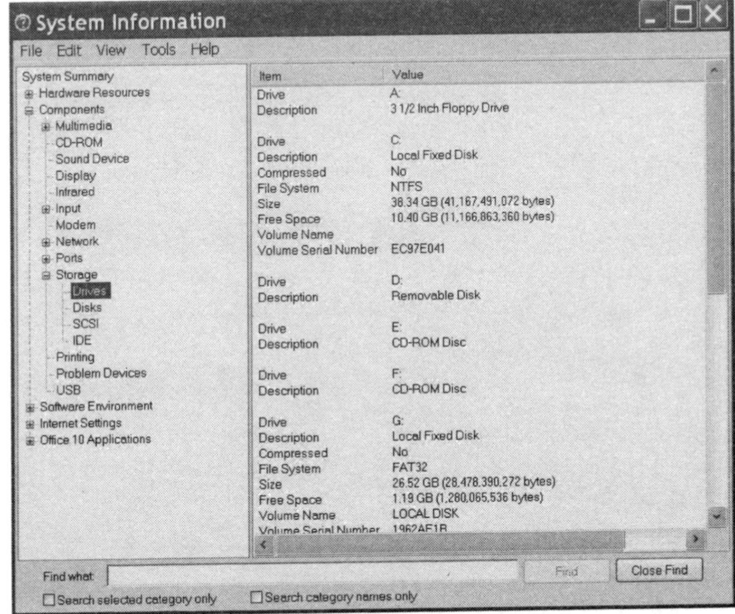

Fig.8.5 The System Information shows the format used for each drive

used on your PC, launch the System Information program and the select Components, Storage, and Drives in the left-hand column. Details of the drives will then be displayed in the main panel (Figure 8.5). Drive C is normally the boot drive, and in this example it is formatted using the NTFS system.

Anyway, the program works effectively in the background detecting the vast majority of viruses, Trojans, etc., so there is little likelihood of a rescue mode being required. However, if you should get unlucky it might be necessary to resort to another antivirus program in order to clear an infection.

In use

AVG does have a useful range of facilities and in other respects it is a very capable program. In common with most antivirus programs you can set it to scan the system on a regular basis, and it also has an automatic update facility. Manual scanning is also available, and this is

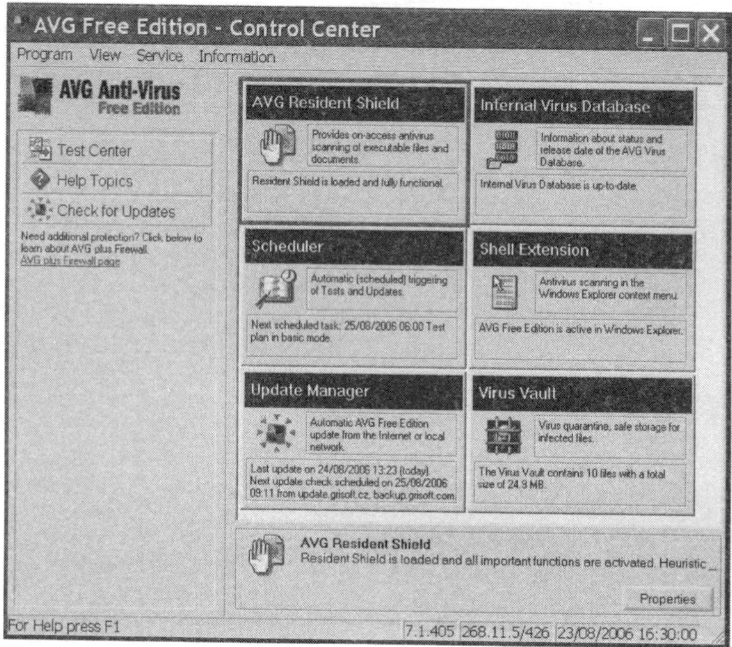

Fig.8.6 The AVG Control Center

another standard feature for this type of software. If you suspect that there might be a virus infection somewhere in the PC you can get the program to do a complete scan of the entire system. Another standard option is to scan one or more of the interchangeable disc drives such as a floppy or CD-ROM drive. This is useful in cases where you suspect that a disc someone has given you might contain a virus.

AVG normally runs automatically at start-up and then runs in the background until the PC is shut down, but it can be started in the normal way from the Start menu. It then appears in a window like the one shown in Figure 8.6. Operating the Test Center button launches a new window that looks like Figure 8.7, which has three large buttons in the main panel. The top button is used when you wish to scan the entire for viruses (Figure 8.8). A window like the one of Figure 8.9 is produced when the process has been completed.

In this case no viruses have been found. The test results will show what action was taken if one or more viruses were detected. The action taken

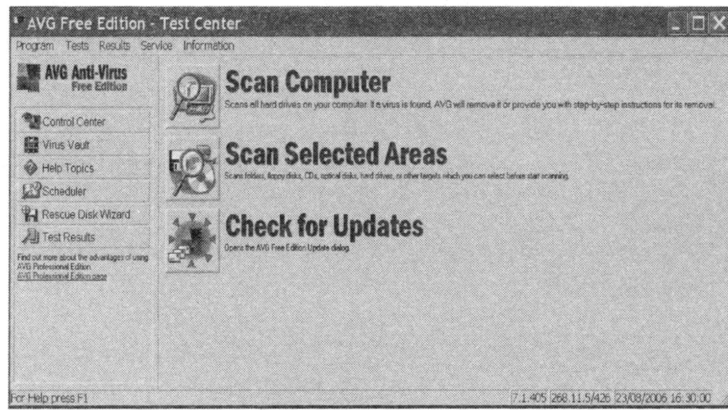

Fig.8.7 The Test Center enables the whole computer or selected drives to be scanned

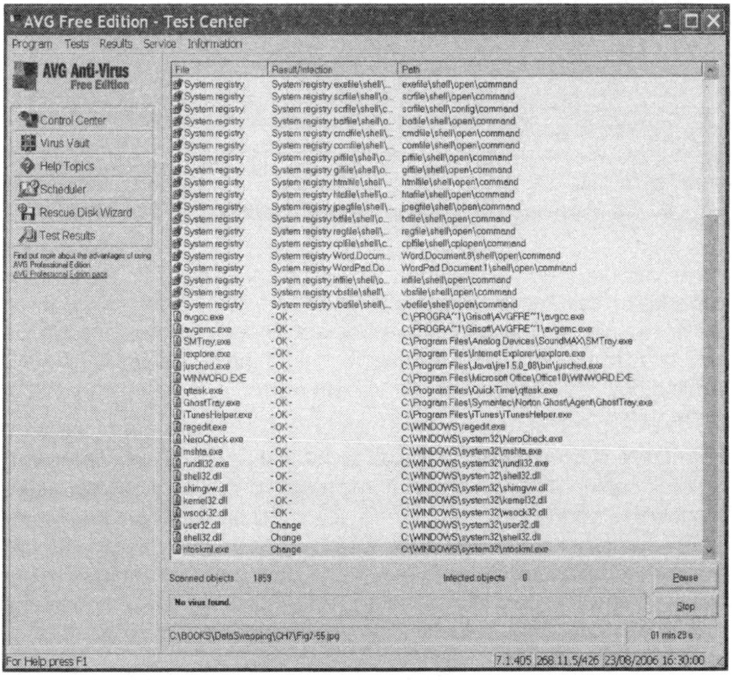

AVG Free Edition - Test Center

Program Tests Results Service Information

AVG Anti-Virus Free Edition

Control Center

Virus Vault

Help Topics

Scheduler

Rescue Disk Wizard

Test Results

File	Result/Infection	Path
System registry	System registry exefile\shell\...	exefile\shell\open\command
System registry	System registry scrfile\shell\o...	scrfile\shell\open\command
System registry	System registry scrfile\shell\c...	scrfile\shell\config\command
System registry	System registry batfile\shell\o...	batfile\shell\open\command
System registry	System registry cmdfile\shell\...	cmdfile\shell\open\command
System registry	System registry comfile\shell\...	comfile\shell\open\command
System registry	System registry piffile\shell\o...	piffile\shell\open\command
System registry	System registry giffile\shell\o...	giffile\shell\open\command
System registry	System registry htmfile\shell\...	htmlfile\shell\open\command
System registry	System registry htafile\shell\o...	htafile\shell\open\command
System registry	System registry jpegfile\shell\...	jpegfile\shell\open\command
System registry	System registry txtfile\shell\o...	txtfile\shell\open\command
System registry	System registry regfile\shell\...	regfile\shell\open\command
System registry	System registry cplfile\shell\c...	cplfile\shell\cplopen\command
System registry	System registry Word.Docum...	Word.Document.8\shell\open\command
System registry	System registry WordPad.Do...	WordPad.Document.1\shell\open\command
System registry	System registry inffile\shell\o...	inffile\shell\open\command
System registry	System registry vbsfile\shell\...	vbsfile\shell\open\command
System registry	System registry vbefile\shell\...	vbefile\shell\open\command
avgcc.exe	-OK-	C:\PROGRA~1\Grisoft\AVGFRE~1\avgcc.exe
avgemc.exe	-OK-	C:\PROGRA~1\Grisoft\AVGFRE~1\avgemc.exe
SMTray.exe	-OK-	C:\Program Files\Analog Devices\SoundMAX\SMTray.exe
iexplore.exe	-OK-	C:\Program Files\Internet Explorer\iexplore.exe
jusched.exe	-OK-	C:\Program Files\Java\jre1.5.0_08\bin\jusched.exe
WINWORD.EXE	-OK-	C:\Program Files\Microsoft Office\Office10\WINWORD.EXE
qttask.exe	-OK-	C:\Program Files\QuickTime\qttask.exe
GhostTray.exe	-OK-	C:\Program Files\Symantec\Norton Ghost\Agent\GhostTray.exe
iTunesHelper.exe	-OK-	C:\Program Files\iTunes\iTunesHelper.exe
regedit.exe	-OK-	C:\WINDOWS\regedit.exe
NeroCheck.exe	-OK-	C:\WINDOWS\system32\NeroCheck.exe
mshta.exe	-OK-	C:\WINDOWS\system32\mshta.exe
rundll32.exe	-OK-	C:\WINDOWS\system32\rundll32.exe
shell32.dll	-OK-	C:\WINDOWS\system32\shell32.dll
shimgvw.dll	-OK-	C:\WINDOWS\system32\shimgvw.dll
kernel32.dll	-OK-	C:\WINDOWS\system32\kernel32.dll
wsock32.dll	-OK-	C:\WINDOWS\system32\wsock32.dll
user32.dll	Change	C:\WINDOWS\system32\user32.dll
shell32.dll	Change	C:\WINDOWS\system32\shell32.dll
ntoskrnl.exe	Change	C:\WINDOWS\system32\ntoskrnl.exe

Scanned objects 1859 Infected objects 0 Pause

No virus found. Stop

C:\BOOKS\DataSwapping\CH7\Fig7-55.jpg 01 min 29 s

For Help press F1 7.1.405 268.11.5/426 23/08/2006 16:30:00

Fig.8.8 The whole system is being scanned for viruses

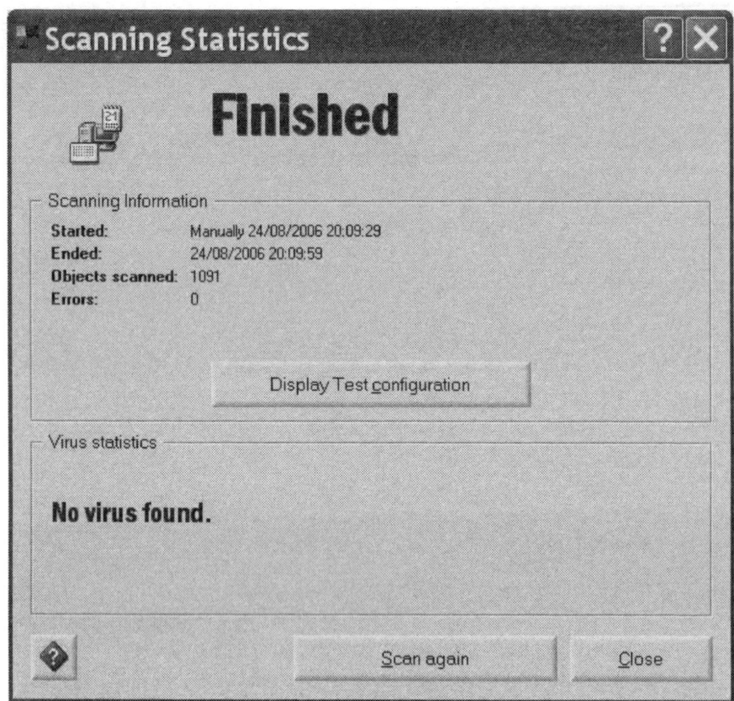

Fig.8.9 The scan has been completed and nothing has been detected

depends on how the program is set up and precisely what it finds. It will leave the infected file unchanged, delete it, or quarantine the file by moving it to the secure folder that is called the "Virus Vault" in AVG terminology. Alternatively, it will do nothing and ask the user to select the required option.

The middle button in the main panel of the Test Center is used when you wish to scan only selected parts of the system. You are provided with a window that shows the parts of the system that can be scanned (Figure 8.10). Simply tick the checkbox for any part that you would like the program to check, and then operate the Scan Selected Areas button. Note that it is not possible to expand the entries for drives and select individual files and (or) folders. The entire contents of a selected drive have to be scanned.

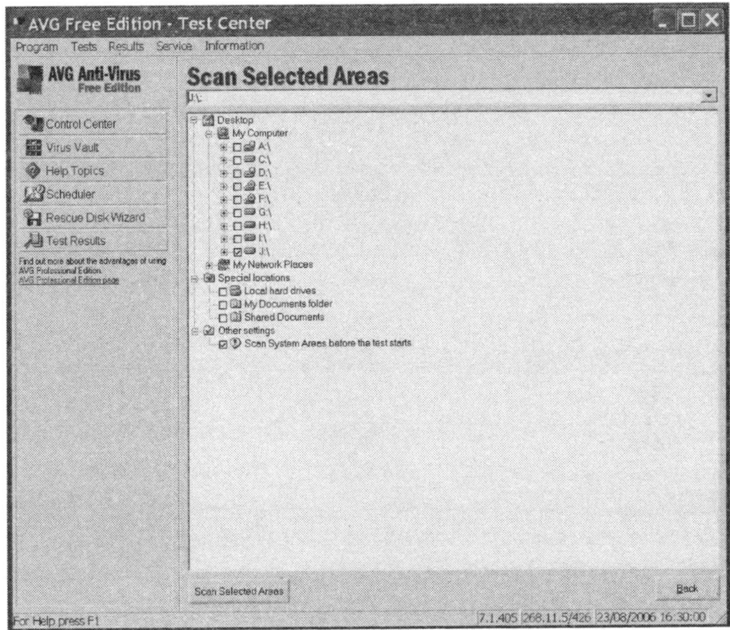

Fig.8.10 This window shows the parts of the system that can be scanned

In general, it is not a good idea to scan part of the system. For example, it is tempting to save time by only scanning the boot drive, but this is leaving the system open to infections. Viruses and other malicious software often have the ability to spread across a system, or to hide themselves on something other than the boot drive. Therefore, it is a good to avoid shortcuts and to scan the entire system.

The ability to scan a selected drive or drives can still be useful though. If someone sends you a disc, it is a good idea to scan it for viruses, but you will probably not wish to scan the rest of the system at the same time. Using this facility of the free AVG antivirus program it is easy to select and quickly scan the CD-ROM, DVD, Flash card, or whatever.

Non-virus

Antivirus programs, as their name suggests, are primarily concerned with the detection and removal of viruses. Most will actually detect a wider range of threats, including most Trojans, spyware, and backdoor

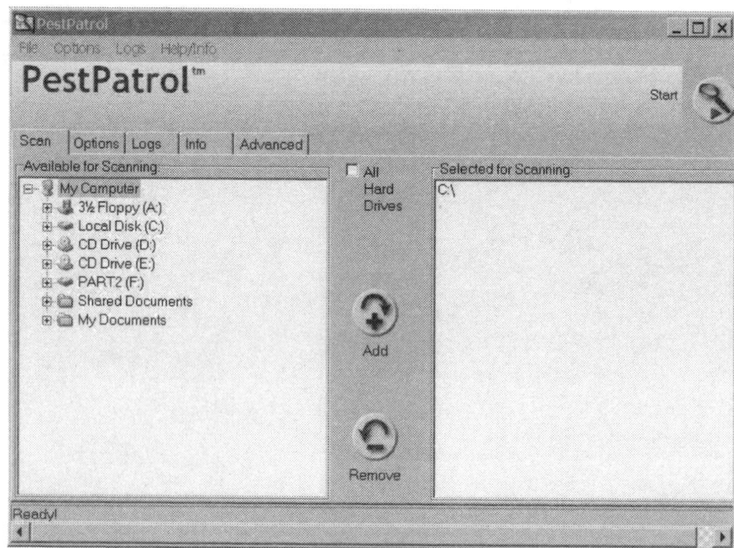

Fig.8.11 The initial screen of Pest Patrol

Trojans. How well these types of threat are detected varies somewhat from one program to another. These days, most antivirus programs will do a good job of detecting any attacks that pose a serious threat to the security of the computer system.

Antivirus programs are not usually designed to detect what could be termed nuisance programs, such as adware programs and their related files. Many of these programs do not present a real danger to the security of the computer, but their nuisance value can be immense. There are programs that are designed to deal with this type of thing, and they will mostly detect some of the more serious threats such as spyware. A new laptop computer is unlikely to be supplied with any preinstalled software of this type, so it is a good idea to install one of these programs yourself.

Pest Patrol is one of the best known programs for removing adware and other nuisance programs, and it is the one that will be used as the basis of this example. The initial screen of Pest Patrol is shown in Figure 8.11, and the first task is to select the drives that will be scanned. This is just a matter of selecting the required drives in the panel on the left using the standard Windows methods. The Add button is then left-clicked in order to add the drives to the list in the right panel. A drive can be removed

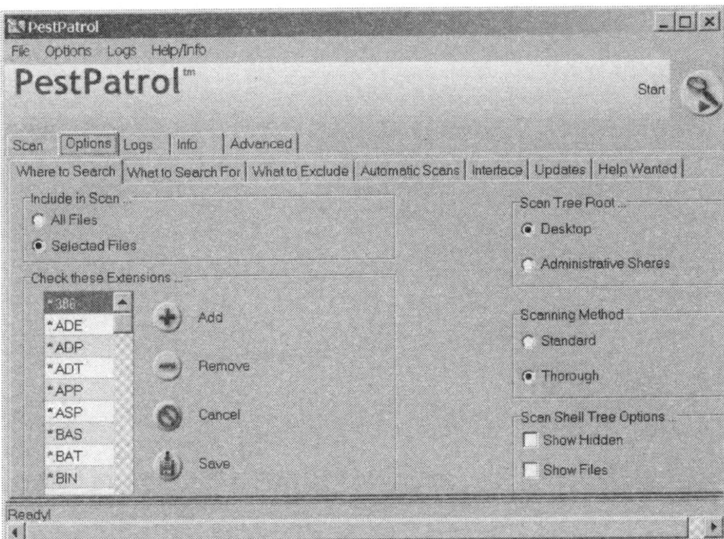

Fig.8.12 The options available here include standard and thorough checking

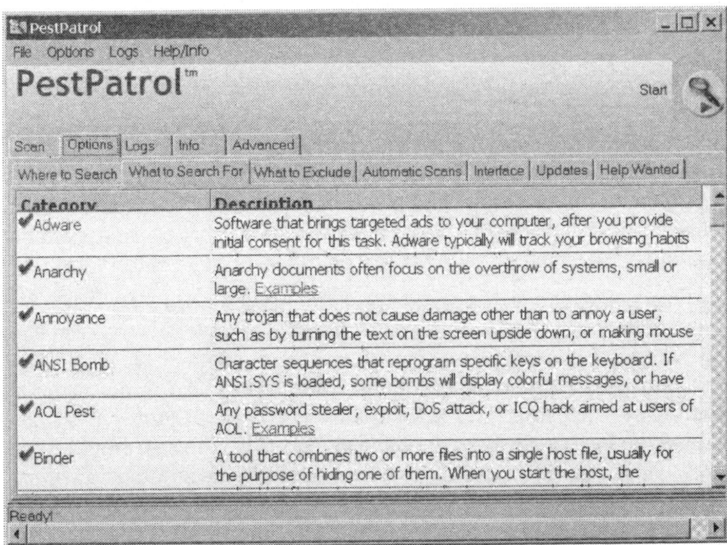

Fig.8.13 Testing can be restricted to certain types of pest

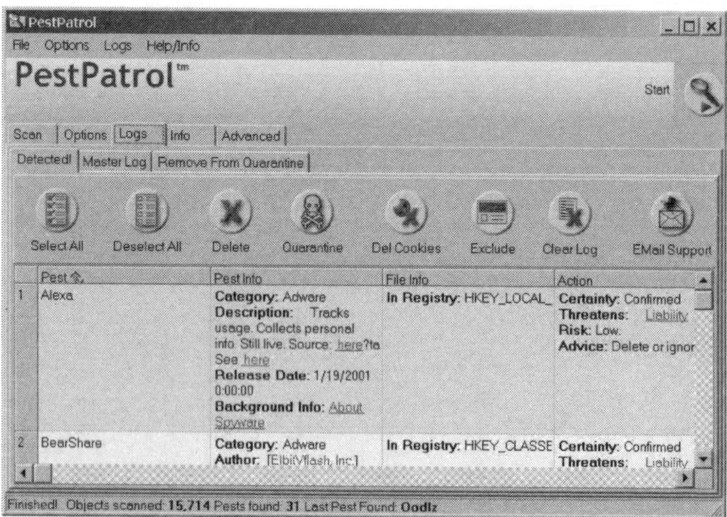

Fig.8.14 A list of scrollable test results is provided

from the list by selecting its entry and operating the Remove button. Simply tick the checkbox if you wish to check all the hard drives.

Operating the Options tab produces a further row of tabs, and these give access to a range of options that control the way Pest Patrol scans the disc. There are standard and thorough options for example (Figure 8.12), and you can also set the program to only look for certain types of "pest" (Figure 8.13). It is by no means essential to do any "fine tuning" though, and the program should work well enough if it scans the discs using the default settings. To go ahead with a scan it is just a matter of operating the Start button in the top right-hand corner of the window.

You are presented with a scrollable list of results once Pest Patrol has finished the scan (Figure 8.14). It is essential to look down the list, item by item, even in cases where there are a large number of entries. What you and Pest Patrol consider to be "pests" could be rather different. Remember that removing adware files could result in any programs supported by that adware becoming inoperative. You are unlikely to get away with installing supported software, disabling the associated adware, and then continuing to use the supported software. Blocking adware with a firewall does sometimes leave the supported application fully operational, but this is a morally dubious practice.

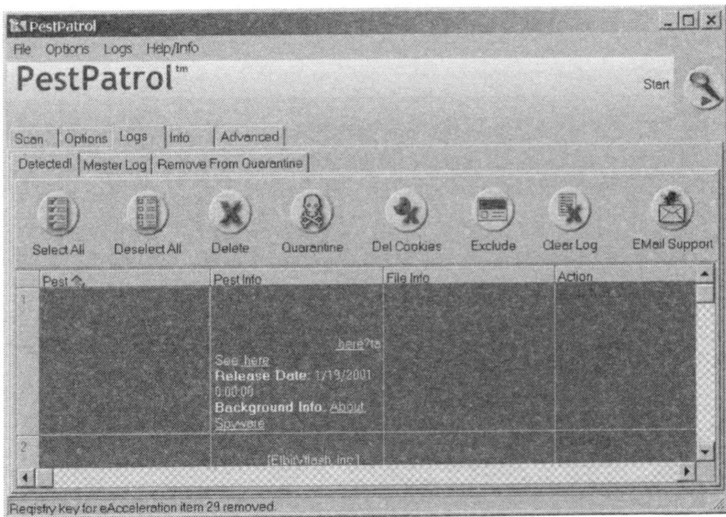

Fig.8.15 The list now shows what has been done to each file

Having decided the fate of the various entries, it is just a matter of selecting each batch and then operating the appropriate button. In this example none of the detected files were required, so they were all deleted. The list changes to show what has been done to each file (Figure 8.15). Note that the program may be unable to delete some files and folders. It will then show the location of the relevant files or folders and recommend manual deletion.

Firewalls

A considerable amount of protection can be provided by using antivirus software, installing a program to deal with nuisance software, and ensuring that the Browser program has sensible settings. Even so, the computer could still be vulnerable to certain types of attack. Further protection can be provided by using a firewall, which can be either a piece of hardware or a program. A firewall's basic function is much the same whether it is implemented in software or hardware.

Although some people seem to think that a firewall and antivirus programs are the same, there are major differences. There is often some overlap between real world antivirus and firewall programs, but their primary aims are different. An antivirus program is designed to scan files on discs and the contents of the computer's memory in search of viruses and other potentially harmful files. Having found any suspect files, the program will usually deal with them. A firewall is used to block access to your PC, and in most cases it is access to your PC via the Internet that is blocked. Bear in mind though, that a software firewall will usually block access via a local area network (LAN) as well.

Of course, a firewall is of no practical value if it blocks communication from one PC to another and access via the Internet. What it is actually doing is preventing unauthorised access to the protected PC. When you access an Internet site your PC sends messages to the server hosting that site, and these messages request the pages you wish to view. Having requested information, the PC expects information to be sent from the appropriate server, and it accepts that information when it is received. A firewall does not interfere with this type of Internet activity provided it is set up correctly.

It is a different matter when another system tries to access your PC when you have not instigated the initial contact. The firewall will treat this attempted entry as an attack and will block it. Of course, the attempt at accessing your PC might not be an attack, and a firewall can result in legitimate access being blocked. Something like P2P file swapping is likely to fail or operate in a limited fashion. The sharing of files and resources on a local area network could also be blocked. A practical firewall enables the user to permit certain types of access so that the computer can work normally while most unauthorised access is still blocked. However, doing so does reduce the degree of protection provided by the firewall.

Windows firewall

There is a firewall program built into the original version of Windows XP, but it is not activated by default. A rather more advanced firewall program is installed as part of SP2 (Service Pack 2), and it is switched on by default, as is the Vista firewall. New PCs are supplied with Vista or a version of Windows XP that already has SP2. Accordingly, there is no need to install SP2, and the firewall will be switched on by default.

The Windows XP/Vista firewall program can confuse users, as it sometimes causes warning messages to appear on the screen when programs are run. This occurs when a program tries to access the Internet and its activity is detected by the firewall. In most cases the program will be something like a media player or web browser that is quite legitimately trying to use the Internet connection.

When asked if you would like to go on blocking the program's Internet access or unblock it, choose to remove the blocking only if you are sure that the program is one that you are using, and that it has good reason to use the Internet connection. Backdoor Trojans, spyware, etc., gather information from a PC and try to send it to hackers via the Internet. The built-in firewall should detect and block most programs of this type provided you do not override it.

The new Windows XP/Vista firewall is certaily better than the original, but it is not as good as most third-party firewall programs. Consequently, if you have an alternative firewall program, in most cases it will be best if this is used and the built-in program is switched off. The built-in firewall will probably not offer any facility that is not available from the third-party alternative.

Ports

When dealing with firewalls you are almost certain to encounter the term "ports". In a computer context this normally means a socket on the PC where a peripheral of some kind is connected. In an Internet context a port is not in the form of any hardware, and it is more of a software concept. Programs communicate over the Internet via these notional ports that are numbered from 0 to 65535. It enables several programs to utilise the Internet without the data for one program getting directed to another program.

Firewalls usually have the ability to block activity on certain ports. The idea is to block ports that are likely to be used by programs such as backdoor Trojans but are not normally used for legitimate Internet traffic. A Trojan could be set to "listen" on (say) port 80, and send the data it has collected once it receives a message from a hacker. By blocking any activity on port 80, the firewall ensures that the Trojan can not send any data, and that it will not be contacted in the first place.

Note that most software firewall programs will block this type of activity anyway, because the firewall will detect that an unauthorised program is trying to use the Internet. It will alert the user and only permit the data to be sent if the user authorises it. Presumably the user would "smell a rat" and deny permission for the Trojan to access the Internet. Most hardware firewalls would prevent the message from the hacker from reaching the Trojan, and would also prevent the attack from succeeding. Even so, it

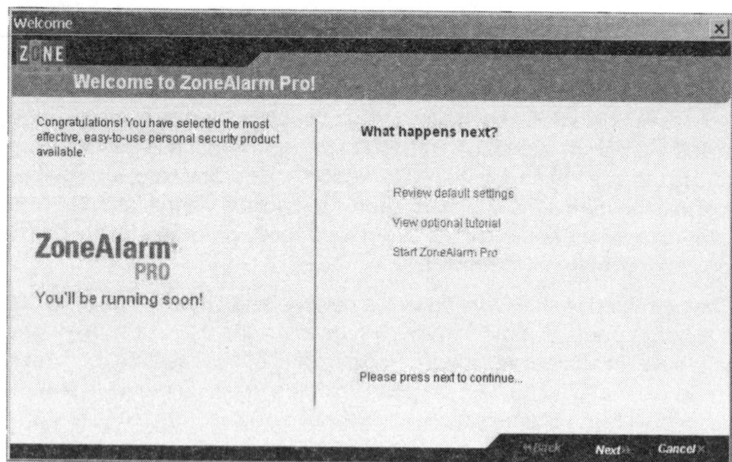

Fig.8.16 Installation has been completed successfully

is useful to block ports that are likely to be used for hacking the system. Doing so makes it that much harder for someone to "crack" your system, which is what Internet security is all about.

False alarms

Many of the early firewall programs had a major problem in that they were a bit overzealous. While you were trying the surf the Internet there were constant interruptions from the firewall as it warned you of supposed attacks on the system. In reality these attacks were wholly or largely nonexistent. What the programs were actually detecting was normal Internet activity, and many of the false alarms could be prevented by setting up the program to ignore certain programs accessing the Internet. Some of these programs were virtually unusable though.

Modern firewall programs mostly operate in a rather less "in your face" fashion, and produce fewer interruptions. Even so, it is usually necessary to go through a setting up process in order to keep down the number of false alarms, and further tweaking may be needed in order to get things working really well. Of course, if you would like to be informed about every possible attack on the system, most firewalls will duly oblige provided the appropriate settings are used. This certainly gives the ultimate in security, but it could make surfing the Internet a very slow and tedious process.

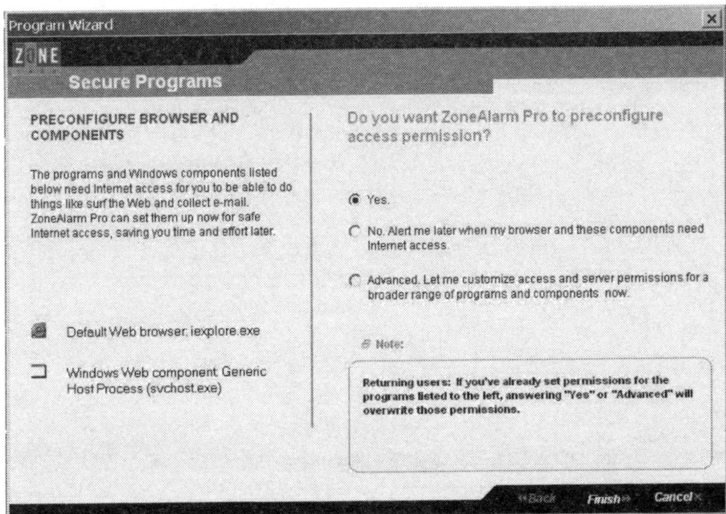

Fig.8.17 Zone Alarm lists programs that will need Internet access

Zone Alarm

There are plenty of software firewalls to choose from, and most of them are capable of providing your PC with a higher degree of security than the built-in firewall. Fortunately, there are several good firewall programs that cost little or nothing. Zone Alarm is a popular firewall, and it exists in free, trial, and full commercial versions. It is quite easy to set up and use, and the free version represents a good starting point for private users wishing to try a good quality firewall at minimum cost. All versions of this program are reasonably easy to set up. Zone alarm Pro will be used for this example, and this program has a few more facilities than the basic (free) version.

Figure 8.16 shows the initial window produced once the installation process has been completed. This simply explains that there are a few processes to complete before the program is ready for use. At the next screen (Figure 8.17) Zone Alarm lists programs that it thinks will need Internet access. The list will include the default browser and any other programs that are required for normal Internet access. By default, these programs will be given Internet access, but other programs will produce a warning message if they attempt to use the Internet. Access will then be allowed only if you give permission. You might prefer to choose which

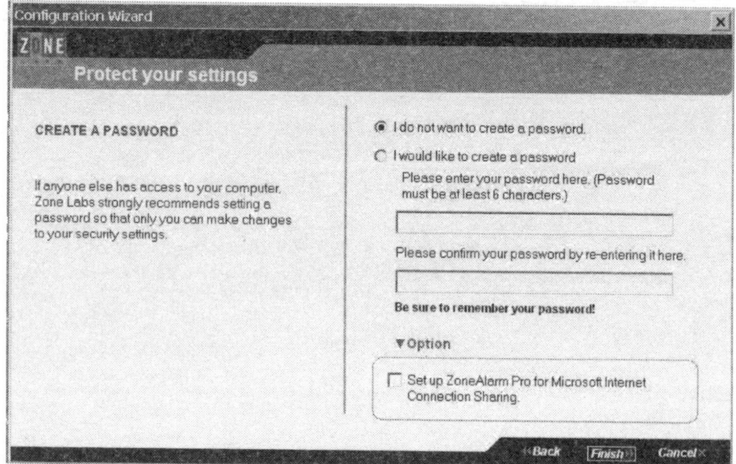

Fig.8.18 The program can be password protected

programs will be granted access during the setting up process rather than dealing with it later as programs try to access the Internet. As most programs do not require Internet access, it is probably easier to grant access as and when necessary.

The next window (Figure 8.18) enables the program to be password protected. This is only necessary if someone else has access to your PC. Things then move on to a window (Figure 8.19) where you choose the types of Internet access that will produce alerts. You can opt to have an onscreen message appear when any access is blocked, or for no alerts to be issued. Note that the program will still continue to block Internet access as and when it sees fit, even if the alerts are completely switched off. The middle option results in an alert being produced when the program considers that attempted access is probably the result of an attack by a hacker. This is the default option and is probably the best choice.

The options available at the next screen (Figure 8.20) are for two of Zone Alarm Pro's optional extras. One of these is a routine that blocks pop-up advertisements and it also blocks third-party "spy" cookies. Pop-ups are now so widespread on the Internet that they have become a major nuisance. Apart from being irksome, they can effectively slow down your Internet connection by increasing the amount of data that has to be downloaded. This can be a serious drag on your surfing, especially for

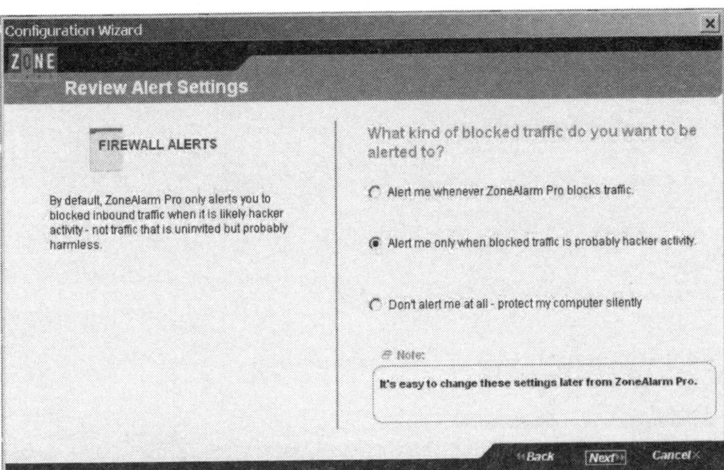

Fig.8.19 Choose the types of Internet access that will produce alerts

those that do not have some form of broadband connection. A pop-up blocker is therefore a very useful feature. However, it is something that is now built into most browsers, so the one provided by Zone Alarm will probably not be needed.

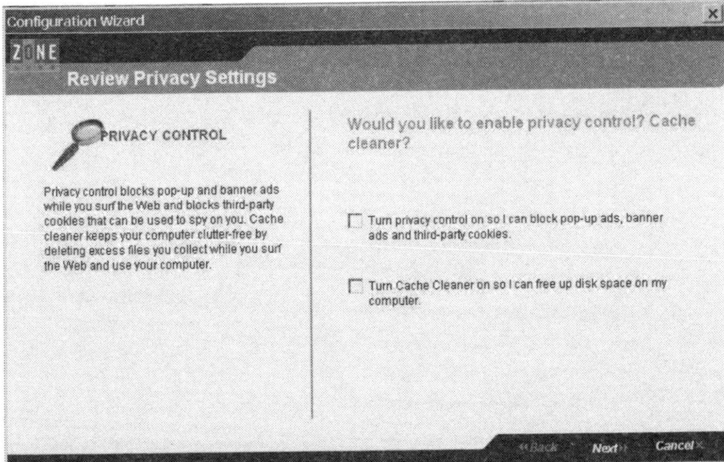

Fig.8.20 Two optional extras can be enabled

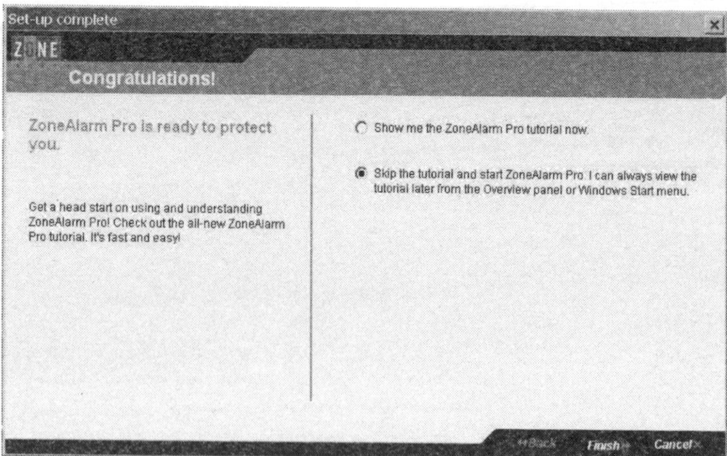

Fig.8.21 A tutorial is available or the program can be started

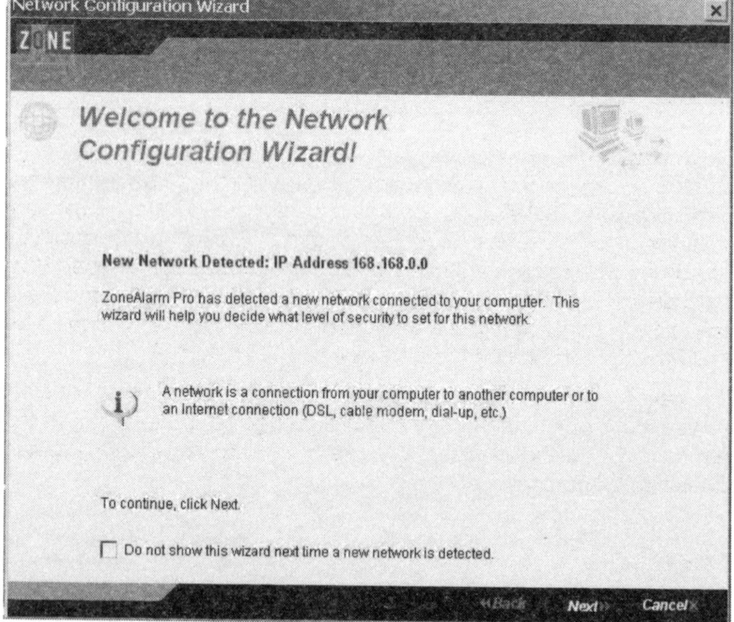

Fig.8.22 Zone Alarm has detected the network

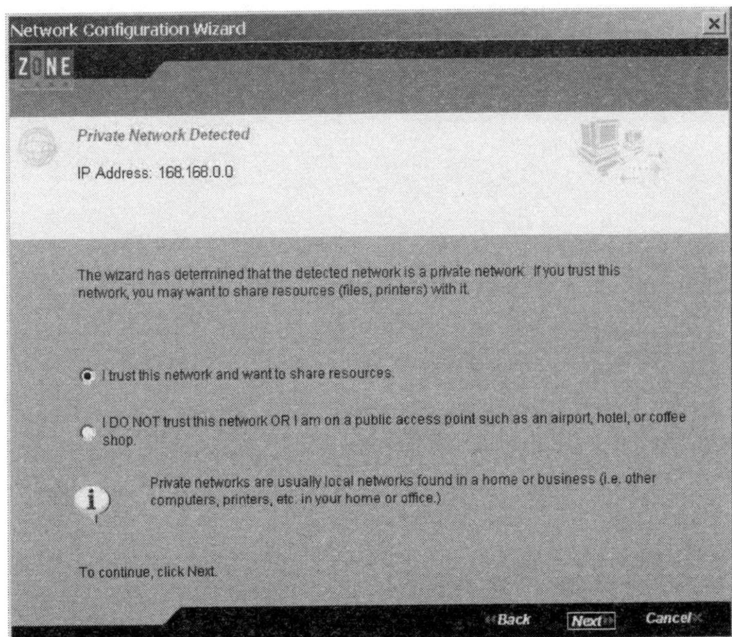

Fig.8.23 The network can be enabled or blocked

Cache cleaning is the other option. Copies of many Internet files are kept on a PC so that they do not have to be downloaded again when the relevant pages are revisited. Anyone undertaking a lot of surfing is likely to end up with many megabytes of cached Internet files on their PC's hard disc. These files should eventually be removed by Windows, but the cache cleaner provides a neater solution by preventing a massive build-up from occurring in the first place.

The next window (Figure 8.21) gives the option of starting the program or viewing a quick tutorial. It is definitely a good idea to look at the tutorial, but it can be viewed at any time by running Zone Alarm Pro and operating the Tutorial button.

Network

The PC used for this demonstration has its Internet connection provided by a broadband modem that has a built-in router, with two other PCs connected to the router. Laptop PCs are often connected into a network

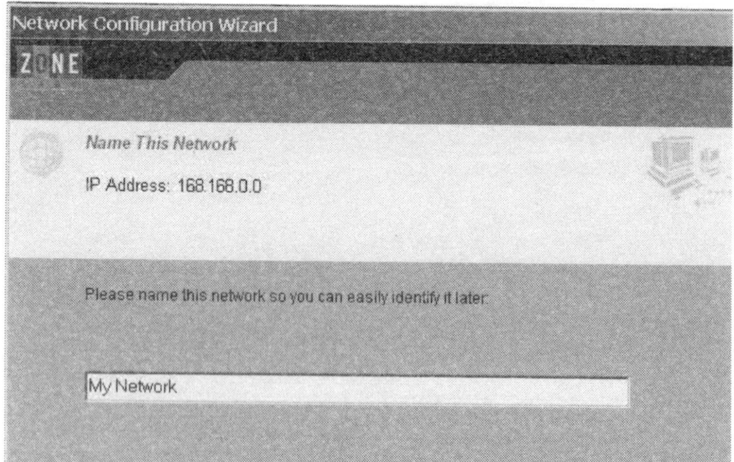

Fig.8.24 The network can be named or the default can be accepted

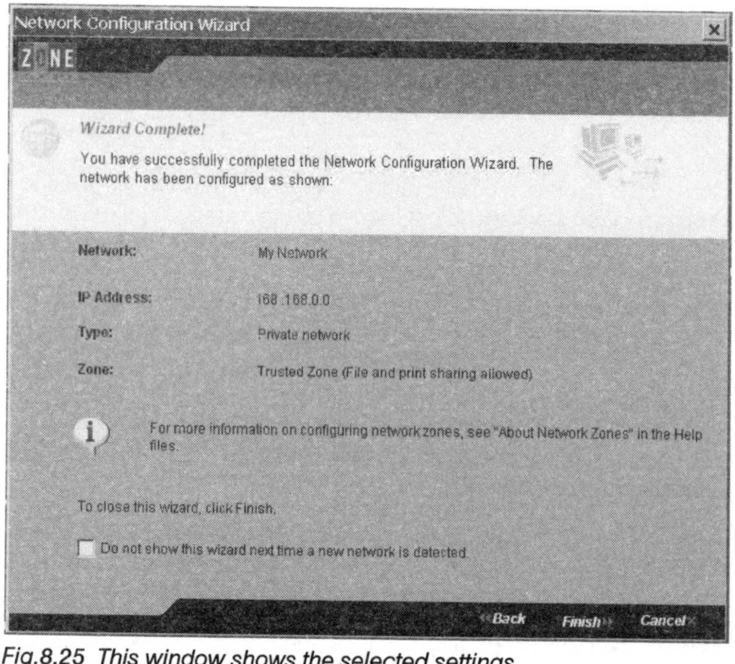

Fig.8.25 This window shows the selected settings

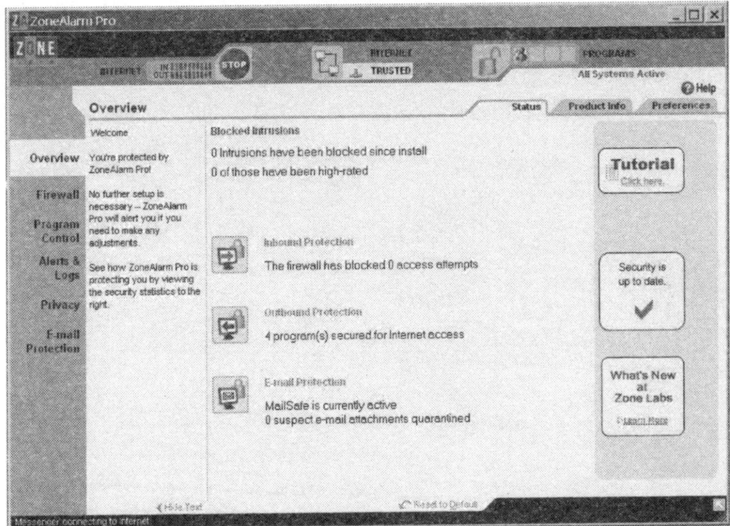

Fig.8.26 Finally, the program is operational

when used back at base, and the firewall program then has to be set up to accommodate this network. Of course, this is not something that you have to bother with if the laptop is used in isolation.

In this example the network was detected by Zone Alarm Pro (Figure 8.22), and the Network Configuration Wizard was launched. Remember that a firewall will block any network access, including the LAN (local area network) variety, unless instructed otherwise. At the next screen (Figure 8.23) you have the option of enabling this network or blocking it. Obviously it must be enabled in order to permit the system to go on working properly.

The window of Figure 8.24 enables the network to be given a name of your choice, or you can simply settle for the default name. The next window (Figure 8.25) simply shows the settings you have chosen and provides an opportunity to go back and change them. Finally, the program is run (Figure 8.26). In normal use the program runs in the background and it is only necessary to go to this screen if you need to make changes to the setup or view the statistics produced by the program.

Operating the Firewall tab switches the window to look like Figure 8.27, and the degree of security in each zone can then be adjusted via the slider controls. Unless there is good reason to change the setting for the

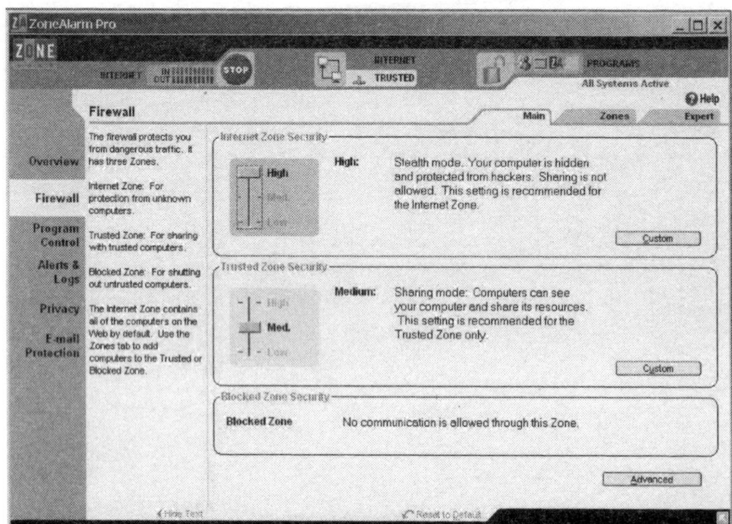

Fig.8.27 Here the Firewall tab has been operated

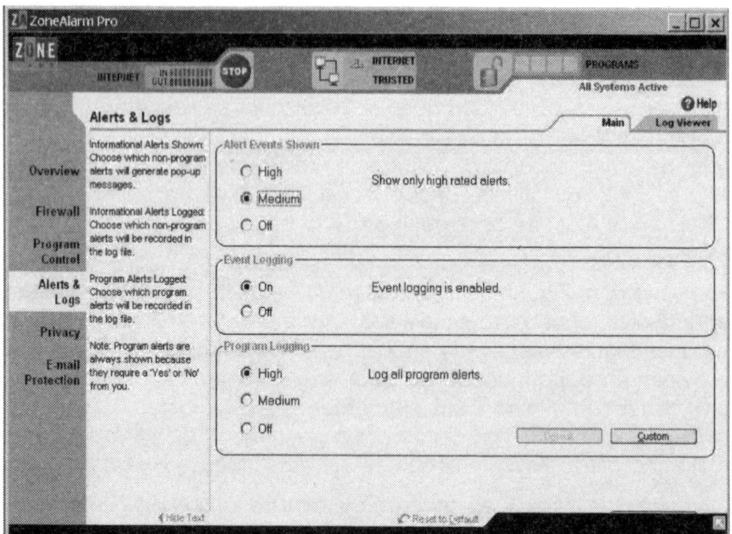

Fig.8.28 The settings can be changed when this tab is selected

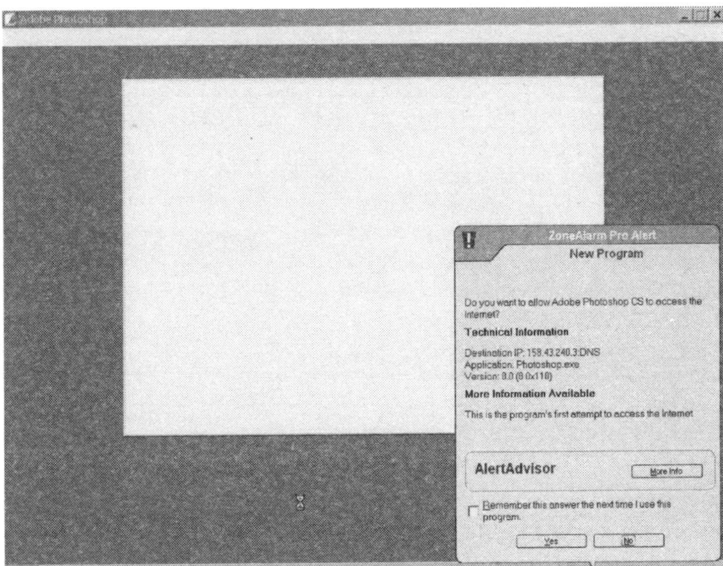

Fig.8.29 A program has generated an alert

Internet Zone, it should be left at High. The other tabs permit easy control of other aspects of the program, such as alerts (Figure 8.28). Therefore, if you find any of the initial settings unsatisfactory it is easy to change them.

In use it is likely that the program will initially query potential problems that are really just a normal part of the PC's operation. In the example of Figure 8.29 an alert has been triggered by an image editing program trying to access the Internet. Although there is no obvious reason for such a program requiring the Internet, many programs these days use the Internet to regularly look for program updates. Operate the Yes button to permit Internet access or the No button to block it. Tick the checkbox if you would like this answer to be used automatically each time the program tries to access the Internet.

Sometimes the alert will genuinely find something that is amiss. In Figure 8.30 the alert shows that a file called msbb.exe has tried to access the Internet. Some delving on the Internet revealed that this is part of the Ncase adware program, which was supposedly uninstalled from the PC a few weeks earlier. Clearly it had not been successfully uninstalled, and some further work was needed in order to banish it from the system.

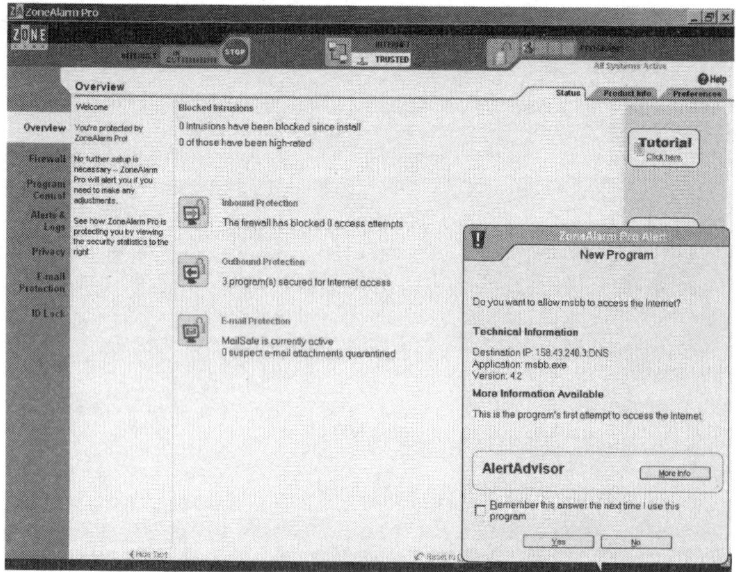

Fig.8.30 The alert was produced by an adware component

Encryption

Many people now use encryption programs to protect their personal or otherwise sensitive data. Encryption first became popular with Emails, probably because this method of communication is something less than totally secure. The basic technique is to scramble the data using an encryption program, so that anyone intercepting the Email finds themselves in possession of a message that appears to be random characters. Of course, the same is true when the intended recipient receives the message. In order to descramble the Email its recipient must have the same program that was used to encrypt it, together with the correct password. The program then decrypts the data to produce the original message again.

Most programs of this type are not only suitable for sending Emails, and can also be used to encrypt any form of data file. You can, for example, encrypt word processor files so that anyone gaining access to your PC will not be able to read them. In fact this is doing things the hard way, because many word processors now have some form of built-in encryption facility. With Microsoft Word for instance, documents can be password protected. This operates at two levels, and at the highest level it is not possible to open a document without giving the correct password first. At a lower level of security it is possible for anyone to open the document and look at its contents, but only authorised users can make any changes to it.

Encrypting sensitive data is important when using a laptop PC, and is especially important if it will be used on the move. The lightweight nature of a laptop means that it is relatively easy to steal. The risk is clearly much greater if the computer is used away from base, where it represents one of the most popular targets for opportunist thieves. There is also a risk of it being lost. If your laptop PC gets into the hands of someone else, there is nothing to prevent them from accessing your data unless it is encrypted.

Take care

Before using any form of password protection for data it is important to realise that modern encryption techniques are extremely powerful. Should you manage to forget the password it is unlikely that you will ever see your data in readable form again. Writing down passwords is not normally considered to be a good practice, but the reduction in security it provides is probably better than finding yourself locked out of you own documents.

Those with poor memories would be well advised to write down the password and hide it away in the bottom of a drawer where no one can find it easily. Many passwords are case sensitive, so it is as well to work on the assumption that they are all case sensitive. That way you should never be caught out by using any letters of the wrong case.

Word

In order to password protect a Word document the document must first be opened. Then select Options from the Tools menu and operate the Security tab on the new window that appears (Figure 8.31). Type the password into the appropriate textbox for the level of security you require, and then operate the OK button. You will have to enter the password into a small pop-up window in order to go back to the document. It will also be necessary to enter the password into a small pop-up window each time you try to open the file or alter it, depending on the level of security selected.

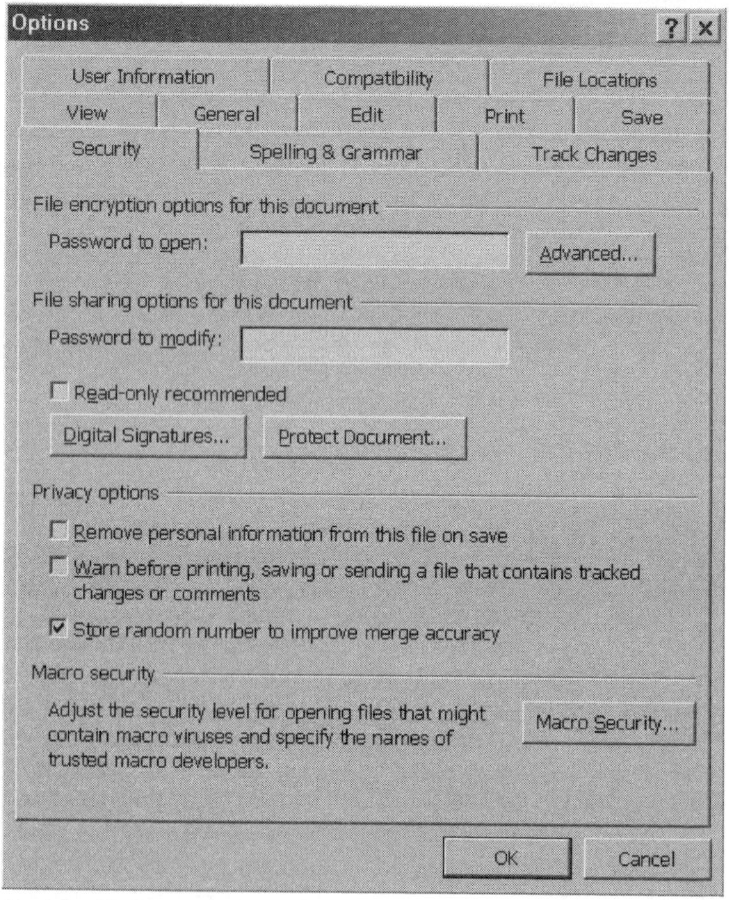

Fig.8.31 *The Security section of Word's Options window*

There are alternatives to using special encryption programs when sending information via Emails. Many data compression programs can provide password protection, so it is possible to use one of these to compress and encrypt a file which can then be sent as an Email attachment. Unfortunately, the free versions of these programs often lack the ability to password protect files, so it might be necessary to buy the full version in order to use this facility.

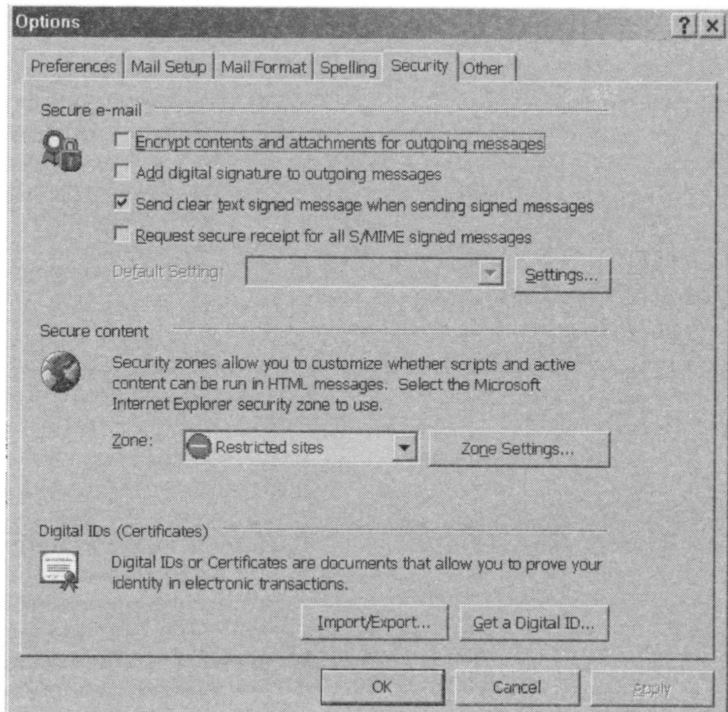

Fig.8.32 The Security section of the Options window in Outlook Express

Users of Outlook and Outlook Express have a built-in encryption facility, but it is of no real use to most users. In order to encrypt a file select Options from the Tools menu and then operate the Security tab in the new window that appears (Figure 8.32). Tick the top checkbox in order to use encryption on your Emails and any attachments. Unfortunately, this method is only usable if you purchase a digital certificate from a company such as VeriSign. The cost is not that great, but probably few private users are prepared to go to the trouble and expense of obtaining one and keeping it up to date.

XP/Vista Encryption

As explained previously, there are programs that can encrypt files on the hard disc of your computer so that they can not be read by others. Windows XP and Vista have a form of built-in encryption facility, but it

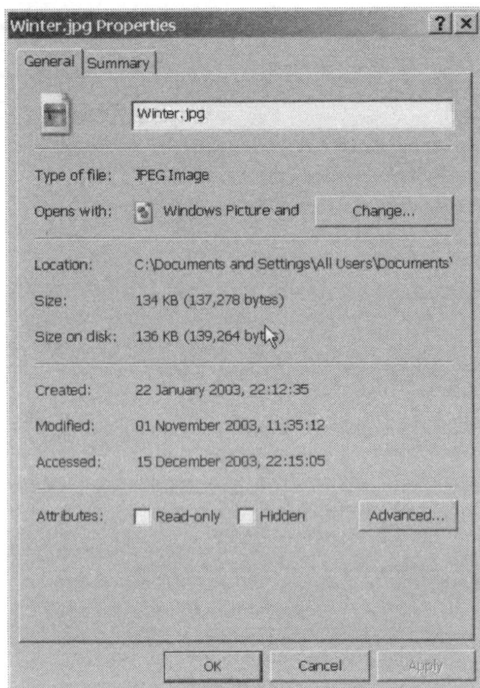

Fig.8.33 The file's properties window

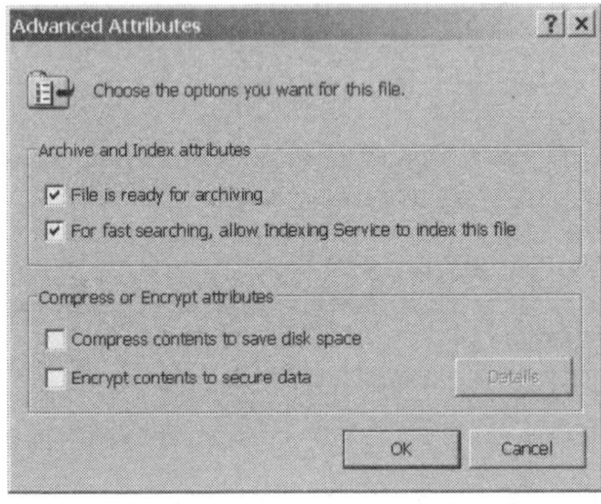

Fig.8.34 The Advanced settings

does not operate in quite the same way as most encryption programs. Although encrypted, the files are still perfectly readable and can be used in the normal way from within Windows.

This does not necessarily mean that they are accessible to anyone that gets hold of your PC, because Windows itself can be password protected. Also, if hackers should gain access to the computer over the Internet, they will not be able to read the encrypted files. Similarly, if someone should copy any protected files to a floppy disc or CD-ROM, the copied files will not be readable on another PC.

In order to protect a file or folder it is first located using Windows Explorer and its entry is then right-clicked. This brings up a small menu where the Properties option is selected. The file's property window will look something like Figure 8.33, and the Advanced button near the bottom of the screen is operated. The new window of Figure 8.34 will then appear, and the bottom checkbox (Encrypt data to secure contents) is ticked. Operating the OK button will produce a warning message (Figure 8.35) if a file rather than a folder is being encrypted, and it is advisable to accept the default and let Windows encrypt the parent folder.

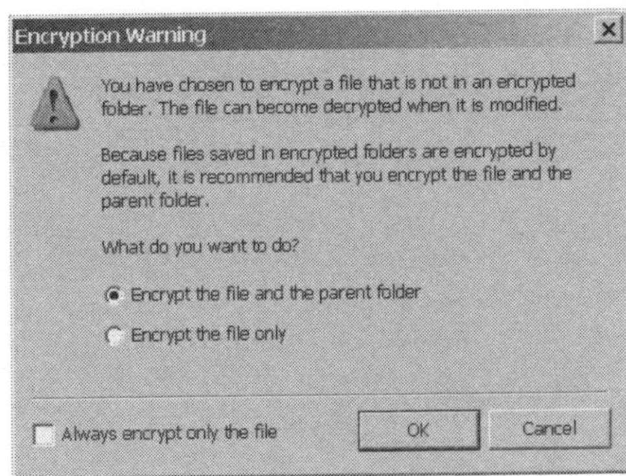

Fig.8.35 Accept the suggested settings

Encrypted files and folders are shown in Internet Explorer in the normal way, but the name of the file is in green text to indicate that encryption

Fig.8.36 The file can be opened and displayed in the normal way despite being encrypted

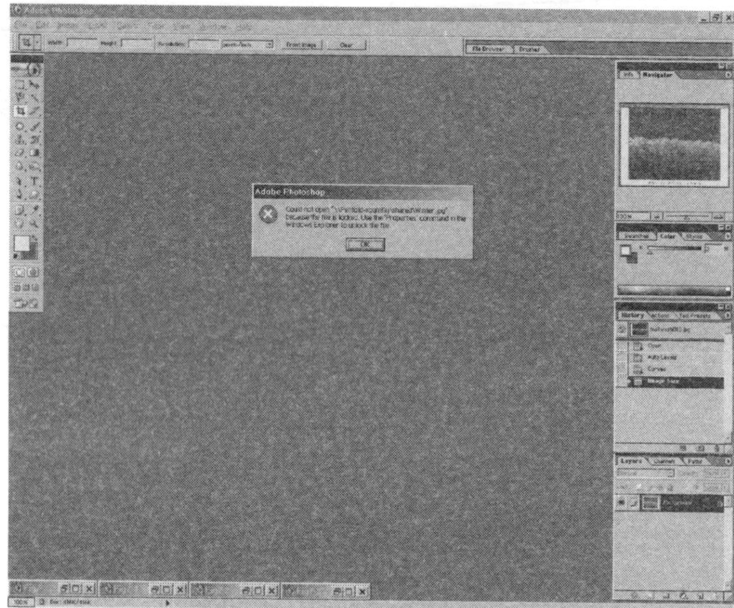

Fig.8.37 The file can not be opened via a network or if copied to another PC

has been used. The encryption is to a large extent transparent to the user. Double-clicking on the Jpg image file used in this example resulted in it being displayed in the usual way (Figure 8.36) with no password being required. Remember that Windows itself must be password protected if you need the files to be inaccessible to anyone gaining access to the computer.

Figure 8.37 shows the result of trying to open the encrypted image file using another PC with the file accessed over a network. The file is encrypted and Photoshop has therefore been unable to open the file. It has therefore produced an error message to this effect. Hackers accessing the computer via the Internet would have the same problem. Even if someone was to steal the PC they would not be able to put the hard disc in another computer and read the encrypted files. Provided Windows itself was password protected they would not be able to boot the PC into Windows and access them either.

An advantage of this built-in encryption is that it is very easy to use. Everything is protected by the Windows password, so there is only one password to remember. Having entered Windows there is no need to

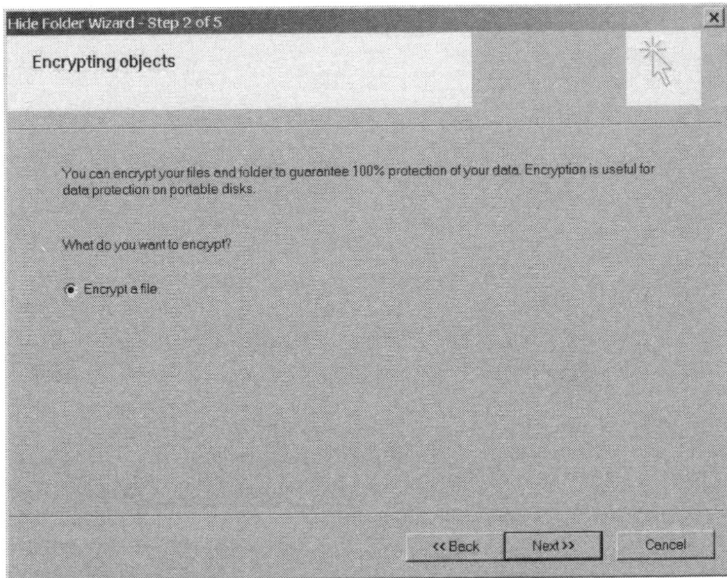

Fig.8.38 The opening window of the Encryption Wizard

use a password when saving or loading encrypted files. They are accessed in exactly the same way as non-encrypted files. In order to remove the encryption it is merely necessary to go back to the properties window again, operate the Advanced button, and then remove the tick from the encryption checkbox.

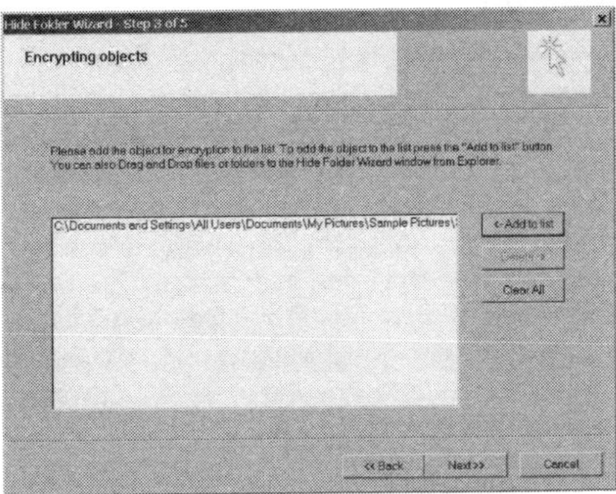

Fig.8.39 Operate the Add to List button

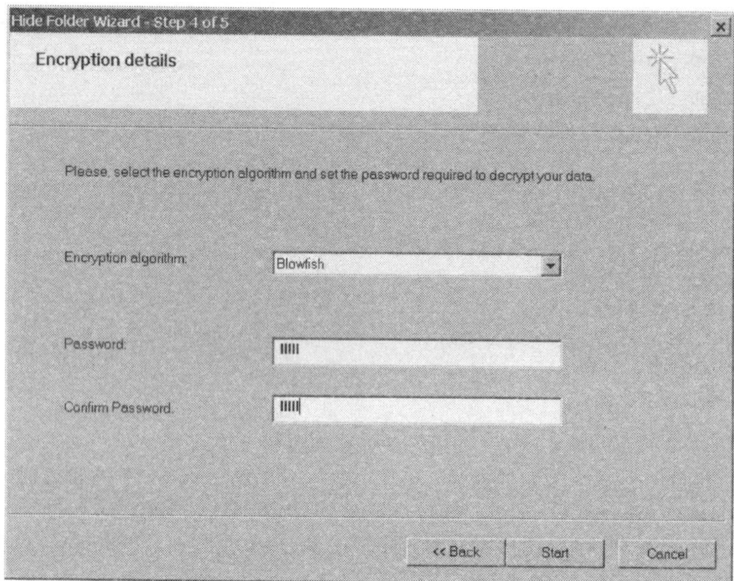

Fig.8.40 Select the required type of encryption

Stealth

Some programs offer a facility to hide folders or files as an alternative to encryption. The hidden files do not show up in Windows Explorer or in the file browsers of applications programs. If prying eyes do not know that the files exist they can not view or alter them. Hide File 3.0 is a program that offers both file encryption and hiding facilities. Using the encryption is very straightforward and an encryption wizard can be selected from the Encryption menu. The first window (Figure 8.38) has only one option (to encrypt a file), and it is really just an introduction to the wizard. At the next window (Figure 8.39) you operate the Add to List button, which launches the usual Windows file browser. This is used to add the required file or files.

Next the required type of encryption is selected (Figure 8.40), and it is advisable to simply accept the default type unless there is a good reason to do otherwise. The password is also entered at this stage, and to avoid mistakes it has to be typed correctly into both text boxes in order to proceed to the next stage. Bear in mind that there is little chance of decrypting a file if you should manage to lose the password. The window

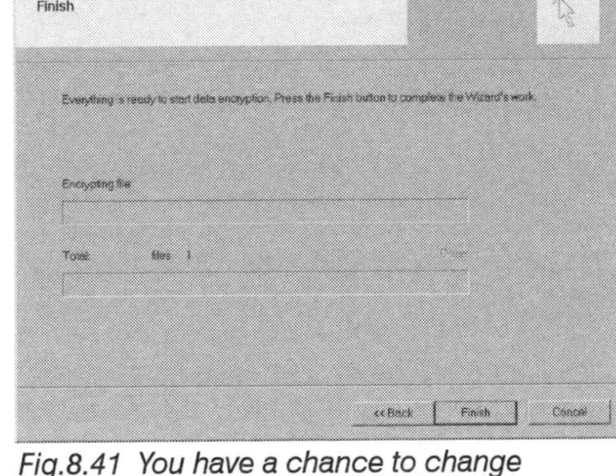

Fig.8.41 You have a chance to change your mind

of Figure 8.41 gives you a chance to change your mind before going ahead with the encryption process, and operating the Finish button completes the process (Figure 8.42). The encrypted file is then added to the list in the main program window (Figure 8.43).

In order to decrypt a file it is just a matter of left-clicking its entry in the list, selecting Decrypt from the pop-up menu, and then adding the correct password into the window that appears (Figure 8.44). Operate the OK button and the file will be decrypted. The file's entry in the list will then change to show that it is no longer encrypted.

To hide a file the Wizard button is operated and the top radio button is selected when the wizard appears (Figure 8.45). At the next window (Figure 8.46) you select the type of object to be hidden, which can be a file, folder, disc, or a group of files. For this example the file option was selected, and two files in a folder were selected and hidden.

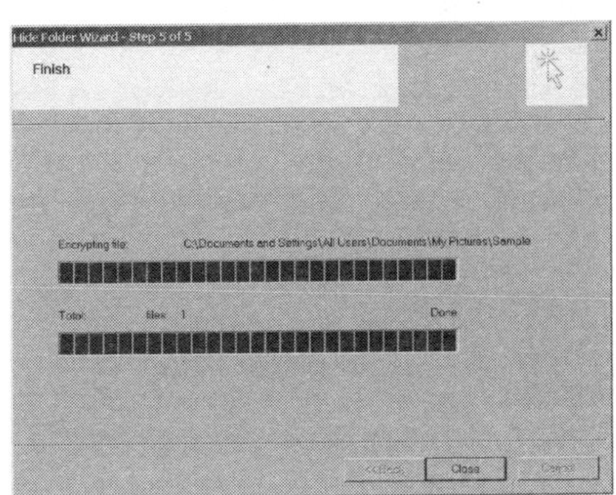

Fig.8.42 The file has been encrypted

Figures 8.47 and 8.48 show "before" and "after" versions of the folder when viewed using Windows Explorer, and the two hidden files have disappeared from view in Figure 8.48. They are still present

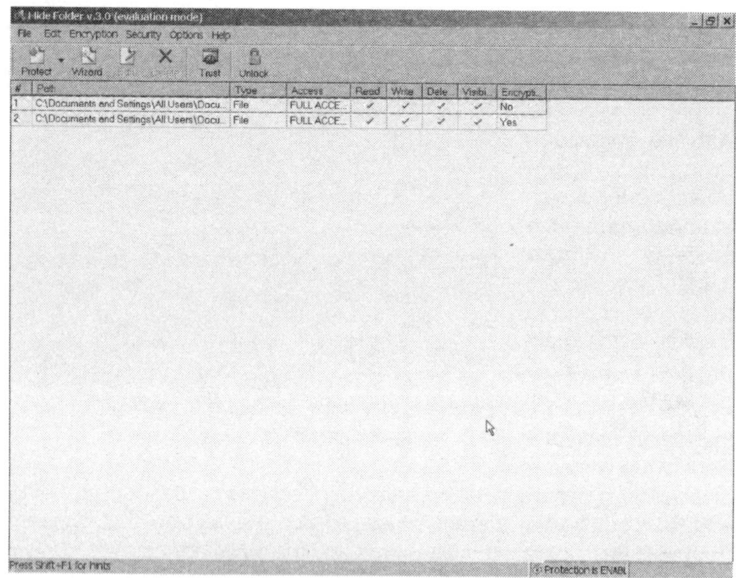

Fig.8.43 The encrypted file has been added to the list in the main program window

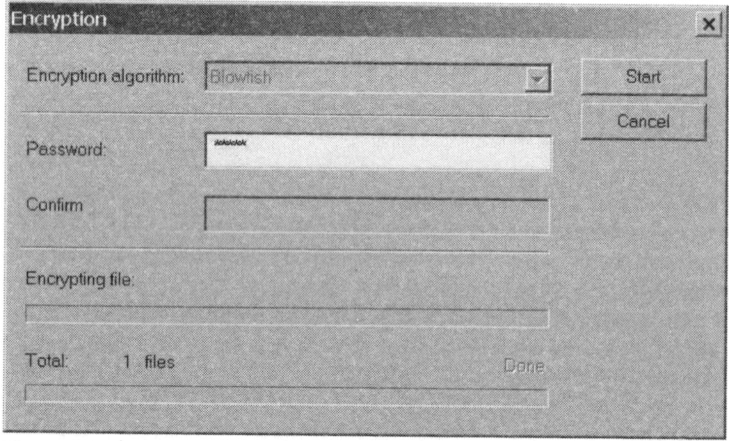

Fig.8.44 The file can not be decrypted without the correct password

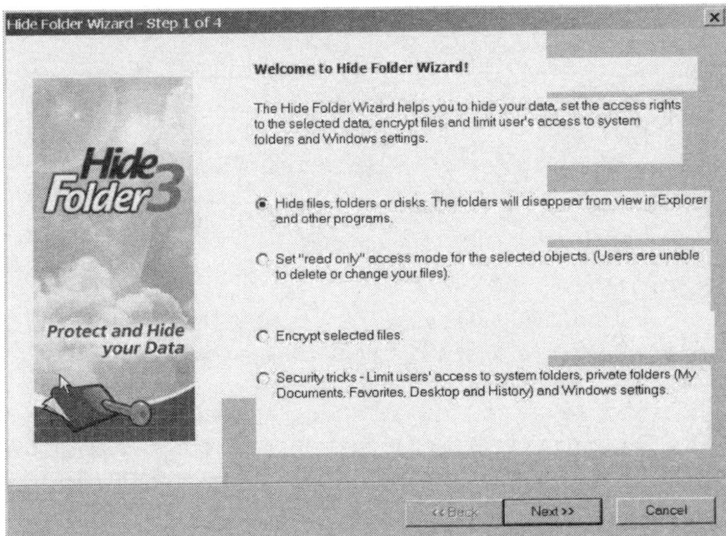

Fig.8.45 The first window of the wizard gives four options

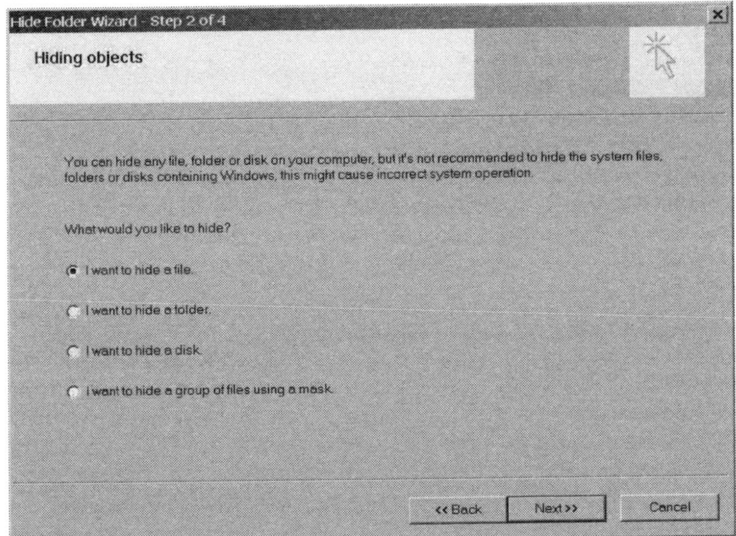

Fig.8.46 Select the type of object to be hidden

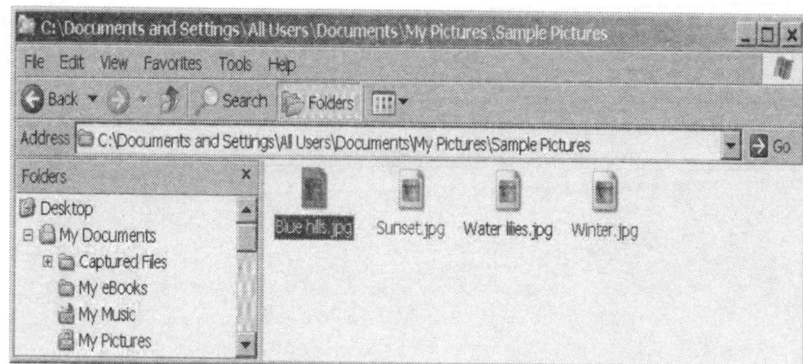

Fig.8.47 The "before" view shows all four image files

on the disc and have not been erased. In order to make a file visible again it is just a matter of going into Hide File 3.0, right-clicking the file's entry in the file list, and selecting Properties from the pop-up menu. This produces the window of Figure 8.49 where the Full Access radio button is selected. Operate the OK button to exit the window and the file will then become visible again.

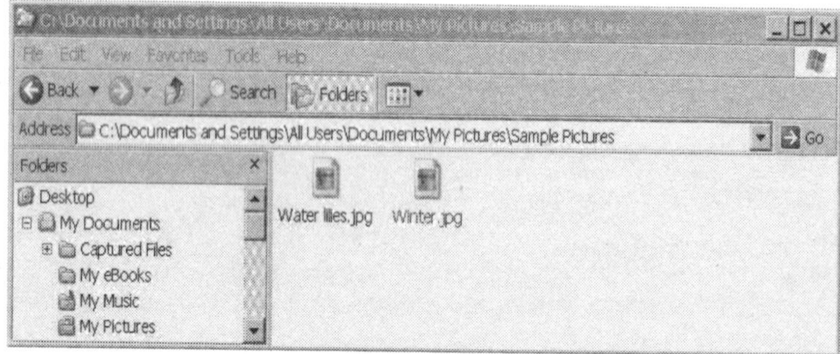

Fig.8.48 Two files have been successfully hidden, but they are still in the folder and intact

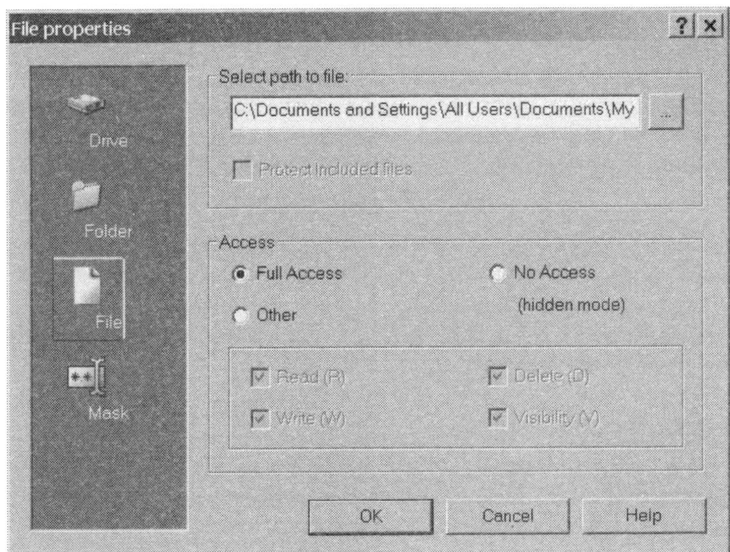

Fig.8.49 Operate the Full Access radio button to reveal the file

Points to remember

Prevention is better than cure. A good antivirus program can cost little or nothing and will immediately spot most viruses. New viruses are appearing all the time, so remember to keep the antivirus program up-to-date. The antivirus programs bundled with many PCs are fully operational, but mostly have update subscriptions that only last for a very limited period. The subscription must be extended in order to keep the program up to date and working well.

It is a good idea to scan discs, including Flash cards, when they are first installed in one of your computer's drives. Most antivirus programs can be set to scan a selected drive, and many will automatically scan any new disc that is introduced into the system.

Some antivirus suites include a set of bootable floppy discs or a bootable CD-ROM so that antivirus checks can be made on a PC that does not have antivirus software installed. Using this type of software, checks can be made on a PC even if it can not be booted into Windows. One drawback of this method is that the antivirus software will not be fully up-to-date.

Antivirus software usually scans for more than viruses, and other harmful files such as Trojans and spyware will usually be found. Things such as adware will not be detected though, as they are often installed legitimately. Programs such as Pest Patrol will scan for adware and the like, and will remove them if required.

Antivirus programs are of limited use against hackers. In order to keep hackers at bay it is essential to use either a software or hardware firewall. Ideally, both should be used if you have some form of broadband connection, especially if it is of the "always on" variety. Windows XP has a built-in firewall program, but there are third-party firewall programs that provide a greater degree of protection.

The Email system is not totally a secure, but it is possible to encrypt the contents and/or attachments to Emails using an encryption program. The recipient usually requires the same program in order to decrypt the files. Most of these programs can be used to encrypt files on your hard disc. Windows XP Professional and Vista have a built-in facility of this type, and password protection is also available in many file compression programs.

Many word processors have a built-in password protection facility. This can be used to prevent others from altering your documents, and can also be used to prevent others from viewing them. Ideal if you wish to keep a personal diary on a PC that will be used by others, for example.

9

Networking

Why network?

On the face of it, any form of network interface is not much use on a computer that will spend most of its working life out and about, and away from other computers. In the real world it is very unusual for a laptop PC that is used on the move to operate in total isolation from other computers. It will usually be necessary for a laptop to communicate with another PC, and other items of networked hardware, once it is back at base.

As explained in chapter 7, many laptop PCs are used away from base, but have data files that need to be synchronised with a desktop PC once back at base. A network connection can be used to provide a high-speed link between the two PCs, making it easy to synchronise files even where large data transfers are involved. A network makes it possible to share resources, enabling a laptop to share a broadband Internet connection and a printer for example. As will be explained later in this chapter, a wireless network adaptor enables a laptop computer to connect to the Internet via the so-called "wireless hotspots" that are found dotted around most towns and cities.

There is insufficient space available here to provide more than some basic details about networking. It should be sufficient to get you started though. BP549, Easy PC Wi-Fi Networking, from the same publisher and author as this book, provides a more in-depth coverage of the subject.

Basic network

With all the PCs in the system equipped with Ethernet ports it is time to design and build the network. The most basic network barely justifies the "network" description, and it just consists of one PC connected direct to the other via their Ethernet ports (Figure 9.1). It is important to realise that Ethernet ports are not primarily designed for this method of connection, and this setup will not work if a normal network cable is used. The cable required when linking two PCs is usually called

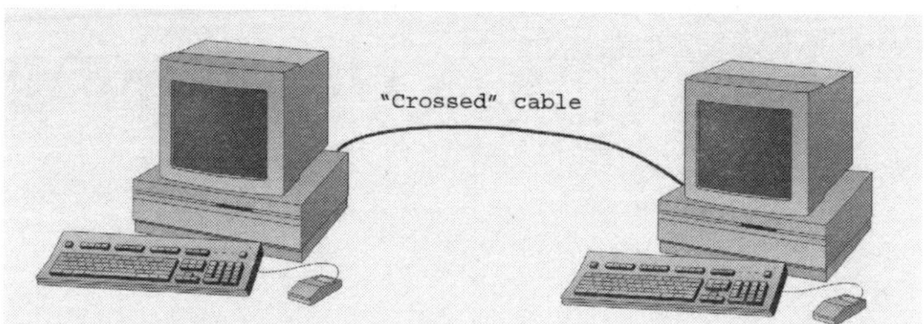

Fig.9.1 The most basic form of network consists of just two PCs and a "crossed" cable

something like a "crossed" or "crossed-over" cable. A normal network lead is usually described as a "straight" cable.

The setup shown in Figure 9.2 is essentially the same as the one of Figure 9.1, and it provides a link between the two PCs. The PCs are linked via a networking router, and the two cables are of the "straight" variety. In the arrangement of Figure 9.1 the crossed-over connections in the cable makes each PC "look" like a router to the other PC. This avoids the expense of the router and it is probably the better method if it will never be necessary to introduce other computers into the system.

A big advantage of using a router is that it will typically have four or more Ethernet sockets, making it easy to add further PCs into the network. Figure 9.3 shows a network having four PCs, and the setup of Figure 9.2 is easily expanded into this configuration. It could probably use the

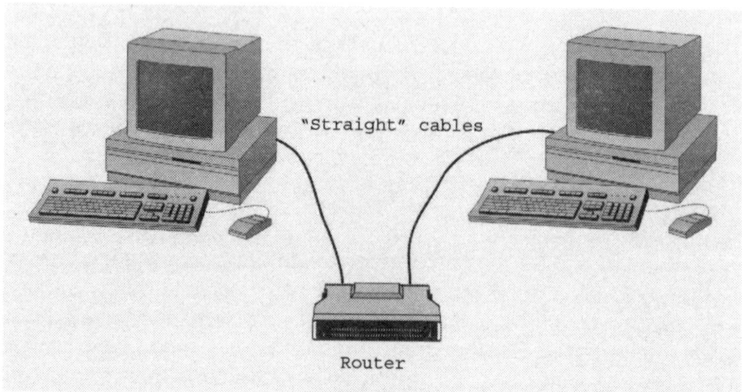

Fig.9.2 A basic network using a router

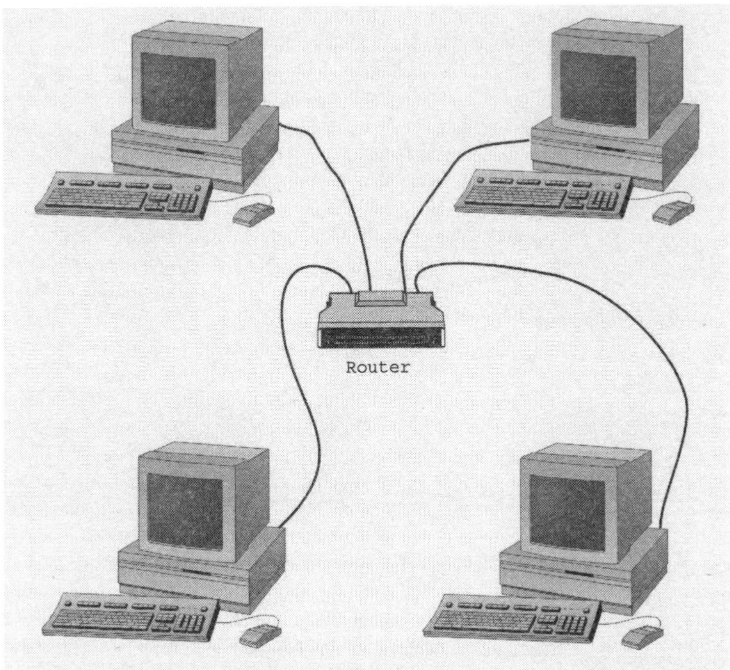

Fig.9.3 More PCs are easily added to the basic network. A router can usually handle at least four PCs

original router, since these mostly have four or more Ethernet sockets. Therefore, the only additional hardware required would be two cables, plus the two extra PCs of course. Networks can become quite involved, but for a home or small business network it should not be necessary to use anything more than a single router to bind the system together.

Network Setup Wizard

Setting up a normal network is largely automatic when using Windows Vista. The easy way to set up networking on PCs running Windows XP is to run the Network Setup Wizard. This is buried quite deep in the menu structure, but it can be accessed by going to the Start menu and then selecting Programs, Accessories, Communications, and Network Setup Wizard (Figure 9.4). The Windows XP and ME versions are slightly different in points of detail, but they are very similar. The Windows XP version is used as the basis of this example.

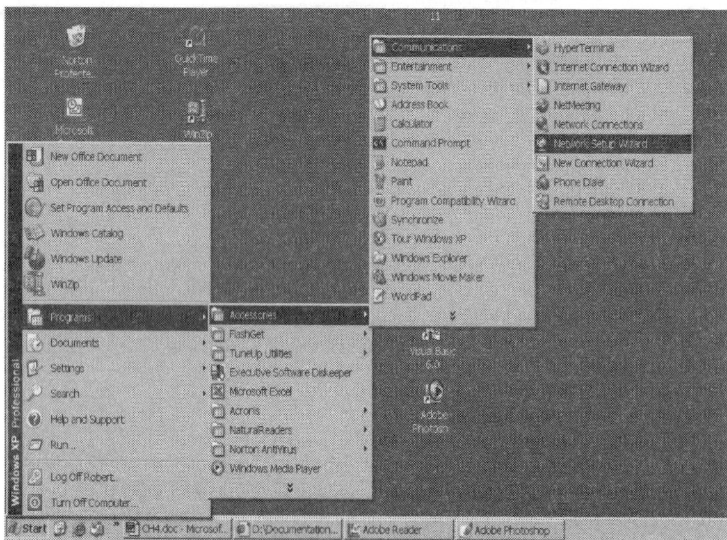

Fig.9.4 The Network Setup Wizard is deep in the menu structure

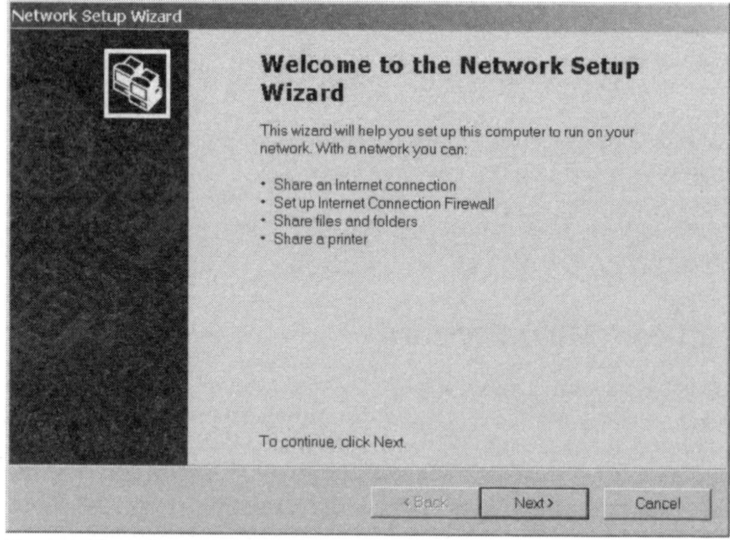

Fig.9.5 The wizard starts with the usual Welcome page

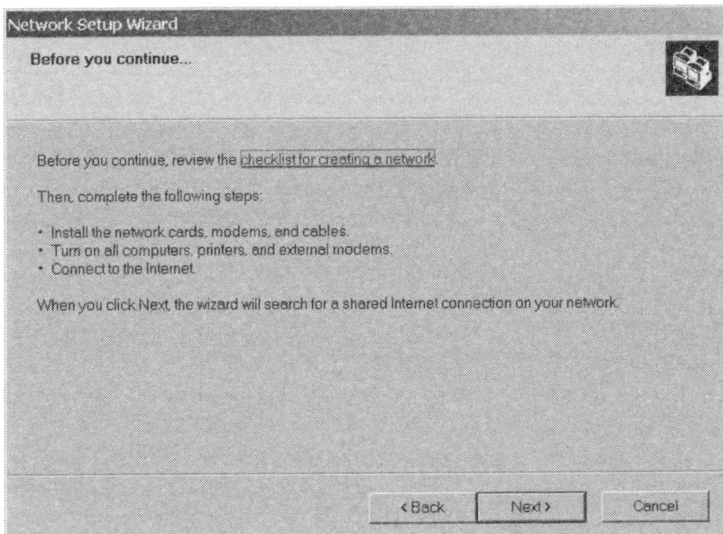

Fig.9.6 This page provides easy access to the relevant parts of the Help system

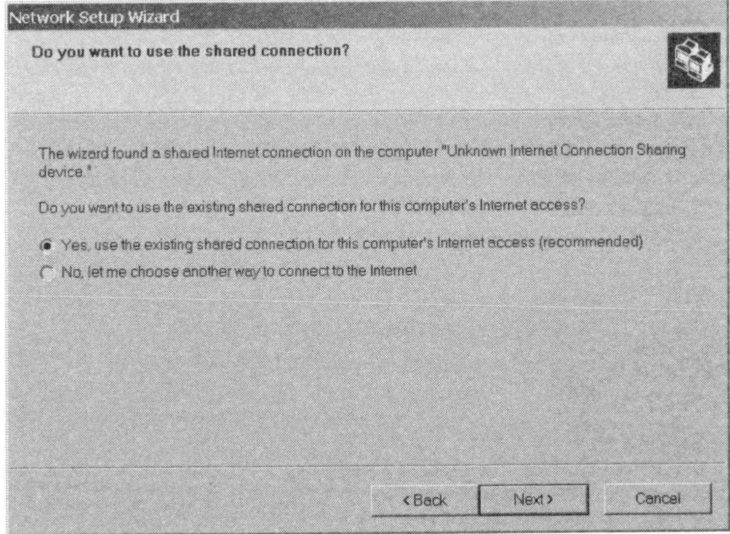

Fig.9.7 The wizard has detected a shared Internet connection

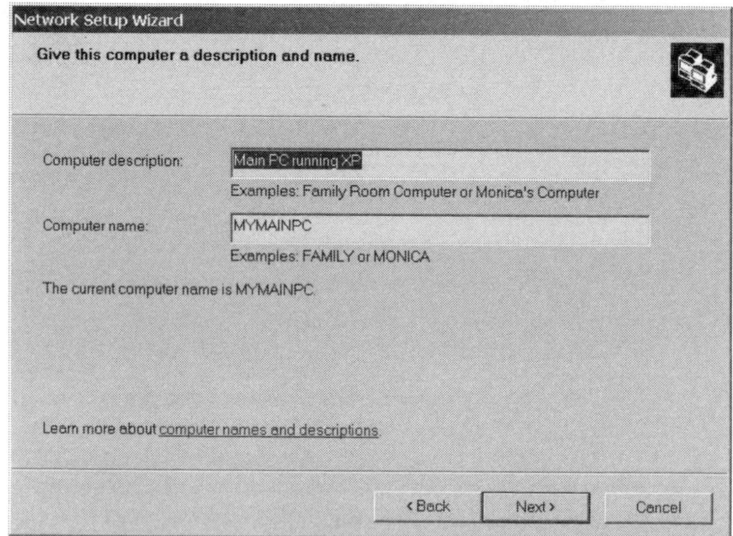

Fig.9.8 Use this page to name the computer and provide a brief description

The initial page (Figure 9.5) simply gives a brief explanation of what the Network Setup Wizard will do. The next page (Figure 9.6) provides an opportunity to obtain background information from the Help system. It also explains that everything in the network must be fully installed, connected together, switched on, and ready to use. The wizard will not help with such things as setting up an Internet connection or installing device drivers for Ethernet or wi-fi cards. It just sets up the network once installation has been completed.

On the next page (Figure 9.7) the setup process starts, and the wizard has detected a shared Internet connection. This is actually provided by a combined access point, router, and ADSL modem. A different Internet connection can be selected or the existing one can be used. In this case there is no alternative available, and the existing Internet connection has to be used. On the following page (Figure 9.8) the computer is given the name that will be used for it on the network, and a brief description can also be added here.

The network (workgroup) name is provided at the next page (Figure 9.9), or you can simply settle for the default name (MSHOME). This completes the setting up process, and a page that shows the selected

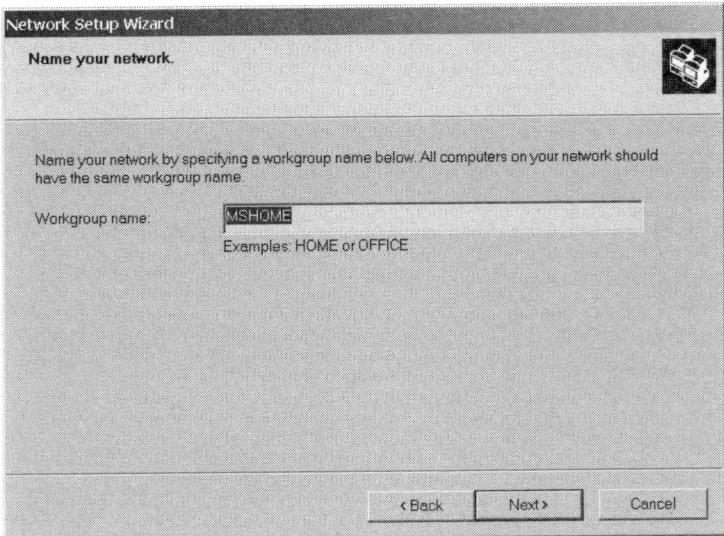

Fig.9.9 Here the name for the workgroup is entered in the textbox

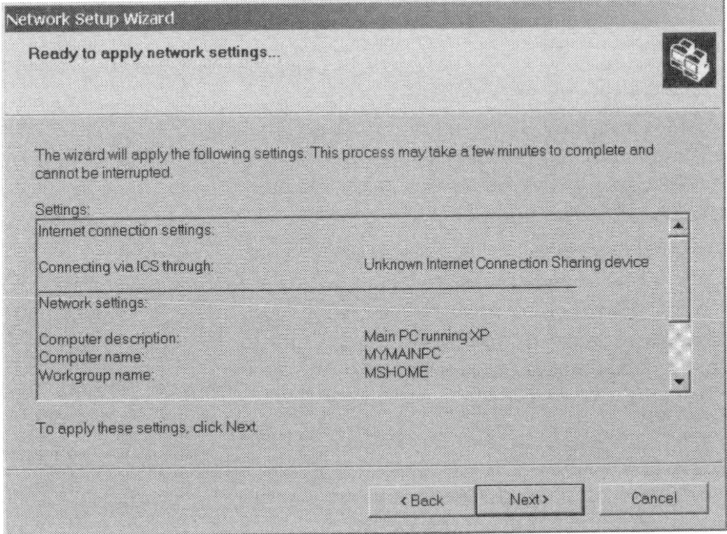

Fig.9.10 This window enables the selected settings to be reviewed

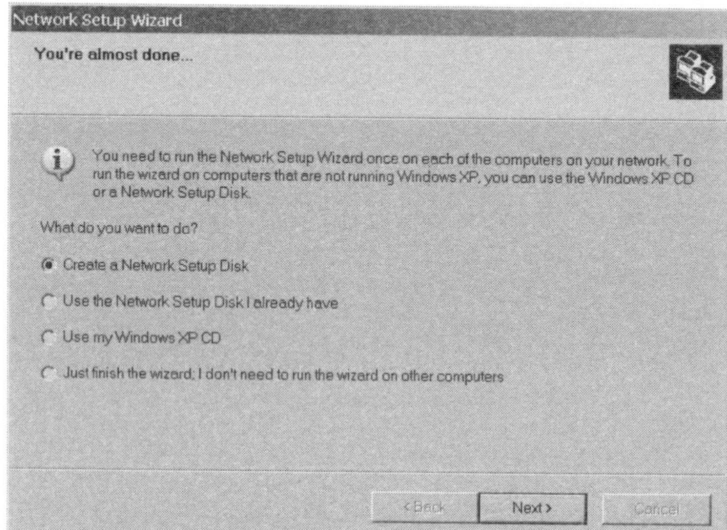

Fig.9.11 There are various options for setting up the network on the other PCs in the system

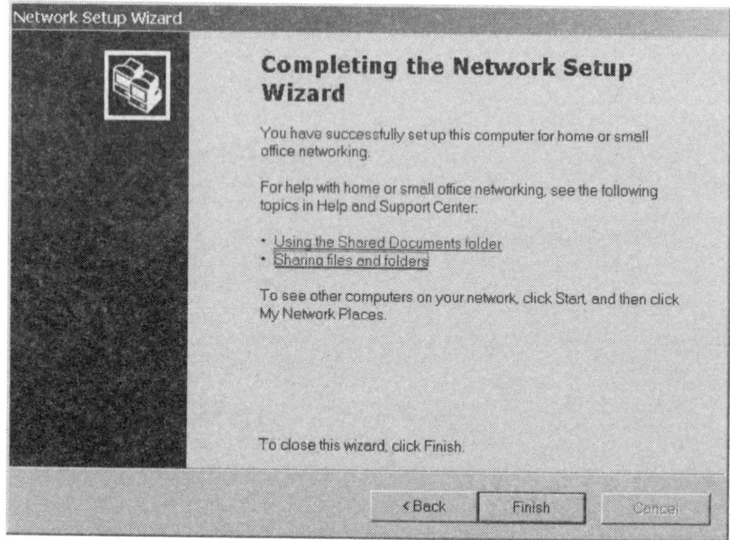

Fig.9.12 The wizard confirms that the process has been completed

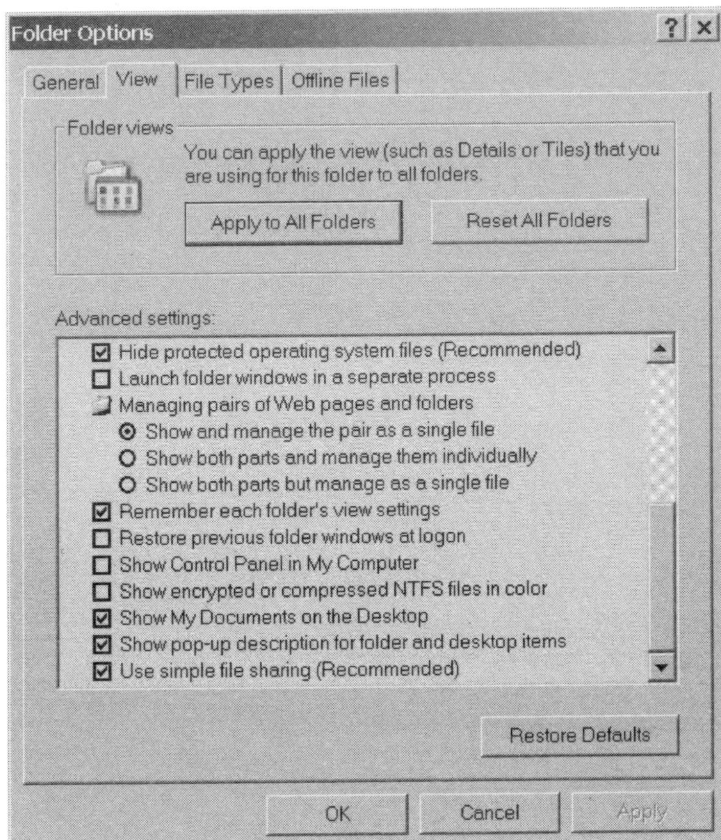

Fig.9.13 The "Use Simple File Sharing" option is suitable for most users

settings is displayed (Figure 9.10) when the Next button is operated. Windows then does some reconfiguring of itself before displaying the page shown in Figure 9.11. This gives various options for setting up networking on the other PCs in the system. You can simply exit the wizard if the other PCs in the network are running Windows ME and/or XP, and then run the Network Setup Wizard in the usual way on those PCs. Finally, the page shown in Figure 9.12 confirms that the process has been completed.

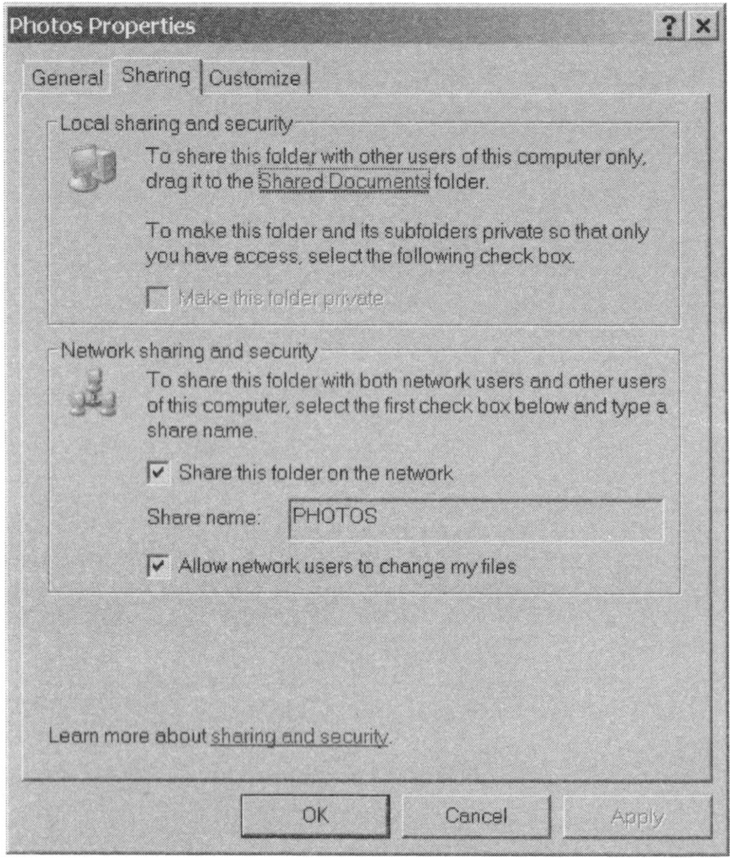

Fig.9.14 Use this window to enable sharing of a folder

Sharing folders

A network is only worthwhile if some resources are shared, but it is not essential to have shared resources on every computer in the network. In order to share the resources of a computer it is necessary to have the appropriate type of sharing enabled. Windows XP Home has a new system of file sharing called "simple file sharing", and this is the default setting for Windows XP Professional. Simple file sharing can be turned off in Windows XP Professional by double-clicking the My Computer

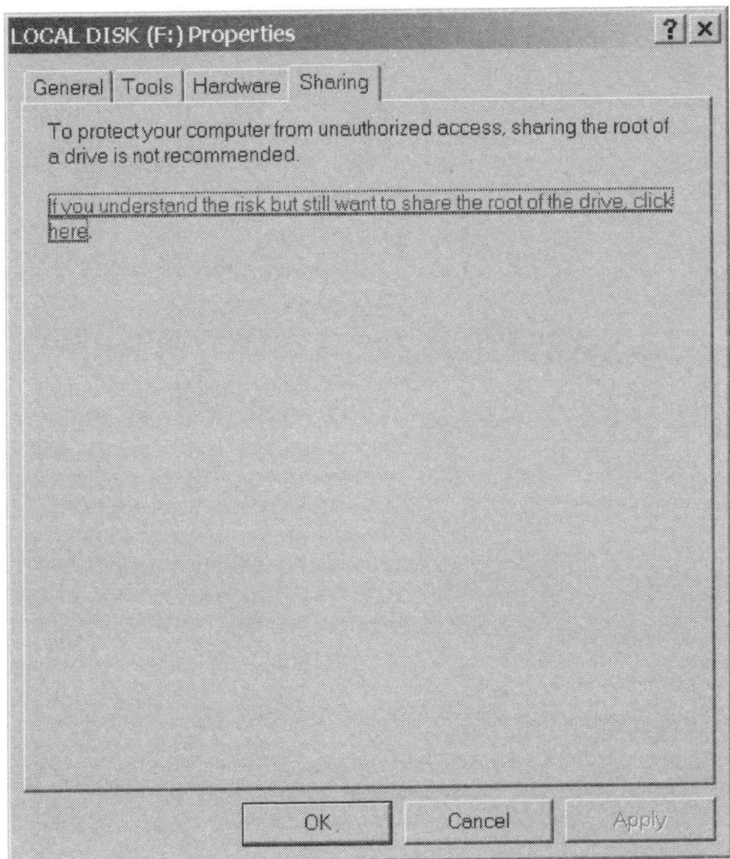

Fig.9.15 This warning message appears if you try to share a disc

icon on the desktop, and the selecting Folder Options from the Tools menu. Left-click the View tab and then scroll down the list in the main part of the window until you find the entry that reads "Use simple file sharing (Recommended)" (Figure 9.13). Remove the tick from its checkbox and then operate the Apply and OK buttons. For most purposes the default setting will suffice, and it is assumed here that the simple file sharing method is used.

In order to share a folder, first locate it using Windows Explorer, and then right-click on its entry. From the pop-up menu select Properties, and

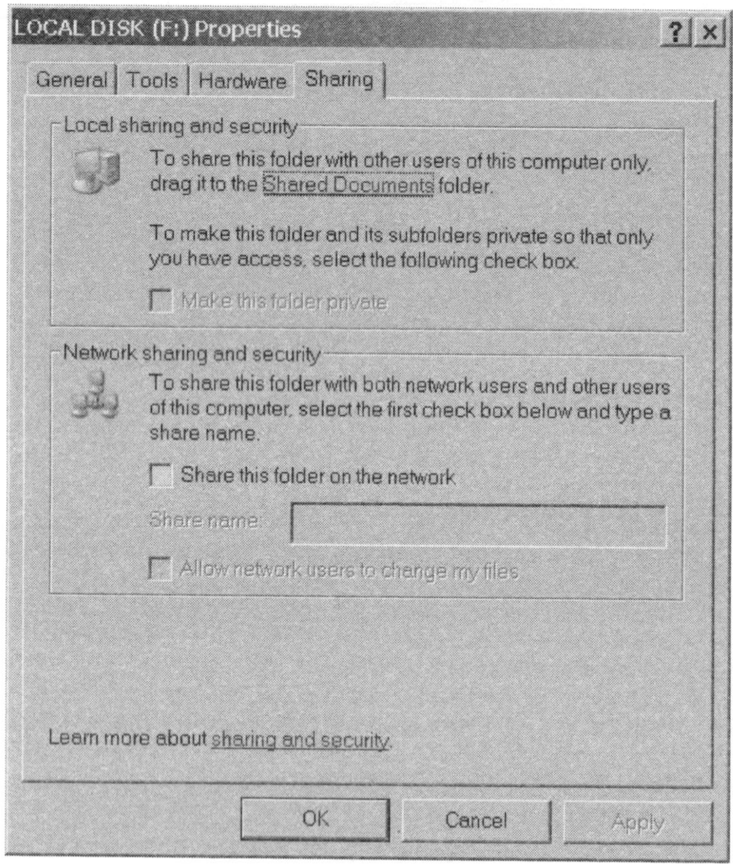

Fig.9.16 A disc can be shared if you are prepared to take the risks

then operate the Sharing tab in the properties window (Figure 9.14). Place a tick in the "Share this folder on the network" checkbox in order to make the folder available to the network. By default, the contents of the folder can be read via the network, but they can not be altered. Full access to the folder can be provided by ticking the "Allow network users to change my files" checkbox. The folder can be shared under its normal name, or a different name can be typed into the Shared name textbox. Operate the Apply and OK buttons to exit the window and make the changes take effect.

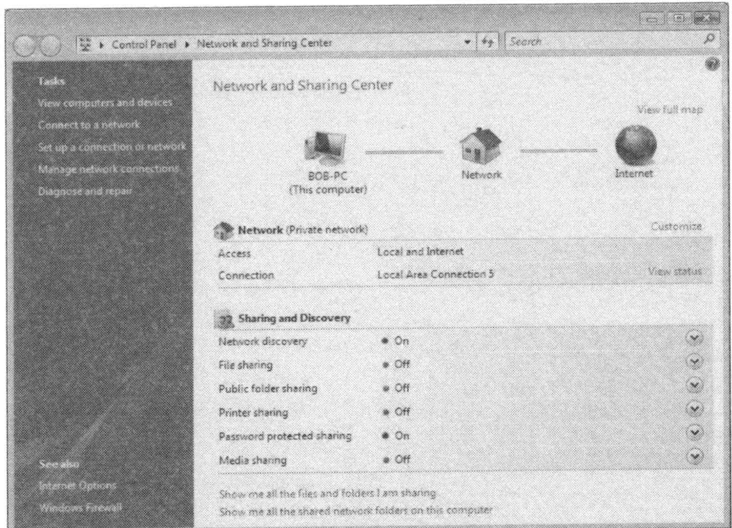

Fig.9.17 This window controls file and folder sharing over a network

Essentially the same method is used to share a complete disc. However, on entering the Sharing section of the disc's Properties window you obtain a warning message (Figure 9.15). If you wish to continue anyway, left-click the link text and the properties window will then change to the normal sharing type. It can then be shared in the same way as a folder (Figure 9.16), but in most circumstances this method of sharing is definitely not a good idea.

Sharing operates in a different fashion with Windows Vista. The normal file sharing window only permits sharing with specified users that have an account and password on that PC. Operating the "Network and Sharing Center" link produces the window of Figure 9.17, where file and folder sharing over a network can be enabled.

Network Places

Having shared a disc or folder, the shared resource can then be added to the Network Places of any PC that will need to access it. In Windows XP start by double-clicking the My Network Places icon on the desktop or select the My Network Places entry in the Start menu. The PC used for this example already has a couple of network places added (Figure 9.18), but when starting "from scratch" the right-hand section of the My

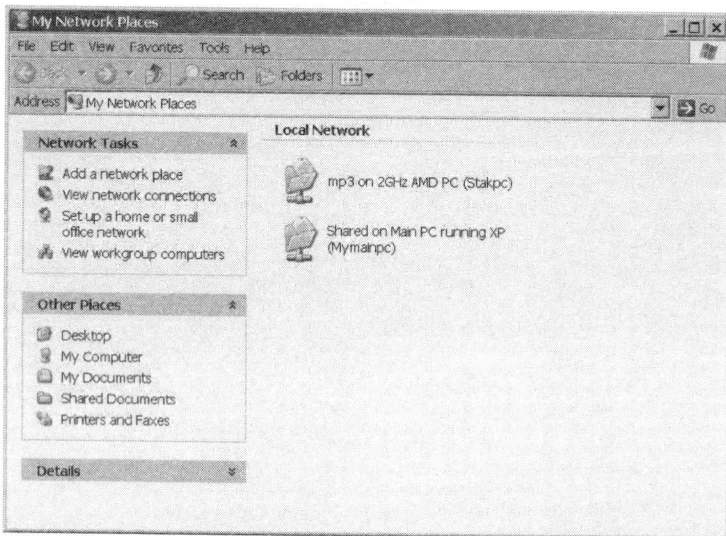

Fig.9.18 The Network Places window

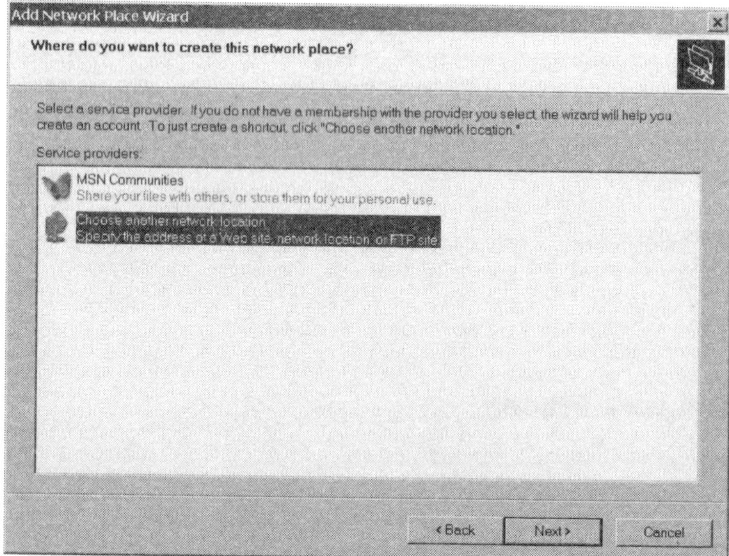

Fig.9.19 Windows is unlikely to find the location you require

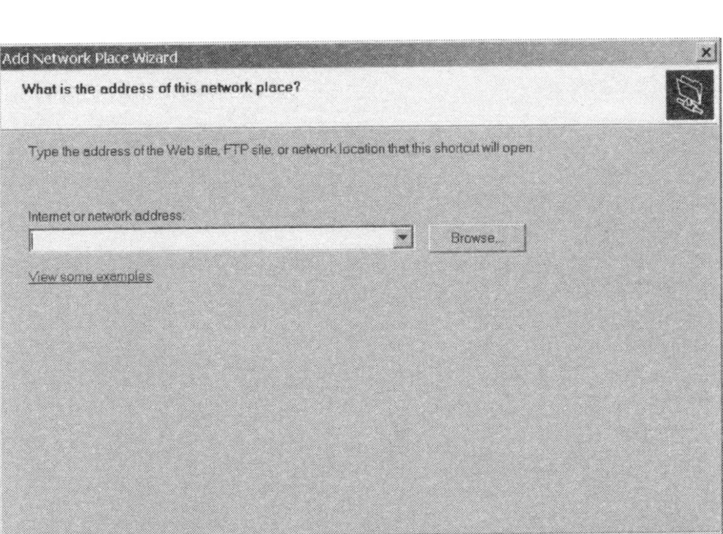

Fig.9.20 Use the Browse button to search for the location you require

Network Places window will be blank. Left-click "Add a network place" in the upper left-hand section of the window, which will launch a new window. This is just a Welcome screen, so operate the Next button to move on to the window of Figure 9.19.

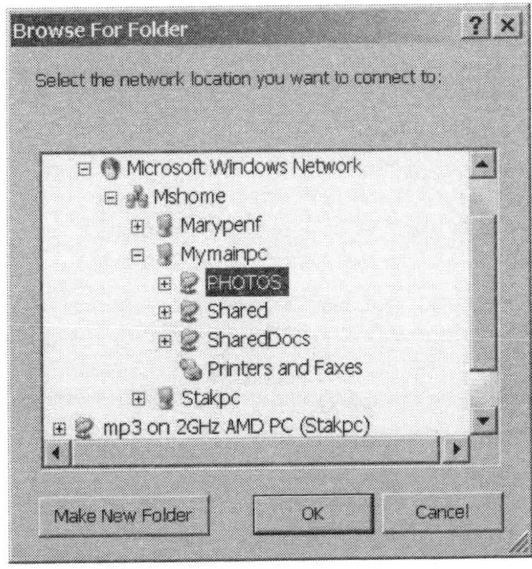

Fig.9.21 The required folder has been found

Windows will search for new network places, but it will not find very much. Consequently, you

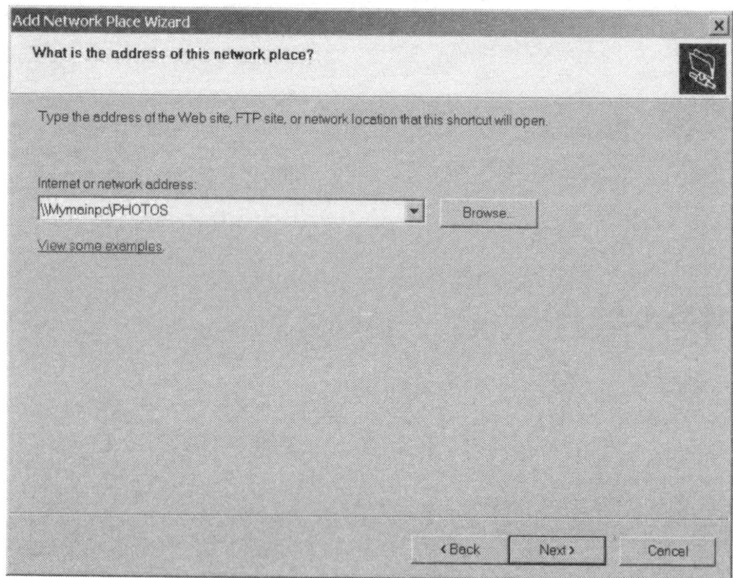

Fig.9.22 The correct folder has been selected

have to choose the option that lets you specify a network location. This moves things on to the window of Figure 9.20, where it is advisable to operate the Browse button and then use the file browser to search for the new network place. The browser provides access to all available parts of the network, and the required PHOTOS folder on Mymainpc was easily located (Figure 9.21). Having selected the correct folder, operate the OK button and the network address will be added to the textbox in the main window (Figure 9.22).

A name for the new network place can be added in the textbox at the next window (Figure 9.23), or you can settle for the suggested default name. The next window (Figure 9.24) simply informs you that the task has been completed. Tick the checkbox if you wish to open the newly added folder in Windows Explorer when the Finish button is operated.

The new network place can be easily accessed using Windows Explorer or the standard Windows file browser built into most applications programs. As one would expect, it will be found in the My Network Places folder, together with any other network places that are installed. In Figure 9.25 the PHOTOS folder has been located in the file browser of

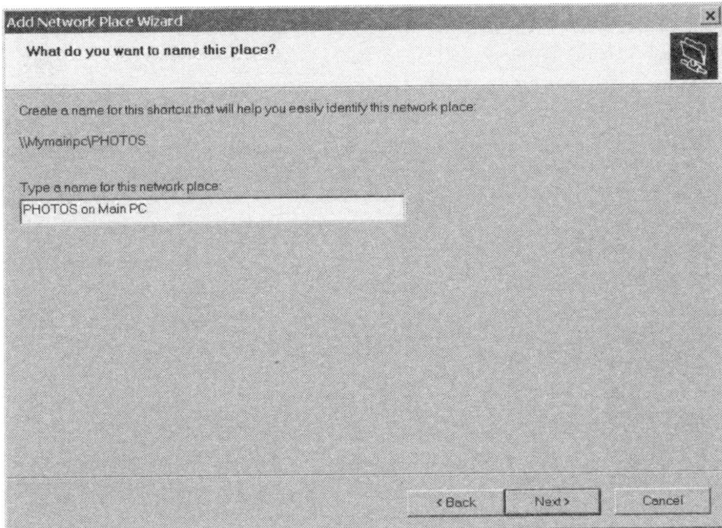

Fig.9.23 A name for the network place can be provided here

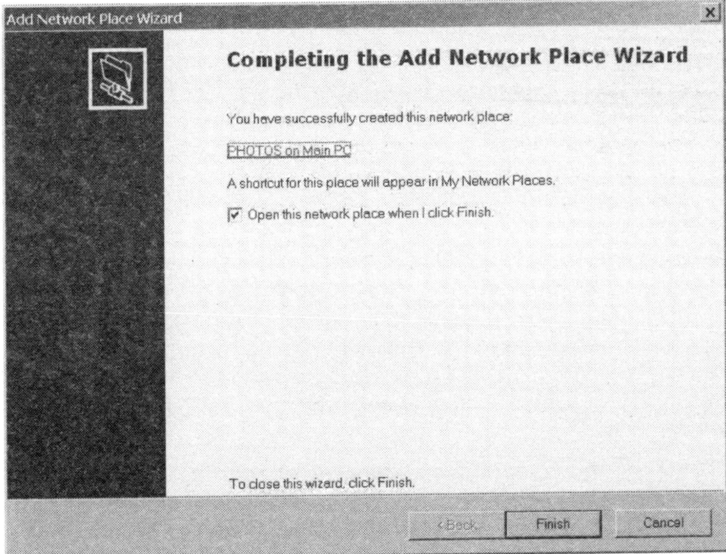

Fig.9.24 This window confirms that the process has been completed

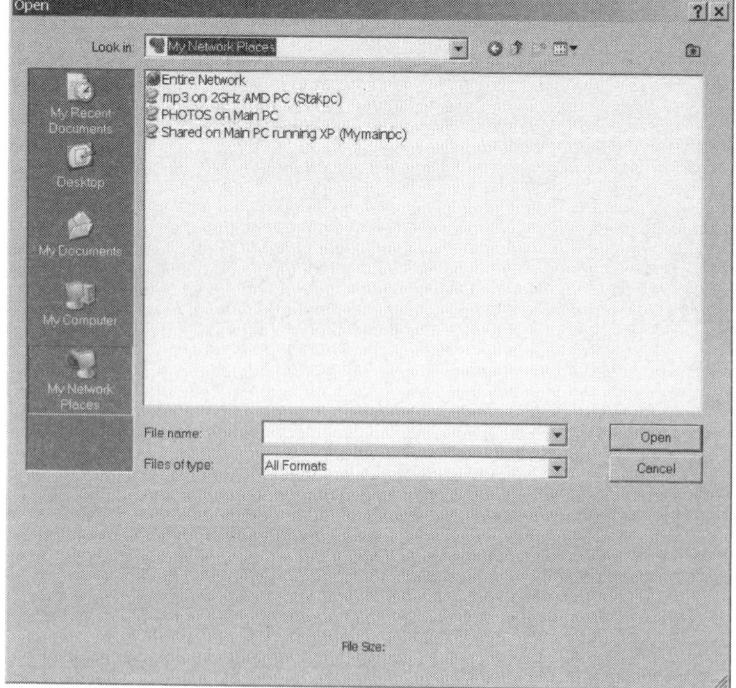

Fig.9.25 The shared folder is available in file browsers

Photoshop CS. It can be opened in the usual way, and then a file can be loaded.

Note that it will only be possible to read files unless you opted to permit changes to files when setting the sharing options for the folder. If changes are permitted, it is then possible to change files in an applications program and save the changes in the usual way. Where permission to alter files has not been given, it is still possible to load and edit them. The edited files must be saved to another folder though, so that the original files are left untouched.

Things are much more straightforward when using Windows Vista. Selecting Network from the Start menu produces the window of Figure 9.26, which has icons for the main items of hardware in the network. Doulble-clicking an icon shows the resources that are available on that hardware, including any shared files or folders (Figure 9.27). In file

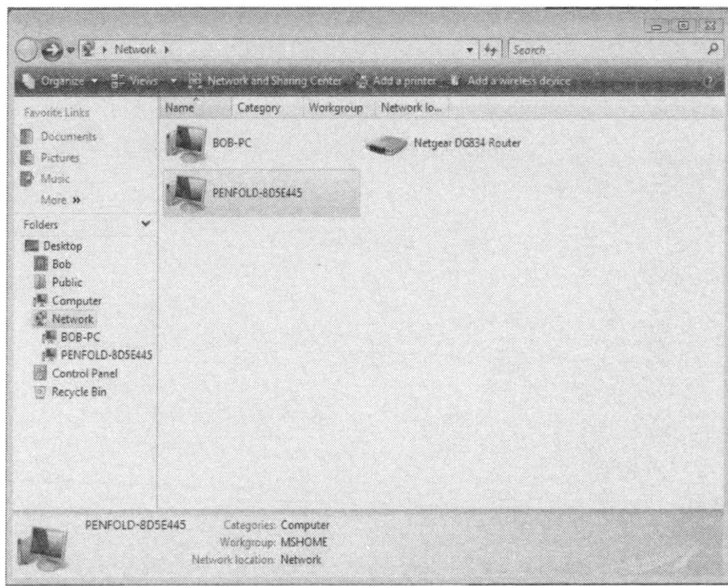

Fig.9.26 The Network window of Windows Vista

browsers the network is accessed, as one would probably expect, via the Network entry.

Why wi-fi?

Although wireless networking technology has been in existence for some time, it has only gained widespread acceptance quite recently. This rise in popularity has no doubt been triggered by the substantial reductions in the prices of wireless networking equipment, or wi-fi equipment as it has become known. Some generic wi-fi adapters can now be purchased for just a few pounds. Many laptop PCs have wi-fi as standard, or as an inexpensive option. This makes wi-fi systems a practical proposition for home and small business users.

Although wireless networking is now reasonably inexpensive, it is still likely to cost somewhat more than an equivalent wired network. Is it worth the extra outlay? The obvious advantage is that it avoids the need to install any wiring. For many users this is really the only advantage of the wi-fi approach, but for most it is a major plus point. A short lead from a computer to a router or other piece of networking equipment is not

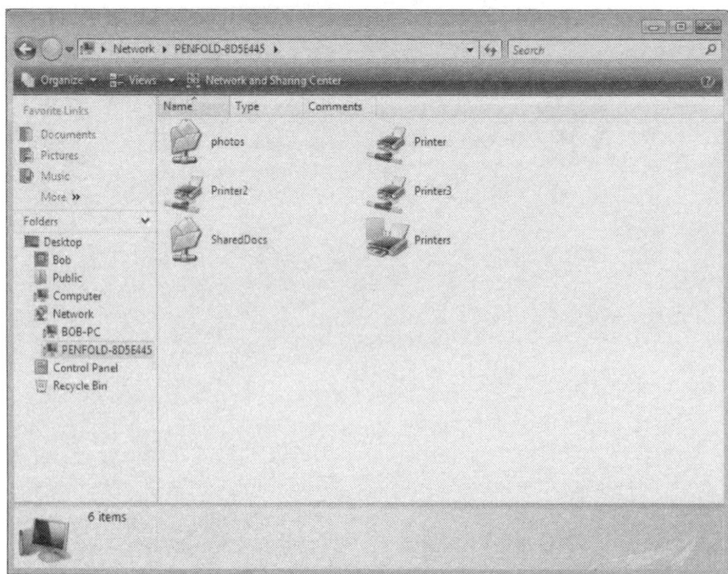

Fig.9.27 The available resources are listed

difficult to implement, particularly if the two pieces of equipment are in the same room. No do-it-yourself skills are likely to be required.

The wired approach is convenient enough where two desktop PCs will be used more or less side-by-side, since the connecting cable can be installed and then left largely forgotten. The situation is different with a desktop PC and a laptop type, where the laptop will often be disconnected and used elsewhere. Over a period of time this inevitable involves a fair amount of plugging in and unplugging, which is not very convenient. It can also result in wear to the Ethernet socket on the laptop PC, which might eventually fail.

All this is avoided by using a wi-fi link. There is no need for any direct connection between the laptop and the rest of the network. You simply place the laptop anywhere in the vicinity of the base unit, switch it on, wait for the connection to be established, and then swap files with other computers in the system, use the network's printer, use the shared broadband Internet connection, or whatever. Wi-fi equipment provides a good operating range, so it is not even necessary for the laptop PC to be in the same room as the other equipment.

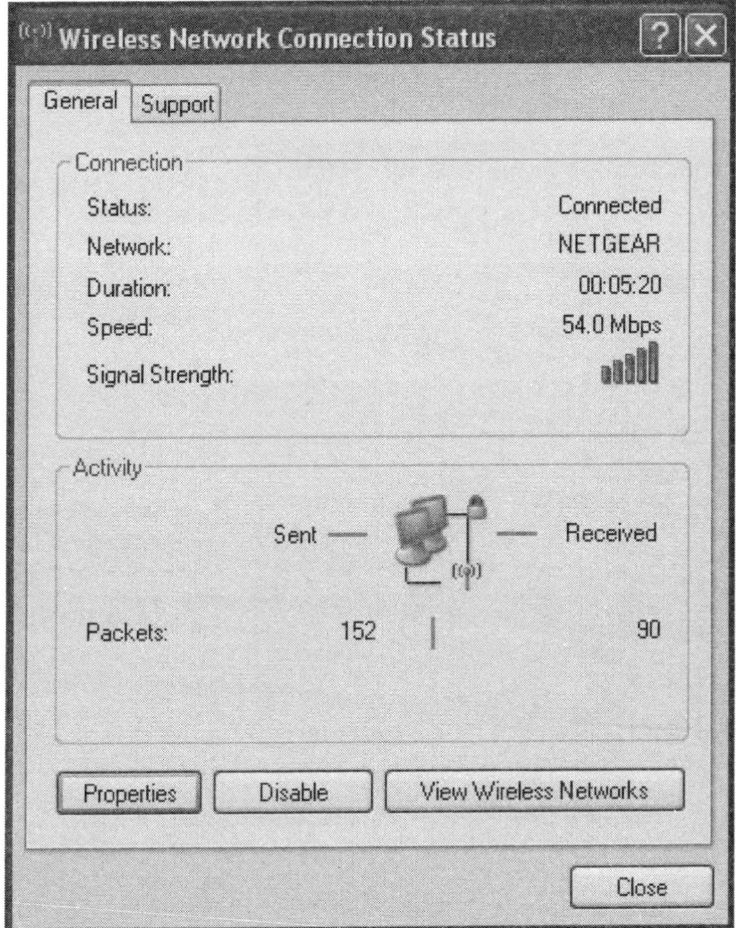

Fig.9.28 The General section of the Connection Status window

Hotspots

It is often possible to access the Internet while on the move using what are called "wireless hotspots". These offer Internet access in numerous locations around the world, with many towns and cities in the UK now having large numbers of these hotspots. A wireless hotspot is a wireless access point that connects to some form of Internet service. This will typically be a high-speed ADSL broadband connection, but it could be some other type of broadband service. It should certainly be something much faster than an ordinary dialup connection, but bear in mind that you might have to share the service with other users, which could noticeably slow things down.

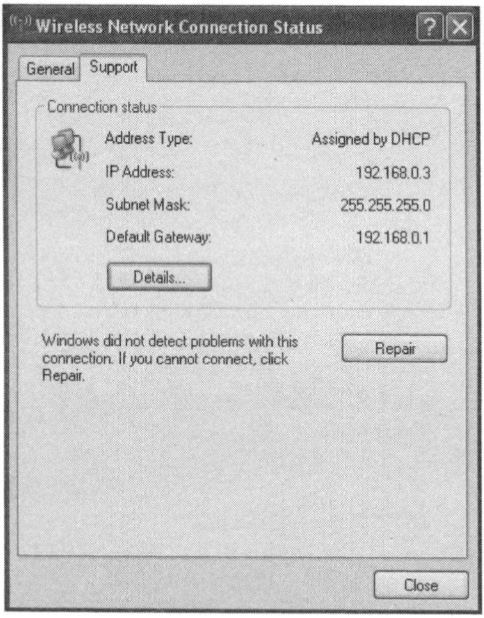

Fig.9.29 *The Support section of the Connection Status window*

The idea is to have hotspots in restaurants, cafes, motorway service stations, hotels, trains, airports, or anywhere convenient for potential users. As one would expect, these services are not usually free, and the hourly connection rates are quite high. Even so, this method can be cost-effective for those requiring Internet access on the move. The speed of the connection is also likely to be much faster than the alternatives, which are unlikely to be significantly cheaper. Some hotspots are provided free of charge, so you might get lucky from time to time and obtain free Internet access.

Hardware

A wi-fi adapter is now offered as an optional extra or even as standard with some laptop PCs. It is advisable to buy a laptop that has a built-in wi-fi adaptor if there is any likelihood that you will ever need this facility. It is something that can be added to any modern laptop via a USB 2.0 port, or via a PCMCIA slot if the laptop is suitably equipped. A built-in wi-fi adaptor is generally more convenient in use though.

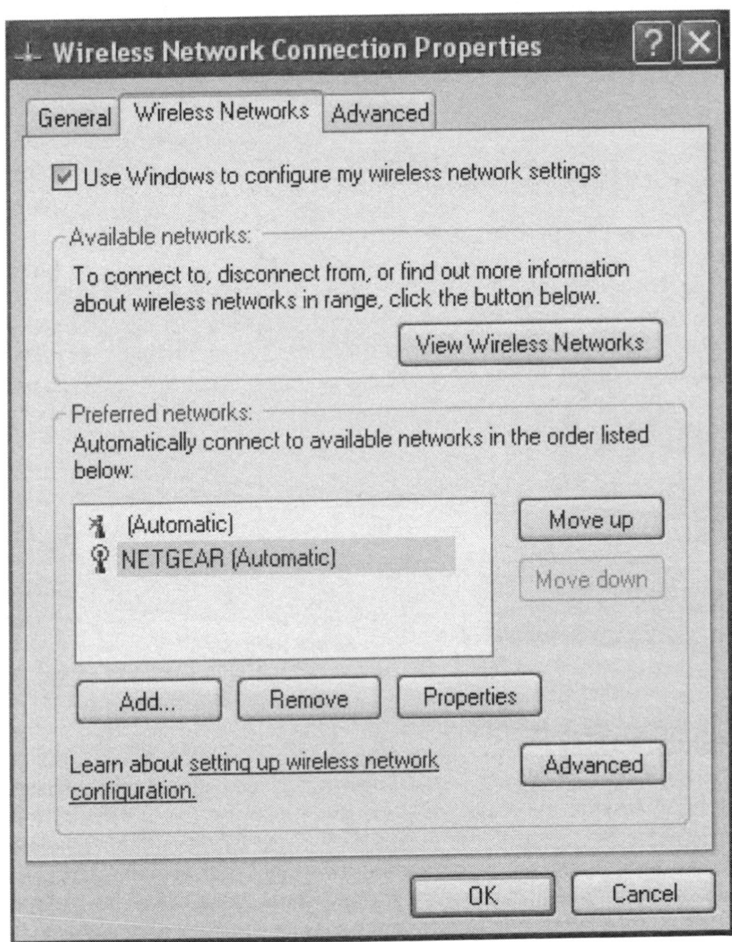

Fig.9.30 The Wireless Network section

At the other end of the wi-fi link the setup is virtually the same as a standard wired network, but the router must be one that also has a wi-fi facility. It is possible to have a network that only uses wi-fi connections, but the more normal approach is to have the router situated close to one PC, and connected to that PC via a cable. There is probably little to be gained by using a wi-fi link for any PC that is close to the router. A wired link will provide a more reliable connection and faster transfer speeds.

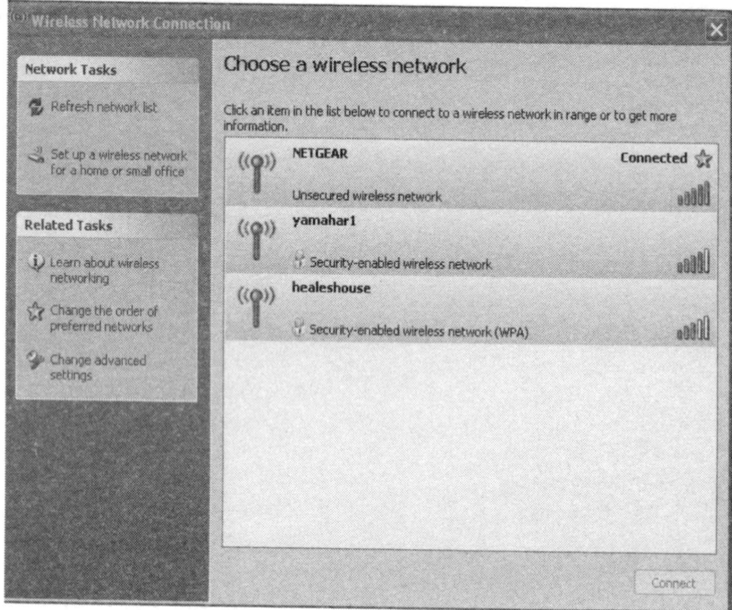

Fig.9.31 A list of the available networks can be provided

Getting connected

The method used to get a wi-fi enabled laptop connected to the network depends on the particular software and hardware that is installed. A window might pop-up automatically, or it could be necessary to launch the software manually. Typically there will be a button in the Windows desktop tray, which is at the left end of the bar along the bottom of the screen. In some cases there will actually be two buttons associated with the wi-fi adaptor, but in this example there is just the one, and operating it produces the window of Figure 9.28.

This window shows the connection status, and this instance the operating system has found a wi-fi network and connected to it. The signal strength meter shows that a strong signal has been obtained. Operating the Support tab produces some basic technical information about the network connection (Figure 9.29), and there is a Repair button that can be useful when the connection with the network is lost. This can happen from time to time with both wired and wi-fi network links.

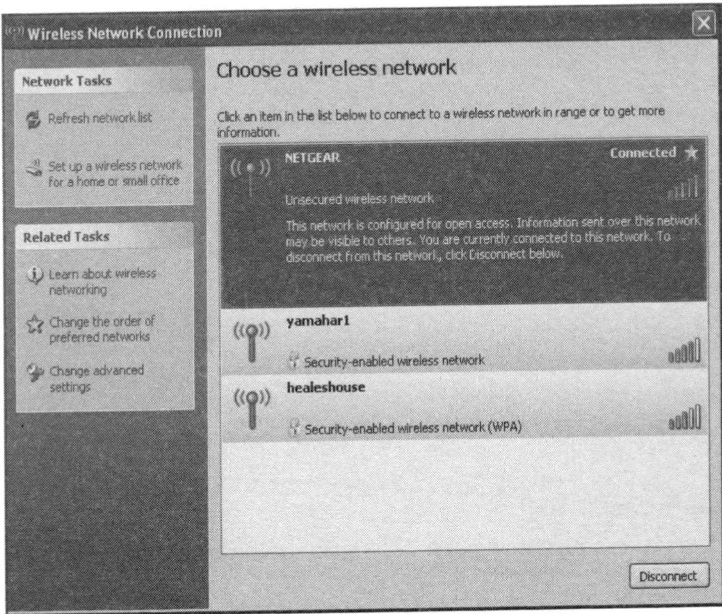

Fig.9.32 Further information can be provided for a network

The wi-fi adaptor in this example has already been set up for use, and it has therefore latched onto appropriate wi-fi base station. You will normally have to undertake this setting up process yourself unless the laptop comes complete with some form of onsite installation package. In this case the first step is to go to the General section of the status window (Figure 9.28) and operate the Properties button.

In the Wireless Networks section (Figure 9.30) there is a list of wireless networks, and the operating system will try to connect to these at boot-up. It tries to connect to the first one in the list, then the next one if that is unsuccessful, and so on until it manages to make a connection or there are no more networks listed. You therefore have the network that will be used most often listed first, the next most important listed second, and so on. Of course, in many cases only one wireless network will be used, and it is then the only network that has to be included in the list.

A list of the available networks (Figure 9.31) can be obtained by operating the View Wireless Networks button. More details of a network can be obtained by left-clicking its entry (Figure 9.32). A connection can be

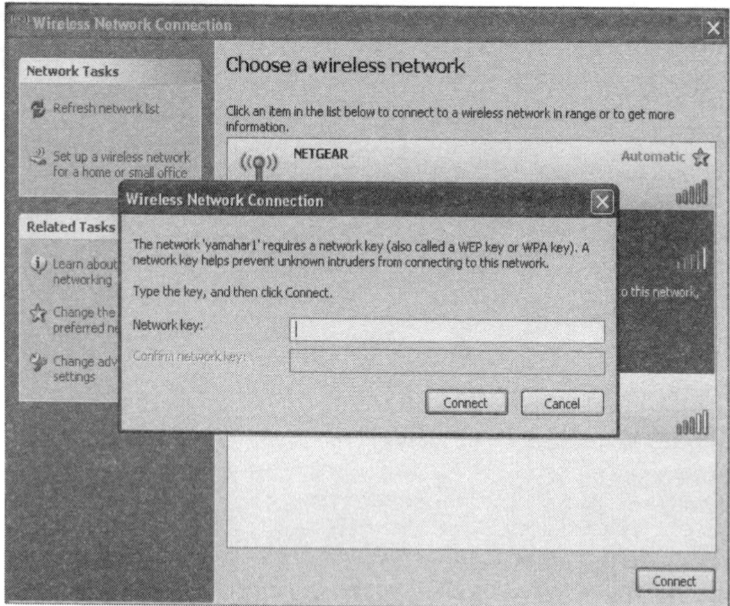

Fig.9.33 A key or password is needed in order to access most networks

made to a network by double-clicking its entry, or by selecting it and operating the Connect button. This will automatically add the network to the network list. The network being used in this example has not been fully set up, and it is open to anyone with a wi-fi equipped PC that is in range. Wi-fi networks are normally protected by encryption and password protection. You will be asked to supply the password on attempting to make a connection (Figure 9.33).

WEP

The original and most basic form of wi-fi security is called Wired Equivalent Privacy, or WEP. This has been used with wi-fi equipment from the outset, and it is based on an encryption and decryption technique. The idea was to make wi-fi links as secure as the wired variety, and it is from this that the name of the system is derived. For WEP to work it is necessary for each wi-fi unit to have it enabled and to use the same key. The key is a large number used in the encryption and decryption process, and it is the WEP equivalent of a password.

An advantage of WEP is that any wi-fi gadget should be capable of using this security system, regardless of its precise function and which company produced it. Note that WEP is only used for wi-fi links and not for the wired variety, which are intrinsically more secure. Even where a network has a mixture of wired and wireless links, WEP security will only be used for the wireless links. Also note that the encryption and decryption process will reduce the speed of data transfers.

WPA

While WEP is adequate to keep casual hackers out of a home or small business network, it is vulnerable to determined hackers armed with the appropriate tools. This deterred larger business users from installing wi-fi links in their networks. With systems carrying sensitive information that could be worth millions to competitors, it was clearly not a good idea to use links that were anything less than totally secure. The equipment manufacturers answer to this problem was a new and improved form of security called WPA-PSK (Wi-Fi Protected Access Pre-Shared Key). These days it is often just called WPA.

Points to remember

Each PC in the network is given a name so that it is easily located when using other PCs in the system. Make sure that each PC is given a different name. The network as a whole is also given a name.

Files and folders are easily shared using the built-in facilities of Windows XP or ME. By default, folders are not shared. Consequently, you must enable sharing for any folder that you wish to make available to the network. Then add the folder to the My Network Places of any PC that will use the folder.

It is possible to share an entire hard disc, but for security reasons it is not a good idea to do so if the network is connected to the Internet.

A wi-fi equipped laptop or notebook PC can be used to access wireless hotspots at cafes, libraries, computer shops, etc. With a few exceptions, use of wireless hotspots is not free though. The cost of access can be quite high, but the same is true of the alternatives. The download speed when using hotspots is usually quite high, and you are normally connecting to a system that is based on a high speed cable or ADSL Internet connection.

A network can use wi-fi for every link, but this is unlikely to be the most practical solution. For short links a wired connection using Ethernet ports will cost less, provide faster transfers, and give better security. Of course, in the case of a laptop there is a big advantage in using a wi-fi link. It avoids the need to plug in and disconnect the laptop each time you return to base.

Wi-fi systems are usually protected from hackers by an encryption system such as WEP or WPA. You have to enter the encryption key when accessing the network for the first time via a wi-fi link.

Index